HUMAN LEARNED HELPLESSNESS
A COPING PERSPECTIVE

THE PLENUM SERIES IN SOCIAL/CLINICAL PSYCHOLOGY
Series Editor: C. R. Snyder
University of Kansas
Lawrence, Kansas

Current Volumes in this Series:

AGGRESSIVE BEHAVIOR
Current Perspectives
Edited by L. Rowell Huesmann

DESIRE FOR CONTROL
Personality, Social, and Clinical Perspectives
Jerry M. Burger

THE ECOLOGY OF AGGRESSION
Arnold P. Goldstein

HOW PEOPLE CHANGE
Inside and Outside Therapy
Edited by Rebecca C. Curtis and George Stricker

HUMAN LEARNED HELPLESSNESS
A Coping Perspective
Mario Mikulincer

PROCRASTINATION AND TASK AVOIDANCE
Theory, Research, and Treatment
Joseph R. Ferrari, William G. McCown, and Judith L. Johnson

SELF-ESTEEM
The Puzzle of Low Self-Regard
Edited by Roy F. Baumeister

SELF-HANDICAPPING
The Paradox That Isn't
Raymond L. Higgins, C. R. Snyder, and Steven Berglas

THE SELF-KNOWER
A Hero under Control
Robert A. Wicklund and Martina Eckert

A Continuation Order Plan is available for this series. A continuation order will bring delivery of each new volume immediately upon publication. Volumes are billed only upon actual shipment. For further information please contact the publisher.

HUMAN LEARNED HELPLESSNESS

A COPING PERSPECTIVE

MARIO MIKULINCER

Bar-Ilan University
Ramat Gan, Israel

PLENUM PRESS • NEW YORK AND LONDON

BF
575
.H4
M55
1994

Library of Congress Cataloging-in-Publication Data

Mikulincer, Mario.
    Human learned helplessness : a coping perspective / Mario
Mikulincer.
        p.   cm. -- (The Plenum series in social/clinical psychology)
    ISBN 0-306-44743-6
    1. Helplessness (Psychology)   I. Title.   II. Series.
BF575.H4M55   1994
155.2'32--dc20   94-34949
                                                               CIP

ISBN 0-306-44743-6

©1994 Plenum Press, New York
A Division of Plenum Publishing Corporation
233 Spring Street, New York, N.Y. 10013

Printed in the United States of America

PREFACE

Hundreds of empirical and theoretical papers on human learned helplessness have appeared in the scientific literature over the past two decades. Although research on learned helplessness was originally confined to the study of learning processes in the laboratory, the concept has had wide appeal; it now captivates the attention of cognitive, social, personality, clinical, and developmental psychologists in a wide variety of settings. As a result, learned helplessness is currently one of the most widely investigated phenomena in psychology, and there is a great need for a comprehensive examination and integration of the literature. Moreover, because there is a large amount of debate in the literature, there is also a need for a single well-articulated framework to encompass the multidimensional and complex nature of the learned helplessness phenomenon.

This book focuses on the cognitive, motivational, and emotional processes that intervene between repeated exposure to uncontrollable events and subsequent helplessness behavior. It goes beyond simple integration of current knowledge to present a new framework for viewing the phenomenon. This framework emerges from a coping perspective of human behavior—the leading current approach to explaining adaptation to stressful events—and assumes that the underlying cause of human learned helplessness is a disruption in the person–environment equilibrium brought on by exposure to uncontrollable events. This disruption mobilizes coping efforts that lead to changes in behavior. Coping is viewed here as a complex process consisting of a number of interrelated activities that all operate in an organized sequence. These include evaluation of the amount of threat to personal goals and self-identity, estimation of the probability of control as a guideline for selecting the type of coping behaviors to employ, the direction of attention inward and the experience of emotions so as to reinforce and sustain coping, mental rumination as a cognitive tool for coping, and effortful engagement in coping behaviors. From this perspective, human learned helplessness is the end result of the person's *active* coping in an uncontrollable environment.

This book incorporates a number of unique features. First, it offers an up-to-date critical review of virtually the entire published literature on the subject of human learned helplessness. Second, the theory presented here is not only logically and conceptually coherent but also supported by systematic empirical research. The theory is based on the many studies conducted by other researchers around the world, as well as on a series of new studies conducted in my laboratory that were specifically designed to test any aspect of the theory that has not yet been addressed in previous research. Whereas most of the previous presentations of the subject have presented competing views of isolated aspects of the processes contributing to human learned helplessness, my theory reexamines these aspects in a meaningful way and clarifies their roles and interrelations as different building blocks in the coping process.

I acknowledge with gratitude the contributions of Toby Mostitcher and Mark Waisman, who provided major editorial assistance. A number of persons read specific chapters and gave me comments and advice; these include Hananya Glaubman, Victor Florian, Aron Weller, and Israel Orbach. Finally, I want to acknowledge the contribution of many undergraduate and graduate students who collaborated with me in carrying out the experiments presented in this book.

MARIO MIKULINCER

Ramat Gan, Israel

CONTENTS

Chapter 1

The Empirical and Theoretical Basis of Human Learned Helplessness   **1**

The Learned Helplessness Phenomenon 2
    Basic Terminology and Distinctions 2
    Early Animal Experiments 3
    Early Human LH Studies 5

The Nature of Helplessness Training 7
    Controllability and Failure 7
    The Experimental Setting 12
    The Subjective Meaning of Helplessness Training 13

The Nature of LH Effects 14
    LH Deficits Defined 15
    The Generalization of LH Effects 16
    Detrimental and Facilitatory Effects of Helplessness Training 18
    Summary 21

Theoretical Accounts 21
    Animal LH Theories 21
    Human LH Theories 23

A Brief Exposition of the Theory 26

Chapter 2

Coping Strategies as Proximal Mediators of LH Effects **33**

Coping Responses: Definition and Taxonomy 34
    The Concept of Coping 34
    Taxonomy of Coping Responses 34

Helplessness Training and Coping Strategies 42
    The Activation of Coping Responses 42
    A Coping Cycle 45

The Coping–Performance Link 49
    Problem Solving 50
    Reappraisal 52
    Avoidance 54
    Reorganization 56
    Empirical Evidence: Coping–Performance Correlations 58
    Empirical Evidence: Predispositional Studies 59

Conclusions 63

Chapter 3

Mental Rumination as a Proximal Mediator of LH Effects 65

Mental Rumination: Definition, Taxonomy, and Functions 66
    The Concept of Mental Rumination 66
    A Taxonomy of Thoughts 66
    Functions of Mental Rumination 67
    The Autonomic Facet of Mental Rumination 72
    Summary 76

Helplessness Training and Mental Rumination 76
    Heightened Cognitive Activity 77
    A Cycle of Mental Rumination 80
    The Intrusion of Autonomic Failure-Related Thoughts 86
    Summary 88

Mental Rumination and Task Performance 88
    Theoretical Statements 88
    Correlational Evidence 91
    Dispositional Studies 94
    Experimental Induction Evidence 96

Conclusions 97

Chapter 4

The Expectancy of Control as a Distal Mediator of LH Effects 99

Preliminary Clarifications 99

The Expectational Effects of Helplessness Training 101
    Theoretical Statements 101
    Helplessness Training and Future Anticipation 102

The Persistence of Expectancy Change 105
Summary 108

The Formation of the Expectancy of No Control 108
The Perception of Control 109
Causal Attribution 112
The Making of Spontaneous Attribution 113
The Dimensions of Causal Attribution 113
The Stability Dimension and Expectancy Change 114
The Globality Dimension and Expectancy Change 114
The Slope of Expectancy Change 115
Epistemic Activity and Expectancy Change 118

Expectancy and Coping 120
Theoretical Statements 120
The Effects of Expectancy on Coping Strategies 122
The Effects of Expectancy on Mental Rumination 124

Expectancy and Task Performance 126
The Expectancy–Performance Correlation 128
Stable–Unstable Attribution and Performance 129
Global–Specific Attribution and Task Performance 133
Disconfirming Attributional Findings 134
Generalized Expectancy of Control 135

Conclusions 138

Chapter 5

Emotional Arousal as a Distal Mediator of LH Effects 139

A Working Model of the Emotion System 140
The Adaptational Function of Emotion 141
Cognitive Appraisal and Emotion 141
Emotion and Coping Actions 142
The Disorganizing Effects of Emotion 143

The Emotional Effects of Helplessness Training 144
The Arousal of Emotion 144
Emotion in Theories of Human LH 145
Empirical Evidence 146
Summary 149

Expectancy and Emotion 149
Expectancy and Anger 150
Expectancy and the Arousal of Anxiety and Depressed Affects 152
A Note on Anxiety and Depressed Affects 155

The Expectancy–Emotion Link in the LH Paradigm 156
Summary 158

The Emotion–Performance Link 159
Emotionality and Performance 160
The Performance Impact of Anger 162
The Impact of Anxiety and Depressed Feelings 164
Summary 170

Conclusions 170

Chapter 6

Perceived Task Value as a Moderator of LH Effects 173

The Valuation Process 174
Perceived Task Importance 174
Perceived Self-Relevance 176
Goals and Self-Identity 178

Perceived Task Value and the Coping Process 179
Perceived Task Value and Coping Strategies 181
Perceived Task Value and Mental Rumination 181
Perceived Task Value and Emotional Intensity 183
Summary 185

Perceived Task Value and LH Effects 185
Task Importance Instructions 188
Achievement Need 190
Type A Personality 191
Task Difficulty Instructions 193
Internal–External Attribution 196
Goal Orientation 198
Self-Identity Confirmation 199
Self-Relevance and Perceived Task Importance 201
Summary 201

The Expectancy–Value Interaction 202

Helplessness Training and Perceived Task Value 204

Chapter 7

Self-Focused Attention as a Moderator of LH Effects 209

Self-Focus Defined 210

Self-Focus and the Coping Process 212
Self-Focus and Coping Strategies 214

Self-Focus and Mental Rumination 215
Self-Focus and Expectancy 216
Self-Focus and Emotional Experience 218
Self-Focus and the Valuation Process 220
Summary 222

Self-Focus and LH Effects 223
The Performance Effects of Self-Focus 224
Self-Focus and the Expectancy–Performance Link 227
Self-Focus and the Impact of Emotion 230
Self-Focus and the Impact of Perceived Task Value 231
Summary 232

Self-Focus: A Component of the Process of Coping with Failure 232
Failure and Self-Focus 233
Perceived Task Value and Self-Focus 235
Affect and Self-Focus 235
Summary 237

Chapter 8

A Coping Perspective of Human Learned Helplessness 239

The Coping Process and Human Learned Helplessness 239
Basic Premises 239
A Mediational Sequence of LH Effects 242
Direct and Indirect Antecedents of LH Effects 250
From Helplessness Training to LH Effects 252

The Nature of Human Learned Helplessness 255
The Helplessness State 255
The Reactance State 258
The Translation of the Helplessness State into Performance Deficits 259
The Translation of the Reactance State into Performance Facilitation ... 260
Functional and Dysfunctional Aspects of LH Effects 260
The Generalization of LH Effects 263

Some Derivates of a Coping Perspective of Human Learned Helplessness   265
The Helplessness-Prone Personality 266
Human LH and Psychopathology 268
Applications of Human Learned Helplessness 271

References 275

Index 307

CHAPTER 1

THE EMPIRICAL AND THEORETICAL BASIS OF HUMAN LEARNED HELPLESSNESS

What happens when an organism is exposed to uncontrollable outcomes? Will it persevere in trying to control the outcome, or will it give up? Will this experience have an impact on the organism's functioning in subsequent tasks and situations? Dealing with these questions, Overmaier and Seligman (1967) and Seligman and Maier (1967) exposed dogs to inescapable shocks and found that the animals apparently gave up trying and passively succumbed to the shock. These behaviors, which reflect the interference produced by uncontrollable outcomes on adaptive responses, have been labeled *learned helplessness* (LH).

In the 25 years since the work of Seligman and his colleagues, LH has become a thriving area of research. Thousands of articles have been published on LH in animals, and the phenomenon has been generalized across species, tasks, stimuli, and responses. Similar effects of uncontrollable outcomes have been reported in humans, and hundreds of studies have extrapolated from these effects to explain human adaptational problems. Several theories of LH in animals and humans have proposed a variety of intervening mechanisms linking uncontrollable outcomes to performance changes. As a result, LH is currently one of the most widely investigated phenomena in psychology.

This book focuses mainly on LH in humans. It presents an account of human LH that integrates the theoretical and empirical advances of the past 25 years. This account is cognitively oriented, emerges from a coping perspective of human LH, and proposes a network of cognitive, motivational, and emotional mechanisms that explain performance changes following uncontrollable outcomes.

In this first chapter, I review the empirical and theoretical origins of human

1

LH. First, I present a critical review of the early studies conducted with animals and humans that found performance changes after exposure to uncontrollable outcomes and set the empirical basis (e.g., apparatuses, operationalizations, tasks, measurements) for studying LH. Then, I deal with the methodological problems of LH studies and delineate the precise parameters of the independent and dependent variables that have been employed to define human LH and which differentiate it from animal LH. Finally, I review alternative theoretical explanations of LH effects and present my account of human LH in a nutshell.

THE LEARNED HELPLESSNESS PHENOMENON

BASIC TERMINOLOGY AND DISTINCTIONS

The phenomenon of learned helplessness is studied in an experimental setting, labeled the *LH paradigm*. This paradigm consists of two phases, the training phase and the test phase. In the training phase, the subject is exposed to uncontrollable outcomes. In the test phase, his or her performance in a related task is assessed to see whether and how it may have been affected by the previous encounter with uncontrollable outcomes.

Over the years, several authors have used the term *learned helplessness* indiscriminately to refer to the deficits observed after uncontrollable outcomes, the operations used to produce these deficits, and the processes that mediate the deficits. For the sake of clarity, I refer to the performance effects of uncontrollable outcomes as *LH effects,* to the exposure to uncontrollable outcomes as *helplessness training,* and to the mediating processes as *LH-related processes.* I use *LH research* as a generic name for the studies that investigate the performance effects of uncontrollable outcomes within the LH paradigm. *Learned helplessness* itself is a descriptive term that refers to the entire person–environment transaction during both the helplessness training and the test phase of the LH paradigm.

I also distinguish between learned helplessness and feelings of helplessness in general. Abraham (1911) was the first to use the term *helplessness* in the psychological literature; he used it clinically, to describe feelings and symptoms in the manic-depressive syndrome. Bibring (1953) likewise placed feelings of helplessness at the core of depression. Though these feelings may be an emotional product of the exposure to uncontrollable outcomes, however, they are neither synonymous with LH effect nor can they define it.

Another necessary distinction is between learned helplessness and the explanation offered by the LH theory (Maier & Seligman, 1976; Seligman, 1975). Several authors have equated them, contending that performance changes produced by uncontrollable outcomes without the intervention of the processes proposed by the theory are false LH effects (e.g., Alloy, 1982). In my terms, the term *LH effects* denotes every performance change produced by the exposure to uncontrollable outcomes within the LH paradigm, regardless of the intervening processes involved. The LH theory is by no means an exclusive explanation of LH effects.

Another important distinction should be made between LH and its application to general human problems. Several social and clinical psychologists have been captivated by the LH phenomenon and have used it to explain a wide variety of human ills, including depression, anxiety, loneliness, victimization, crowding, unemployment, health problems, and even death (see Peterson, 1985; Peterson & Bosio, 1989, for reviews). In doing so, however, they assign explanatory status to what is essentially a descriptive term—without examining the adequacy of their extrapolation, and, more important, without really understanding the psychological meaning of LH itself. When applying the concept, it is important to delineate the psychological processes that underlie LH effects and to evaluate whether these processes parallel those in the targeted human problems.

A final distinction should be made between animal and human LH research. Though LH in both animals and humans refers to the performance changes produced by uncontrollable outcomes, the operationalizations, research concerns, and theoretical orientations of animal and human LH research are quite different. Animal LH research attempts to delineate the environmental boundaries of the phenomenon and is guided mainly by neobehavioristic and biological approaches. Human LH research attempts to delineate the contribution of both the environment and the person to the LH effects, and it is guided mainly by a cognitive orientation that emphasizes the subjective experience of uncontrollability. In addition, other basic issues, like the operationalization of uncontrollable positive events and the generalization of the LH effects, seem to differentiate between animal and human LH research. The present book focuses on human LH and tries to explain why it occurs when it does. This is not to say, however, that one can negate the contribution of animal LH research and theory. In fact, every review of LH should initially focus on the early animal LH experiments and theories.

EARLY ANIMAL EXPERIMENTS

Performance deficits produced by uncontrollable outcomes were reported before Seligman's initial studies in several animal learning studies (see Maier & Seligman, 1976; Seligman, Maier, & Solomon, 1971, for reviews). These early experiments, however, did not examine the possible causes of the performance deficits (Maier & Seligman, 1976). The mere comparison of the performance of subjects exposed to uncontrollable outcomes with that of subjects not exposed to a training task, or to any prior outcome, does not prove lack of control necessarily produces performance deficits; the training task may have exposed those who performed it to other stimuli that those who did not perform it did not receive. To demonstrate LH effects, studies by Seligman and Maier (1967) and Overmaier and Seligman (1967) thus compared the performance of subjects in the "helplessness training" group with that of subjects who were exposed to the same outcomes in the training phase but exerted control over them. In these studies, the authors used what they called a "triadic design" with three basic training conditions: no training, training with outcomes that were beyond control, and training with outcomes (the same ones) that were under control.

In the studies by Seligman and Maier (1967) and Overmaier and Seligman (1967), one group of dogs (the control group) received no shock while in a Pavlovian hammock. A second group (the escape group) received 64 electric shocks of 6.0 mA intensity for 5 sec; the dogs could escape these shocks by pressing a panel located on either side of their heads. In the third group (the "helplessness training" group), each dog was "yoked" to a dog in the escape group. The two dogs received the same number, duration, and pattern of shocks, and the shocks ended at the same time for both of them. The animals differed only in their control of the shock termination: While the escape-group dog ended shocks by its own responses, the yoked dog could not control the end of the shocks (which came only when the escape-group dog delivered the required response).

Twenty-four hours after the training phase, all the dogs performed a controllable test task. They were placed in a shuttle box that had two compartments separated by a barrier. The floor was an electrified grid through which an electric shock of 4.5 mA was administered to either compartment after a 10-sec tone (discriminant signal). Dogs were given 10 trials, and the requirement for shock termination in each trial was that they jump over the barrier to the other side of the compartment (escape). The shock could be avoided if the jumping response occurred during the 10-sec tone.

Separate comparisons of the helplessness-training group to the escape and control groups demonstrated the performance changes produced by uncontrollable outcomes. Dogs in the helplessness-training group were much slower to escape from the shock in the test task than dogs in both the escape and control groups. The helplessness-training dogs seemed to accept the shock without any resistance and were unlikely to cross the barrier to escape from it. They were also slow to learn to avoid the shock even when they discovered the contingency between responding and shock termination. Although they jumped over the barrier occasionally and in so doing stopped the shocks, they rarely jumped again on the next trial; instead, they stopped running altogether until the shocks came to an end.

Significantly, although the dogs in the escape group also were exposed to aversive shocks in the training phase, in the escape/avoidance test task they performed as well as the dogs in the control group. This finding implies that it was lack of control and not the mere prior exposure to aversive shocks that produced the deficits observed among the helplessness-training dogs.

Subsequent animal LH studies using the triadic design found LH effects under different types of training and test procedures and in a wide variety of species (see Maier & Seligman, 1976, for a review). In addition, animal LH studies demonstrated LH effects when a reward was given independently of the organism's response (e.g., Goodkind, 1976; Welker, 1976). Seligman also examined the conditions that could prevent LH effects. Seligman and Maier (1967), for example, found that dogs who received escapable shocks before training with the inescapable shock ("immunization") did not show performance deficits in the test task. Seligman, Maier, and Geer (1968) found that forcibly dragging yoked dogs from side to side in the shuttle box during the test task, thus demonstrating the new contingency between responses and shock termination ("therapy"), was sufficient to prevent the LH effects.

EARLY HUMAN LH STUDIES

Once LH was demonstrated in animals, the next step was to see whether something similar would happen in human experiments. The experiment of Hiroto (1974) was one of the earliest of this research trend. Hiroto exposed one group of college students to 50 trials of unsignaled loud noise, which they could terminate by pressing a button four times (escape group). A second group (helplessness-training group) was exposed to inescapable noise that ceased independently of their responses—as a result of responses by a subject from the escape group. The two groups received the same amount, duration, and pattern of noise, and the noise ended at the same time for the two groups. Like the yoked dogs in the animal experiments, these paired students also differed in the degree of control they had over the outcome. A third group of subjects was not exposed to any noise.

In the test phase, subjects were exposed to 20 trials of loud noise, which they were told to stop by moving the handle of a finger shuttle box from one end of the box to the other. All of the subjects could control the end of the noise. The results paralleled those observed with animals: Subjects exposed to helplessness training were less likely to learn to escape the noise than subjects in the other two groups; subjects in the escape group did not show any impairment and performed as well as subjects in the no-noise group.

Early human research also demonstrated LH effects following exposure to unsolvable cognitive problems. Hiroto and Seligman (1975), for example, asked subjects to perform three 10-trials Levine concept formation tasks. In each trial, two different geometrical patterns (each composed of five attributes) appeared on each side of a card. The subjects were asked to figure out which of five attributes the experimenter had arbitrarily designated as the target attribute. In each of the trials, subjects indicated whether the target attribute appeared on the right or left side of the card, and the experimenter told them whether their choice was correct or not. After the tenth card, subjects indicated what they thought the target attribute was and received feedback on the correctness of their solution.

One group of subjects (the control group) performed no task in the training phase. A second group (the solvable group) received feedback similar to that provided in the escape condition of Hiroto (1974). Subjects received veridical feedback on each trial and at the end. This procedure enabled subjects to learn the target attribute and to control the experimenter's feedback by their own responses. If they made the right choice, they could produce the "correct" feedback and avoid the "incorrect" feedback. A third group (the unsolvable group) were exposed to uncontrollable feedback. For them, the experimenter did not select any attribute, instead providing a predetermined, random schedule of "correct" and "incorrect" responses during the trials. After the tenth trial, subjects in this group were uniformly told "incorrect" each time they gave a solution. This procedure prevented subjects from learning any response that could either control the experimenter's feedback or avoid failure in problem solving.

In the test phase, subjects were exposed to 20 trials of a noise escape task in the same finger shuttle box as that used by Hiroto (1974). Again, the results paralleled the animal LH effects. Subjects in the unsolvable condition were less likely to learn how to end the noise than subjects in the solvable and no-problem conditions; no difference was found between the solvable and the no-problem group.

Early research also found LH effects in humans after vicarious experiences with inescapable noise or unsolvable problems. For example, DeVellis, DeVellis, and McCauley (1978) exposed observers to participants who were either successful or unsuccessful in avoiding loss of reward on an instrumental task. On a subsequent instrumental task, both observers and participants in the success condition scored better on a response latency measure than those in the failure condition. Brown and Inouye (1978) similarly found that observation of a competent model who ostensibly failed on an anagram task resulted in reduced persistence in a subsequent anagram task. Chartier and Friedlander (1981), however, failed to find any performance change after either direct or vicarious experience with inescapable noise.

At the beginning of human LH research, some investigators tried to induce LH effects by means of verbal instructions about the uncontrollability of the outcomes (e.g., Glass & Singer, 1972; Sherrod & Downs, 1974; Thornton & Powell, 1974). As human LH research advanced, however, the use of verbal instructions disappeared as findings suggested that it did not fit well with the operationalization of helplessness training. It became apparent that telling subjects from the outset of the training phase that outcomes were uncontrollable created a particular psychological state that prevents rather than induces LH effects (see Chapter 5). In 1994 the standard helplessness training consists of actual exposure to inescapable aversive events or unsolvable problems.

Research also demonstrated that human LH effects are not circumscribed to deficits in noise escape learning. Such effects were found in a wide variety of cognitive problem-solving tasks, including anagrams, intelligence tests, block designs, digit-letter substitution, discrimination learning, and Raven matrices (see Miller & Norman, 1979; Roth, 1980, for reviews). To date, there is no standard task that defines the test phase of LH experiments. Any task that requires the selection, organization, and implementation of voluntary responses to solve a problem can be used to examine the performance effects of uncontrollable outcomes.

Studies have also demonstrated that humans, like animals, can be immunized against LH effects by being exposed to controllable events beforehand (e.g., Thornton & Powell, 1974). Jones, Nation, and Massad (1977) and Nation and Massad (1978), however, found that immunization procedures interacted with schedules of reinforcement. Specifically, only partial success pretraining was found to prevent the development of LH effects produced by unsolvable problems.

THE NATURE OF HELPLESSNESS TRAINING

In this section I elaborate on the basic objective task and contextual features that define helplessness training. In addition, the subjective representation of helplessness training is discussed. The question addressed is this: What are the meanings that people habitually attach to helplessness training?

CONTROLLABILITY AND FAILURE

The distinction between controllable and uncontrollable outcomes is central to defining helplessness training. To make this distinction, Seligman et al. (1971) proposed that in every instrumental conditioning situation the organism is exposed to two conditional probabilities: (a) the conditional probability (p) of reinforcement (RF) following a certain response (R), and (b) the conditional probability (p) of reinforcement (RF) following the absence of that response (R'). An outcome is controllable whenever there is something that the organism does or refrains from doing that affects the occurrence of the outcome. Specifically, a response controls the occurrence of a reinforcement if and only if

$$p(RF/R) \neq p(RF/R').$$

In this case, the two probabilities are not the same. The occurrence of a reinforcement is *contingent* on responses, and subjects receive different amounts of reinforcement depending on whether or not they make the required response. They can learn to alter what they get by making or withholding a response, and they can draw conclusions about the effectiveness of their responses for manipulating the environment.

A response does not control an outcome when it does not change what one gets. In other words, uncontrollability exists when

$$p(RF/R) = p(RF/R').$$

The occurrence of an outcome is *noncontingent* on responding; the two probabilities are the same. Here, subjects receive the same amount of reinforcement whether or not they make a response. When this is true for all responses, the outcome is totally uncontrollable, and nothing the subject does matters. Subjects learn about the noncontingency between responses and outcomes and about the inability of their responses to alter the environment.

The dogs in the escape and helplessness-training groups in the Seligman and

Maier (1967) experiment received different levels of contingency between outcome (shock termination) and responding. Dogs in the escape group were exposed to response–outcome contingency: They changed the probability of shock termination by pressing a panel. In contrast, dogs in the helplessness-training condition were exposed to response–outcome noncontingency: The probability of the shock's ending remained the same whether or not they pressed the panel or made any other response. On this basis, Seligman (1975) concluded that response–outcome noncontingency is a sufficient condition to define helplessness training. In his own words, "a person or animal is helpless with respect to some outcome when the outcome occurs independently of all his voluntary responses" (p. 17).

One implication of Seligman's reasoning is that the valence of the uncontrollable outcome is irrelevant to defining helplessness training. Seligman (1975) claimed that "not only trauma occurring independently of responses, but noncontingent positive events can produce helplessness" (p. 98). In both cases, there is nothing the individual can do to increase the occurrence of a positive outcome or to decrease the occurrence of an aversive outcome.

Another implication is that the dimension of success–failure—the absolute probability of obtaining a positive outcome or avoiding a negative one—is irrelevant for defining helplessness training. A positive outcome that *always* is obtained without regard to one's actions (uncontrollable success) should induce the same LH effects as a positive outcome that is *never* obtained (uncontrollable failure). Accordingly, the LH effects produced by a negative outcome that is always noncontingently avoided should be the same as those produced by the same outcome that is never avoided. LH effects result from either a string of successes or from a string of failures, as long as they befall people independently of their responses. The only relevant factor is that responses and outcomes be independent of one another.

Although Seligman's reasoning is straightforward and can be easily examined in animal LH research, it faces unsurmountable difficulties when applied to human LH research. For while helplessness training in animals has been operationally defined exclusively by lack of control, in humans it has been inextricably combined with an additional component: the experience of failure.

This is evident, first of all, in the way that helplessness training typically has been operationalized in human LH research. As mentioned above, experiments generally have been based on either an inescapable noise or an unsolvable problem. In the noise escape task, subjects receive two outcomes after responding: noise termination and a light feedback indicating whether or not they terminated the noise by their responses. When they make the correct escape response, a green light flashes; when they fail to do so on any given trial, a red light accompanies the noise ending. In helplessness training, both outcomes are uncontrollable: There is no response that can end the noise (its termination is controlled by the responses of escape-group subjects) or lead to a green light. These two uncontrollable outcomes, however, have different absolute probabilities of occurrence: The noise sometimes ends after an escape-group subject makes a correct response, but the green light is never obtained. Therefore, helplessness training includes uncontrollable failure: The probability of obtaining a green light is always zero.

This confusion between lack of control and failure also characterizes the standard unsolvable problem task. Here, too, subjects receive two types of outcomes. At each trial they receive feedback on the correctness of their guesses, and at the end of the problem they are told whether or not they arrived at the correct solution. In helplessness training, both these outcomes are uncontrollable—there are no responses on the part of subjects that can alter the experimenter's feedback. The outcomes, though, have different probabilities of occurrence: Whereas "correct" feedback at each trial is given at random according to a predetermined schedule (50% of the trials), this feedback is never obtained at the end of the problem. Subjects therefore learn that the probability of obtaining a "correct" feedback at the end of the problem is zero no matter what response they make.

The experience of failure in human helplessness training is accentuated further by the instructions people receive at the outset of the experiment and by the choice of tasks. In contrast with the animal experiments, human subjects are not simply placed in a setting that exposes them to certain reinforcement contingencies. They are first instructed to pursue certain goals (e.g., to learn how to end an aversive noise or to solve a cognitive problem). There is thus an explicitly stated aim that they must try to achieve. Subjects are posed with a challenge, and they know that there are only two possible outcomes: failure or success. Moreover, although the task in helplessness training is actually chance-dependent, and the outcome is objectively independent of responses, subjects in most of the LH studies receive deceptive instructions emphasizing the dependence of the outcome on their responses (e.g., "There is a particular response that will end the noise"). Subjects are thus led to believe that success or failure on the task depends solely on their own ability to arrive at the correct response. Subjective concern over failure or success is emphasized yet again by the choice of tasks. In most human LH studies the tasks are universally recognized to reflect individual skills and abilities (e.g., anagrams), to the extent that all LH researchers recognize the need for careful debriefing at the end of the experiment in order to prevent any possible loss of self-worth.

The combination of choice of tasks and instructions may thus be so powerful that they alone may produce the perceived link between lack of control and failure, regardless of the actual probabilities of reinforcement. When presented together with a zero probability of reinforcement, it seems virtually inevitable that absence of a green light (indicating that one has terminated the noise by one's own response) or the absence of "correct" feedback at the end of a cognitive problem will be interpreted by the subject to reflect personal incompetence. Helplessness training is thus transformed into a failure situation.

The recognition that helplessness training includes both lack of control *and* failure has led to several studies trying to separate these two factors experimentally. One series of such studies has attempted to demonstrate that the introduction of feedback at the end of cognitive problems is unnecessary for producing LH effects

(Cohen, Rothbart, & Phillips, 1976; Kofta & Sedek, 1990; Sedek & Kofta, 1990). These studies used the original triadic design, but they added a new uncontrollable condition in which subjects exposed to response–outcome noncontingency at each trial of unsolvable cognitive problems (random "correct" feedback) received no feedback at the end as to whether they solved the problems. Results were in line with Seligman's reasoning: Subjects in the two uncontrollable conditions, with or without feedback at the end of the problem, performed worse than those in the control condition.

The observed performance deficit, however, cannot be taken as serious evidence. Although subjects did not receive explicit messages, they could readily reach the conclusion that they failed to solve the problem on their own. The provision of random feedback at each individual trial refuted any hypothesis that subjects may have raised about the concept to be learned, essentially preventing them from reaching the conclusion that they had solved the problem correctly. In such conditions, people learn not only that responses and the "correct" feedback are noncontingent, but also that they personally were unable to solve the problem. They do not need the experimenter to tell them in order to become aware of their poor performance.

Another series of studies examined the independent contribution of the dimensions of controllability and success–failure to LH effects. Four studies (McReynolds, 1980; Tennen, Drum, Gillen, & Stanton, 1982; Tiggemann, 1981; Tiggemann, Barnett, & Winefeld, 1983) used the inescapable noise procedure and manipulated the amount of "bogus" green lights subjects received after each trial, indicating that they ended the noise by their responses. The results were contradictory. On the one hand, Tennen et al. (1982) and Tiggemann (1981) found that task performance was worse after inescapable than after escapable noise, regardless of the frequency of green lights. On the other hand, McReynolds (1980) and Tiggemann et al. (1983) showed that LH deficits were recorded mainly when subjects experienced noncontingent tone offset and were never shown the green light. Provision of a bogus green light after the uncontrollable termination of the noise prevented LH effects.

Similar inconclusive findings emerge from three other studies, each of which used different experimental devices for separating lack of control and failure in the noise escape task. Two of the studies were in line with Seligman's hypothesis. Winefeld, Barnett, and Tiggemann (1985) found that subjects exposed to inescapable noise performed worse in a subsequent noise escape task than those exposed to escapable noise, even if they were told that they performed better than other subjects (successful social comparison feedback). Tennen, Gillen, and Drum (1982) similarly found that subjects exposed to inescapable noise exhibited worse anagram performance than subjects in control conditions, even if they were successfully rescued from the noise by a powerful other. In contrast, Koller and Kaplan (1978) found no performance deficit after exposure to protracted noncontingent noise termination (in which virtually all responses were positively reinforced) and did find performance deficits following exposure to rapid noncontingent noise termination (in which virtually no response could be positively reinforced).

Six studies separated lack of control and failure in unsolvable cognitive problems. Again, the results were contradictory. Four studies (Buys & Winefeld, 1982; Griffith, 1977; Lamb, Davies, Tramill, & Kleinhammer-Tramill, 1987; O'Rourke, Tryon, & Raps, 1980) found that performance was worse in all the uncontrollable conditions than in the controllable conditions. The type of feedback provided at the end of the problem or the amount of money received did not affect performance. Two studies (Benson & Kenelly, 1976; Eisenberg, Park, & Frank, 1976), however, found that the bogus success feedback at the end of unsolvable cognitive problems prevented performance deficits in subsequent test tasks, and only random feedback in each trial accompanied by failure feedback at the end of the problem produced worse performance than control conditions.

Unfortunately, most of the studies reviewed above have basic methodological problems that make it difficult to separate out the performance effects of uncontrollable success. First, the uncontrollable success conditions usually contained at least a hint of failure. In the O'Rourke et al. (1980) study, for example, subjects in the noncontingent condition who received money after responding were told that the money was a "gift"; it was given, not earned. This message may have left the subjects feeling that they had failed to carry out the experimenter's explicit instructions, which were to *earn* the money. Similarly, in the Tennen, Gillen, and Drum (1982) study, it was obvious that the subjects who were rescued from inescapable noise by a powerful other had not ended the noise by themselves.

In addition, the uncontrollable success conditions were more deceptive than the failure conditions. In the latter, only the instructions were deceptive (subjects are told that the unsolvable problems are solvable, or that the inescapable noise can be ended with a correct response). In the success conditions, however, the deception was twofold—embedded in both the initial instructions and in the outcomes. Providing a green light indicating that responses end what really is an uncontrollable noise or telling subjects that they solved what is really an unsolvable problem is clearly deceptive, and it may lead subjects to become suspicious. Several LH theorists have pointed out that extensive use of deception alone may suffice to produce performance deficits (e.g., Wortman & Brehm, 1975). Subjects who became aware of the deceptive nature of the experiment may have become less motivated to perform the tasks, or they may have adopted a negativistic attitude toward the deceiver ("I will not expend effort every time the experimenter asks me to perform well"). The greater deceptiveness of the uncontrollable successes may thus have been responsible for some of the observed performance deficits.

More importantly, the above studies lack ecological validity. Though the dimension of success–failure and the dimension of control–lack of control are conceptually orthogonal and can be experimentally separated, it is difficult for people to make this distinction subjectively. It is uncertain whether people exposed to "true" uncontrollable success really perceive themselves as free of failure. Jones and Berglass (1978) argue that uncontrollable success makes people feel insecure and worried about the possibility of failing in the future. They may perceive their success as a temporary, fortuitous event and be unsure that they possess the skills and abilities to guarantee success the next time around. They are concerned with the prospect of failure, and they are afraid to discover that they are not as capable as they appear to be. Jones and Berglass claim that in cases of uncontrollable success failure may still be experienced, but in an anticipatory-symbolic way. This threat of potential failure activates psychological mechanisms that may alter task performance.

In addition, there is accumulating evidence that laypersons are unable to perceive and learn uncontrollability when exposed to uncontrollable success. Some of the studies reviewed above assessed subjects' perceptions of control and consistently found that subjects believed that they had higher levels of control in uncontrollable success conditions than in uncontrollable failure conditions (e.g., Griffith, 1977; Tiggemann, 1981; Tiggemann et al., 1983). Accordingly, Jenkins and Ward (1965) and Alloy and Abramson (1979) demonstrated that subjects apprehend objective lack of control more easily when they do not obtain a reward than when they do get one. In fact, people generally take credit for uncontrollable successes and believe that their actions caused them (Langer, 1975). They subjectively link success with control and failure with lack of control.

On this basis, the experimental separations of lack of control and failure may have nothing to do with the way people subjectively represent lack of control. More important, it is erroneous to generalize from animal LH research and claim that uncontrollability alone is the defining feature of helplessness training in humans. Rather, the combination of lack of control with the experience of failure seems to describe better the nature of the training, as Miller and Norman (1979) state: "Both the contingency and the nature of the obtained outcome are critical to learned helplessness" (p. 98). Peterson (1985) also notes this distinction between animal and human LH research traditions: "In animal experiments, appetitive helplessness is straightforwardly operationalized by presenting noncontingent food. In human studies, appetitive helplessness is less straightforwardly created, since noncontingent success is a contradiction in terms" (p. 251).

THE EXPERIMENTAL SETTING

A generalization from animal to human LH research is also prevented by differences in the nature of the setting in which LH is studied. One difference is that humans, unlike animals, receive general instructions before starting the helplessness training. They are presented with the problem and told to figure out a solution. They are thus oriented to solving the problem before they start and are asked to focus their actions and cognition on the problem at hand.

Though most LH researchers take them for granted, the initial instructions are an essential component of helplessness training. If the subjects were not asked to try to solve a problem, they would emit no response, there would be no outcome, and they would experience no lack of control. If they were not told to use the information that the experimenter provides to solve the problem, they would pay no attention to the noncontingency between their responses and the outcomes. Finally, if no problem-solving situation is created, the subjects would experience no failure. Only when they are oriented to problem solving and execute pertinent problem-solving actions is feedback that they made incorrect responses experienced as signaling failure.

More important, the standard instructional set implies that the problems are solvable. By telling subjects to solve the problems, the experimenter deceptively informs them from the very outset of the training phase that the problems can be solved. Subjects thus begin the helplessness training believing in the controllability of the outcomes and may be surprised and disappointed as they gradually learn that the latter are uncontrollable.

In this way, the human LH setting is completely different from the animal LH setting. Animals begin the helplessness training without any external demand to solve a problem—they do not know that they are going to receive an electric shock—and without any anticipatory cognition about the controllability of the outcomes. They can predict neither the events that will occur in the helplessness training nor the level of response–outcome contingency. Although the shock they receive is an unexpected event for these animals, the lack of contingency between their responses and shock termination does not discomfirm any prior expectancy. In contrast, human subjects would not be surprised by the sequence of task events in the helplessness training (e.g., noise emission, clue card presentation), but the lack of response–outcome contingency would discomfirm their prior expectancies (Burger & Arkin, 1980; Douglas & Anisman, 1975).

In general, the experimental setting in human LH research can be defined as a problem-solving setting in which the uncontrollability of the outcome does not accord with the beliefs held by the person at the beginning of the task. In other words, human helplessness training is essentially *the experience of uncontrollable failure to solve a problem originally perceived as solvable.*

THE SUBJECTIVE MEANING OF HELPLESSNESS TRAINING

The definition of helplessness training in human LH research should also include the way a person subjectively represents the task situation. The experience of no control depends not only on objective noncontingencies but also on the individual's schema of control and his or her knowledge of the task. Moreover, a low probable outcome may be taken as a sign of failure only when it touches on the person's goals.

On this basis, it is erroneous to analyze human LH from the exclusive standpoint of what the exposure to uncontrollable outcomes does to people—that is, without knowing the beliefs, goals, concerns, and history of the particular person exposed to these outcomes. A similar error would be made if one ignores the way a person subjectively construes what is happening between him or her and the world.

To understand human LH, one should analyze the meaning a person attaches to the uncontrollable failure. This meaning summarizes the personal harms of the failure from the standpoint of well-being and adaptation. It involves the appreciation of what a person with particular values and concerns believes he or she can lose in the helplessness situation.

The subjective meanings of helplessness training center around the consequences attached to the *person–environment mismatch* that uncontrollable failure creates. Helplessness training is a goal-oriented setting; subjects set a goal (to solve a problem) and implement instrumental actions for attaining it. But whereas the implementation of instrumental responses in other settings may culminate in goal attainment, in helplessness training the goal is unattainable, and a mismatch is created between what the environment allows and what a person wants. Subjects form well-organized plans for attaining a goal, but they are blocked by uncontrollable failure. This interruption is discrepant with the imaginal construction of successful performance, and it may go against what a person feels one should do in the task situation. In this way, the helplessness training may be appraised as a *goal-incongruent* (Lazarus, 1991) transaction with the environment—a relationship that thwarts personal goals.

The mismatch created by helplessness training means a personal loss. Numerous losses occur in the typical helplessness training. These include loss of a sense of control over outcomes, loss of positive consequences of success, and possibly loss of the sense of self-worth and other important aspects of the self. Basically, the uncontrollable failure means the loss of the pursued goal and the frustration of other goals that are instrumentally related to it.

Helplessness training may also imply a threat to personal views of the self and the world. Uncontrollable failure may undermine beliefs about the controllability of the environment as well as about one's own skills in effecting control. Moreover, uncontrollability creates uncertainty about both the responses required to attain goals and the course of events. People are not sure about either what will happen in such an uncontrollable situation or what to do about whatever it turns out to be. They may feel at the mercy of external, random, and uncertain forces that threaten the meaning they habitually give to experience.

In the above reasoning, however, I do not mean to say that all the above relational meanings would be common to all individuals in all LH settings. Rather, the meanings will depend on the goals, values, and beliefs that a particular person brings into the LH situation. They may also depend on the particular objective task and contextual features of helplessness training.

THE NATURE OF LH EFFECTS

This section will deal with the basic features of LH effects. I first delineate the nature and components of LH deficits. Then I focus on two issues that demand theoretical and empirical attention: (a) the generalization of LH effects, and (b) the improvement of task performance after a small amount of helplessness training (reactance).

LH DEFICITS DEFINED

Seligman defines the LH deficits in humans as any performance change after helplessness training that reflects motivational and/or cognitive difficulties in performing a task. This definition implies two basic features of LH deficits that signal the presence of difficulties in performing a task. One is the lack of any trade-off or compensation among different performance classes—speed and accuracy, for example. LH deficits are said to occur when deficits are found in at least one performance class without any improvement in any other class. Slow response after helplessness training is a LH deficit when there is no improvement in another performance class, but not when it is offset by increased accuracy; in the latter case, slow performance is a performance strategy used to make few errors. The other basic feature is the lack of congruence between task performance and task demands. LH deficits are always those performance changes that fail to meet task demands. Slow response is a LH deficit only when subjects are required to solve the problems quickly or within a given time, but not when they are required to perform slowly and accurately.

Seligman's definition stipulates that LH deficits are both motivational and cognitive. Helplessness training reduces motivation to initiate instrumental actions for molding the environment and interferes with learning how responses produce outcomes. In animal LH studies, the motivational deficit is reflected in slow escape/avoidance from aversive events, and the cognitive deficit is manifested in the animal's inability to connect the termination of the shock to its own responses. These two components can be also distinguished in human LH studies. The motivational deficit has been hypothesized to be manifested in the time or number of trials subjects take to push a button or pull knobs to end an aversive event. The cognitive deficit has been hypothesized to be manifested in the extent to which subjects fail to repeat successful responses in next trials of an escape task.

The distinction of motivational and cognitive deficits is problematic, however, because there is no necessary equivalence between the performance classes assessed and the hypothesized motivational and cognitive variations. Take, for example, the motivational deficit. Levis (1976) stated that "not performing a given response class in no way a priori suggests anything definitive about the energy or motivational properties of the organism. . . . An organism can be under a high drive state and at the same time behaviorally be immobile" (pp. 55–56). Accordingly, the nonrepetition of a successful response may equally reflect a cognitive deficit or the subject's unwillingness to make that response, as well as any number of other cognitive interferences (e.g., lack of concentration, distraction).

This conceptual problem is aggravated in the frequent use of anagrams for assessing LH deficits. Generally subjects perform a series of solvable anagrams with the same solution order, and three dependent measures are computed: (a) number of trials to reach the criterion (solution order), (b) number of failures to solve the attempted anagrams, and (c) mean anagram solution latency. Seligman hypothesized that the number of trials to criterion reflects the cognitive deficit, with more trials implying a retardation of the learning of the solution to the anagrams, whereas the other two measures reflect the motivational facet of LH effects, with longer latencies and more failures reflecting stronger motivational deficits.

Douglas and Anisman (1975), however, claimed that latency measure is a poor measure of motivation because it involves both the time to find the correct word mentally and the time to a make a motor response. A long latency may reflect equally the lack of motivation to respond and cognitive difficulty in finding the correct word. The trials to criterion measure is also problematic. Buchwald, Coyne, and Cole (1978) stated that "difficulty in seeing a pattern in anagrams is not equivalent to difficulty in learning that responses produce outcomes" (p. 181). Moreover, a large number of trials to reach a criterion may reflect either difficulty in connecting responses and outcomes, difficulties in problem solving, or general intellectual deficiencies. Nor is this measure free of a motivational component, because unmotivated subjects (who may not expend cognitive efforts in solving the problem) would take more trials to reach the criterion.

In general, it is difficult to separate the motivational and cognitive components of LH deficits in humans. The performance deficits observed following helplessness training may have a cognitive basis, a motivational one, or both. The only thing that is certain is that LH deficits reflect problems in meeting task demands in a problem-solving setting. These problems could be manifested in retarded responses, inaccuracy, and/or an inability to figure out the solution to a problem.

THE GENERALIZATION OF LH EFFECTS

Another basic definitional feature of LH effects is the transfer of the performance changes produced by helplessness training to a new controllable test task. LH effects are demonstrated if and only if subjects exposed to a training task in which responses do *not* control outcomes show performance changes in a later situation in which responses *do* control outcomes. The observation of performance changes in the original helplessness-training task is not an instance of LH effects. These changes become LH effects only when they are transferred to new controllable tasks.

The centrality of the generalization of LH effects raises questions as to the mechanisms and slope of that generalization. One possibility is that the performance changes produced by helplessness training automatically generalize to a wide variety of tasks and situations. Another possibility is that these performance changes are restricted to tasks and situations similar to the original helplessness training. A third possibility is that the performance changes can be generalized to different tasks and situations, but the degree of generalization and the mechanisms that control it are a matter of study.

Animal LH research favors the first alternative, suggesting that LH effects are automatically generalized across tasks and situations. A large number of animal studies demonstrate LH effects in test tasks that involve apparatuses, stimuli, and response demands quite different from those of the original helplessness training (see a review in Maier & Seligman, 1976). Maier and Seligman (1976) argued that what is learned when the environment is uncontrollable can have an impact on a wide range of behavior.

This reasoning faces difficulties, however, when it is applied to human LH research. First of all, most of the LH studies with humans have not investigated the degree of generalization of LH effects. Though these studies have appropriately demonstrated LH effects by examining performance changes in a controllable test task, they have either used test tasks that are similar to the training task (e.g., noise escape tasks, cognitive tasks) or constructed similar training and test situations (e.g., using the same room). In most of the studies, the training and test tasks are part of the same experimental setting. A series of four LH studies by Hiroto and Seligman (1975) illustrates the problems of assessing the generalization of LH effects. In these studies, LH deficits were generalized from a noise escape task to cognitive problems (concept formation, anagrams) and vice versa. Hiroto and Seligman claimed that the findings demonstrate the generalization of LH effects. Both instrumental and cognitive tasks, however, are problem-solving tasks. Whether the task is to push a button or to unscramble a word, the subject must figure out the right response to solve a problem. Moreover, in all four studies (as in most LH studies), the training and test phases could readily be perceived as part of the same problem-solving setting.

Studies in which the test phase was situationally dissimilar from the training phase (e.g., different experiments, different experimenters, different rooms) were effectively no better at proving the automatic generalization of LH effects in humans, because their results were highly inconclusive (see Miller & Norman, 1979; Roth, 1980, for reviews). Moreover, these studies have sometimes failed to clearly separate the training and test phases. For example, take the finding by Sherrod and Downs (1974) that subjects exposed to inescapable noise were less prone to volunteer to participate in a new experiment and to do mathematical problems than subjects exposed to escapable or no noise. The authors concluded that the detrimental effects of inescapable noise are generalized to altruistic behavior. Their dependent measure, though, can equally reflect altruism or persistence at a cognitive task.

Inconclusive results have also been reported in studies that compare LH effects across similar and dissimilar test phases. On the one hand, some studies indicate that LH effects tend to dissipate when the training and test phases become dissimilar. Cole and Coyne (1977), for example, found LH effects only when the training and test phases were conducted in similar settings (same room, same experiment, same experimenter). Trice and Woods (1979) and Tiggemann and Winefeld (1978) accordingly found LH effects only when the training and test phases involved similar tasks. Eckelman and Dyck (1979), interestingly, found that immunization against LH effects also dissipates when the controllable pretraining phase and the test phase were conducted in dissimilar settings and used dissimilar tasks.

On the other hand, other studies found that LH effects could be generalized under certain situational conditions and among certain groups of subjects. For example, Cohen et al. (1976) found that subjects with a high external locus of control showed generalized performance deficits following helplessness training across different tasks and settings. Similarly, generalized LH effects were found by Alloy, Peterson, Abramson, and Seligman (1984) among subjects who attributed lack of control to global rather than to task-specific factors.

On this basis, one cannot say, as Maier and Seligman (1976) do, that the generalization of LH effects occurs automatically after exposure to helplessness training. Neither can one say, however, that LH effects are not generalized to different tasks and situations. In our present state of knowledge, the best account of the reviewed findings is that LH effects in humans may potentially be generalized across dissimilar tasks and situations, but how and when this generalization takes place requires empirical research and theoretical effort.

DETRIMENTAL AND FACILITATORY EFFECTS OF HELPLESSNESS TRAINING

From the beginning of LH research with humans, it has been clear that the effects of helplessness training are not restricted to impairment of task performance. There are cases in which helplessness training instead produces *reactance,* an improvement in test task performance. Several theorists have postulated that although a large amount of helplessness training produces performance deficits, a small amount improves performance. Seligman (1975) briefly suggested that the typical reaction to a small amount of helplessness training is heightened arousal, which gives way to passivity as people are exposed to repeated failures. Similar predictions, though based on different theoretical reasoning, were made by Wortman and Brehm (1975), Roth (1980), and Zuroff (1980).

Analyzing the consequences of loss of incentive, Klinger (1975) also proposes an invigoration–deterioration cycle. He claims that the initial reaction to failure to obtain desired outcomes is invigoration: "After an organism has launched an instrumental sequence, it responds to an obstacle with increased vigor, taking the form of more powerful motions, more rapid responses, more intense concentration" (Klinger, 1975, p. 8). Eventually, though, when people repeatedly fail to attain a desired outcome, they lose interest in the goal, disengage from goal-oriented activity, and exhibit performance deficits.

Thornton and Jacobs (1972) were the first to report the facilitatory effects of helplessness training. Subjects who received inescapable shock while performing a reaction-time button-pressing task showed *improved* performance in tests of mathematical and verbal reasoning and perceptual organization than subjects who received escapable or no shocks. The problem with Thornton and Jacobs's findings is that the observed performance facilitation might have resulted from other factors than lack of control. One may have been that subjects in the inescapable-shock condition were told from the very outset that outcomes were chance dependent, preventing any painful experience of failure. Another may have been that the test task was presented before the helplessness training, facilitating the learning that outcomes are controllable and thus acting as an buffer against LH deficits.

Roth and Bootzin (1974) also found a reactance effect. After being exposed to no, one, or two unsolvable problems, subjects completed a series of solvable problems, during which the experimenter induced an equipment malfunction that prevented the completion of the task. Relative to no failure, a higher percentage of subjects exposed to one or two failures attempted to cope actively with the obstacle by seeking out the experimenter and asking him or her to correct the problem. In addition, of those who did seek out the experimenter, subjects exposed to one or two failures stood up to get him or her sooner than subjects in the no-failure group. Roth and Bootzin interpreted these findings as implying that uncontrollable outcomes lead people to react with invigorated problem-solving responses.

Roth and Bootzin's findings also suggest that reactance is found mostly after a small amount of helplessness training. Roth and Bootzin exposed subjects to only one or two unsolvable problems. whereas most of the studies that have found the classic detrimental effects of helplessness training on task performance exposed subjects to three, four, or six such problems. One should recall, however, that Roth and Kubal (1975) made no attempt to compare performance effects of different amounts of helplessness training.

Complete and systematic investigation of reactance and LH deficits requires that subjects be exposed to at least three amounts of helplessness training (no, small, and large) and that their performance variations be followed up in a subsequent task. This research strategy was adopted by Pittman and Pittman (1980), who exposed subjects to either no, two, or six unsolvable problems. Data on subsequent anagram performance showed that two unsolvable problems produced better test task performance than the no-problem condition, and six unsolvable problems produced significantly worse performance.

Similar findings were obtained by Baum and his colleagues (Baum, Aiello, & Calesnick, 1978; Baum & Gatchel, 1981) in two studies of students' reactions to living in crowded dormitories. Residence in long-corridor-design dormitories (32–40 residents) was designed as the helplessness-training condition, and residence in short-corridor-design dormitories (6–20 residents) was designed as the control condition. These naturalistic studies fulfill the defining criteria of helplessness training in that crowding has been consistently related to lack of control over outcomes (e.g., Baron & Rodin, 1978; Baum & Valins, 1979), and residents of long-corridor dormitories have been found to report less ability to regulate the nature, frequency, and duration of social interactions than residents of short-corridor dormitories (Baum & Valins, 1979).

During the first five weeks of residence, subjects exposed to the "helplessness training" showed more signs of invigoration than controls: Long-corridor residents gave more competitive responses in a prisoner's-dilemma game than short-corridor residents. After the sixth week, though, the percentage of competitive responses among long-corridor residents fell abruptly to the level of the short-corridor residents. At this point, long-corridor residents began to show signs of helplessness. Their rate of withdrawal responses in the prisoner's-dilemma game increased significantly in comparison both to their rate during the first five weeks of residence and to the withdrawal rate of short-corridor residents. In general, findings suggest that "natural" helplessness training first promotes invigoration and then withdrawal.

One recent study, however, failed to corroborate the hypothesized invigoration – deterioration cycle. Barber (1989) conducted a parametric LH study in which subjects were asked to try to stop a series of 5, 10, 15, 20, 25, or 30 escapable or inescapable tones. Subjects in the inescapable-tone condition performed as well as controls after 5 trials. This was followed by worse performance after 10 trials, no performance differences after 15 and 25 trials, and again worse performance after 30 trials. Barber (1989) concluded that performance deficits are found at two points in the continuum from a small to a large amount of helplessness training, and that these points are separated by a period in which the training has no performance effect.

Barber's findings are open to two major methodological questions. First, because the test and training tasks used similar stimuli and response devices, they may have been perceived as a single task. Consequently, the study may not have measured the generalization of LH effects to a new task. Second, questionnaire data on perceived control indicated that subjects become aware very early in the experiment, even after 5 inescapable tones, that responses and tone termination were noncontingent. This early perception of uncontrollability raises doubts about the procedure, because research has pointed to difficulties in perceiving uncontrollability even after a large amount of training (e.g., Ford & Neale, 1985).

To overcome these shortcomings, I conducted a recent parametric laboratory study. Subjects were exposed to either zero, one, two, three, four, or five unsolvable concept-formation problems and subsequently were asked to perform a letter cancellation task. Performance accuracy data (see Figure 1.1) were consistent with the invigoration–deterioration cycle. Subjects exposed to one unsolvable problem performed better than subjects exposed to no problem. Two unsolvable problems had no significant effect, but three, four, and five unsolvable problems produced worse performance than no problem.

In general, the presence of reactance is supported by four of the five studies that assess the link between amount of helplessness training and performance. It is further validated by most of the LH studies that examine the interaction between amount of helplessness training and other situational and personality factors (see next chapters). These findings enlarge the nature of the LH effects and require that any theory account for both the detrimental effects of a large amount of helplessness training and the facilitatory effects of a small amount of helplessness training.

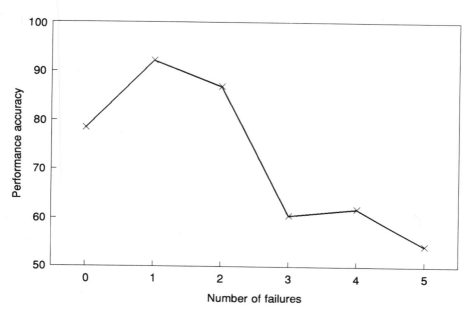

FIGURE 1.1. Means of performance accuracy according to number of failures.

SUMMARY

LH deficits are defined by the presence of cognitive and/or motivational deficiencies in performing a new, controllable task after being exposed to helplessness training. Thus any theory of human LH should explain how uncontrollable failure produces these deficiencies in controllable tasks. Moreover, such theory should also present some statements about the mechanisms that underlie (a) the generalization of LH effects, and (b) the performance facilitation produced by a small amount of helplessness training.

THEORETICAL ACCOUNTS

ANIMAL LH THEORIES

The first and dominant theoretical account of animal LH is the original Learned Helplessness theory (Maier & Seligman, 1976; Seligman et al., 1971). It states that LH effects result from learning that outcomes are independent of responses. Every organism exposed to uncontrollable outcomes learns that these outcomes are beyond its control. This learning leads to the formation of the expectation that outcomes will remain independent of responses in the next tasks, which in turn reduces the motivation to initiate instrumental responses and impairs task performance. It is the formation of the expectancy of no control for the test task that explains subsequent LH deficits.

Maier and Seligman (1976) presented two alternative explanations of animal LH; these focus on the general changes in motivation that inescapable shock can produce in animals. The *adaptation* hypothesis proposed that animals pretreated with inescapable shock may adapt to the shock and feel less pain than the animals in the escape condition. This in turn would reduce their motivation to escape the shocks in the test task. The *sensitization* hypothesis argued that the animals may develop an oversensitivity to the possibility of inescapable shock that might interfere with their organization of responses.

As animal LH research advanced, both these explanations were refined and developed to account for empirical findings. Maier and Jackson (1979) proposed that adaptation to inescapable shock is brought about by the release of endorphins that cause the organism to feel less pain during shock presentation. The sensitization hypothesis has been modified and refined by research on the fear-producing property of inescapable shock (e.g., Jackson & Minor, 1988; Minor, Trauner, Lee, & Dees, 1990). In this view, prolonged exposure to inescapable shock results in context fear conditioning, overarouses the organism, and elicits inappropriate responses that interfere with task performance.

Other alternative hypotheses explain the performance deficits produced by inescapable shock in terms of the learning of incompatible motor responses (e.g., Anisman & Waller, 1973; Bracewell & Black, 1974; Levis, 1976). Bracewell and Black (1974), for example, argued that any active response is punished during helplessness training, and the organism thus learns to hold still. Accordingly, Anisman and Waller (1973) and Levis (1976) argued that animals exposed to inescapable shock learn that their habitual responses are ineffective in ending the shock and that passivity or "freezing" may be the most appropriate coping reaction. Anisman, DeCatanzaro, and Remington (1978) and Weiss, Glazer, and Pohorecky (1974) favor neurochemical-based "incompatible motor response" explanations of animal LH. Weiss et al. contended that LH deficits stem from the depletion of the norepinephrine needed to initiate movement; Anisman et al. claimed that cholinergic mechanisms were involved.

Another incompatible-response account was formulated by Boyd (1982) on the basis of Amsel's (1972) model of behavioral persistence. In Boyd's view, LH effects result from the fixation and persistence of responses that are appropriate to the helplessness training but inappropriate to the test task. Organisms exposed to inescapable shock may fixate on responses acquired during helplessness training, which in turn may delay the acquisition of new, more appropriate responses in the test task. Though Boyd's account resembles other incompatible-response explanations, it does not restrict LH effects to the learning of passivity. Boyd contends that any response set—motor or cognitive—that is transferred from helplessness training to the test task is responsible for the LH effects.

An entirely different explanation was presented by Lubow, Rosemblat, and

Weiner (1981), who contended that LH effects result from conditioned inattention to the inescapable shock. In their terms, helplessness training entails exposure to lack of contingency between a repeatedly presented event and any other event in the environment, which in turn teaches the organism not to attend to the noncontingent event. This conditioned inattention, which can be prevented by systematically exposing the organism to another event after the shock, impedes the conditioning of instrumental responses to the shock and impairs performance in the test task.

Lee and Maier (1988) also proposed that attentional mechanisms may underlie animal LH. In these authors' terms, animals exposed to inescapable shock have difficulty in focusing on task-relevant cues and in inhibiting attention to task-irrelevant stimuli. Lee and Maier suggest that this attentional deficit may result from a high level of fear or from the depletion of norepinephrine produced by inescapable shock. In addition, they raise the possibility that animals exposed to inescapable shock may be unable or unwilling to pay attention to internal response-related cues, and that this may further exacerbate their difficulties in selecting appropriate escape responses.

I will not review in this book the findings supporting or disconfirming the various hypotheses, nor will I discuss the arguments for and against them. The theories apply mainly to animal LH deficits and cannot be directly extrapolated to explain human LH. First, most of the hypotheses reviewed above apply only to the effects of inescapable shocks. They cannot explain the psychological effects of unsolvable cognitive problems, which constitute one common operationalization of helplessness training with humans. Second, most of the hypotheses explain retarded motor responses in escape tasks or retarded learning in simple instrumental or classical conditioning settings. But they cannot explain cognitive difficulties, such as inaccuracy in anagrams, after helplessness training in humans. Third, the reviewed hypotheses have little to say about the generalization of human LH effects, the reactance effects, and the issue of individual differences.

To explain human LH, we need constructs that are much broader and inclusive than those derived from animal studies. They must be able to explain motor and cognitive deficits in either simple or complex problem-solving settings that are produced by either inescapable aversive stimuli or unsolvable cognitive problems. They must take into account the complexity of human motives: the tendency of human beings to be reflective, to appraise and reappraise both themselves and their environment during and after helplessness training, and to assign personal meanings to their experiences. In other words, theories must consider the roles of high order mental processes and be able to deal too with findings that are unique to human LH.

HUMAN LH THEORIES

The Learned Helplessness theory has also been the dominant account of human LH (Abramson, Seligman, & Teasdale, 1978; Alloy & Seligman, 1979; Seligman, 1975). In its original version, the theory claimed that LH deficits in both animals and humans are caused by the expectancy of no control. In its reformulated version (Abramson, Seligman, & Teasdale, 1978), the theory proposed that animals and humans differ in the formation of the expectancy of no control: Although simple learning processes suffice to explain expectancy changes in animals, the same changes in humans require also that the person subjectively attributes his or her failure to particular causes. Irrespective of causal attribution, however, the reformulated Learned Helplessness theory still views the expectancy of no control as the sufficient precursor of LH deficits. No matter which attribution a person makes, if he or she expects lack of control after failure, he or she will exhibit LH deficits.

With empirical tests of both the original and reformulated Learned Helplessness theories, however, it became clear that the expectancy of no control and its attributional antecedents are not sufficient to explain the pattern of results obtained. Although performance decrements are found when the expectancy of no control is formed, this link is confined to particular conditions and to particular persons. Moreover, other cognitive and emotional factors have been found to influence the strength of LH deficits. It is for these reasons that during the past 15 years investigators have formulated alternative theories of human LH. They have proposed a variety of psychological factors that may constrain the effects of the expectancy of no control and/or account by themselves for LH effects.

Two theories have followed Seligman's reasoning that the expectancy of no control leads to LH deficits, but they have added other factors that moderate the expectancy–performance link. In their integrative model of reactance and helplessness, Wortman and Brehm (1975) proposed the perception of the importance of the training and test tasks as one of these moderators. The expectancy of no control may impair performance mainly when people assign high importance to the tasks. The assignment of low importance may inhibit LH deficits, even after a person expects to fail in the test task. In addition, Wortman and Brehm suggested that the individual's affective reactions to helplessness training may intensify LH effects, with anger strengthening reactance, and anxiety and depressed mood strengthening LH deficits.

In their cybernetic model of human behavior, Carver and Scheier (1981) claimed that the direction of attention inward (self-focus) is an additional moderating factor. Unfavorable expectancies produce LH deficits only under conditions that encourage self-focus or among persons who habitually tend to direct attention inward. In addition, Carver and Scheier introduced the concept of mental withdrawal—a mental dissociation from task attempts—as the mechanism that underlies LH deficits.

Other theories have taken a step further away from the Learned Helplessness theory and propose that psychological factors other than the expectancy of control may account for LH effects. The cognitive interference hypothesis emphasizes the role of anxiety and off-task thoughts (Coyne, Metalsky, & Lavelle, 1980; Lavelle, Metalsky, & Coyne, 1979; Mikulincer, 1989a). This hypothesis, which is based on anxiety theory and research (Mandler, 1972; Sarason, 1975; Wine, 1971), maintains that exposure to unsolvable problems provokes anxiety and related self-focused off-task thoughts, including worry about one's negative characteristics, self-doubts, and self-deprecation. These self-concerned cognitions divert attention away from task-relevant activities and thereby impair task performance. Any treatment designed to reduce task-irrelevant self-preoccupation will thus weaken cognitive interference and LH deficits.

In his action control theory, Kuhl (1981, 1984) introduces the dimension of action–state mental rumination as an intervening factor in the sequence of events leading to LH effects. Action rumination is defined by purposive thinking on goal-directed problem solving. State rumination is represented by both purposive and autonomic thinking about the past, present, and future state of the self. Kuhl (1981) postulates that exposure to uncontrollable failure initially enhances action rumination and focuses the person on the problem at hand. This process may underlie reactance effects. Repeated uncontrollable failure may induce a change from action to state rumination, which diverts attention away from task-relevant actions, creates a state of cognitive interference, and thereby impairs task performance.

The egotism hypothesis (Frankel & Snyder, 1978) suggests that LH deficits are a result of lack of effort stemming from the desire to protect self-esteem from the threat created by a failure. As stated earlier, uncontrollable failure may not only lead to the belief that outcomes are independent of responses but also may threaten self-esteem. To protect self-esteem, people might lower their efforts in the test task in order to rationalize any potential failure as attributable to lack of effort rather than lack of ability. They may adopt what Jones and Berglas (1978) have termed self-handicapping strategies—the creation of impediments to performance which give people an excuse for failure. These strategies protect self-esteem by controlling the causes of failure, but at the price of performance deficits.

In a somewhat related account, I viewed self-handicapping strategies as one way that people may cope with uncontrollable failure (Mikulincer, 1989b,c). This position was based on the premise that people exposed to helplessness training may mobilize a variety of coping resources to manage the threatening implications of failure. It is also based on Lazarus and Folkman's (1984) contention that coping actions have an impact on adaptational outcomes. Specifically, I hypothesized that problem solving and a variety of reappraisal strategies (e.g., excuse making) may improve task performance, whereas the use of off-task coping strategies (e.g., mental disengagement or effort withdrawal) may contribute to LH deficits.

All of the above explanations of human LH have had a strong impact on the conceptualization of human LH and have generated a wealth of empirical research, some of which has supported each of them. At the same time, each of these theories has provoked a wave of criticism and studies aimed at attacking its arguments and disconfirming its predictions. Extensive examples of controversial findings and theoretical attacks and counterattacks are presented by Abramson, Seligman, and Teasdale (1978), Alloy (1982), Frankel and Snyder (1978), Kuhl (1981), Lavelle et al. (1979), and Silver, Wortman, and Klos (1982). All these studies were designed to demonstrate the validity of one hypothesis and to rule out the others. None have tried to integrate the various contentions and arrive at a single, integrated position.

In reaction to this polemical and controversial nature of human LH literature, I will present an integrative approach that converges the conflicting hypotheses into a single, well-articulated position. I try to avoid fruitless debate regarding the sufficiency of isolated factors; instead I suggest that most of the above explanations of human LH may be right, because each of the proposed mechanisms may contribute in one way or another to LH effects. As Maier and Jackson (1979) stated with regard to animal LH, perhaps "all of us were right (and wrong)."

The position I present throughout this book is that human LH is a multidimensional phenomenon and that LH effects reflect the action of a network of cognitive, emotional, and motivational factors that may be responsive to helplessness training and may alter task performance. Factors such as the expectancy of control, the perception of task importance, the experience of a threat to self-identity, the direction of attention inward, the arousal of anger, anxiety, and depression, the engagement in action- or state-oriented ruminations, and the adoption of particular coping strategies may all contribute to LH effects and may accomplish particular functions in the process leading to these effects. Moreover, they may be interrelated, and each of them may constrain the performance effects of the other factors. I will propose a theory that delineates the roles of the above factors in human LH and their interrelationships and constraints. I will attempt to integrate the multiple intervening factors so as to reach a single, well-articulated account of the complex nature of human LH.

A BRIEF EXPOSITION OF THE THEORY

In this section I present a brief preview of the theory that will be developed in detail throughout the book. The theory emerges from a coping perspective of human behavior and integrates prior theoretical accounts of human LH with pertinent empirical evidence. It assumes that the process of coping with the person–environment mismatch created by uncontrollable failure is the most crucial aspect of human LH. It further assumes that the cognitive, motivational, and emotional intervening factors proposed by previous theories are part of this process. In this theory, coping strategies are the direct mechanisms of change in the environment and/or the person. The expectancy of control determines the *type* of coping response activated after failure, the perceived importance of the failure and the individual's focus of attention determine its *strength*, emotion supports the activation of the coping response, and mental rumination is its cognitive substrate.

The theory further specifies the sequence of psychological events in a causal chain hypothesized to culminate in LH effects. Specifically, it delineates sequences that explain the improvement in performance produced by a small amount of helplessness training (reactance) and the impairment in performance produced by a large amount of training (LH deficits). In these sequences, the cognitive, motivational, and emotional factors noted above are categorized according to their sequential relationships to LH effects: *distal* factors operate quite early in the causal sequence, before LH effects become apparent, whereas *proximal* factors operate relatively late in the causal pathway and may occur immediately prior to, or concurrent with, performance changes.

The theory is based on the following three premises adapted from Lazarus's model of coping and adaptation (Lazarus, 1991; Lazarus & Folkman, 1984):

1. *Helplessness training disrupts the person–environment equilibrium and activates a coping process.* After failure, people will generally experience a mismatch with the environment. This leads them to evaluate the importance/self-relevance of the failure by directing their attention inward and appraising the extent to which this failure threatens their mental structures (e.g., goals, schemas). The results of this evaluation determine whether the person opts to mobilize coping efforts to manage the mismatch. If the decision is to cope with the failure, then the person will estimate the probability of control as a guideline for selecting the type of coping behaviors to employ, will experience emotions that reinforce and sustain the chosen way of coping, will engage in mental rumination as a cognitive tool for coping, and will effortfully undertake the chosen coping strategy that is designed to bring events and goals into better alignment.

2. *Once coping efforts have been mobilized, recurrent failure will change control expectancies, emotions, cognitive activities, and coping responses.* This sequence begins with the effects of each consecutive failure on the expectancy of control. Changes in control expectancies cue revision of coping strategies and ruminative thoughts, and these evoke the emotions needed to reinforce and sustain the coping activities. After a small amount of failure, ordinary, well-functioning people typically hold a moderate to high expectancy of control, which in turn leads to task-oriented coping and rumination and also to angry affect. After a large amount of helplessness training, however, people typically lower their expectancy of control; this leads to off-task coping and rumination and to anxious or depressed emotion.

3. *Changes in coping strategies after failure are manifested in task performance.* Coping strategies (a) orient people toward or away from the task, (b) either correspond with or are antagonistic to task efforts, and (c) are reflected in either improved or impaired task performance. In addition, certain coping strategies may produce dysfunctional cognitions and emotions that lead to LH deficits.

The first derivate of the above premises is that coping strategies are *proximal* precursors of LH effects. Reactance results from coping strategies that direct resources toward the solution of the problem and facilitate task-relevant activities. LH deficits result from coping strategies that move people away from a task and compete with task activities for resources. For example, the person may direct resources toward distracting activities or toward self-schemas and personal priorities. Under some conditions, LH deficits may also result from some dysfunctional side effects of coping strategies, such as the intrusion of autonomic thoughts and affects.

In these terms, both reactance and LH deficits are a product of coping attempts. The problem with the coping strategies that lead to LH deficits is that they are carried out at the expense of task performance and may have some dysfunctional side effects. Beyond reflecting a functional trade-off by which task performance is sacrificed in exchange for mitigation of distress and/or adaptation to environmental constraints, LH deficits may therefore also reflect the cognitive interference produced by autonomic thoughts and affects.

The cognitive substrate of coping, *mental rumination,* also contributes to LH effects. It may alter task performance by filling the thought flow with particular types of ideations that create the cognitive context for the organization of coping strategies. Reactance results from rumination that fills the thought flow with task-relevant ideations and creates a cognitive context favorable to problem solving. LH deficits result from rumination that fills the thought flow with off-task ideations and creates a cognitive context that may interfere with task-relevant activities.

A second derivate of my premises is that every factor that influences coping actions is a *distal* precursor of LH effects. One of these factors is the *expectancy of control,* the "secondary appraisal" (Lazarus & Folkman, 1984) component of the coping process that acts as a "psychological watershed" in that it determines the choice of a particular coping strategy. After failure, people assess the extent to which they can control the failure and restore the loss; based on these assessments, they select what they perceive to be the most suitable coping actions. On this basis, expectancies may indirectly contribute to the performance changes that coping actions may produce. That is, the expectancy of control may lead to reactance or LH deficits by favoring the undertaking of coping actions that either improve or impair task performance.

Another factor that may indirectly contribute to LH effects is *emotional arousal.* In my terms, emotional arousal reinforces and sustains the coping actions cued by the expectancy of control. The expectancy of control merely indicates which coping actions are to be preferred. Emotions are the mechanisms by which those actions are initiated and sustained until their ends are attained; they are specialized to mobilize particular action tendencies in response to dangers and threats, to prepare the person for undertaking those actions, and to provide the "fuel" for completing them. In this way, emotions contribute to LH effects by acting on the coping actions that either improve or impair task performance: They strengthen the link between expectancy of control and coping actions and sustain these actions in face of obstacles or alternative motivational tendencies.

The individual's *focus of attention* and the *perceived importance/self-relevance* of failure are also distal precursors of LH effects. These two factors seem to determine the intensity of whatever coping actions people undertake and therefore the strength of any resulting LH effect. During and after helplessness training, attentional focus can be directed either toward or away from the self. The direction of attention toward the self facilitates the appraisal of the self-relevant threats

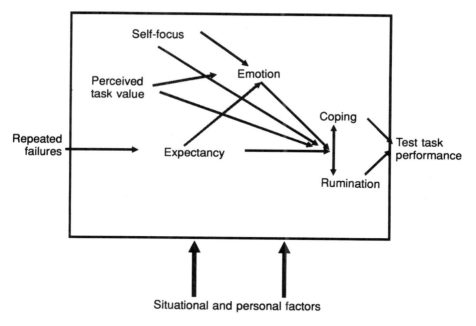

FIGURE 1.2. The coping process.

implied by failure, favoring the activation of the entire coping process and thus intensifying the resulting performance changes. A self-focused person can realize the personal implications of failure, feel a pressure to undertake coping actions, and thereby may show the reactance and LH deficits resulting from these actions.

Before taking any coping action, however, self-focused persons assess the relevance of the failure to their goals and self-identity and evaluate whether these personal structures are threatened and whether there is a resulting need to activate actions to manage the threat. The assignment of high value to failure implies that important things are at stake and favors the mobilization of coping actions, either of the sort that may be reflected in reactance or LH deficits. The appraisal of low value means that there is nothing of importance to lose, reduces the need for coping, and thus prevents any positive or negative performance change that coping actions could cause.

Figure 1.2 summarizes the above reasoning. Expectancy of control, emotions, mental rumination, and coping strategies seem to *mediate* between helplessness training and performance changes. They are altered by helplessness training and contribute to reactance and LH deficits. This mediational sequence, though, is *moderated* by the perceived importance of failure and the person's focus of attention. No coping action, ruminative thought, emotion, or performance change will be recorded when failure does not imply any threat or people lack the cognitive mechanism to detect the threat (low self-focus).

In this schema, LH deficits and reactance are preceded by markedly different expectancies, emotions, cognitions, and coping strategies. Both LH effects, however, are characterized by high levels of perceived task value and a high degree of self-focus. This schema also differentiates between factors that mediate LH effects (expectancy, emotion, rumination, coping strategies) and factors that moderate them (perceived task value, self-focus). In addition, the schema emphasizes that helplessness training alone will not alter test task performance; two additional conditions

TABLE 1.1. Summary of the Studies Presented throughout the Book

Study	N	Independent variables	Training task	Test task	Dependent variables
Study 1	60	Number of failures (0, 1, 2, 3, 4, or 5)	Concept formation	Letter cancellation	Accuracy; ratings of control, attribution, expectancy, emotion, rumination, coping action
Study 2	64	Feedback × proneness to problem solving × proneness to reappraisal	Concept formation	Letter cancellation	Performance accuracy
Study 3	64	Feedback × proneness to avoidance × test delay	Concept formation	Letter cancellation	Performance accuracy
Study 4	64	Feedback × proneness to reorganization × test delay	Concept formation	Letter cancellation	Performance accuracy
Study 5	48	Number of failures (0, 1, or 4) × type of learned material (action, state)	Concept formation	Recognition task	Study time, memory accuracy
Study 6	48	Number of failures (0, 1, or 4) × instructions to suppress task thoughts (no, yes)	Concept formation	Thinking aloud task	Number of mentioned task-related thoughts
Study 7	30	Feedback	Concept formation	Contingency learning	Judgments of control

(continued)

TABLE 1.1. (*Continued*)

Study	N	Independent variables	Training task	Test task	Dependent variables
Study 8	40	Feedback × self-efficacy for problem solving (low, high)	Concept formation	Letter cancellation	Accuracy; ratings of expectancy, emotion, rumination, coping action
Study 9	48	Number of failures (0, 1, and 4) × trait emotional intensity (low, high)	Concept formation	Letter cancellation	Accuracy; ratings of expectancy, emotion, rumination, coping action
Study 10	48	Number of failures (0, 1, and 4) × trait anger (low, high)	Concept formation	Letter cancellation	Accuracy; ratings of expectancy, emotion, rumination, coping action
Study 11	48	Number of failures (0, 1, and 4) × messages of task importance (low, high)	Concept formation	Letter cancellation	Accuracy; ratings of expectancy, emotion, rumination, coping action
Study 12	48	Number of failures (0, 1, or 4) × induction of self-focus (low, high)	Concept formation	Letter cancellation	Accuracy; ratings of expectancy, emotion, rumination, coping action
Study 13	64	Feedback × induced self-focus × task importance instructions	Concept formation	Letter cancellation	Performance accuracy

Note: Feedback = comparison of no feedback versus failure.

must be met. Changes will be observed after helplessness training only when failure both threatens the achievement of important goals and elicits self-focus. Moreover, any personality and situational factor that influences expectancies, coping strategies, mental rumination, or emotion may temper the link between helplessness training and task performance. Finally, the schema implies that the expectancy of control influences task performance only indirectly (via coping strategies) and only under conditions of high perceived task value and high self-focus.

In the following chapters, I will elaborate on the specific hypotheses derived from a coping conceptualization of human LH. Each of Chapters 2 through 7 presents one of the factors that underlie LH effects in detail. In these chapters, I elaborate on the function of these factors for human LH, present some basic hypotheses on their antecedents and effects, review relevant statements of other theories of human LH, and survey pertinent research. In addition, I present a series of 13 unpublished LH studies that I conducted in my laboratory for this book (see a summary in Table 1.1). In Chapter 8, I present an integrative view of the mediational sequence leading to reactance and LH deficits, and I elaborate on the theoretical significance and implications of a coping perspective of human LH.

COPING STRATEGIES AS PROXIMAL MEDIATORS OF LH EFFECTS

A major issue in the analysis of human LH as a coping process is how people cope with lack of control and the impact of their coping responses on task performance. By coping I mean any and all cognitive and behavioral responses intended to resolve a mismatch between environmental outcomes and the individual's wants or, at least, to minimize the threat implied by the mismatch (e.g., Lazarus & Folkman, 1984; Lazarus, 1991). These coping responses are shaped by the appraisal of the situation (e.g., goal relevance, controllability) and may have a wide variety of motivational, cognitive, emotional, and functional effects (e.g., Lazarus & Folkman, 1984; Smith, 1990).

Coping responses occupy a central position in my conceptualization of human LH. Coping responses may be activated in reaction to the uncontrollable failure and may alter test task performance. After helplessness training, people may mobilize coping efforts to manage the person–environment mismatch that thwarts their goals and threatens their self-identity. These responses may be oriented toward or away from the task, may support or compete for resources with task-relevant activities, and hence may directly contribute to the improvement or impairment of performance in a solvable test task.

My basic hypothesis is that coping responses mediate between helplessness training and LH effects. A small amount of failure typically leads to task-oriented coping strategies, which in turn improve performance. A large amount of training leads to off-task coping strategies, which in turn impair performance. This chapter presents theoretical and empirical knowledge pertinent to these mediational sequences.

33

COPING RESPONSES: DEFINITION AND TAXONOMY

THE CONCEPT OF COPING

Like most contemporary accounts of coping, my ideas rely on Richard Lazarus's cognitive appraisal model (Lazarus & Folkman, 1984). This theory defines coping responses "as constantly changing cognitive and behavioral efforts to manage specific external and/or internal demands that are appraised as taxing or exceeding the resources of the person" (Lazarus & Folkman, 1984, p. 141). In this definition, coping responses are directed toward a particular person–environment transaction and are responsive to changes both in the environment and the person. The definition also emphasizes the contextual construction of coping responses. People do not react automatically to environmental changes. Rather, they appraise the demands implicit in the situation, the resources they have for managing them, and the consequences of their responses before acting. In addition, coping responses are not synonymous with adaptive outcomes. They encompass all the person's attempts to deal with life adversities, whether or not the attempts are successful.

The above definition also emphasizes the functional nature of coping responses. According to Lazarus and Folkman (1984), coping responses serve to manage a mismatch between an actual course of events and what a person wants in the situation. Some responses are designed to restore the disrupted equilibrium between the person and the environment by attempting to change either the environment or oneself. Other responses are designed to modify the meaning of the problematic situation so that it becomes less threatening. Though such responses cannot directly end a mismatch, they may facilitate adaptive changes by reducing the distress that may otherwise interfere with such activities. Still other responses are designed to distance people from the problematic situation as a means of managing the distress without resolving the mismatch.

None of the above coping responses, however, preclude the possibility of dysfunctional consequences. In fact, every adaptive mechanism may entail the danger of maladaptation when it is improperly used. Similar ideas are implicit in accounts of self-regulation (Carver & Scheier, 1981; Rothbaum, Weisz, & Snyder, 1982) and adaptation (Snyder & Higgins, 1988; Taylor & Brown, 1988).

TAXONOMY OF COPING RESPONSES

Scholars have found a very large variety of possible coping responses. For example, Amirkhan (1990) compiled an exhaustive list of 161 distinct coping responses derived from existing measures. Lazarus and his colleagues developed a measure they called Ways of Coping (Folkman & Lazarus, 1980, 1985) that includes 66 different thoughts or actions used by people to deal with negative events. This diversity is also evident in one of my phenomenological studies (Mikulincer & Ben-Artzi, 1990), in which subjects who were asked to report their habitual responses to negative life events provided 76 distinct coping strategies.

Numerous studies have attempted to make a taxonomy of this large range of coping responses (e.g., Aldwin & Revenson, 1987; Amirkhan, 1990; Endler & Parker, 1990; Folkman & Lazarus, 1980, 1985; McCrae, 1984). Every study, though, presents a different taxonomy. The lack of consensus may stem from the use of different research tools, the assessment of different populations and negative events, or, as Carver, Scheier, and Weintraub (1989) pointed out, from a lack of clear focus in the items in the self-report scales. In my view, the lack of consensus may also derive from the use of different labels for similar coping categories as well as from the use of a wide variety of self-report scales rather than a uniform scale validated across samples and life events.

Despite the lack of uniformity of coping taxonomies, a detailed examination of the studies reveals that some categories recur under different labels. These categories include problem solving, reappraisal of the event in positive terms, acceptance of the problem and reorganization of self-views and priorities, cognitive avoidance of the threat by focusing on fantasies (wishful thinking), cognitive and behavioral detachment from the situation, sedative/distracting activities, and seeking social support.

On a theoretical level, attempts have been made to organize coping responses into high-order categories. One classic taxonomy was proposed by Lazarus and Folkman (1984), who divide coping responses on the basis of their focus. *Problem-focused coping* entails making changes in the environment to bring it into line with the person's wants; people try to remove obstacles that block the realization of their strivings. *Emotion-focused coping* entails making intrapsychic changes to minimize a mismatch or to reduce its threatening implications; people try to alter their appraisal of the mismatch, their attitudes toward it, and/or their priorities.

Lazarus and Folkman's emotion-focused coping category, however, is too simple (e.g., Scheier, Weintraub, & Carver, 1986; Tobin, Holroyd, Reynolds, & Wigal, 1989). The wide range of responses it encompasses—including reappraisal, acceptance, wishful thinking, and avoidance—differ appreciably, and some are inversely correlated (e.g., Aldwin & Revenson, 1987; Carver et al., 1989). Though all the strategies reflect intrapsychic changes, some of them impair problem solving (e.g., avoidance), whereas others may aid it (e.g., reappraisal). In addition, whereas some strategies may distort reality, others lead to the acceptance of the problematic situation.

Another proposed high-order categorization of coping responses differentiates between approach and avoidance strategies (Horowitz, 1979; Kobasa, 1982; Miller, 1980; Roth & Cohen, 1986). In its simplest form, this pair of concepts refers to activities oriented toward or away from threatening stimuli. Whereas approach strategies deal with a person–environment mismatch by confronting its threatening implications and are designed to manage it actively, avoidance strategies are designed to deny the mismatch and to escape/avoid any direct or symbolic confrontation with its threatening consequences. Several studies support the approach–avoidance categorization (e.g., Gentry & Kobasa, 1984; Kobasa, 1982; Parkes, 1984).

The problem with the approach–avoidance categorization is that although problem solving and acceptance are both clearly approach strategies, they use different tactics to manage a mismatch. This problem was first acknowledged by Scheier et al. (1986), who subsumed all problem-focused coping strategies under the approach category, then divided emotion-focused coping strategies into those that reflect a cognitive and affective "stay" in the problematic situation and those that reflect a "flight" from the threat. In this way, Scheier et al. (1986) integrated the approach–avoidance distinction with Lazarus and Folkman's problem-focused– emotion-focused distinction and proposed three categories: problem-focused, emotion-focused/approach, and emotion-focused/avoidance coping. This taxonomy was empirically validated by Endler and Parker (1990) and Tobin et al. (1989).

Nonetheless, although all emotion-focused/approach strategies aim at intrapsychic change, they are not homogeneous in the purpose and product of the change. *Reorganization* strategies entail the accommodation of mental structures to reality; people work through the mismatch and reorganize existing cognitive-motivational structures to bring them more in line with reality constraints. *Reappraisal* coping tries to alter the appraisal of events, emphasizing their positive sides and dismissing any need to change stable inner structures.

Whereas reorganization strategies produce changes in self-perception and priorities, reappraisal strategies may keep these structures intact. Though the former result in the acceptance of the problem and its incorporation into mental structures, the latter result in a partial denial of the threat and its fragmentation from these structures. Finally, reorganization can truly put an end to a mismatch by finding substitute goals, whereas reappraisal can provide only an illusory, temporary resolution of the mismatch and, in fact, may delay a real solution until changes occur in the environment or person.

On this basis, I propose four higher-order categories: problem-focused, reappraisal, reorganization, and avoidance strategies. As for seeking support, this includes a wide variety of responses that span the various high-order factors. Some forms of support seeking are problem focused (information seeking), others entail reappraisal (i.e., making social comparisons with other people), and still others are avoidant (i.e., talking about distracting subjects with others).

Coping strategies can be oriented toward the person–environment mismatch (problem solving, reappraisal, reorganization) or away from it (avoidance). Of the approach strategies, reorganization and reappraisal are designed to make intrapsychic changes, and problem solving is designed to make a change in the environment. Finally, of the intrapsychic strategies, reappraisal distorts reality, and reorganization entails the acceptance of reality and a change of priorities.

Problem-Focused Coping

Problem-focused strategies are designed to reduce a person–environment mismatch by molding the problematic events and maintaining intact existing mental structures. In a task situation, this sort of coping encompasses the generation and organization of task-relevant responses to remove external obstacles and to over-come any actual or anticipated failure. This coping strategy is what Hartmann (1939) calls "alloplastic adaptation."

Problem-focused coping consists of a vast array of cognitive and behavioral procedures (e.g., see Aldwin & Revenson, 1987; Lazarus & Folkman, 1984; Mc-Crae, 1984). In a factor analytic study, Carver et al. (1989) found four different problem-focused strategies: (a) active coping—procedures to remove obstacles from the goal; (b) planning—thinking about action strategies and about how to solve the problem; (c) suppression of competing activities—disengagement from other goals and activities; and (d) restraint—holding back actions and avoiding premature decisions.

Problem-focused coping is also manifested in two other cognitive activities. One is epistemic activity, which consists of the generation of functional knowledge about the alternative paths for solving a problem, the testing of these paths against available evidence, and the selection of the most appropriate path. The other in-volves a metacognitive process: the generation of knowledge about cognitive func-tioning. People generate hypotheses about the competences necessary for problem solving and about how to control distraction, monitor the solution process, organize incoming information, and retrieve stored information.

Reorganization Strategies

Reorganization strategies may be used when people cannot adjust events to their wishes and instead try to minimize the person–environment mismatch by accommodating their wishes to the events. This is what Hartmann (1939) calls "autoplastic adaptation."

The adjustment of mental structures entails intrapsychic changes to make them fit both the reality constraints and the person's basic ends and global self-definition. Studies have found that people cope with unsurmountable undesirable events by reordering their priorities (Taylor, 1983), their plans and life projects (Weisman & Worden, 1975), and/or their personal views of the world and them-selves (Cornwell, Nurcombe, & Stevens, 1977), as well as by adopting new goals, discovering what is important to them, or learning new things that provide oppor-tunity for growth and change (Carver et al., 1989; McCrae, 1984). This reorgani-zation task is also implicit in Lindemann's (1944) concept of "grief work" and Janis's (1958) concept of the "work of worrying." It is also consistent with Horowitz's (1979) idea of "completion tendency," by which mental structures are revised to remain tuned to reality.

Reorganization entails a better accommodation to reality: the pursuit of more realistic goals and the adoption of a more realistic view of oneself. It may also result in a more flexible and rich self-system as people become aware of their strengths and weaknesses and learn new things about themselves and the world. Though they abandon some of their immediate goals and projects, they need not feel powerless, but they may find alternative projects and goals that renew their sense of self-worth.

Reorganization does not involve a complete giving up of basic ends or a rejection of one's global self-definition. Rather, it entails the replacement of the immediate goal pursued in a task (which is only one of several alternative ways of attaining superordinate goals and confirming global self-definition) with a more realizable goal. In fact, an unsurmountable person–environment mismatch only means that the subordinate goals pursued are inappropriate and maladaptive for the attainment of basic ends and should be replaced with more reality-attuned and effective ones. Reorganization coping is directly designed to find these alternative goals. At the expense of some adaptive change in lower-level goals, it thus minimizes the person–environment mismatch and maintains the core parts of the goal hierarchy intact.

Adaptive changes may be classified according to their pervasiveness. Marris (1974) spoke about three types of changes. The least pervasive change is substitutive in nature and reflects the replacement of means for meeting existing needs. Growth reflects a more pervasive change in which people incorporate existing beliefs and goals within a broader understanding or range of interests. Loss is thought to be the most pervasive change: People reinterpret what they have learned about the self and the world, "tying past, present, and future together again with rewoven strands of meaning" (Marris, 1974, p. 21). Of course, the pervasiveness of a change may be directly reflected in the amount of immediate distress produced by the reorganization task and by the amount of time that the task requires.

The reorganization task involves a series of self-evaluative and self-reparative activities. First, people must accept that the problem is unsurmountable. Acceptance of the irremediability of the mismatch and the abandonment of useless activities are basic steps in adapting mental structures. They reflect an attempt to come to terms with the situation by changing one's own schemas rather than by trying to force reality to conform to them. Second, people must work through the distressing experience and reflect upon their existing cognitive-motivational structures in order to evaluate the damage. Third, people must restructure these structures to incorporate the threatening event, generate alternative projects, and put aside the old inappropriate goals and unrealistic self-aspects.

Reorganization is similar to problem solving in that both these approaches restore the equilibrium between the person and the environment by removing the obstacles that block the attainment of goals and the confirmation of global self-definition. The simple difference between the two types of coping resides in the type of obstacles removed: Whereas problem-focused coping destroys and conquers environmental obstacles, reorganization removes internal obstacles.

Reappraisal Strategies

Unlike problem solving and reorganization, reappraisal leaves the person–environment mismatch unresolved. This does not necessarily imply, however, that reappraisal will interfere with the person's attempts to end a mismatch. In fact, reappraisal may facilitate these attempts by reducing the distress that may otherwise interfere with the resolution of the mismatch.

Reappraisal consists of attempts to alter the cognitive construction of the unresolved mismatch and to make it less threatening (Lazarus & Folkman, 1984; Pearlin & Schooler, 1978). Lazarus and Folkman included under the heading of reappraisal not only changes resulting from a realistic interpretation of the events but also those derived from the distortion of reality. Snyder and Higgins (1988) called this way of coping "negotiation with reality"—a compromise with the threat that reduces its overwhelming power. Taylor and Brown (1988) called it "cognitive adaptation" by which people distort negative information and represent it in an unthreatening manner.

In my terms, reappraisal is an intrapsychic manifestation of alloplastic adaptation. Like problem solving, reappraisal serves to assimilate the environmental events into existing mental structures, and it also attempts to manage a mismatch by molding the environment rather than the person's own mental structures. Reappraisal, however, differs from problem solving in its target. Whereas problem solving is aimed at altering the real environment, reappraisal only alters the person's subjective construction of the environment.

The literature points out several reappraisal strategies. The most common is what Lazarus and Folkman (1984) call focusing on the positive aspects of a mismatch. It involves the use of selective attention on positive information and the denial of negative aspects of reality, as well as such other cognitive maneuvers as thinking positive thoughts, making positive self-statements, using humor (Billings & Moos, 1981, 1984; McCrae, 1984), finding side benefits, imagining worse events, making positive social comparisons (Stone & Neale, 1984), refusing to dwell on the problem (Aldwin & Revenson, 1987), and appraising the events as purposeful and meaningful (Taylor, 1983; Thompson, 1985, 1991).

The tendency to focus on the positive aspects of threatening events has been reported in several studies (see Taylor & Brown, 1988, for a review). Thompson (1985), for example, found that some of the victims of a major fire reported that they felt lucky that the experience was not worse, that they judged themselves to be well off compared to others, that their experience had some incidental benefits, or that they were able to put the negative aspects aside. Taylor (1983) and Taylor, Wood, and Lichtman (1983) found that when negative events could not be denied, some subjects attempted to find meaning or benefit in them. Studies of victims of traumatic events have found that many subjects convinced themselves that the trauma served some useful purpose (e.g., Chodoff, Friedman, & Hamburg, 1964; Helmrath & Steinitz, 1978; Mages & Mendelsohn, 1979; Mechanic, 1977).

Another reappraisal strategy is excuse making—redefining the causal agent of the bad event (Snyder & Higgins, 1988). Snyder and Higgins (1988) define excuses as cognitive maneuvers that either raise consensus ("Anyone would perform as poorly as I did"), raise distinctiveness ("I generally succeed in other tasks") or lower consistency information ("I solved this problem in the past"). Expecting everyone to fail suggests that the situation itself may be responsible for a failure. Claiming that the failure is not generalizable to other tasks and over time suggests that circumstances or unstable self-aspects are responsible for it. Though the mismatch created by failure remains intact, it tells nothing of relevance to self-identity and does not demand inner reorganization. As one can readily note, the attribution of failure to external, unstable, and specific causes is a prototypic excuse-making procedure.

An interesting excuse-making maneuver is the claim of self-handicaps (Arkin & Baumgardner, 1985; Leary & Shepperd, 1986), which consists of the self-report of physical or psychological problems and the attribution of a person–environment mismatch to them rather than to more central self-aspects. A number of studies have documented the claim of self-handicaps as a means of coping with threats (e.g., DeGree & Snyder, 1985; C. R. Snyder & Smith, 1982, 1986).

People can also reappraise the threat indirectly by compensatory cognitions (Steele, 1988). These include emphasizing successes in other important areas or affirming basic values. These cognitions may devalue the importance of the negative events and reduce their detrimental impact on the self system. Baumeister and Jones (1978) and Greenberg and Pyszczynski (1985) found that people compensated for a failure by biasing memory to positive aspects of the self or by inflating the evaluation of other self-dimensions.

Avoidance Strategies

Avoidance also leaves the mismatch unresolved and instead attempts to reduce its threatening implications. A wide range of avoidance strategies is found in the literature. One large group consists of cognitive procedures designed to prevent the intrusion of threat-related thoughts and affects into consciousness. Among these procedures, one can find suppression of thoughts about the threat; distancing by thinking about task-irrelevant matters or engaging in distracting activities; wishful thinking by daydreaming, imagining a better place and time, or waiting for a miracle; active forgetting or putting the problems out of mind; and the numbing or inhibition of emotion (Aldwin & Revenson, 1987; Carver et al., 1989; Folkman & Lazarus, 1980, 1985; McCrae, 1984).

Horowitz (1979) states that cognitive avoidance may be manifested in perception, attention, consciousness, and ideational processing. It is reflected in the inhibition of associations related to the problem situation, in a subjective sense of indifference toward the problem, in a switching of attitudes to such a degree that thoughts about the problem are confused, in narrowing of attention and focusing it away from stimuli related to the problem, in failure to determine the meaning of the problem or to explore alternative meanings, in an inability to remember what happened, and in an excessive focus on fantasy, all of which help to avoid facing the problem and its implications. According to Horowitz, cognitive avoidance reflects the operation of controls over information processing that serve actively to inhibit any material that may increase distress and discomfort.

Another group of avoidance strategies consists of behavioral disengagement: the withdrawal of task-oriented efforts. This strategy has been variously called passivity, effort withdrawal, and problem avoidance (e.g., Aldwin & Revenson, 1987; Carver et al., 1989; Stone & Neale, 1984). Behavioral disengagement can protect self-identity by breaking the responsibility link between the person and the mismatch. Withdrawing effort from a threatening activity, people can discount the self-relevant threat and manage their inner tension by attributing any potential failure to lack of effort rather than lack of ability. This strategy, which Jones and Berglas (1978) called behavioral self-handicapping, has been documented empirically (i.e., Pyszczynski & Greenberg, 1983; Rhodewalt, Saltzman, & Wittmer, 1984).

The literature has also noted another avoidance strategy—alcohol/drug consumption. This strategy is a classic behavioral self-handicap as it creates an impediment to adequate performance and enables people to attribute their failure to a substance rather than to lack of ability (e.g., Jones & Berglas, 1978). Alcohol and drug consumption also reduce self-awareness (e.g., Hull & Young, 1983) and distract people, thereby assisting cognitive avoidance.

Cognitive avoidance and behavioral disengagement provide mutual support for each other. Because effort expenditure in problem solving may recall the unresolved problems, lead to the intrusion of threatening thoughts, and counter cognitive avoidance, behavioral disengagement may support cognitive avoidance by keeping people away from any activity reminiscent of the original problem. Cognitive avoidance may support behavioral disengagement by making people unaware of their defensive maneuvers. Jagacinski and Nicholls (1990) noted that "a conscious decision to reduce effort is inconsistent with the goal of establishing that one is competent" (p. 19).

Avoidance coping shows some similarities and differences with other intrapsychic strategies. Like reappraisal, avoidance also leaves the mismatch unresolved and reduces distress by distorting reality. These two coping strategies differ, however, in the extent and the consequences of the distortion. Whereas reappraisal entails a *partial* denial of the threatening aspects of the problem situation, avoidance strategies entail a *total* denial of the mismatch along with complete behavioral and cognitive disengagement from the situation. Moreover, whereas reappraisal facilitates active confrontation with the problem, avoidance prevents any kind of active confrontation. In my terms, reappraisal reflects optimism regarding the possibility of resolving a mismatch and a cognitive means for maintaining this orientation. In contrast, avoidance reflects pessimism about one's chances of resolving the mismatch and a conviction that the only solution and the only way to reduce distress is to avoid any confrontation with the problem.

Avoidance is also similar to reorganization in that both entail a movement away from the task and disengagement from problem-focused efforts. But whereas the disengagement that makes avoidance serves merely to mitigate distress and leaves the mismatch that causes it intact, the disengagement produced by reorganization reflects the direction of resources toward self-reflective activities designed to end the mismatch. Moreover, whereas people who adopt avoidance sacrifice the adaptation of mental structures to reality in exchange for immediate positive affect, those who adopt reorganization sacrifice immediate good feelings for long-term adaptation. The two types of coping may also inhibit each other. Avoidance may lead to disengagement not only from the problem at hand but also from dealing with the mismatch through reorganization; reorganization may keep the person occupied with the mismatch and thereby impede avoidance.

At the same time, avoidance and reorganization can be activated sequentially. For example, reorganization may sometimes activate painful self-relevant material and increase tension and distress, which may lead the person to adopt avoidance coping. Alternatively, avoidance may sometimes result in problems in functioning and may not reduce the distress, which may lead the person to tackle the mismatch more actively.

There is one more distinction that needs to be made between avoidance and the other coping strategies: Whereas the other three types of coping will eventually reach completion, avoidance may be endlessness. In problem solving and reorganization, the coping task ends when the person and the environment are brought into better alignment; in reappraisal, it ends when internal or external conditions allow for problem solving. With avoidance, however, the coping task has no natural end because the mismatch continues to exist, both in reality and in memory. Any external stimuli reminiscent of the mismatch may reinstate it in awareness, thereby renewing distress and requiring further coping. Similarly, any inner thoughts or feelings that reactivate the memory of the mismatch may also increase distress and lead to further avoidance coping. Avoidance coping may thus be viewed as leading to a chronic state of alertness and vigilance and to intermittent resumption of coping efforts.

HELPLESSNESS TRAINING AND COPING STRATEGIES

In examining the role of coping responses in the path going from helplessness training to performance, it is necessary to delineate the effects of helplessness training on these responses. In this section, I present theoretical and empirical knowledge on the hypotheses that (a) coping responses are set in motion by helplessness training, and (b) small and large amounts of training typically activate different types of coping responses.

THE ACTIVATION OF COPING RESPONSES

In my theory, coping efforts are mobilized to deal with helplessness training and may remain active during the subsequent test task. The activation of coping strategies is one basic outcome of the exposure to failure. Helplessness training may interrupt a person's actions, generate and/or enlarge actual–ideal discrepancies, thwart personal goals, and produce self-relevant threats and losses. In response, people may adopt coping strategies aimed at managing the mismatch and its threatening consequences.

To be sure, the mobilization of coping efforts is not an automatic response to failure. Rather, it is a product of people's appraisal of the situation and their resources, and it may be moderated by an array of personal and situational factors involved in the appraisal process. One major moderating factor may be the extent to which the failure threatens personal interests and self-views. Coping efforts may be a direct function of the relevance of the failure for goal hierarchy and self-identity. People may engage in energetic coping attempts when they encounter difficulty in realizing their aims only when they perceive that something of personal importance is at stake.

Another set of factors relevant to the activation of coping after failure consists of the conceptions of the self and the world. These conceptions may help determine what is relevant to the realization of the person's strivings and which environmental events may threaten them. Such beliefs may contribute to the appraisal of which expectancies have been violated and which self-aspects threatened, as well as to the delineation of the benefits likely to result from any coping response.

The complexity and flexibility of the individual's cognitive structures may also moderate the activation of coping. The interruption of goal-oriented actions may lead to coping efforts mainly when people perceive their goal as the only means of attaining their wishes or meeting their needs. People with more complex and flexible cognitive structures might be better able to discover or devise alternative plans and goals that could facilitate their leaving the distressing situation and engaging in more fruitful and satisfactory activities, thereby obviating any need to cope. The activation of coping may also be affected by the person's coping resources. Any situational factor that may impair the person's capability to engage in effortful coping activities (fatigue, disease, drugs, alcohol, etc.) might inhibit the coping process.

Obviously, these few examples do not exhaust the personal and situational factors that may moderate the activation of coping after failure. People's views, cognitive schemas, and coping resources, however, may be a good place to start a search for relevant coping processes within human LH.

Though no theory of human LH makes explicit statements about the process of coping with failure, one can find several references to the activation of particular coping responses after helplessness training. For example, Frankel and Snyder (1978) assumed that people tend to react to helplessness training with reappraisal and avoidance activities. Specifically, they suggested that people may attempt to attribute their failure to bad luck or high task difficulty (a typical reappraisal strategy) or may defensively reduce the efforts they spend in the test task (a typical behavioral avoidance strategy). These authors also claim that reappraisal may be inadequate in the typical LH paradigm, and people may prefer to adopt an avoidance attitude: "Luck was either implausible as an excuse or else would have evened out over trials, and to say that a task is particularly difficult in the absence of evidence that others have also found it difficult may suggest a lack of ability" (p. 1146). Similar views were expressed by Zuroff (1980).

Carver and Scheier (1981) suggest that people exposed to failure either redouble their efforts in organizing and executing problem-focused actions or attempt to distance behaviorally from the failure situation. They also propose that when the social/physical environment or their self-representations do not permit their physical withdrawal, people may withdraw mentally by directing their attention to distracting, off-task matters. Somewhat similarly, Kuhl (1981) suggested that people exposed to uncontrollable failure may either generate action alternatives that could help to overcome failure or concentrate on the past, present, and future state of the self and "edit" their damaged self-schemas.

The problem with these theories is that they do not encompass the entire coping process and do not conceptualize the hypothesized responses as part of the coping task. Moreover, they may lead to the erroneous conclusion that lack of control cues some particular coping responses instead of activating the response that people themselves choose. In contrast, I see helplessness training as a constellation of events that may instigate coping efforts without cuing any particular action. What helplessness training does is to set in motion a process that includes the appraisal of a mismatch, the mobilization of coping efforts, and the selection and execution of coping strategies.

There is extensive evidence that coping strategies may be activated in response to failure. Several studies found that failure induces excuse making (see Bradley, 1978; Snyder & Higgins, 1988; Zuckerman, 1979, for reviews). It has been consistently shown that failure, relative to success, leads people to make more external, unstable, and specific attributions. As stated earlier, this attributional pattern is a typical reappraisal response, for external attribution increases consensus, unstable attribution reduces consistency, and specific attribution raises distinctiveness.

Excuse making was also found in a typical LH study (Mikulincer & Marshand, 1991) in which subjects exposed to four unsolvable problems attributed their performance less to internal and global factors than did no-feedback subjects. Interestingly, the subjects in the study did not attribute their failure to unstable causes. This may have had to do with the credibility of the reappraisal strategies in the LH paradigm. Four failures may be unrepresentative of the outcomes students generally obtain in achievement settings. This may facilitate their view of the situation as distinct and their attribution of responsibility to external factors, but it is more difficult to convince either oneself or others that four failures are transient and do not represent the entire chain of outcomes in a given task.

A number of studies have also documented the use of cognitive avoidance strategies after helplessness training. Rozensky, Tovian, Stiles, Fridkin, and Holland (1987) found that unsolvable problems fostered more Rorschach responses reflecting withdrawal from the external situation than did solvable problems. Miller (1976) found that subjects who failed in a social perceptiveness task claimed to have exerted less effort than did those who succeeded. Though the subjects' retrospective accounts may represent a reappraisal strategy to excuse the failure rather than real behavioral disengagement, more direct evidence was offered by Sigall and Gould (1977), who found that failure in unsolvable problems produced lower levels of effort in the preparation for the next task than did success.

Research has also found that helplessness training increases the consumption of drugs and alcohol—another behavioral avoidance strategy. Weidner (1980) showed that relative to subjects exposed to solvable problems, those exposed to unsolvable problems chose more performance-inhibiting drugs than neutral drugs when given an opportunity to do so. Noel and Lisman (1980) found that unsolvable problems led to more beer consumption in a taste rating task than did the solvable problems. The finding did not reflect a mere increase in general beverage consumption, because there was no difference in the amount of ginger ale consumed by the two groups. Rather, helplessness training leads to a differential increase in alcohol consumption.

All the reviewed findings demonstrate that helplessness training may activate a wide array of coping strategies without cueing any specific strategy. It is true that the findings can be explained by other psychological processes. The external unstable-specific attribution may result from cognitive biases; effort withdrawal may result from a rational analysis of personal gains; alcohol consumption may reflect uncontrollable behavior, and so on. These alternative explanations, though, are partially ruled out by findings showing that these reactions are a functional response to the need for coping. For example, studies consistently found that the higher the perceived importance of a failure, the stronger the tendency to use excuse attributions (see Snyder, Stephan, & Rosenfield, 1978, for a review), to withdraw effort from the task (Pyszczynski & Greenberg, 1983), and to distance oneself cognitively from the failure (Mikulincer, 1989b).

Beyond the above studies of single coping strategies, one of my studies showed that problem-solving, reorganization, and avoidance responses are all present in subjects' accounts of their real-life helplessness experiences (Mikulincer & Caspy, 1986, Study 1). Subjects recalled some situations in which they felt helpless and freely described their responses to them. A content analysis of the reports yielded the following coping categories: (a) 86% of the subjects reported avoidance responses, including strategies, such as cognitive distancing, suppression of affect and thought, behavioral disengagement, and the adoption of a passive and giving up attitude; (b) 79% of the subjects reported problem-focused strategies; and (c) 63% of the subjects reported reorganization strategies, consisting of attempts to work through the helplessness situation, analyze its meaning, and adopt new goals.

A Coping Cycle

If coping responses mediate the reactance produced by a small amount of failure and the LH deficits produced by a large amount, different responses should be typically activated after different amounts of failure. Whereas a small amount of failure should activate coping responses that improve performance, a large amount should activate responses that impair performance. Therefore one can hypothesize that a small amount of failure may activate problem solving and reappraisal, which (as will be discussed in the next section) lead to reactance, and a large amount of failure may activate avoidance and reorganization, which lead to performance deficits.

Study 1 of the studies I present in this book (see Chapter 1) provides supportive evidence for the hypothesized coping cycle. After being exposed to zero, one, two, three, four, or five unsolvable problems, subjects completed 4 items tapping the extent to which they used problem-solving, reappraisal, reorganization, and avoidance strategies during the experiment. Each item presented a concise description of one strategy and subjects gave their answers in a bipolar 7-point scale, ranging from "not at all" (1) to "very much" (7). The results revealed that both small and large amounts of failure were able to induce coping efforts, but that whereas subjects exposed to one or two failures reported having used more problem-solving and reappraisal strategies than no-failure subjects, subjects exposed to three or more failures reported having used more avoidance and reorganization strategies than no-failure subjects (see Figure 2.1).

Reliance on problem-solving and reappraisal strategies reached its peak after one or two failures and steadily decreased as the number of failures increased. In

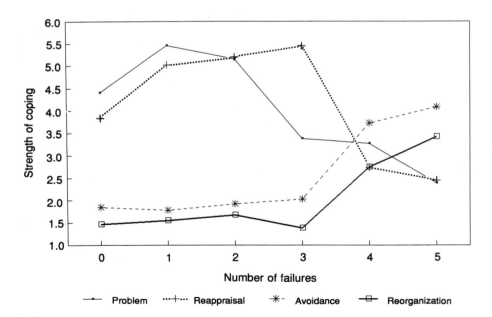

FIGURE 2.1. Means of coping strategies according to number of failures.

Table 2.1. Means and F-Ratios of Coping Scores according to Number of Failures

Coping category	Study number	No failures	One failure	Four failures	F
Problem solving					
	9	4.25	4.81	3.12	12.14[b]
	10	4.68	4.62	3.25	6.28[b]
	11	4.18	4.93	2.31	25.01[b]
	12	4.18	4.56	3.00	8.02[b]
Reappraisal					
	9	3.50	4.06	3.87	0.62
	10	1.62	2.87	1.81	11.36[b]
	11	1.75	1.87	1.68	0.22
	12	1.43	3.69	2.87	22.51[b]
Reorganization					
	9	1.69	2.02	2.69	5.14[b]
	10	1.50	1.75	2.25	4.72[a]
	11	1.43	1.37	2.18	5.49[b]
	12	1.62	1.62	2.50	5.01[a]
Avoidance					
	9	2.06	1.62	3.12	10.16[b]
	10	1.62	1.37	2.50	9.29[b]
	11	1.62	1.50	2.37	9.10[b]
	12	1.37	1.69	2.68	13.44[b]

[a] $p < .05$
[b] $p < .01$

contrast, reliance on avoidance and reorganization reached its maximal value only after three failures. Similar patterns of differences were found in four of the studies that I present in this book, which exposed subjects to zero, one, or four failures and asked them to answer the 4 coping items (see Table 2.1).

It appears that people exposed to helplessness training initially respond to failure with problem-focused and reappraisal efforts, then shift to avoidance and reorganization strategies only after repeated failure. Initial coping efforts seem to have an approach orientation, with problem-focused attempts to reassert control and reappraisal to manage interfering emotions. After repeated failure, people give up problem solving and prefer to adopt either avoidance or reorganization strategies, apparently having reached the conclusion that the best way to deal with the threat produced by endless failure is to distance themselves from the task situation and/or to find substitutive goals and plans.

This observed cycle of coping may have an adaptive significance. When faced with the choice of altering either the environment or their own schemas, people may initially prefer to alter the world. Schemas are the devices that allow people to understand the world, predict the future, control environmental events, and direct and organize actions. There may, therefore, be considerable survival value attached to protecting existing mental structures at times of adversity. Any change in these structures is likely to be painful and may be experienced as an imminent threat of self-disintegration and disorientation. Upon the recognition of a mismatch, the starting point will thus usually be that one's mental structures are right and that the world is wrong. People tend to adopt a conservative attitude that prevents changes in habitual beliefs and demands more discrepant information before initiating any inner reorganization. Until this information is received, people attack the world, attempt to remove sources of threat, and try to keep their schemas intact.

Only after repeated failure to mold the environment in accord with their needs will people abandon active fighting and alloplastic ways of coping. They will then either avoid the problem situation or try to accommodate their schemas to reality constraints. That is, people may engage in "flight" from a situation and give up some of their goals, or they may decide that their schemas are wrong, work them through, and replace some of these goals and self-views. Avoidance and reorganization are thus considered here to be activated after a large amount of repeated failure, when alloplastic coping attempts fail to produce beneficial adaptive outcomes.

The above reasoning is consistent with Piaget's analysis of cognitive development. The child initially attempts to assimilate incoming discrepant information into his or her existing schemas; and only after futile assimilatory attempts does he or she try to accommodate the schemas to reality constraints. It is also consistent with the conservative impulse posited by Marris (1974) to defend the validity of what one has learned and to change mental structures only after recognizing the futility of one's defenses. The reasoning is also in keeping with egotism theories (Snyder et al., 1978), which claim that people are motivated to protect their schemas via active fighting or cognitive maneuvers.

Interestingly, the findings also suggest that reorganization and avoidance do not form an ordered sequence, and that people exposed to a large amount of helplessness training tend to rely equally on each of these strategies. That is, people replace problem solving by either an autoplastic or an escapist orientation. Though these two coping alternatives reflect a disengagement from problem solving, they may have different implications for the individual's psychological state, as well as for the restoration of disrupted equilibrium.

Variations in coping responses may reflect underlying changes in the subjective appraisal of the situation. For instance, people's convictions that problem-focused actions may be effective, their confidence in their abilities to carry them out (Bandura's sense of self-efficacy), and their beliefs that the outcome is controllable may all be eroded by repeated failure, leading to the observed changes in coping reactions. After a single failure, people may still believe in the controllability of the outcome and may opt to engage in problem-focused coping. After successive failure, however, they may conclude that problem solving is useless and choose intrapsychic strategies of avoidance or reorganization.

No matter which mechanism underlies the coping cycle, the findings support the idea that helplessness training sets in motion the coping process, and that a small amount of failure activates alloplastic coping attempts (e.g., problem solving and reappraisal), whereas a large amount of failure activates avoidance and reorganization.

THE COPING–PERFORMANCE LINK

The next task in evaluating the role of coping in human LH is to establish whether coping actions affect performance. In this section I present data and elaborate on the coping–performance link and the particular coping responses that underlie reactance and LH deficits.

In my terms, the coping strategies people use to deal with failure are proximal antecedents of performance changes. Being effortful cognitive and behavioral maneuvers that support or interfere with task-relevant activities, they can either improve or impair task performance. Coping responses congruent with task demands would facilitate task performance; responses incongruent with task demands would impair task performance. Specifically, problem-solving and reappraisal strategies may support task-relevant activities and improve performance, whereas avoidance and reorganization strategies may interfere with those activities and impair task performance.

Coping responses may alter task performance through two paths. The first path involves the allocation of resources. Every coping response entails the allocation of resources to particular activities, which have repercussions on task performance. Problem-focused coping directs resources toward analysis of task-relevant features, making of problem-solving plans, and engagement in task-relevant activities. This allocation fits well the task demands and may facilitate task performance. Avoidance and reorganization coping, in contrast, diverts resources away from the task, to distracting thoughts (avoidance) or to the revision of self-schemas (reorganization). Either way, this allocation does not fit task demands, may deplete the resources needed for task-relevant activities, and thus impairs task performance.

The second path involves dysfunctional thoughts and affects. The detection of a mismatch is generally accompanied by at least some distressing thoughts and affects that may urge the person to take coping steps. Though these thoughts and affects may facilitate the coping process, they may sometimes take a dysfunctional form, overwhelming the cognitive system and disorganizing and paralyzing volitional actions. In other words, they may produce dysfunctional "cognitive interference" with task-relevant activities, which is directly manifested in performance deficits. In my terms, whether cognitive interference occurs may depend on the person's way of coping. Whereas reappraisal strategies may enable the person to manage inner distress and inhibit cognitive interference, avoidance may sometimes favor the intrusion of dysfunctional thoughts and affects and thus contribute to performance deficits.

It is important to distinguish between coping efforts and task efforts. The two are virtually synonymous when the attempt to manage the person–environment mismatch takes the form of efforts to alter the environment. They are quite different, and possibly even antonymous, when the attempt takes the form of cognitive distancing or the accommodation of the person's mental structures to the reality constraints. Performance facilitation can be expected only in the first instance, performance deficits in the second.

At the same time, it is important to emphasize that LH deficits do not result from lack of coping. Both reactance and LH deficits are outcomes of coping. The term *lack of coping* is meaningless; people exposed to failure always do *something* to cope with the threat. Off-task coping strategies, such as avoidance and reorganization, should not be confounded with passivity and lack of coping. Although these strategies reflect a passive attitude toward the task and a retreat from problem solving, they reflect an active attempt to cope with the mismatch. This is true even where they produce dysfunctional outcomes, such as the flood of distressing affects and thoughts that disorganize and paralyze volitional actions. This cognitive interference may simply be one of the unwanted products of avoidance coping.

Nor can certain coping strategies always be considered adaptive and functional, and others maladaptative and dysfunctional. My hypotheses are not derived from the traditional view of coping (e.g., Andrews, Tennant, Henson, & Vaillant, 1978; Haan, 1977; Vaillant, 1977), which differentiates between adaptive and maladaptive strategies on the basis of predetermined evaluative criteria (i.e., whether their degree of organization, level of maturity, or extent of reality contact). The traditional conceptualization does not take into account situational characteristics, which in my view can in and of themselves determine whether any particular coping attempts are adaptive or not (Haan, 1977; Hartmann, 1939). Nor does it accord with evidence that so-called "immature" coping strategies—namely, avoidance and denial—can produce positive outcomes when no alternative strategies prove effective in reducing distress (Collins, Baum, & Singer, 1983).

I adopt the flexible concept of coping effectiveness offered by Lazarus and Folkman (1984), who distinguish between coping efforts and adaptational outcome: "No strategy is considered inherently better than any other. The goodness . . . of a strategy is determined only by its effects in a given encounter and its effects in the long term" (p. 134). That is, the effectiveness of coping strategies varies across domains, situations, and time, and it depends on the features of and adaptational requirements of the situation. Thus, to evaluate the effectiveness of a coping strategy within the LH paradigm, I analyze the adaptive task posed by the LH situation and the range of response options available for accomplishing it.

PROBLEM SOLVING

The use of problem-focused coping during the test task may improve task performance, lead to reactance, and prevent LH deficits. The test phase of the LH paradigm is a problem-solving situation in which outcomes are controllable and people can minimize the discrepancy of their prior failure by shaping the environment to their wants. To overcome the failure of the helplessness training and restore the equilibrium with the environment, they are required to engage in effortful problem solving. Problem-focused coping implies a constructive cognitive-behavioral approach to a task, which enables good functioning and prevents any detrimental effect of prior failure on task performance.

In addition, by inhibiting inner distress, problem solving prevents cognitive interference. First of all, problem-focused coping helps to remove the environmental sources of the harm that can create distress and interference. Second, it helps to reinstate in the person a sense of self-efficacy and mastery and to reduce self-doubts and negative feelings. Third, the very act of dealing actively with the problem may make people feel better (Folkman & Lazarus, 1988).

The beneficial effects of problem-focused coping, however, are limited to the typical test phase of the LH paradigm. Problem-focused coping may not be effective when the test task is uncontrollable. Here reliance on problem-focused strategies would not facilitate performance or minimize person–environment discrepancies, but it might rather increase self-relevant threats and distress as people realize their powerlessness. Folkman (1984) asserts that problem-focused coping efforts lose their adaptive value in uncontrollable situations, when the abandonment of these efforts is the basic key for managing threat.

The positive impact of problem-focused coping has been cited more or less explicitly in several theories of human LH. According to both the original and reformulated Learned Helplessness theories, the abandonment of problem-solving attempts results in LH deficits. Accordingly, Sedek and Kofta (1990) view LH deficits as a "cognitive exhaustion"—a reduction in active problem solving—whereas C. Peterson (1978) explains the deficits in terms of inappropriate problem-solving plans. In addition, Carver and Scheier (1981), Diener and Dweck (1978), and Kuhl (1981) all argue that problem-solving orientation underlies reactance.

In addition, research in the field of stress and coping supports the hypothesis that problem-focused coping has beneficial outcomes. Reliance on problem-focused coping has been found to be inversely related to psychiatric symptomatology, psychological distress, and such particular types of emotional problems as depression, anxiety, loneliness, panic disorders, and posttraumatic stress disorders (e.g., Billings & Moos, 1984; Felton & Revenson, 1984; Nezu & Carnevale, 1987; Solomon, Mikulincer, & Avitzur, 1988). The use of problem-focused coping has also been found to be positively related to several measures of physical health and health-related habits (e.g., Brown & Nicassio, 1987; Nowack, 1989). Similar positive effects of problem-focused coping have been found on measures of positive affectivity and functioning, for example, life satisfaction, psychological adjustment, high morale, subjective well-being, and performance quality (e.g., Compas, Malcarne, & Fondacaro, 1988; Epstein & Meier, 1989; McCrae & Costa, 1986).

There is also evidence that problem-focused coping is particularly beneficial in attenuating the detrimental effects of highly stressful events. For example, the adoption of problem-focused coping has been found to minimize the damage of stressful events on well-being (Headey & Wearing, 1990), to reduce the psychiatric symptomatology that follows upon extreme stress (Aldwin & Revenson, 1987), and to improve functioning after extreme stress (Billings & Moos, 1981; Holahan & Moos, 1990; Pearlin & Schooler, 1978). Solomon, Mikulincer, and Flum (1988) found that problem-focused coping buffers the detrimental effects of negative life events on psychiatric symptomatology in a sample of combat stress reaction casualties.

At the same time, research has also pointed to the limitations of problem-focused coping. It has been consistently found that problem-focused coping has positive outcomes only in controllable situations (e.g., Collins et al., 1983; Kaloupek & Stoupakis, 1985; Kaloupek, White, & Wong, 1984). For example, Ashford (1988) interviewed employees before a major organizational transition and found that active attempts to structure the situation—over which they had no control—either failed to affect or increased their distress. Compas et al. (1988) and Forsythe and Compas (1987) found that children who use problem-focused coping to deal with uncontrollable stressors showed increased levels of distress and problems in functioning. Collins et al. (1983) reported that in the case of Three Mile Island accident, where the stressor was chronic and the sources of stress could not be easily changed, problem-focused coping had no positive effect on well-being.

REAPPRAISAL

Like problem-focused coping, the use of reappraisal strategies during and after helplessness training may also improve performance, produce reactance, and prevent LH deficits. Though reappraisal does not directly lead to the allocation of cognitive resources in task-relevant activities, it may indirectly facilitate task performance by supporting problem solving.

Reappraisal is an approach-oriented strategy that support problem solving. The very act of seeking task-relevant information that could promote a more positive attitude keeps the person involved in the task. The cognitive activities involved in reappraisal—finding a meaning in the task, analyzing the positive aspects of the task, rationalizing the task outcomes—are essentially task oriented. Moreover, by promoting a positive attitude, reappraisal reduces the need to flee from the threat and thus fosters the adoption of a problem-solving orientation. Indeed, several studies have found a positive correlation between the use of reappraisal and the use of problem-focused strategies (i.e., Aldwin, Folkman, Schaefer, Coyne, & Lazarus, 1980; Folkman & Lazarus, 1985; Folkman, Lazarus, Dunkel-Schetter, DeLongis, & Gruen, 1986).

In addition, reappraisal may facilitate problem-solving and test task performance by keeping the person's distress at a manageable level. Highlighting the positive aspects of a failure, finding meaning to the failure, and discounting any link between the failure and the self, these reappraisal strategies could alleviate failure-related threats and thus prevent distress from interfering with task performance.

These strategies reduce the subjective aversiveness of the person–environment mismatch potentially created by helplessness training and may thus enable the person to undergo the test task without being overwhelmed by negative emotions and thoughts.

In this way, reappraisal would lead to full concentration on task-relevant stimuli, full engagement in task-relevant actions, and hence performance improvement in solvable tasks. Moreover, it may keep the person's optimism and sense of self-efficacy alive (e.g., the failure is seen as a temporary, personally irrelevant outcome), which Folkman (1984) suggested reinforces the decision to undertake problem-focused coping. It may also keep people alert to any positive changes in the situation, especially in the controllability of the test task, and lead them to take advantage of these changes.

The positive effects of reappraisal are all the more valuable because the threat created by helplessness training cannot be immediately managed by problem solving. Where the problem is unsolvable, any attempt to minimize a mismatch by influencing the environment must be ineffective and would lead only to frustration and distress. What are called for are coping responses that make threat-reducing intrapsychic changes without promoting off-task cognitive activities or otherwise distancing the person from the task.

Just as problem-solving strategies have their limitations, though, so does reappraisal. Reappraisal can be expected to have positive effects only when it is used as an auxiliary to problem solving. Although persons who rely exclusively on reappraisal might cope well with the unsolvable problems, they would not perform well on the test task. That requires problem-solving efforts. The upshot of this reasoning is that the LH situation requires varied and flexible coping: the use of reappraisal during the helplessness training, and problem-focused coping during the test task.

Both theory and research support the idea that reappraisal may promote positive adaptational outcomes. For example, Snyder and Higgins (1988) argue that discounting the link between failure and the self minimizes self-relevant threats, sustains problem solving, and thereby facilitates performance. Similar assertions are made by Taylor and Brown (1988), who analyzed the adaptational outcomes of three strategies of focusing on the positive: unrealistically positive self-evaluation, exaggerated perceptions of control, and unrealistic optimism. The need to use both reappraisal and problem solving has also been emphasized by Lazarus and Folkman (1984), who argue that emotional equilibrium and functioning depend on both the management of inner tension and the solution of the problems at hand.

Research has consistently found that people who discover something positive in threatening events show less distress than those who do not (e.g., Menaghan, 1982; Pearlin, Lieberman, Menaghan, & Mullan, 1981; Pearlin & Schooler, 1978). Research has also documented the effectiveness of making positive social comparisons (Bennett & Holmes, 1975; Burish & Houston, 1979). Other studies show that downward comparison (comparing one's situation with that of others worse off than oneself) is linked to lower levels of anxiety and depressed affects and to higher levels of life satisfaction and adjustment (e.g., Affleck, Tennen, Pfeiffer, & Fifield, 1988; Gibbons & Gerrard, 1989; Gibbons & McCoy, 1991). Finding meaning in a threat has been also shown to be a highly effective strategy for managing distress (see Taylor & Brown, 1988; Thompson, 1991, for reviews).

At the same time, research shows that exclusive reliance in reappraisal without the concomitant use of problem-focused coping might be maladaptive. Mattlin, Wethington, and Kessler (1990) found that positive reappraisal strategies reduced anxiety and depression caused by the death of a loved one, but increased these distressing emotions following low-threat or practical situations when the strategies were used without concomitant problem-focused coping. The authors concluded that reappraisal can lead to poor adaptation if it is not accompanied by problem-solving activities.

Finally, there is evidence that the joint use of reappraisal and problem-focused coping produces the most positive adaptational outcomes. Martelli, Auerbach, Alexander, and Mercuri (1987) found that patients who had been taught a combination of emotion- and problem-focused strategies adjusted better to the stress of surgery than patients who had been taught only one of the strategies. Retrospective accounts by former concentration camp inmates and prisoners of war similarly indicate that those who adjusted best used a combination of problem-focused and reappraisal strategies (e.g., Schmolling, 1984).

AVOIDANCE

Avoidance coping can regulate the inner tension produced by the helplessness training, but it is detrimental to test task performance. Cognitive and behavioral disengagement from the threat produced by helplessness training might alleviate distress. Not thinking about the failure, denying its meaning and personal implications, and engaging in wishful thinking can keep it from threatening one's goal hierarchy and self-identity and from overwhelming the cognitive system. Suppressing and splitting off negative feelings can remove the threat from awareness. Withdrawing effort and disengaging from the task make it possible to sever any link between the failure and the self and to channel one's resources into distracting task-irrelevant activities.

The problem with avoidance begins during the solvable test task. Avoidance keeps people detached from the task situation, impedes task-oriented efforts, and inhibits problem solving. It diverts cognitive resources from task-relevant activities reminiscent of the prior unsolved problem and leaves insufficient resources available for task performance. The person is occupied with distracting matters, his or her mind wanders to other times and places, and he or she is unwilling or unable to allocate resources to the task. Furthermore, a prolonged use of avoidance coping also contributes to the erroneous transfer of the beliefs developed during helplessness training to the test task. By diverting attention from the task and hence inhibiting analysis of the features and demands of the new task, avoidance prevents recognition of the controllability of the test task and makes it seem a continuation of the helplessness situation. Thus cognitive and behavioral avoidance may produce an unnecessary constriction of functioning and cause a person to miss opportunities for reinstating a realistic sense of self-worth and mastery.

Impairment in functioning is especially evident when behavioral disengagement strategies, such as alcohol/drug consumption and effort withdrawal, are used. Excessive consumption of drugs and alcohol can disorganize behavior and interfere with the planning and execution of problem-solving actions. Similarly, the defensive withdrawal of effort from a task makes it impossible to take advantage of the solvability of a problem. Frankel and Snyder (1978) and Carver and Scheier (1981) have already stated that this behavioral disengagement is the direct antecedent of LH deficits. Moreover, although effort withdrawal may initially reduce self-relevant threats by enabling the person to discount his or her lack of ability, it leads to negative evaluative reactions from others, which in turn can increase personal threat in the long run (Baumgardner & Levy, 1988; Smith & Strube, 1991).

On the intrapsychic level, although avoidance coping may initially reduce self-relevant threats and distress by suppressing failure-related thoughts and affects, in the long run it may increase distress as a result of the unwanted, autonomic intrusion of these thoughts and affects into consciousness (see Chapter 3). The suppression of threatening material that has not been worked through or incorporated into one's meaning structures leaves it in memory, awaiting any opportunity to intrude into consciousness (e.g., Horowitz, 1979). The test task, in which failure is possible, may provide that opportunity by reminding the person of his or her prior failure. This sequence of events may develop into a self-exacerbating cycle of avoidance coping and intrusion/distress, in which each can impair task performance. Whereas avoidance directly constricts functioning, the subsequent intrusion of failure-related thoughts and affects may overwhelm the cognitive system and disorganize action.

The above reasoning is based on theoretical and empirical knowledge gained in the study of stress and adaptation. Roth and Cohen (1986) concluded that avoidance may be beneficial, but only as long as it provides the person with time to assimilate the stressful event and to mobilize efforts to manage it, and only if it is followed by problem-focused coping. Accordingly, Lazarus (1983), for example, claimed that avoidance is often a valuable form of coping during an uncontrollable trauma—when nothing can be done to alter events, and/or emotional and cognitive resources are limited—but that its usefulness may be short-lived. Continued after the traumatic episode ends or after one's resources have been replenished, avoidance would prevent people from taking advantage of opportunities to influence the environment.

This is not to say that avoidance is always maladaptive. I only mean that it would cause performance deficits and other emotional problems when it is used in the solvable test task. According to Lazarus, avoidance is destructive when direct actions to reinstate an equilibrium are useful or when people are strong enough to rely on problem-focused coping. It would be also destructive when failure can potentially be encountered again and again in new tasks. All these conditions are present when ordinary, well-functioning people perform a solvable test task after helplessness training.

A large number of studies show that the reported use of avoidance coping is positively related to reported levels of distress, psychiatric symptomatology, and a number of emotional problems, and that it exacerbates the detrimental effects of stressful life events on mental health (e.g., Amirkhan, 1991; Holahan & Moos, 1990; Kuiper, Olinger, & Air, 1989; Solomon, Mikulincer, & Avitzur, 1988). In addition, avoidance coping was found to be inversely related to life satisfaction, psychological well-being, marital satisfaction, social functioning, and psychological adjustment (e.g., Hanson, Cigrang, Harris, & Carle, 1989; Headey & Wearing, 1990; Solomon, Avitzur, & Mikulincer, 1989). Collins et al. (1983), however, found that avoidance coping may help psychological adjustment to uncontrollable stressors, such as the Three Mile Island nuclear incident.

The use of avoidance coping has also been found to be inversely related to health and positively linked to physical complaints, self-reported pain, and a variety of disorders, including migraine, high blood pressure, problems in metabolic control of diabetes patients, eating disorders, drinking, heart disorder, and asthma, as well as to cortisol level (e.g., Hanson et ai., 1989; Moos, Brennan, Fondacaro, & Moos, 1990; Nowack, 1989). In this context, it is important to underline Pennebaker's work (e.g., Pennebaker & Susman, 1988), which demonstrated that inhibition of thoughts related to traumatic events results in an increase of ANS activity and psychosomatic diseases.

REORGANIZATION

Like avoidance coping, the use of reorganization strategies can help to manage the threat produced by helplessness training, but at the same time may have detrimental effects on test task performance. On the one hand, reorganization eliminates self-relevant threats, as well as enables the person to learn something new about the self and the world and to obtain a more integrative and realistic view of his or her competences and skills. On the other hand, the adoption of reorganization may produce some cognitive changes that impede engagement in problem solving and thereby impair task performance. Reorganization entails a temporary disengagement from the task situation and the diversion of cognitive resources away from task-relevant activities. Instead of trying to alter the environment and solve the problems at hand, people engage in a series of effortful reflective activities that have nothing to do with task performance. Because resources are limited, few resources may be available for the generation and organization of problem-solving plans, attention may be not directed to task-relevant features, and people may be unable to expend effort in performing well. All these cognitive changes may lead to performance deficits in the test task.

Moreover, the "editing" of inner structures may have some cognitive products that lead to LH deficits. In the course of their mental reorganization, people may activate painful self-relevant memories, thoughts, and affects that absorb their attention, distract them from task-relevant activities, and further interfere with task performance. For reorganization entails a painful recognition that the existing mental structures are somehow wrong. In addition, it may sometimes result in temporary negative beliefs about the self and the world, and it may raise temporary doubts about one's self-efficacy and worth.

Reorganization may also produce motivational changes that have detrimental effects on performance. Reorganization entails the replacement of one goal with another. But until the new goal is set and integrated into their goal hierarchy, people are in a motivational vacuum. If they put aside the goal they previously pursued in the task before they establish a new goal to guide their actions, they may suspend goal-oriented actions in the task, find no meaning or value in it, and not be motivated to expend effort on it. This motivational detachment may be directly manifested in LH deficits.

The performance deficits produced by reorganization coping are short-lived, however, and may disappear when the person completes the working-through process. In this case, cognitive resources can be withdrawn from elaboration of off-task material to become available for problem solving, cognitive interference ceases, and task effort may be renewed in the pursuit of the substitute goals. Having changed their priorities, people could stop thinking on the prior failure and engage freely in task activities without being occupied with the failure any longer.

On this basis, one can suggest that though both reorganization and avoidance detach people from the task and impair task performance, the LH deficits they produce may be different in their temporal parameters and meaning. First of all, the deficits resulting from avoidance may be more enduring than those produced by reorganization. Whereas the latter cease with the substitution of goals and the resolution of the mismatch, the former may have no natural end, because the painful experience is not integrated into the mental structures and so may continue to control the person's cognitions and actions. Moreover, whereas the deficits produced by reorganization reflect a temporary sacrifice of task performance for future adaptive benefits, those produced by avoidance reflect a sacrifice of equilibrium with the environment for the sake of immediate emotional benefits. The task detachment involved in reorganization is the result of the direct confrontation with the person–environment mismatch, whereas that involved in avoidance reflects an escape from painful confrontation.

One can also delineate the various situational and personal factors that may moderate the performance effects of reorganization. The centrality of the goal that is to be replaced in the person's goal hierarchy may be one of them. The more central the old goal is, the more parts of the mental structures must be reorganized, the longer the working-through process will take, and the more pervasive and enduring the resulting LH deficits might be. In addition, the more important the goal, the more painful the reorganization process could be expected to be. This pain might in turn trigger the adoption of avoidance coping and the sustenance of LH deficits over time. Another factor might be the number of means available for attaining higher-order goals. The more alternative means for realizing their basic ends people could have, the more rapidly they could replace the inadaptive mean without enduring long-term performance deficits.

The idea that reorganization may produce temporary deficits is implicit in various theories of coping and motivation. In his model of reaction to crisis, Schontz (1975) held that when people work through a negative experience and face painful reality, they may experience distressful emotions and thoughts that can be so overwhelming that they inhibit the ability to plan and engage in active problem solving. Schontz also argued that these problems are not necessarily maladaptive, however, but may contribute to growth and adaptation.

Accordingly, Horowitz (1982) claims that the working-through process is marked by recurrent cycles of intrusion of painful self-relevant material and defensive retreat from threat-related stimuli that may interfere with and constrict functioning, and that these cycles occur progressively less frequently until they disappear when the inner reorganization is completed. Working from a different perspective, Klinger (1975) suggests that when people initially abandon a nonattainable goal and search for new goals, they may experience apathy, passivity, and pessimism (labeled "depression"). Over time, though, the loss becomes less relevant in the person's mental structures, and this change enables him or her to renew his or her commitment to goals, interest in the world, optimistic beliefs, and active task attempts: "Depression involves a gradual decline in the affective value of the lost incentive and a gradual shift in adaptation level to permit a recovery of other values" (p. 11).

EMPIRICAL EVIDENCE: COPING–PERFORMANCE CORRELATIONS

The hypothesized coping–performance link receives considerable support in six of the LH studies that I present in this book (see Table 1.1). Though these studies used correlational techniques and thereby told nothing about the causal directionality of the relationships, they establish the existence of concurrent relationships between the use of reported coping strategies and test task performance after helplessness training.

In these studies, the coping–performance link was first examined by Pearson correlations between subjects' coping scores, as measured by my four coping items, and performance accuracy in a letter cancellation task. Then task performance was regressed on coping strategies in order to examine the unique contribution of each strategy. Table 2.2 presents the pertinent results.

The pattern of results was quite consistent across the studies. Regressions showed that the set of coping scores made a significant prediction of performance accuracy after helplessness training in all the studies and explained between 34% and 45% of the performance variance. Pearson correlations revealed that problem

TABLE 2.2. Correlations and Standardized Regression Coefficients of Performance Accuracy as Predicted by Coping Scores

Study number	Problem solving	Reappraisal	Reorganization	Avoidance
1 $F = 5.59^b$ $R^2 = 34\%$				
r	$.52^b$	.21	$-.39^b$	$-.41^b$
Beta	$.41^b$	.03	$-.10$	$-.29^a$
8 $F = 9.18^b$ $R^2 = 46\%$				
r	$.36^a$	.18	$-.51^b$	$-.65^b$
Beta	.16	.08	.02	$-.61^b$
9 $F = 12.53^b$ $R^2 = 54\%$				
r	$.61^b$	$.33^a$	$-.48^b$	$-.53^b$
Beta	$.40^a$	.09	$-.22$	$-.26^a$
10 $F = 7.94^b$ $R^2 = 42\%$				
r	$.44^b$	$.29^a$	$-.46^b$	$-.51^b$
Beta	$.38^a$	$-.01$	.15	$-.28^a$
11 $F = 5.63^b$ $R^2 = 35\%$				
r	$.37^a$	$.27^a$	$-.36^a$	$-.39^a$
Beta	$.39^a$	.22	$-.07$	$-.18$
12 $F = 5.22^b$ $R^2 = 37\%$				
r	$.33^a$	.07	$-.41^b$	$-.49^b$
Beta	.08	$-.09$	$-.08$	$-.39^a$

$^a p < .05$
$^b p < .01$

solving and reappraisal were positively correlated with performance accuracy, whereas avoidance and reorganization were inversely correlated with it. These correlations were statistically significant in most of the studies. In keeping with my predictions, coping strategies were shown to be related to performance after failure, with problem solving and reappraisal being related to more accurate performance, and avoidance and reorganization to less accurate performance.

The regressions also pointed to the differential impact of each coping strategy. They revealed that the unique contributions of problem solving and avoidance to task performance were stronger and reached statistical significance in more studies than those made by reappraisal and reorganization (see Table 2.2). This finding implies that problem solving and avoidance are directly associated with task performance and do not need the intervention of other coping strategies, whereas the observed effects of reappraisal and reorganization on task performance reflect the presence of a third factor (possibly other coping strategies).

EMPIRICAL EVIDENCE: PREDISPOSITIONAL STUDIES

Further support for the coping–performance link is found in four of my studies that examine how subjects differing in their habitual ways of coping react to helplessness training. In the earliest study (Mikulincer, 1989c), I selected subjects according to their propensity to adopt problem solving and reappraisal coping (as measured by the Ways of Coping Checklist, Folkman & Lazarus, 1980), and then tested their performance in a letter cancellation task after either failure or no feedback in four unsolvable problems.

The findings support the hypothesis that a large repertoire of coping responses, both problem and emotion focused, prevents LH deficits. A large amount of helplessness training produced worse performance than no feedback among subjects who had a low propensity to either problem solving or reappraisal. It failed, however, to impair performance among subjects who tended to rely on both problem solving and reappraisal. In fact, these subjects performed well—and better than the other coping groups—after failure or no feedback.

Though the above study brought important information about the positive performance effects of problem solving and reappraisal, it only partly tests the role of these strategies in human LH, for it did not examine whether they underlie the facilitatory effects of a *small* amount of helplessness training. To fill in this gap, I recently replicated that research in my Study 2 (see Table 1.1) but exposed subjects to only one unsolvable problem instead of four.

The findings fill out the picture provided by the Mikulincer (1989c) study and demonstrate that reactance depends on the combined use of problem solving and reappraisal (see Figure 2.2). A single failure produced better performance than no

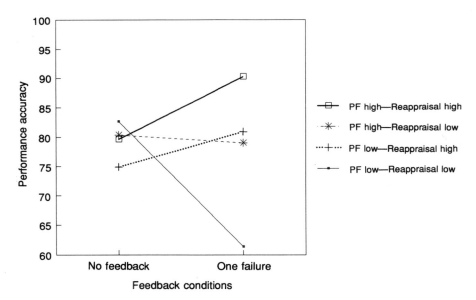

FIGURE 2.2. Means of performance accuracy according to feedback, problem-focused coping, and reappraisal coping.

feedback, a classic reactance effect, only among subjects who had high propensity to both problem solving and reappraisal. It did not improve performance among subjects who did not tend to rely on either problem solving or reappraisal. Moreover, subjects with low propensity for both problem solving and reappraisal reacted to even a single failure with performance deficits.

Together the correlational and predispositional data delineate the following effects of problem solving and reappraisal. On the one hand, problem solving may have a direct effect on task performance after both small and large amounts of helplessness training. It improves performance, raises the likelihood of reactance, and reduces the risk for LH deficits. These positive effects seem to be maximized by the simultaneous or sequential use of reappraisal strategies, which facilitate the allocation of cognitive resources in task-relevant activities. On the other hand, reappraisal strategies seem to be only auxiliary to problem solving and to have beneficial effects on task performance only when people are problem oriented.

In Studies 3 and 4 of my series of studies (see Table 1.1), I found supportive evidence for the detrimental effects of reorganization and avoidance. The instruments and procedure were identical to those used in the Mikulincer (1989c) study. Subjects in Study 3 were divided according to their scores on the avoidance subscale of the Ways of Coping Checklist, however, and subjects in Study 4 were divided according to their scores on a scale tapping the extent to which they tend to reorganize their priorities after negative life events (Taylor et al., 1983).

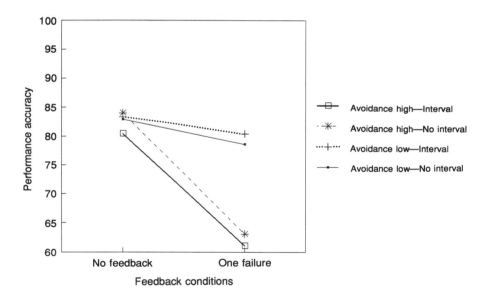

FIGURE 2.3. Means of performance accuracy according to feedback, avoidance coping, and time interval.

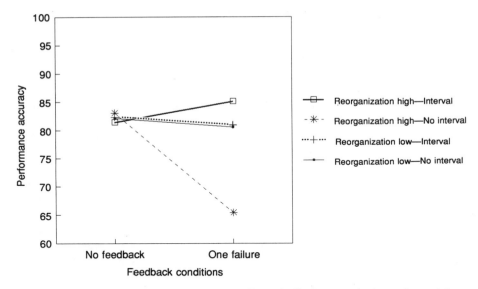

FIGURE 2.4. Means of performance accuracy according to feedback, reorganization coping, and time interval.

In the two studies, I also manipulated the time interval between the training and test phases. Half the subjects performed the test task immediately after the training task; the remaining subjects waited for 15 minutes before performing the test task. The expectation was that if LH deficits caused by reorganization cease after goal substitution, they should be short-lived and disappear with time. It was also expected that this would not happen to LH deficits that result from avoidance, where the problematic mismatch remains unsolved and the new task (even after a delay period) may renew the personal threat implied in the helplessness training and reactivate avoidance and LH deficits.

The results show that when there is no delay period LH deficits may result either from reorganization or avoidance (see Figures 2.3 and 2.4). Helplessness training produced less accurate performance than no feedback in an immediate task only among subjects who had propensities to avoidance or reorganization; subjects without these propensities showed no LH deficit. After a delay period, however, helplessness training produced performance deficits only among subjects with a tendency to avoidance coping. No delayed LH deficit was found among subjects without that propensity, nor was any found among subjects with a tendency toward intrapsychic reorganization after negative events.

Both reorganization and avoidance were found to have detrimental effects of task performance; however, they differed in the temporal nature of these effects.

Although both coping strategies contributed to immediate LH deficits, only the detrimental effects of avoidance resisted the passage of time. Reorganization seems to produce only short-lived deficits, which, as stated above, reflect a temporary disengagement from the task.

CONCLUSIONS

This chapter discussed the role that coping responses may play in human LH. Specifically, it took up two main issues: (a) whether problem solving and reappraisal contribute to the reactance effects observed after a small amount of helplessness training, and (b) whether avoidance and reorganization contribute to the LH deficits observed after a large amount of helplessness training.

It has been consistently proven that helplessness training reliably activates the four main categories of coping responses: problem solving, reappraisal, avoidance, and reorganization. In addition, there is evidence that whereas a small amount of helplessness training mainly activates problem solving and reappraisal, a large amount of training promotes avoidance and reorganization. In this context, the process nature of coping responses is emphasized. These responses grow out of the cognitive appraisal of the situation and are altered by changes in the person and the environment.

Moreover, both theory and research support the hypothesis that coping responses alter task performance after helplessness training and directly contribute to both reactance and LH deficits. Whereas problem solving and reappraisal have been found to improve task performance and to underlie reactance effects, avoidance and reorganization have been found to impair performance and to promote the classic LH deficits. Thus both reactance and LH deficits seem to reflect directly the use of coping responses that orient people either toward or away from the task and that support or compete for resources with task-relevant activities.

On this basis, one can delineate the following sequences: A small amount of helplessness training activates problem-solving and reappraisal strategies, which improve test task performance. A large amount of helplessness training activates avoidance or reorganization, which impair test task performance. In other words, coping responses may thus be one mechanism by which helplessness training alters functioning.

CHAPTER 3

MENTAL RUMINATION AS A PROXIMAL MEDIATOR OF LH EFFECTS

A cognitive process that contributes to coping and may directly affect the shaping of LH effects is mental rumination. It involves the conscious processing and elaboration of information related to coping with a mismatch (Kuhl, 1984; Martin & Tesser, 1989). It helps the coping process by filling consciousness with thoughts needed for altering the environment (action thoughts), accommodating mental structures (state thoughts), or avoiding a direct confrontation with a mismatch (task-irrelevant thoughts). Various theoretical propositions have focused on the process of rumination (Kuhl, 1984, Martin & Tesser, 1989), and research has shown its effects on coping and functioning (Kuhl, 1984, 1985).

I hypothesize that helplessness training leads to the passage from non-deliberative to deliberative thinking and the heightening of mental rumination (Kuhl, 1984; Martin & Tesser, 1989). I also hypothesize that these changes are the cognitive substrate of coping responses and may be proximal antecedents of reactance and LH deficits. A small amount of failure typically leads to rumination on task-oriented, action thoughts, which facilitates the organization of problem-solving strategies and thus contributes to the observed reactance effects. A large amount of failure typically leads to rumination on off-task thoughts, which helps reorganization and avoidance coping, thereby contributing to the observed LH deficits.

The present chapter is organized in the following way. First I present a theoretical position regarding the nature and functions of rumination; then I deal with its mediating role in human LH. I focus on (a) the effects of helplessness training on mental rumination, and (b) the performance consequences of this cognitive activity.

MENTAL RUMINATION: DEFINITION, TAXONOMY, AND FUNCTIONS

THE CONCEPT OF MENTAL RUMINATION

The phenomenon of mental rumination is becoming an important topic of study in psychology. It seems to be a typical response to ordinary life situations, related to other psychological processes, and involved in several psychological disorders (Beck, 1976; Kuhl, 1984; Sarason, 1975). I have limited the discussion in this chapter, however, to those thoughts that are relevant to human LH: ruminations that occur while working on the training and test tasks. I do not refer to thoughts in LH-irrelevant settings, or those not related to failure.

Mental rumination while working on a task is defined as controlled, purposive thinking on a particular issue over a relatively long period of time (e.g., Martin & Tesser, 1989). This definition distinguishes rumination from transient ideations and free associations, and it emphasizes the purposive nature of rumination. Rumination must be construed as intended thoughts that are developed via conscious design.

Mental rumination reflects a "mindful" state of mind (Chanowitz & Langer, 1980)—that is, engagement in effortful information processing. People actively search for information, encode situational cues, and retrieve memories that could be relevant for dealing with their transaction with the environment. They analyze stored and incoming information in depth, and they develop anticipatory cognitions and behavioral plans based on that analysis. In addition, the central processing space of their working memory is filled with ideations about the person–environment transaction, and new associative pathways are created among these ideations.

Several authors, however, have recognized the accompanying presence of some unwanted, intrusive thoughts that occur without conscious control (e.g., Horowitz, 1979; Martin & Tesser, 1989). These thoughts do not accomplish any function, are hard to suppress, and may be a sign of "cognitive autonomy" (Logan, 1989). Moreover, they may compete for resources and interfere with more organized and purposive thoughts. In my view, these autonomic thoughts are not a definitional feature of rumination, but rather one of its consequences. What began as a purposive activity may become a dysfunctional, autonomic experience.

A TAXONOMY OF THOUGHTS

Though a large variety of ruminative thoughts can occur in task situations, there is consensual agreement (e.g., Kuhl, 1984; Martin & Tesser, 1989; Sarason, 1984; Sarason, Sarason, Keefe, Hayes, & Shearin, 1986) on the following taxonomy: (a) action rumination (task-relevant thoughts about problem-solving actions), and (b) two types of off-task ruminations—state rumination (thoughts about the state of the actor performing the task) and task-irrelevant rumination (thoughts on issues that are irrelevant to the task situation).

Action rumination is strategic in nature (Kuhl, 1984, 1985). People elaborate on ways to succeed in a task; they effortfully search and process information bearing on alternative problem-solving plans and strategies. They selectively encode task-relevant stimuli and inhibit any off-task cognition. In general, their cognitive system focuses on instrumental actions, and their thought flow is filled with pertinent cognitions.

Off-task thoughts can be divided into state rumination and task-irrelevant rumination. The common denominator of these thoughts is that they do not focus on task features, problem-solving plans, or instrumental actions. State rumination, however, is still focused on a particular portion of the task situation: the person performing the task and the state of his or her goals and schemas during and after the task. Task-irrelevant rumination totally abandons the task situation and distracts people from both the problem and their own state.

State rumination is analytic and reflective (Kuhl, 1984, 1985). People ruminate on their present, past, or future states. They process information on the state of their inner structures (goal hierarchy, self-identity) and on the changes in these structures that the task situation may imply. They engage in self-evaluative thoughts and activate any stored material that bears on the state of their inner structures. Cognitions typical of state rumination include those related to self-worth, those linked to the personal effects of success and failure, and those involved in a "rehashing" of the meaning of the situation.

Kuhl mentioned three subtypes of state ruminations: failure oriented, extrinsic, and vacillating. The failure-oriented types are thoughts on the self-relevant damage and threats implied by a failure. The thought flow is full of worries about the implications of the failure, painful memories of past failures, and catastrophic ideations. Extrinsic state ruminations are thoughts about the goal to be attained. Attention is obsessively directed toward the aspired state of the self, and the thought flow is full of ideations about what will happen once the goal is or is not attained. The vacillating type of state ruminations are worries and doubts about leaving frustrating tasks and partaking instead in more pleasurable activities.

Task-irrelevant rumination consists of thoughts about issues that have nothing to do with the task situation. People ruminate about past transactions with the environment, imagine other possible transactions, and think about other people, inanimate objects, tasks, or goals that are completely irrelevant to their current relationship with the world. They engage in thoughts that have nothing to do with either the problem at hand or the state of their mental structures. Though these persons may not physically abandon the task situation, they are mentally disengaged from it, and their mind wanders to other places and times.

FUNCTIONS OF MENTAL RUMINATION

By definition, mental rumination is a functional, purposive activity. One may ask, however, what is the specific psychological function of mental rumination?

In his action control theory, Kuhl (1984, 1985) focuses on action and state ruminations and claims that they mediate between intention and action; they are the mechanism that controls the preservation and enactment of intentions. In Kuhl's terms, an intention is a cognitive structure stored in the declarative memory. It is activated by environmental features, and it is linked with action programs designed to produce a change in the environment. The importance of rumination resides in the fact that the activation of an intention to do something does not guarantee the enactment of the intended action. Both external and internal forces may impede the execution of the action so that the intervention of self-regulatory efforts are required for the action to be carried out. Rumination is one such basic self-regulatory mechanism; although motivation may fluctuate, rumination keeps the goal active.

Kuhl has suggested that action rumination serves a metastatic, change-inducing function. It facilitates the removal of obstacles to the enactment of an intended action by focusing the person on the task at hand and engaging the cognitive system in the analysis of alternative ways for producing a desired change in the environment. State rumination, in contrast, accomplishes a catastatic, change-preventing function. It facilitates the preservation of an intention that is irremediably blocked by external or internal forces. Thinking only about the intention keeps the intention alive and prevents any change in superordinate goals, even when no action can be carried out.

In addition, Kuhl (1984) suggests that state thoughts accomplish an editing function: They contribute to the evaluation and reorganization of damaged mental structures, such as self-schemas and goal hierarchies. In Kuhl's terms, state rumination can be viewed "as serving a similar purpose as the editing of a program . . . reflecting on ineffective parts of the program without executing any of the steps that are being analyzed" (p. 144).

Alternative, but not contradictory, ideas have been raised by other authors. From a self-regulatory perspective, Kanfer and Hagerman (1981) claim that conscious thinking helps the person to sustain goal-directed actions. This is manifested in the monitoring of behaviors, the comparison of the actual state of events to a standard, and the programming of behavior by responding with self-reward if the behavior meets the standard and with self-punishment if it falls short. In Kanfer and Hagerman's terms, the function of rumination is to protect one's goal-oriented strivings in face of adversities.

Based on Kelley's attributional analysis, Pittman and her colleagues (Pittman & D'Agostino, 1985; Pittman & Heller, 1987) argue that the main reason for engaging in effortful information processing is to render one's world predictable and potentially controllable. People ruminate in order to acquire an accurate understanding of the causal agents of environmental events that could facilitate the assertion of control. So the more a person is motivated to take control, the more likely he or she is to process available information and to engage in conscious thinking.

In his analysis of posttraumatic reactions, Horowitz (1979, 1982) stated that rumination helps the person to assimilate threatening information. Rumination facilitates the working through of failures and losses, the evaluation of personal damage, and the reorganization of inner structures in such a way that the events become less dangerous to the integrity of the self-system. In this way, rumination helps the person to incorporate a threat into the self-system with minimal damage. It acts as a buffer against the damage that failures and losses may cause to inner structures, integrating old and new self-referent information and promoting better adaptation. In a similar vein, Martin and Tesser (1989) claim that rumination has a self-reparative function. They hypothesize that mental rumination is elicited every time some part of the self is injured by environmental events. To repair it, people engage in controlled information processing and ruminative thoughts aimed at symbolically making whole the damaged part of the self.

In my terms, rumination accomplishes a coping function: It helps people manage a person–environment mismatch. Rumination may provide the cognitive context for molding the environment in accord with one's goals, accommodating inner structures to reality constraints, or avoiding a direct confrontation with a mismatch. It is a means of searching for and organizing the information needed to execute a chosen coping strategy.

Action rumination may help people to remove a source of harm from the environment. It facilitates the molding of the environment and helps people to overcome failure and to reach their goals. Elaborations on self-views, personal aspirations, and priorities (state rumination) may help people to work through the threatening implications of a mismatch, fine-tune inner structures, and find substitute goals. Phenomenologically, state rumination is experienced as a painful awareness of one's self-state and personal aspirations; it is necessary in order for the person to preserve his or her superordinate goals and central aspects of self-identity in situations where a threat cannot be removed by instrumental actions. Rumination on task-irrelevant issues may help people to distance themselves cognitively from the threatening situation, to imagine better places and times, and thus to reduce the distress that the direct confrontation with a mismatch may produce. All these types of rumination provide the cognitive tools for bringing the person and the environment into better alignment, or at least for reducing the threats and distress produced by a mismatch.

The coping function of mental rumination is implicit in the theoretical statements reviewed above. It is present in statements that rumination helps people enact intended actions (Kuhl, 1981), attain personal goals (Kanfer & Hagerman, 1981), and assert control (Pittman & Heller, 1987). What is implicit here is that rumination may help people to cope with a person–environment mismatch by changing the negative course of events and bringing the environment more in line with their goals. The same idea is also present in statements that rumination helps people preserve and edit blocked intentions (Kuhl, 1981), work through threatening events (Horowitz, 1979), and repair damaged self-aspects (Martin & Tesser, 1989). Here it is implicit that rumination helps coping with a mismatch by reorganizing inner structures and accommodating them to reality constraints.

The hypothesized link between coping responses and mental rumination, however, does not mean that rumination determines the type of coping strategy chosen. Rather, the content of any rumination may be determined by the coping orientation that people have already adopted on the basis of their appraisal of the situation, their response repertoire, and other personal preferences. Only after these processes have come into play do they activate information processing and engage in rumination that could help achieve the objectives of the strategy chosen.

Action rumination may thus be seen as a tool employed for problem solving and reappraisal. Problem-focused coping requires a systematic analysis of the problem, the retrieval of both declarative knowledge on problem-solving situations and procedural knowledge on problem-solving strategies, and deliberative thinking about how the environment can be altered. In support of this view, Erwin and Marcus-Mendoza (1987) found that the frequency of action rumination was related to the adoption of an active problem-solving approach in a midterm exam. Action rumination is also helpful in reappraisal strategies, because any attempt to reappraise a task situation positively should be based in an analysis of the task and the processing of its positive aspects. Snyder and Higgins (1988) have already suggested that excuse making (a kind of reappraisal strategy) requires a focus on problem solving and action alternatives, and that it may be inhibited by focusing attention on the state of the self.

By definition, state rumination may be seen as a tool for reorganization coping. This way of coping requires the processing of the meaning and self-implications of a mismatch, the retrieval of relevant self-schemas, the evaluation of personal damage, and the formulation of hypotheses about the most suitable rearrangement of inner structures. All these requirements may be fulfilled by ruminating on the past, present, and future state of one's self-identity and goal hierarchy.

The three types of Kuhl's state-oriented thoughts may contribute to reorganization. Failure-oriented thoughts ("Where did I go wrong?") help the person to work through the damage caused by a mismatch to the self system. Extrinsic thoughts on aspirations and priorities may assist in evaluating threats to the future state of the self and in finding substitute goals. Vacillating thoughts may delay mental disengagement from a task situation until the working-through process is completed.

Task-irrelevant rumination may be viewed as a tool for avoidance coping. Avoidance coping may put an end to rumination (either action or state oriented) on the task situation and lead people to ruminate on task-irrelevant, distracting information. Avoidance coping, however, may paradoxically lead to the intrusion into consciousness of autonomic state thoughts related to the failure (Lazarus & Folkman, 1984; Horowitz, 1982; Janis, 1958). I will elaborate on this idea in dealing with the autonomic facet of state rumination.

Supportive evidence for the hypothesized links between coping responses and mental rumination is found in six of the LH studies that I present in this book (see Table 1.1 for details). Subjects completed the four coping items described in Chapter 2 and three items tapping the frequency of action, state, and task-irrelevant thoughts. Each item presented a concise description of one type of thought, and subjects gave their answers in a bipolar 7-point scale ranging from "not at all" (1) to "very much" (7). As can be seen in Table 3.1, most of the studies found that the use

TABLE 3.1. Pearson Correlations of Rumination Scores and Coping Scores

Rumination	Study	Problem solving	Reappraisal	Reorganization	Avoidance
Action					
	1	−.02	.26[a]	−.05	.17
	8	.53[b]	.10	−.38[a]	−.29[a]
	9	.41[b]	.45[b]	−.35[a]	−.36[a]
	10	.38[a]	.33[a]	−.34[a]	−.36[a]
	11	.54[b]	.10	−.31[a]	−.33[a]
	12	.34[a]	.15	−.22	−.08
State					
	1	−.47[b]	.06	.64[b]	.58[b]
	8	−.35[a]	.01	.26	.24
	9	−.36[a]	−.17	.44[b]	.38[a]
	10	−.33[a]	.01	.66[b]	.51[b]
	11	−.51[b]	−.08	.49[b]	.54[b]
	12	−.25	−.35[a]	.50[b]	.52[b]
Task-irrelevant					
	1	−.66[b]	.05	.48[b]	.53[b]
	8	−.38[a]	−.32[a]	.36[a]	.59[b]
	9	−.39[a]	−.40[a]	.37[a]	.43[b]
	10	−.50[b]	−.06	.53[b]	.64[b]
	11	−.41[a]	−.05	.45[b]	.48[b]
	12	−.44[b]	−.27[a]	.48[a]	.43[b]

[a]$p < .05$
[b]$p < .01$

of problem-focused coping was positively correlated with the frequency of action rumination and inversely correlated with the frequency of state and task-irrelevant ruminations. Most of the studies also found that reliance on reappraisal was positively related to action thoughts, though the correlations were relatively low. In contrast, the use of reorganization and avoidance strategies was inversely correlated with the frequency of action rumination and positively correlated with the frequency of state and task-irrelevant thoughts.

Interestingly, the findings presented in Table 3.1 showed that avoidance coping includes rumination not only on distracting, task-irrelevant material but also on painful state thoughts. It is possible that the findings reflect the intrusion of autonomic state thoughts into consciousness upon the adoption of avoidance coping. One should take this interpretation with extreme caution, however, because my rumination items cannot differentiate between purposive and autonomic thoughts. Alternatively, the findings may suggest that state rumination after failure—which is the cognitive substrate of reorganization coping—is so painful and distressing that it may lead people to distance themselves temporarily or permanently from the threat as a means for mitigating the heightened distress. Again, caution should be also taken here because of the cross-sectional nature of the assessments. What one can say with certainty is that avoidance coping and state rumination are not antagonistic activities. Instead, they can be possible steps in a recursive sequence of avoidance and confrontation with a threat.

To summarize, action rumination helps to shape the environment, generate action alternatives, and construct new problem-solving plans; state rumination helps to reorganize mental structures; and task-irrelevant rumination facilitates avoidance coping. All three types of rumination serve a coping function and may continue until a person-environment mismatch is minimized, or at least until its threatening implications are managed.

THE AUTONOMIC FACET OF MENTAL RUMINATION

Though mental rumination is conceptualized as a purposive activity, several authors have noted that it may be accompanied by an unwanted side effect: the intrusion of autonomic failure-related thoughts into consciousness (e.g., Horowitz, 1982; Martin & Tesser, 1989). These thoughts run ballistically on to completion, are irrelevant to one's intentions, and are hard to suppress. They fill the cognitive system, but although they are related to the failure situation, they do not contribute to the management of the mismatch and its threatening implications. Rather, they exacerbate tension and distress. Phenomenologically this cognitive material is experienced as an "uninvited intruder" (Horowitz, 1982), "unintended thoughts" (Uleman & Bargh, 1989), or "autonomic cognitions" (Logan, 1989).

Horowitz (1979, 1982) views these autonomic thoughts as the basic component of what he calls "intrusion states." According to Horowitz, these thoughts typically alternate with avoidance and denial and can be found after every type of serious failure or loss. They seem to be accompanied by uncontrollable pangs of emotion, somatic hyperactivity, excessive alertness and vigilance toward the surrounding world, reenactments of personal responses to the stressful event, bad dreams, intrusive sensations and images while trying to sleep, misperceptions and pseudohallucinations. In general, the cognitive system seems to be flooded by repetitive thoughts, affects, images, and behaviors that the person cannot stop from intruding into consciousness.

The intrusion of autonomic failure-related thoughts may also interfere with the controlled facets of mental rumination. It absorbs attention and resources that could have been invested in coping with the mismatch. It includes painful self-relevant material (directly or symbolically related to a mismatch) that may augment inner tension and distress. On the whole, the intrusion of autonomic state thoughts may overwhelm the cognitive system with material that impairs rather than helps the coping task. In extreme cases, it may completely disrupt and paralyze organized coping.

When people deliberate about a mismatch, stored material relevant to this issue is purposively activated in the "associative memory network" (Anderson & Bower,

1973) and can be incorporated into the thought flow. This activation, however, is also spread over other units of information connected with the relevant material by existing pathways in the associative network (Anderson, 1990). In this way, cognitive material that is not purposively activated is made accessible for processing and may intrude into conscious thinking.

In some cases, the rapid autonomic spread of activation may be overridden by a controlled processing that selectively incorporates into conscious thinking only material that is relevant to the coping task (Clark & Isen, 1982). Here the heightened information processing proceeds along with inhibitory mechanisms that control the access to consciousness and suppress autonomic thoughts. In other instances, though, autonomic memory activation overwhelms conscious thinking with associations, images, sensations, and themes that are irrelevant to the coping task. Here a configuration of heightened rumination and cognitive autonomy is created in which inhibitory mechanisms are weakened, and autonomic thoughts intrude into consciousness.

The main questions here are the following: (a) What are the contents of the autonomic thoughts? (b) What are the psychological mechanisms that produce them? With regard to the first question, several authors have suggested that autonomic thoughts after failure are mainly focused on the state of the person performing the task (e.g., Kuhl, 1984; Martin & Tesser, 1989). They consist of distressing associations and images of the personal damage produced by the failure, memories of prior failure and loss experiences, reflections about one's weakness and powerlessness, and catastrophic fantasies. Horowitz (1979) also contends that common intrusive thoughts and feelings deal with the loss and its personal implications, such as one's responsibility, vulnerability, and reactions to the loss. The material that intrudes into consciousness thus deals mainly with the past, present, and future state of the damaged mental structures. On this basis, any consideration of state thoughts should include reference to both purposive and autonomic cognitive products. State rumination may facilitate the accommodation of mental structures to reality constraints; however, some state thoughts may be autonomically activated and may have no obvious coping function.

With regard to the second question, I suggest a two-stage sequence. In the first stage, the mere occurrence of a personally important failure may activate autonomic failure-related thoughts. This is what Horowitz (1979) calls a period of "outcry," in which the cognitive activation may spread from the "failure" node in the associative memory network to other related thoughts, affects, and sensations. At this stage, people who have insufficient resources to master this onslaught of intrapsychic events may experience a rupture in their defenses and become overwhelmed by failure-related thoughts. Adequately functioning people, however, are generally able to channel these thoughts into purposive mental rumination and are able to control their entrance into consciousness. That is, they may take advantage of the failure-related thoughts to resolve the mismatch and to reach a new level of adaptation. Alternatively, they may adopt avoidance coping by totally inhibiting the access of failure-related thoughts into consciousness and distracting themselves with thoughts about other matters. Either way, they are able to put an end to a brief state of intrusion.

In the second stage, some purposive attempts to cope with a mismatch, which originally have increased the control over failure-related thoughts, may lead to the recurrence of the autonomic intrusion of these thoughts into consciousness. Here the activation of autonomic failure-related thoughts may occur as an unintended outcome of efforts to manage the mismatch, and it results from a choice of coping strategies that involve bad trade-offs. This reasoning is consistent with the psychoanalytic argument that dysfunctional symptoms reflect unsuccessful attempts to solve problems.

The main path by which coping may lead to the intrusion of autonomic state thoughts is by excessively prolonged avoidance strategies. As stated earlier, the aim of avoidance coping is to suppress mental rumination on a mismatch via rumination on task-irrelevant issues. When important self-aspects are implicated in a mismatch, however, suppression may be unsuccessful, and the suppressed material may return to consciousness. Folkman and Lazarus (1988) wrote that "we are impressed with how difficult it is to achieve distancing when one wants to, for example, in situations in which one must await a decision in which one has a strong stake" (p. 473). The to-be-suppressed thoughts may stay active in memory, and any related stimuli may automatically call them into mind. In this way these thoughts return to consciousness as autonomous intruders rather than as wanted material.

The idea that the adoption of avoidance strategies may be followed by the occurrence of autonomic state thoughts is explicitly stated by Horowitz (1979, 1982) in his model of adaptation to stress. In this model, autonomic state thoughts are inherent products of every avoidance attempt, even the most successful, because the to-be-suppressed material is repeatedly activated until cognitive processing reaches completion. Information that is unacceptable might be temporarily prevented from reaching consciousness, but it remains active in memory, exerting a constant demand for processing and intruding into consciousness every time internal or external stimuli call it up. Avoidance, according to Horowitz, inevitably leaves the work unfinished, because it splits the bad event from the self and leads the suppressed thoughts to press continuously for intrusion into consciousness.

Horowitz claims that the person's reactions to serious stressful events are guided by a "completion tendency"—the tendency to mobilize coping effort and process pertinent material until the person and the environment are brought into better alignment and disrupted equilibrium is restored. This tendency remains active after people decide to avoid any confrontation with a threat, because avoidance coping by definition implies the inhibition of all the activities that could truly resolve the mismatch (see Chapter 2). Intrusion reflects the fact that the coping task is unfinished. It may be viewed as a demand for a reduction in avoidance so as to solve the problem or work through the failure. Avoidance coping, which inhibits problem solving and inner reorganization, may thus be interrupted by intrusion states in which the suppressed material returns to consciousness and demands processing until the mismatch is resolved.

This intrusion may lead to two very different sequences of intrapsychic events. In the adaptive sequence, the intrusion of failure-related material into consciousness may lead people to abandon (or at least reduce) avoidance coping and to expend effort in working through the loss until their mental structures and the new reality are integrated. When the working-through process is completed, a new level of adaptation is reached, and failure-related thoughts cease to be activated or to intrude into consciousness. In short, the intrusion of failure-related thoughts may be seized as an opportunity to engage in purposive mental rumination and to resolve the distressing mismatch.

In the maladaptive sequence, the intrusion of failure-related material into consciousness may lead people to increase (rather than decrease) their avoidance defenses, thinking that this will put an end to the intrusion state and prevent its recurrence in the future. These people may constrict their functioning even further and may begin also to avoid some new situations (e.g., those connected with the last intrusive episode). They may also suppress new thoughts that, although not directly related to the failure episode, may be related to the stimuli that caused the most recent intrusion state. This increase in avoidance is likely, however, to lead to another episode of intrusion, because more and more external and internal stimuli are becoming associated with the failure episode—thus gaining the power to recall it and to activate additional autonomic failure-related thoughts and affects. A self-exacerbating cycle of avoidance and intrusion may thus develop that leaves the person "stuck" with the failure, prevents adaptation, and creates problems in functioning.

The above ideas have weighty theoretical and empirical support. Freud (1914/1957) noted that attempts to deny or repress unwanted thoughts lead to preoccupation with those thoughts and to the intrusive "return" of the repressed material. Lindemann (1944) and Lazarus (1983) observed that suppression of thought can result in subsequent obsessive concern and distress. Janis (1958) found that patients who avoided thinking about an upcoming operation were preoccupied with it afterward. The same pattern was found among people who attempted to inhibit the expression of thoughts about a traumatic experience (Burstein & Meichenbaum, 1979; Foa & Kozak, 1986; Rachman, 1980; Silver, Boon, & Stones, 1983) and among people who were induced to suppress a particular thought (Conway, Howell, & Giannopoulus, 1991; Wegner, Schneider, Carter, & White, 1987; Wegner, Schneider, Knutson, & McMahon, 1991). In addition, Rholes, Michas, and Smith (1987) found that the frequency of autonomic state thoughts in stressful episodes was positively related to the adoption of avoidance coping.

An additional, but unusual, path by which coping may lead to the intrusion of autonomic state thoughts is via the adoption of reorganization coping. Under some conditions, working through a failure demands a great deal of effort and time because many mental structures (some of them quite fundamental) may need to be reorganized in order to end the person–environment mismatch. This working through is generally accompanied by extensive and painful state rumination that may become "channeled" (Martin & Tesser, 1989) into autonomic thoughts that can intrude into consciousness without serving any coping function. According to Martin and Tesser, the longer purposive rumination goes on, the greater the number of other cognitions that will become associated with the current failure. As a consequence, a broader net of autonomically activated ideations will make the failure situationally available and call the associated state thoughts to mind, even after working through is completed. This will result in autonomic state thoughts being easily and frequently cued by the environment.

This is not to say, however, that autonomic state thoughts will always follow prolonged reorganization coping. Rather, this sequence of cognitive events depends on a number of personal and situational factors, such as the level of the individual's inner controls and the complexity of his or her associative network. People who have strong inner controls and more differentiated associative networks may be able to engage in extensive reorganization and purposive rumination about the state of the self without suffering the intrusion of autonomic thoughts.

SUMMARY

On the whole, mental rumination seems to participate in the coping process. Its controlled, purposive facets are the cognitive substrate of coping responses and may provide the cognitive context over which these responses are organized. The autonomic facets of mental rumination are unwanted products of the coping process; they may mainly follow avoidance coping. In both ways, either as an auxiliary of coping responses or as an unwanted derivate of these responses, mental rumination may have repercussions on the way people cope with a mismatch and thereby may contribute to LH effects.

HELPLESSNESS TRAINING AND MENTAL RUMINATION

The first target of inquiry in the mediating role of rumination within the LH paradigm should be its association with helplessness training. One should assess whether mental rumination is heightened by lack of control and, if so, what kind of rumination is encouraged. Based on a coping perspective of mental rumination, I propose three main hypotheses. First, helplessness training—which sets in motion a coping process—may heighten effortful cognitive activity, which is manifested in the magnitude of mental rumination and other aspects of the processing of information (e.g., search, encoding, retrieval). Second, different kinds of thoughts will be elicited by different amounts of helplessness training: A *small* amount of failure, which typically activates problem-solving and reappraisal strategies, will lead to action rumination, whereas a *large* amount of failure, which typically activates off-task coping strategies (e.g., avoidance and reorganization) will lead to off-task rumination (either state or task-irrelevant). Third, a large amount of failure will increase the intrusion into consciousness of autonomic failure-related thoughts.

HEIGHTENED COGNITIVE ACTIVITY

My first hypothesis is that helplessness training is a precursor of purposive mental rumination. This hypothesis is based on the idea that helplessness training, which creates a person–environment mismatch (see Chapter 1), may threaten well-being and initiate the coping process, which always involves some kind of cognitive activity. In trying to cope with a failure, either by problem-solving or off-task strategies, people may search, process, and ruminate on stored and incoming information that could help them to protect well-being. Moreover, their thought flow consists of cogitations that organize appropriate coping responses and facilitate the management of the mismatch. Having encountered no failure and having no need to cope with a mismatch, people adopt a "mindless" state of mind (Chanowitz & Langer, 1980). As Martin and Tesser (1989) suggested, "Consciousness is often a troubleshooting process. . . . Consciousness becomes consequential when the environment does not permit behavioral scripts to unfold in their expected way" (p. 311). Similar ideas have been mentioned in several works (Dweck & Leggett, 1988; Kuhl, 1981; Pittman & Heller, 1987; Wicklund, 1986).

The heightening of cognitive activity after failure may also reflect the desire to understand the meaning of the situation. Helplessness training generates ambiguity about the causes and meaning of environmental events. People do not expect the failure and do not understand why they have failed in the task. They therefore focus their thoughts on organizing their experience, integrating it with their cognitive structures, and ruminating purposively on the meaning and implications of their current transaction with the environment.

Uncontrollable failure may also lead people to stop current actions and to delay any further action until they find more appropriate coping ways. Recurrent failure signals that the habitual response repertoire is ineffective for minimizing a mismatch and that its automatic repetition may only augment the distress. Therefore failure may lead people to think before they act—that is, to organize new action programs. This demand may be reflected in the engagement in mental rumination, which may lead people to discover new action programs by bringing remotely associated contents into direct juxtaposition and creating new associative paths among them.

Whatever the purpose, failure may open up the cognitive system in order to construct and test new, more valid knowledge. It may lead people to put aside inappropriate problem-solving plans and to replace them with more suitable strategies. It may also lead people to learn something new about themselves, to enrich their mental structures, and to organize substitute goals and projects. In other words, failure indicates that one's actions and/or priorities do not fit reality constraints and that one should ruminate on existing response repertoires and mental structures. In terms of the lay epistemic theory of Kruglanski (1989), helplessness training may be a situational antecedent of the need for cognitive closure; a desire for an answer—any answer—on a given topic is preferable to confusion and ambiguity. Failure refutes knowledge, creates cognitive confusion, and thus increases the need for new answers that could end ambiguity and distress.

According to this reasoning, the heightening of mental rumination after failure will depend on the extent to which existing knowledge has been violated, the centrality of this violation for well-being, the level of the resulting distress, and the consequent demand for coping actions. It may also depend on such dispositional factors as a person's tendency to ruminate, his or her tolerance of ambiguity, and his or her need for cognitive closure, as well as the complexity of the cognitive structure and the availability of cognitive resources. The higher the tendency to ruminate, the lower the tolerance of ambiguity, the greater the need for cognitive closure, the more complex the cognitive structures, and the more available the resources, the more intensive will be the elaboration of information pertinent to the coping task.

In addition, one can propose a "stop rule" for heightened mental rumination that goes into effect whenever the coping task succeeds. This is the case when the meaning of the failure is understood, new action programs are generated, and a mismatch is ended. At this time, there are no more personal threats, ambiguities, or demands for coping actions. It is now possible to cease effortful information processing and begin to act in a nondeliberative way. This stop rule however, can be disrupted by autonomic thoughts that overwhelm the cognitive system and keep the person occupied with the failure situation. In this case, rumination (mainly off-task oriented) may persist without accomplishing any coping function.

Several studies have documented the heightening of mental rumination following helplessness training. One series of studies has focused on the reported frequency of ruminative thoughts. Morris and Liebert (1973) and Morris, Davis, and Hutchings (1981) found that the frequency of self-preoccupative worry, as assessed by the Emotionality-Worry Scale, increases after the experience or anticipation of failure. Klinger (1984) found that free reports of self-preoccupation increase with poor performance in a task. Kuhl (1984) reported that perseverative thoughts on a task after working in other tasks for about 20 minutes were more frequent after failure than after no feedback, and that this effect occurred mainly among subjects with a tendency to state rumination.

LH research conducted in my laboratory also provides evidence that helplessness training increases the reported frequency of both state and task-irrelevant thoughts (Mikulincer, 1989a, b, c; Mikulincer, Glaubman, Ben-Artzi, & Grossman, 1991; Mikulincer & Marshand, 1991; Mikulincer & Nizan, 1988). In these studies, the frequencies of state and task-irrelevant thoughts and the reported frequency of mind wandering as assessed by the Cognitive Interference Questionnaire (CIQ; Sarason et al., 1986) were higher after failure in four unsolvable cognitive problems than after no feedback. In addition, failure was found to increase any tendency to engage in state and task-irrelevant thoughts. This was true for people who habitually engaged in off-task thoughts or who were diagnosed as suffering from mild depression. Findings also indicated that the effects of failure on state and task-irrelevant thoughts were weakened by reappraisal procedures (excuse making). This last finding is far from being unexpected and reflects the inhibitory links between reappraisal coping and off-task thoughts.

Another series of studies conducted by T. S. Pittman and her colleagues has focused on the cognitive operations involved in mental rumination: the effortful search, encoding, and retrieval of information. In the first study, Pittman and Pittman (1980) assessed attributional activity after zero, two, or six unsolvable problems. Subjects were given a written essay and information on the motives for its writing. Half of the subjects were told that the essay was written for payment (mand condition), and the other half were told that it was not written for publication (tact condition). The dependent variable was the extent to which people attributed the essay's writing to external or internal causes. If helplessness training activates deliberative thinking, it would make people attentive to attribution-relevant cues and prone to process and use them when making causal judgments.

Results showed that failure subjects adopted a mindfulness attitude and encoded attributional-relevant cues efficiently. In the two unsolvable groups, the mand-tact information had greater impact on self-reported attributions than it did in the no-feedback condition. Whereas subjects in the no-feedback condition were not influenced by the attributional information, subjects exposed to lack of control attributed the writing to more internal and less external motives in the tact than in the mand condition. The findings were replicated, with the same manipulations and materials, by Liu and Steele (1986).

In another study, Swann, Stephenson, and Pittman (1981) found that helplessness training fosters the active search for information. In interviewing another person, subjects exposed previously to unsolvable problems freely asked more questions that contributed to learning about the interviewee (diagnostic questions) than did subjects exposed to no feedback. The former also selected more diagnostic issues to examine further from those that the interviewee had already answered; in fact, no-feedback subjects tended to end the examination after the interviewee answered the questions.

Conceptually similar findings have been found in memory tasks. Hypothesizing that lack of control leads people to invest effort in the encoding and retrieval of information, Pittman and D'Agostino (1989) gave subjects previously exposed to zero or six unsolvable problems a list of sentence pairs to study, followed by a recognition test consisting of sentences from the list, inferences based on these sentences, and new sentences. Results were in keeping with the hypothesis: Subjects exposed to helplessness training were more accurate in recognizing inferences as either old or new sentences than were no-feedback subjects. The same results were obtained in a subsequent study (Pittman & D'Agostino, 1989, Experiment 2) that examined the learning and recognition of a short text.

In general, evidence suggests that helplessness training triggers the effortful search, encoding, and retrieval of information. Pittman and D'Agostino (1989) conclude that "an experience with failure to control one's outcomes is a danger signal that produces an increased desire to construe subsequent situations accurately. Toward this end subjects engage in effortful information acquisition . . . and new information is processed carefully and deeply (a style that could be characterized as more systematic, bottom up, or data-driven)" (p. 479).

Interestingly, the cognitive effects of helplessness training resemble those of positive mood. Several studies have found that experimentally induced positive mood has an impact on memory, categorization, information search, creativity, and problem solving (see Isen, 1984, 1987, for a review), enriching and deepening the encoding, analysis, and elaboration of stored and incoming material. In a recent study, one of my students (Tzarfati, 1992) found that a positive mood triggers deliberative thinking and leads people to generate new knowledge instead of relying on faulty preconceptions.

But how can it be that helplessness training, which seems to induce negative affect, alters cognitive operations in the same way as positive affect? In my terms, both failure and positive mood lead people to open up their cognitive system in order to enhance their psychological well-being. Effortful cognitive activities after failure are aimed at restoring disrupted well-being, whereas the same cognitive operations after a positive mood is established are aimed at maintaining this level of well-being (Clark & Isen, 1982; Isen, 1987).

Though helplessness training and positive mood may produce similar cognitive changes, however, they have different performance effects. Whereas the cognitive effects of both positive mood and helplessness training may be reflected in the improvement of problem-solving performance (e.g., Isen, 1984, 1987), the heightened cognitive activity elicited by helplessness training may also lead to performance deficits. For example, Pittman and Pittman (1980) found that although failure led to increased utilization of attributional-relevant cues (heightened information processing), it produced poor performance on an anagram task.

The opposing effects of cognitive activity on task performance after helplessness training may be attributable to the fact that the person can be oriented either toward or away from the task. Deliberative thinking may improve performance when it focuses on the processing of action alternatives. It may impair performance, however, when it focuses on the processing and rumination of state-related material or on other task-irrelevant material (e.g., thoughts about self-worth). Whereas the former involves the person with the problem at hand, the latter may divert attention from the task and interfere with task performance. For this reason, we cannot draw firm conclusions regarding type of performance change (reactance or LH deficits) from findings of increased cognitive activity following helplessness training.

A Cycle of Mental Rumination

My second hypothesis is that helplessness training creates a specific cycle of purposive mental rumination. Initially, failure heightens action rumination. People exposed to lack of control focus on action alternatives and engage in task-relevant thinking. If the failure continues despite the person's persistent effort and no action alternative can overcome the failure, however, people begin to move their attention and their thoughts away from the task, either by focusing on the self or on other task-irrelevant issues. Thoughts about the self concern the state of the self, the damage caused by the failure, and related feelings, as well as the cost and benefit of the current and alternative activities and ways to reach a compromise between their goals and reality constraints. Task-irrelevant thoughts concern issues that distract people from the failure situation and distance them from the threat.

Cycles of rumination also have been construed by Kuhl (1981) and Martin and Tesser (1989). These previous conceptualizations have also emphasized the shift from task-relevant to off-task thinking following repeated failure. They do not, however, relate to the possibility that there may be two broad categories of off-task thoughts that have different functions and may lead to different outcomes. Although these theories acknowledge that a large amount of helplessness training may result in state-oriented thinking, they do not mention the occurrence of distracting thoughts. In addition, Martin and Tesser (1989) propose a third stage in the cycle of rumination (a "helplessness state") that, in my terms, does not reflect purposive information processing but rather the intrusion of autonomic failure-related thoughts into consciousness.

It is not my intention to claim that people necessarily go through a fixed ruminative sequence; any of the stages, and even the entire cycle, may be skipped. For example, a person with a tendency to depression may, after only a single failure, refrain from further task-relevant thinking and move directly to off-task thinking. Or, in the case where the failure is not perceived as important, the person may not engage in any rumination at all. What I mean is that in adequately functioning people, off-task thoughts are more likely to occur when problem solving is perceived to be ineffective for managing a mismatch (i.e., when they have difficulties in finding actions to overcome failure). This perception may result from either actual experience with successive failures or generalized expectancies and limited response repertoire. Indeed, Wicklund and Braun (1987) found that failure increased the frequency of off-task ruminations mainly among people with a small repertoire of instrumental actions.

This cycle of mental rumination resembles the cycle of coping responses observed in Chapter 2. In fact, both of these cycles may result from the person's subjective construction of the situation. After one failure, people may fail to recognize the lack of control, may still expect to control future outcomes, and may think that they can cope with failure by problem solving, which would lead to action rumination. After successive failures, however, they perceive the uncontrollability of the outcome, adopt off-task coping, and therefore engage in off-task thoughts. They may conclude that the best way to cope with a seemingly intractable unpleasant situation is either to avoid it by engaging in distracting, task-irrelevant thoughts or to accommodate mental structures to the new reality constraints by engaging in state rumination.

Direct support for the hypothesized cycle of mental rumination is found in four of the studies that I present in this book; these studies exposed subjects to either no, one, or four failures and asked them to complete the three rumination items (see Table 1.1 for details). The findings show that lack of control may evoke both task-relevant and off-task thoughts, and that the amount of failure determines the relative proportion of each type of rumination. Relative to no feedback, small amounts of failure heightened action rumination but had no effect on the two types of off-task thoughts. A large amount of failure, however, heightened both state and task-irrelevant ruminations (see Table 3.2); the frequency of action rumination was reduced after four unsolvable problems. These effects are well illustrated in Study 1, which showed that the frequency of action thoughts was highest after one or two failures, whereas the frequencies of state and task-irrelevant thoughts were highest after four or five failures (see Figure 3.1).

Indirect support for the above cycle of rumination is found in four studies that have assessed the impact of small and large amounts of failure on information processing. In a study by Mikulincer, Kedem, and Zilcha-Segal (1989), subjects were exposed to either no, one or four unsolvable problems, then performed a letter cancellation task under three conditions. One group of subjects were given the task with no additional cue. A second group received task-relevant cues whose utilization facilitated performance (pairs of parentheses that signaled the space holding the target letters). A third group received the same task with task-irrelevant cues whose utilization interfered with performance (randomly located pairs of parentheses).

Based on the theory of cue utilization (Easterbrook, 1959; Geen, 1980), we

TABLE 3.2. Means and F-Ratios of Rumination Scores by Number of Failures

Rumination	Study number	No failures	One failure	Four failures	F
Action					
	9	4.00	4.71	2.93	6.35[a]
	10	3.87	4.22	2.12	19.00[b]
	11	4.37	5.00	2.75	15.30[b]
	12	4.00	4.50	3.12	4.73[a]
State					
	9	1.68	1.50	2.56	6.60[a]
	10	1.50	1.37	2.87	17.73[b]
	11	1.37	1.62	2.37	4.47[a]
	12	1.75	1.87	3.00	7.12[b]
Task-irrelevant					
	9	1.75	1.43	2.62	6.72[a]
	10	1.62	1.68	2.75	11.75[b]
	11	1.43	1.31	2.44	6.98[b]
	12	1.50	1.62	2.94	14.26[b]

[a] $p < .05$
[b] $p < .01$

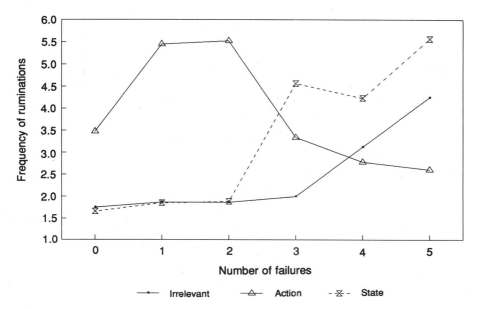

FIGURE 3.1. Means of mental ruminations according to number of failures.

assumed that people's ruminations would be reflected in the way they employed cues. Those who engaged in action thoughts, including the search for problem-solving cues, and whose inner controls inhibited the diversion of their thoughts from the task at hand would make use of relevant cues and ignore irrelevant cues. Behaviorally, one would see (a) performance facilitation with the addition of task-relevant cues, and (b) no performance change with the addition of task-irrelevant cues. In contrast, subjects who engaged in off-task thoughts, which divert atten-tion from task features, would use neither task-relevant nor task-irrelevant cues. Behaviorally, their off-task thoughts would be reflected in no performance change with the addition of relevant or irrelevant cues. Our prediction was that if subjects exposed to a small amount of failure engaged in action rumination, task-relevant cues would improve their performance, whereas irrelevant cues would lead to no performance change. Moreover, if subjects exposed to a large amount of failure engaged in off-task rumination, neither relevant or irrelevant cues would affect their performance.

Results indeed indicated that subjects exposed to one failure were more accu-rate in the task-relevant cue condition than in the no-cue condition, and that the addition of task irrelevant cues did not affect their performance. Results also showed that subjects exposed to four failures showed no performance change after the addition of either task-relevant or -irrelevant cues. In all the conditions, these subjects performed worse than no-feedback subjects. It appears that people react to small amounts of failure with action thoughts and to larger amounts with off-task thoughts. In support of this view, the frequencies of state and task-irrelevant thoughts, as assessed by the CIQ, was found to increase only after four failures.

Study 5 (see Table 1.1) also brings indirect evidence on the cycle of rumination. It examines the sort of material that the person is ready to process in LH settings. If after a small amount of failure the cognitive system is really action oriented, the person would focus mainly on processing information relevant to problem solving. In contrast, if rumination after a large amount of failure is more state oriented, the person would focus mainly on processing material on the state of the self. On this basis, I predicted that the extent of information processing would be qualified by the cycle of rumination. A small amount of failure would enhance only the processing of action-related material, whereas a large amount of failure would augment only the processing of state-related information.

I tested these predictions using Pittman and D'Agostino's (1989) recognition test. Subjects previously exposed to no, one, or four unsolvable problems were asked to study either a text on the use of strategies for solving cognitive problems (action-oriented text) or a text on the worries of a student who failed an important exam (state-oriented text). Results were in keeping with the above predictions (see Table 3.3). Relative to no-feedback subjects, (a) one failure heightened study time and recognition accuracy of the action-oriented text, and (b) four failures heightened study time and accuracy of the state-oriented text. In addition, a small amount of failure was found to have no effect on the processing of the state-oriented text. When the text encouraged the processing of action alternatives, however, a large amount of training produced shorter study time and less accurate recognition than did no feedback.

The findings support the cycle of rumination. People react to a small amount of failure with action rumination, and they are prone to learn mainly action-related material. After repeated failures, people tend to engage in state rumination, are prone to process mainly state-related material, and show problems in the processing of problem-focused material. The last finding suggests that the performance deficits

TABLE 3.3. Means and Standard Deviations of Study Time and Recognition Accuracy by Number of Failure and Type of Learned Text (Study 5)

	No failures		One failure		Four failures	
	Action	State	Action	State	Action	State
Study time (minutes)						
Mean	3.25	4.12	5.25	3.25	2.62	5.75
Standard deviation	1.48	1.96	1.67	1.49	1.68	2.12
Recognition accuracy						
Mean	75.50	76.12	82.12	77.75	64.00	84.75
Standard deviation	8.57	8.28	8.50	6.01	7.09	5.97

observed after large amounts of failure may reflect an inability or unwillingness to deal with action-related information when resources are allocated in the processing of state-related material. It also implies that LH deficits depend on the individual's cognitive orientation. These deficits occur mainly when mental rumination competes for resources with task-relevant activities.

The findings reviewed above emphasize that the link between failure and information processing is not fixed. It may depend on the person's stage in the cycle of rumination, as well as on the kind of material being processed. In fact, helplessness training triggers information processing only when the material fits the type of rumination in which the person is currently engaged. It increases the processing of action-related material among persons who are in the stage of task-related thinking, and the processing of off-task material among those involved in off-task thoughts.

Relevant data is also provided by two experiments conducted by one of my students (Dekel, 1993) on stereotypical thinking and the primacy effect. By definition, stereotypical thinking and the primacy effect reflect a disengagement from effortful information processing. Stereotypical thinking reflects the tendency to perceive a person through the commonly accepted features of that person's group, without expending the effort needed to analyze his or her unique characteristics. The primacy effect reflects the reluctance to spend the resources needed to revise a hypothesis built on the basis of an initial impression, even after receiving contradictory information (Kruglanski & Freund, 1983).

Experiment 1 by Dekel (1993) examined stereotypical thinking; after no, one, or four unsolvable problems, subjects were asked to evaluate an essay written by a fourth grader and were provided information about the child's socioeconomic status (low versus high). Experiment 2 examined the primacy effect: after no, one, or four unsolvable problems, subjects were given a two-paragraph description of a person and were asked to rate the person's level of sociability. Half of the subjects received an information sequence that first described the person as open to social contacts and then as closed to these contacts. The remaining subjects were given a reversed sequence of information. In the two experiments, subjects completed the CIQ (tapping their current state and task-irrelevant thoughts).

The two experiments showed a consistent pattern of results. Subjects exposed to only one failure reported frequencies of state and task-irrelevant thoughts similar to those of the no-failure subjects. In addition, their judgments were found to be less influenced by stereotypes and initial impressions than were those of the no-failure subjects. In contrast, subjects exposed to four failures reported more state and task-irrelevant thoughts, and their ratings were found to be influenced more by stereotypes and initial impressions, than was the case for the no-failure subjects. The findings imply that people initially react to failure with effortful information processing, as manifested in a reduction of stereotypical thinking and primacy effect. A large amount of failure creates a reluctance to invest effort in processing task material, however, as reflected in increased stereotypical thinking and primacy effect.

Dekel's findings indirectly support the hypothesized cycle of rumination. The reduction in stereotypical thinking and primacy effect observed after a small amount of failure may be a manifestation of action rumination. As elaborated earlier, action rumination involves the processing of all incoming information relevant to task performance. In Dekel's study, this heightened cognitive activity might have fostered the revision of hypotheses that free the person from preconceptions and initial impressions. The increase in stereotypical thinking and primacy effect observed after a large amount of failure may be a manifestation of off-task thoughts (state or task-irrelevant). Because resources were directed to the analysis of off-task information, the person was left with insufficient resources for processing incoming task-relevant material and therefore tended to rely more on preconceptions and initial impressions.

On the whole, helplessness training seems to set in motion a cycle of mental rumination. A small amount of helplessness training increases the frequency of action rumination and focuses the cognitive system on the processing of action-related material. After a large number of failures, people come to report higher frequencies of state and task-irrelevant thoughts and to focus the cognitive system on the processing of off-task material.

THE INTRUSION OF AUTONOMIC FAILURE-RELATED THOUGHTS

My third hypothesis is that a large amount of helplessness training may foster the occurrence of autonomic failure-related thoughts. This hypothesis is based on two findings reviewed in this and the previous chapter: (a) A large amount of helplessness training may lead people to adopt behavioral and cognitive avoidance coping strategies, and (b) the adoption of avoidance coping is usually accompanied by the weakening of inner controls and the intrusion of unwanted thoughts into consciousness (Horowitz, 1982; Janis, 1958; Lazarus, 1983). Therefore a large amount of helplessness training, which leads to the adoption of avoidance coping, may indirectly foster the occurrence of autonomic failure-related thoughts.

Study 6 (see Table 1.1) provides direct support for this hypothesis, using a thought suppression paradigm (Wegner et al., 1987). If helplessness training fosters autonomic thoughts, people may have difficulties suppressing failure-related thoughts even after they are required to do so. That is, they may show more frequent intrusions of the to-be-suppressed thoughts than do no-failure subjects. In the study, subjects were asked to write down their thoughts for a period of 10 minutes after being exposed to no, one, or four failures. Half of the subjects (thought suppression group) were asked to try *not* to think about the experiment and to keep it out of mind; the other half of the subjects (control group) did not receive this additional instruction. Judges who were blind to the experimental conditions counted the number of times that the experiment was referred to in each report.

Table 3.4 presents an interesting pattern of differences. Among control subjects, more thoughts on the experiment were found after one and four failures than

TABLE 3.4. Means and Standard Deviations of Number of Mentioned Task-Related Thoughts by Number of Failures and Suppression Instructions (Study 6)

	No failures		One failure		Four failures	
	Control	Suppression	Control	Suppression	Control	Suppression
Mean	7.87	1.50	13.87	2.12	14.12	14.62
Standard deviation	3.64	1.92	4.79	1.64	4.61	5.85

after no failures. This finding converges with previous evidence suggesting that both small and large amounts of failure heighten the frequency of ruminative thoughts. The most important finding, however, was observed in the thought suppression group, where subjects exposed to four failures made more mentions of the to-be-suppressed thoughts than those exposed to one or no failures. In short, people exposed to a large amount of failure seemed to be unable to inhibit the intrusion of unwanted thoughts. This conclusion is supported also by comparing the thought suppression groups to the controls: Whereas subjects in the no-failure and one-failure conditions showed a significant reduction in mentions of the unwanted thoughts after being asked to suppress them, subjects in the four-failure condition failed to show such a reduction.

Integrating the findings, one can draw the following conclusions: In a no-failure situation, there will be little or no tendency to think about the task after its completion. A small amount of failure will tend to increase the frequency of task-related rumination, but at this level of failure it is still under the individual's control. A large amount of failure will also heighten the frequency of ruminative thoughts, but at this level the person is already beginning to lose some degree of control over the failure-related thoughts. That is, some of the off-task thoughts that characterize people exposed to a large amount of failure seem to run on autonomically.

At first sight, these findings may seem to contradict Pittman's results on controlled information processing after helplessness training. On the one hand, Pittman's findings indicate that people purposively try to think about the failure situation. On the other hand, the occurrence of autonomic thoughts suggests that the cognitions are beyond the individual's control. Moreover, the uncontrolled thoughts may even interfere with the purposive thoughts by absorbing attention and resources. These findings raise some perplexities about the coping process. It appears that helplessness training, which has been found to mobilize coping efforts, may also foster autonomic thoughts that have nothing to do—and may even interfere—with coping attempts. That is, helplessness training may be a precursor of both organized coping actions and disorganized mental activity.

In my view, the apparent contradiction can be resolved by assuming the existence of a cycle of coping–disorganization. That is, people may initially react to helplessness training with controlled information processing, and only after repeated failure will they become overwhelmed by autonomic thoughts. At first, people try to manage the mismatch created by failure via problem solving, and they purposively engage in action rumination. This cognitive activity is under the individual's control and facilitates the generation and organization of problem-solving plans. After repeated failure, people increasingly rely on reorganization or avoidance coping and begin to ruminate on either state or task-irrelevant material. Though avoidance coping is also a purposive activity, it may have some autonomic, dysfunctional side effects. At some point it may weaken inhibitory mental processes, and this may lead to the intrusion into consciousness of autonomic failure-related thoughts elicited by the failure or by other external or internal stimuli. These thoughts are a sign of inner disorganization and paralysis.

SUMMARY

In general, helplessness training seems to produce three coping-related cognitive changes: (a) the passage from nondeliberative to deliberative thinking, (b) the passage from task-relevant to off-task (state or task-irrelevant) rumination, and (c) the passage from mental organization to disorganization. Whereas the first and second changes are a reflection of the individual's attempts to cope with an uncontrollable failure, the third change seems to be an unwanted by-product of avoidance coping.

MENTAL RUMINATION AND TASK PERFORMANCE

The next task in evaluating the mediating role of rumination in human LH is to examine the path going from mental rumination to task performance. This section aims to examine the hypotheses that (a) mental rumination can alter task performance after helplessness training, and (b) its absence prevents LH effects.

THEORETICAL STATEMENTS

Mental rumination is a proximal antecedent of LH effects. It affects task performance because it provides the cognitive context to, and facilitates the organization of, coping actions that improve or impair task performance. On the one hand, action rumination invigorates performance because it enables full concentration on the problem at hand and facilitates the organization of task-relevant problem-solving strategies. On the other hand, off-task (state or task-irrelevant) rumination impairs performance because it draws away resources from the processing of task-relevant information and from the generation of problem-solving plans. In addition, off-task rumination may lead the person to adopt a passive attitude toward the task at hand, with subsequent performance impairments. As Kuhl (1982) puts it, "A person is passive . . . when he or she is preoccupied with activities that are not intended to transform a present state into a desired future state" (p. 148). Finally, off-task rumination may be accompanied by intrusive thoughts that overwhelm the cognitive system and interfere with action.

Kuhl (1981) presented similar ideas with regard to action and state thoughts, though he did not mention the effects of task-irrelevant thoughts. Kuhl began his analysis by examining the roles of the expectancy and value constructs, concluding that they are insufficient to explain performance changes. LH deficits are found in the presence of high perceived task value, which is expected to facilitate performance, and many subjects exhibit these deficits without having generalized the expectancy of no control. According to Kuhl, these findings suggest a third determinant of LH effect: the dimension of "action versus state orientation."

As Kuhl (1984, 1985) explains it, the dimension of action–state rumination may influence performance via parsimonious information processing, emotional control, and the replacement of frustrating activities. Whereas action rumination might optimize the processing of information and permit a rapid translation of intentions into actions, state rumination might complicate such processing and delay action. Whereas action rumination can regulate interfering emotions, state rumination has no inhibitory mechanism that could prevent emotions from overwhelming the cognitive system. Whereas action rumination fosters persistence in reaching only attainable goals, state rumination alienates the person from the instrumental value of an activity. State-oriented people remain stuck with unattainable goals. Evidently, the extent to which information processing is optimized, emotions are controlled, and goal substitution is enabled affect task performance.

In my view, action, state, and task-irrelevant ruminations may influence task performance after failure via four alternative pathways. One is through attentional direction, in which conscious thinking directs the person's attention to those aspects of the person–environment transaction that aid in coping with failure. People ruminate on some aspects of their transaction with the environment and activate memories, ideas, and fantasies related to them while withdrawing attentional focus from those aspects of the transactions that are irrelevant to or impede coping.

The second pathway is through the allocation of resources in conscious thinking. Cognitive resources are essential for (a) the search and activation of cognitive material; (b) the rehearsal and maintenance of the activated ideations in the central processing space of the working memory, where they can be easily accessible for information processing and rumination; and (c) the generation of alternative hypotheses and the programming of alternative courses of actions in the course of rumination. Ruminative thinking is not a passive stream of thought, but an active processing of information in which people attempt to understand the nature of failure and its personal significance, to make alternative plans, to imagine more positive scripts, or to distract themselves from a threat.

Because cognitive resources are limited (e.g., Kahneman, 1973), their allocation in rumination would reduce their availability for other activities and for the processing of other cognitive material. This reduction in available resources would make it difficult to process information and engage in activities that have nothing to do with the way people choose to cope with failure. The ruminative process thus draws resources to itself and away from competing activities.

The third pathway is through the preemption of working memory space by ruminative thinking with coping-related ideations. In the course of rumination, ideations that may help cope with failure are activated and incorporated for processing in working memory. Material associated with these ideations and made accessible via spread of activation may also be processed in working memory (Anderson & Bower, 1973). In other words, working memory space would be taken up with material that is directly or remotely associated with the process of coping with the failure.

Because working memory is also limited, with a finite central processing space (Baddeley & Hitch, 1974; Eysenck, 1982), the preemption of some portion of this limited capacity with ruminative thought would also reduce the space available for the processing of other cognitive material or incoming information. Ruminative thought would thus not only fill up working memory space but also impede the processing of information irrelevant to the current rumination.

The fourth pathway is via the complex cognitive context that rumination creates for the processing of information. During rumination, large quantities of diverse material come to mind and create a cognitive context that becomes increasingly complex as the newly developed associative pathways are elaborated. In my view, the complex cognitive context would facilitate the generation of knowledge and plans as the latter are nourished by the material elaborated in rumination. The frequency of relevant knowledge and plans would thus depend on the complexity of the cognitive context created during rumination, and their content would depend on the material that comes into mind most readily.

These four cognitive pathways can be expected to result in either positive or negative performance changes, depending on the content of the mental rumination. Specifically, task-relevant action rumination facilitates performance, and off-task rumination (state or task-irrelevant) undermines it.

When rumination is directed to restoring control and overcoming failure (action rumination), it would have a positive effect on task performance. Attention would be directed to task-relevant features, working memory filled with task-relevant action ideations, cognitive resources fully allocated in task-relevant cognitive activities, and a complex context created that would facilitate the generation of problem-solving plans. At the same time, attention would be purposely drawn away from off-task features, relatively few cognitive resources and little working memory space would be available for processing off-task cognitive material, and the cognitive context would inhibit the generation of knowledge irrelevant to solving the problem. These cognitive changes would converge in full concentration on the task at hand and in performance improvement in a solvable task.

When rumination is state-oriented or task-irrelevant, it would have a negative effect on task performance. In this case, attention would be directed to off-task features of the transaction, working memory filled with off-task ideations, cognitive resources allocated in off-task activities, and a complex cognitive context created that would facilitate the generation of knowledge about one's personal state or other task-irrelevant matters. At the same time, attention would be purposely drawn away from features, including task-relevant ones, that distract from the off-task activity; relatively few cognitive resources and little working memory space would be available for processing problem-focused material; and the cognitive context would inhibit the generation of problem-solving plans. These cognitive changes distract the person from the task at hand and interfere with instrumental actions, thereby deteriorating performance.

These deleterious effects may be exacerbated by the instigation of autonomic state-related thoughts. The autonomically activated material may also divert attention away from task-relevant features, compete for resources and working memory space with task-relevant activities, and create a cognitive context that interferes with task performance. This cognitive interference has no trade-off quality, however, and it does not reflect any temporary, adaptive disengagement from the task. Rather, it reflects the individual's inability to organize his or her thoughts and to inhibit material that has nothing to do with the coping process. In other words, the deficits produced by autonomic failure-related thoughts may reflect the failure of coping attempts and the disorganization of cognitive processing.

On this basis, I propose that the reactance–helplessness cycle produced by helplessness training depends on rumination. Without mental rumination, no cognitive resources would be directed toward or away from the task, no pertinent material would be activated and rehearsed in working memory, and no complex cognitive context would be created. In this case, people would be less able to engage in coping activities that move them toward or away from task-relevant activities, and thus would be less likely to show LH effects.

One can also propose that the extent of LH deficits is a direct function of the attentional demands of the test task. Helplessness training would lead to performance deficits in tasks that place high demands on attentional resources, because off-task rumination competes for the resources necessary for optimal performance. LH deficits would not be recorded in tasks that demand few resources, because the resources that would be left for task activities would be sufficient.

A related idea is that rumination contributes to the generalization of the LH effects. People who engage in action rumination in order to reverse failure may continue to try to reverse it in the test task, and thus they would exhibit all the positive performance effects. Accordingly, people who engage in off-task rumination as a means to accommodate inner structures or to avoid/escape a threat during helplessness training may undertake the test task still occupied with off-task thoughts and show generalized LH deficits.

CORRELATIONAL EVIDENCE

The link between rumination and performance has been most extensively supported in correlational studies. First of all, they indicate that action rumination is positively related to task performance and functioning. For example, Peterson, Swing, Braverman, and Buss (1982) found that the frequency of action thoughts during achievement tests was associated with performance improvement. Rosenbaum and Ben-Ari (1985) found that engagement in action thinking during a task was positively related to the possession of an extensive repertoire of self-control skills for coping with bad events.

Evidence has also been accumulated on the inverse correlations between off-task thoughts and task performance. Traitlike measures of self-preoccupative worry were found to be inversely related to academic examination scores, anagram and psychomotor performance, and course grades; and the frequencies of state rumination, task-irrelevant thoughts, and mind wandering while working on a task were found to be inversely correlated with task performance in both natural and laboratory settings (see Deffenbacher, 1980; Hamilton, 1975; Wine, 1971 for reviews). Importantly, these correlations were also found when emotionality and other components of distress and anxiety were controlled for, implying that the link between off-task thoughts and performance is not a mere reflection of the individual's affective state (Deffenbacher, 1980).

The connection between rumination and performance was also supported by six of my LH studies, which assessed both rumination and task performance following helplessness training (see Table 1.1). In these studies, Pearson correlations and regression analyses were computed between subjects' rumination scores (as measured by my three rumination items) and performance accuracy in a letter cancellation task. Regressions showed that the set of rumination scores made a significant prediction of performance accuracy after helplessness training in all the studies and explained between 24% and 45% of the performance variance. Pearson correlations revealed that the frequency of action thoughts was positively correlated with performance accuracy, whereas the frequencies of state and task-irrelevant thoughts were inversely correlated with it (see Table 3.5). These correlations were statistically significant in most of the studies. The regressions also revealed that the three rumination scores made unique contributions to task performance in most of the studies (see Table 3.5).

Because the data are correlational, it is of course impossible to be certain whether rumination alters performance or reflects concerns arising from performance. Despite their opposite directions, however, the two suppositions are not mutually exclusive. For example, as state rumination becomes more frequent after failure, it may produce poor performance in subsequent solvable tasks, which in turn may further increase the frequency of state rumination, and so on.

A number of studies have also shown a link between off-task thoughts and the deterioration of other aspects of information processing. For example, one of my students (Paz, 1989) found that the tendency to engage in state and task-irrelevant thoughts as measured by the Thought Occurrence Questionnaire (TOQ; Sarason et al., 1986) was related to the sorting of semantic information into a large number of small categories, the rejection of nonprototype items from membership in a semantic category, and the lack of perception of relatedness among members of a category.

TABLE 3.5. Correlations and Standardized Regression Coefficients of Performance Accuracy as Predicted by Rumination Scores

Study number		Action	State	Task-irrelevant
1	$F = 10.82^b$ $R^2 = 38\%$			
	r	$.42^b$	$-.48^b$	$-.54^b$
	Beta	$.25^a$	$-.22^a$	$-.34^b$
8	$F = 12.07^b$ $R^2 = 41\%$			
	r	$.41^b$	$-.58^b$	$-.46^b$
	Beta	$.22^a$	$.41^b$	$-.26^a$
9	$F = 8.34^b$ $R^2 = 36\%$			
	r	$.44^b$	$-.45^b$	$-.57^b$
	Beta	$.22^a$	$-.05$	$-.41^b$
10	$F = 5.47^a$ $R^2 = 22\%$			
	r	$.42^b$	$-.43^b$	$-.39^b$
	Beta	$.31^b$	$-.30^b$	$-.02$
11	$F = 5.84^a$ $R^2 = 24\%$			
	r	$.27^a$	$-.49^b$	$-.44^b$
	Beta	$.12$	$-.34^b$	$-.19$
12	$F = 12.02^b$ $R^2 = 45\%$			
	r	$.16$	$-.52^b$	$-.53^b$
	Beta	$.11$	$-.41^b$	$-.36^b$

[a]$p < .05$
[b]$p < .01$

These findings suggest that off-task rumination reduces the depth of task-relevant information processing. The depletion of resources available for the processing of task-relevant stimuli and the preemption of working memory space by off-task thoughts may be responsible for the damage.

Interestingly, these findings resemble those reported by one of my students (Herbert, 1990) in two LH studies. Relative to no-feedback subjects, those exposed to four unsolvable problems rejected more nonprototypical items from membership in a semantic category and created a larger number of semantic categories in a sorting task. These effects of helplessness training may reflect the underlying action of off-task rumination. In support, Herbert found that the frequency of off-task thoughts, both state and task-irrelevant (as measured by the CIQ), was higher after helplessness training than after no-feedback.

Studies have also found that engagement in self-preoccupative worry is positively related to the time required to categorize semantic stimuli and spent on solving everyday problems (Tallis, 1989). This response retardation is particularly evident when stimuli are ambiguous (e.g., Metzger, Miller, Sofka, Cohen, & Pennock, 1983). It seems that state rumination leads to response retardation either by diverting attention away from the task or by highlighting potential threats to one's self-identity—thereby making one hesitant to respond at all (Geen, 1987; Tallis, 1989), or inducing one to collect a great deal of information so as to be sure of responding correctly.

Using the Action–State Scale, Kuhl and various colleagues conducted a series of studies on the effects of rumination on various aspects of information processing. Kuhl (1984) reported that action-oriented persons had a higher ability to focus efficiently on task-relevant stimuli than state-oriented persons, and that when subjects predisposed to action rumination made parsimonious choices, state-oriented persons chose nonparsimonious decision strategies. Kuhl and Eisenbeiser (1986) found that the predisposition to state rumination seems to "stick" people with unattractive and frustrating activities, preventing them from going on to a new, more attractive task. Kuhl and Wassiljew (1983) found that the stronger subjects' proclivity to state rumination was, the less complex were the strategies they used for solving a problem. Interestingly, this finding was not significant after failure, when all subjects engaged in state thought regardless of their prior disposition. On the whole, the findings support the hypothesis that action rumination is positively related to problem-focused information processing, whereas state thoughts deteriorate any cognitive activity that may contribute to task performance.

DISPOSITIONAL STUDIES

To assess the effects of rumination in the LH paradigm, Brunstein and Olbrich (1985) measured the reactions to unsolvable problems of subjects who habitually tended to engage in action rumination or state rumination. As expected, the thought flow of action- and state-oriented subjects differed significantly. Whereas action-oriented subjects engaged in making efficient plans, analyzing the task, and instructing themselves to do better, state-oriented subjects ruminated on their loss of ability and other self-evaluative topics. Moreover, although action- and state-oriented subjects did not differ in their use of efficient or inefficient hypothesis-testing strategies during solvable problems, they showed a significant difference after failure. Action-oriented subjects showed a reactance effect, increasing their use of efficient problem-solving strategies and decreasing the use of inefficient ones. State-oriented subjects showed LH deficits, increasing their use of inefficient strategies and decreasing the use of efficient ones.

In a second study, Brunstein (1989) examined the effects of individual differences in action and state ruminations on the generalization and chronicity of LH effects. It was hypothesized that subjects who habitually tended to engage in state rumination would be plagued by state thoughts during the training task and that these thoughts would become rekindled as soon as difficulties arose during the test task, thereby interfering with task performance. In contrast, subjects who habitually tended to engage in action rumination would confront their failures with increased problem-focused coping, showing performance improvement in the test task.

The training task involved failure or no feedback in discrimination learning, and subjects were required to think aloud during the task. The test task consisted of problems of logical transformation. The test session took place either immediately after the training phase or 24 hours later, and the test task was presented as measuring either similar or dissimilar things from those measured in the training task. Immediately after the test session, subjects were asked to rate the frequency of failure-related thoughts during the test activity.

The findings were unambiguous. For subjects who tended to engage in action rumination, the thinking-aloud protocols reflected self-instructions and how they could improve their performance and solve the problems. In contrast, subjects who tended to engage in state rumination were troubled by their lack of ability and their inefficacious solution strategies. Consistent with the training phase, the questionnaire data on thoughts during the test task revealed that the thoughts of state-oriented subjects focused on the experience of failure, lack of ability, and giving up. Action-oriented subjects expressed feelings of increased coping with the test task.

The above cognitive differences were also reflected in test task performance, particularly when there was a delay of 24 hours between the training and test sessions. In both similar and dissimilar conditions, helplessness training produced better performance than no feedback among action-oriented subjects and worse performance among state-oriented subjects. In making a detailed inspection of the data, Brunstein revealed that these performance differences occurred only after the second test problem. Apparently there was a need to reactivate the helplessness training in the first test problem, as new difficulties were encountered, in order to transfer the LH effects to the test session. This possibility was also emphasized by Pasahow (1980), who found LH deficits in an anagram task only if the most difficult anagrams were presented at the beginning of the session.

Brunstein's findings illustrate the crucial role of ruminative thinking in the LH paradigm. Helplessness training improves performance only among subjects who are predisposed to, and actually engage in, action rumination while experiencing failure. It damages performance only among subjects who are predisposed to, and actually engage in, state ruminations while experiencing failure.

One of my LH studies (Mikulincer, 1989a) supported the above conclusion and extended it to both state and task-irrelevant thoughts. Subjects were preselected according to their habitual tendency to engage in off-task rumination, either state or task-irrelevant (as measured by the TOQ; Sarason et al., 1986); they were exposed to failure or no feedback on four unsolvable cognitive problems, and their performance was assessed in a letter cancellation task. Results showed that failure, as compared to no feedback, decreased performance accuracy in a letter cancellation task only among subjects who habitually engaged in off-task rumination. Subjects who did not were impervious to helplessness training. This finding supports the hypothesis that an excessive engagement in off-task thoughts is an important antecedent of LH deficits.

Not every type of off-task ruminations, however, was equally associated with LH deficits. A regression analysis revealed that the predisposition to engage in task-irrelevant thoughts, particularly when these thoughts denoted an escape from the task, made a stronger unique contribution to performance deficits after helplessness training than the predisposition to engage in state rumination. This finding is consistent with the correlational findings reviewed above that the reported frequency of task-irrelevant rumination while performing the training and test tasks was more strongly related to LH deficits than the frequency of state rumination. It is also consistent with findings reviewed in Chapter 2 that avoidance coping made a more direct and stronger contribution to LH deficits than reorganization coping. In general, the findings support the idea that LH deficits reflect subjects' attempts to distance themselves from the failure.

Three other findings from this experiment aid in refining the conditions and processes by which off-task rumination impairs performance after failure. First, mind wandering during the experimental task was significantly associated with performance accuracy after helplessness training. The more mental wandering subjects reported, the more omission errors they made. This finding supports the contention that an excessive engagement in off-task rumination, whether as a result of a habitual tendency or of situational constraints, is related to LH deficits.

Second, subjects predisposed to engage in off-task rumination made more errors than subjects not so predisposed in the letter cancellation task, but did not scan fewer letters. This finding suggests that off-task rumination impairs performance by drawing attention away from task features rather than by reducing speed.

Third, the effect of off-task rumination depended on the number of letters subjects had to remember. Subjects predisposed to engage in off-task rumination were less accurate than subjects not so predisposed only in the 6-letter version of the test task, but not in the 2- and 4-letter versions. It may be that the subjects' reduced attentional resources remained sufficient for the less demanding versions but proved inadequate when the demands were increased.

Both my findings and those of Brunstein and Olbrich (1985) suggest that off-task thoughts moderate LH deficits. Brunstein and Olbrich suggest that these performance deficits reflect a deterioration in information processing (type of hypothesis-testing strategy chosen), whereas my findings suggest that the decline derives from the withdrawal of attention from the task and depend on the cognitive demands it makes.

EXPERIMENTAL INDUCTION EVIDENCE

Another method for examining the role of rumination involves the experimental manipulation of this variable. This research strategy was first adopted in two experiments by Kuhl (1981). In the first, subjects were exposed to either failure or no feedback in four unsolvable problems and tested in a letter cancellation task. Upon the training task, state rumination was induced in one group of subjects by having them respond to a questionnaire that asked them to describe and evaluate their current emotional state. In a second group, action rumination was induced by having subjects engage in a nonachievement activity: reading an essay and judging how interesting, informative, and well written it was.

The results partially support the hypothesized roles of state and action thoughts. As expected, failure subjects performed worse than controls only under the state-thoughts condition. The induction of action thoughts made the failure ineffective in producing LH deficits. Contrary to expectations, however, the induction of action rumination did not produce performance facilitation after failure. Kuhl suggested that the essay reading task was not achievement related, and so it may not have been enough to direct attention toward problem solving. As a consequence, the task might have kept people from the state thoughts that impair performance while not producing the action thoughts that enhance performance above baseline levels.

Kuhl's second experiment was designed to overcome this flaw by a better induction of task-relevant thoughts (subjects were asked to state their problem-solving hypotheses explicitly during the experiment) and by measuring predispositions for mental rumination. Though subjects with a propensity for state rumination performed worse than action-oriented subjects after failure, the difference was eliminated among those who were induced to engage in action thoughts. More important, failure produced better performance than no feedback—a reactance effect—among both action-oriented subjects and subjects who were asked to verbalize their problem-solving hypotheses. In general, the diverse findings point out that helplessness training impairs performance among people who tend to engage in off-task rumination and invigorates performance among those who react to failure with action rumination, whether by preselection or induction.

These findings were replicated and extended by Kuhl and Weiss (1983) and Mikulincer and Nizan (1988, Experiment 3). Kuhl and Weiss found that LH deficits were reversed by the induction of action rumination. Mikulincer and Nizan found that asking subjects to verbalize their hypothesis-testing strategies while working on unsolvable problems not only eliminated the performance deficit produced by helplessness training but also attenuated the detrimental effects of a global attribution of failure. That is, action rumination seems to facilitate appropriate test task performance, even among subjects who expect a failure to recur in the new task.

CONCLUSIONS

In this chapter I have explored the role of rumination in human LH. I dealt with the activation of and changes in rumination after helplessness training, as well as its effects on task performance. With respect to the antecedents of rumination, my view is that rumination is a coping device elicited in response to a threatening mismatch. This idea is supported by findings, reviewed throughout the chapter, which demonstrate that failure activates rumination and that this activation occurs along with coping activity. A small amount of failure seems to elicit task-relevant action rumination, which is used in problem solving. A large amount of failure seems to elicit off-task thoughts, with state rumination aiding in reorganization coping and task-irrelevant rumination helping with avoidance coping. In addition, a large amount of failure may lead to the intrusion of autonomic failure-related thoughts into con-sciousness, which may be a side effect of excessive avoidance coping.

The performance effects of rumination were also examined in this chapter, and several hypothetical paths were discussed. Action rumination seems to improve task performance and also to contribute to reactance. The two types of off-task rumina-tion (state and task-irrelevant) seem to impair task performance and to contribute to LH deficits. In addition, off-task rumination has an autonomic facet that may overwhelm the cognitive system and exacerbate performance deficits. On this basis, it is possible to outline that a small amount of failure will activate action rumination, and this may lead to reactance. Enough additional failure will eventually activate off-task rumination, which will lead to LH deficits.

THE EXPECTANCY OF CONTROL
AS A DISTAL MEDIATOR
OF LH EFFECTS

A coping analysis of LH effects should not only take into account the way coping strategies alter performance, but also specify the sequence of events in a causal chain that begins with helplessness training and ends with the undertaking of coping strategies. According to my coping conceptualization of human LH, the expectancy of control is an important factor that intervenes in the above sequence, determines the type of coping strategy that a person will undertake, and thereby determines the type of the resulting LH effects (reactance or LH deficits). The expectancy construct has had a long history in psychology and provides the cornerstone in cognitive theories of coping (Lazarus & Folkman, 1984). It involves the assessment of what one can do to cope with a particular failure, and it helps people to choose among coping alternatives. The expectancy of control acts as a "psychological watershed" (Carver & Scheier, 1981) in that it directs a general coping effort to particular coping strategies.

In my coping conceptualization of human LH, the expectancy of control people hold after failure is a distal antecedent of LH effects: It mediates the link between helplessness training and task performance indirectly via the coping actions it produces. Specifically, I propose three basic hypotheses on the mediating role of expectancy. First, although a single failure has typically no expectancy effect, repeated failure can reduce the expectancy of control. Second, a favorable expectancy leads to problem solving, and an unfavorable expectancy leads to off-task coping (either avoidance or reorganization). Third, the effects of expectancy on coping would be reflected in LH effects: High expectancy of control would lead to reactance; the expectancy of no control would lead to LH deficits.

In this chapter I examine the mediating role of the expectancy of control.

Specifically, I explore (a) the expectational effects of helplessness training, and (b) the effects of expectancy on coping and performance. I also put special emphasis on the precursors of expectancy change during helplessness training, because the path from failure to expectancy is not simple and automatic. These factors may be distal contributors to coping strategies, mental rumination, and performance changes.

PRELIMINARY CLARIFICATIONS

Before dealing with the possible role of the expectancy of control, I wish to make some clarifications regarding the operationalization of the expectancy construct. This is an important preliminary task, because the expectancy of control has more than one meaning and some of its operationalizations may lead to inadequate results and interpretations.

The first issue concerns whether the expectancy of self-efficacy is an adequate operationalization of the expectancy of control. Bandura (1977, 1986) and Abramson, Seligman, and Teasdale (1978) assert that the expectancy of control results from two different beliefs: (a) the expectancy of self-efficacy—the extent to which people believe they have the appropriate abilities for executing responses required to obtain outcomes, and (b) outcome expectancy—the extent to which they believe that the outcome is dependent on certain responses.

People expect to have control over outcomes *only* when they believe that there are responses that can obtain these outcomes and that they can successfully execute these responses. Either low self-efficacy or low outcome expectancy creates the expectancy of no control. People may expect to have no control because they lack the necessary skills or abilities (*personal helplessness*) or because they believe that no response can obtain outcome (*universal helplessness*). The same distinction, though with different names, has been made in other conceptualizations of the expectancy construct (Feather, 1982; Heckhausen, 1977; Skinner, 1985).

On this basis, when outcome is perceived as chance dependent, self-efficacy expectancy does not necessarily correspond with the expectancy of control. The belief that no response alters outcome occurrence reduces the expectancy of control, regardless of a person's sense of self-efficacy. Only when the outcome is perceived to depend on skill does the expectancy of self-efficacy directly influence the expectancy of control. The higher the belief in the possession of the necessary skills, the higher the expectancy of control.

Both the instructions on the skill dependence of outcomes and the tasks in the typical LH experiment create a correspondence between self-efficacy expectancy and control expectancy (see Chapter 1). Furthermore, both theory and research indicate that people tend to perceive outcomes as signs of their self-efficacy even in chance-dependent tasks (e.g., Ayeroff & Abelson, 1976; Langer, 1975). Using Heider's (1958) ideas on internal–external attribution, Snyder et al. (1978) suggested several reasons for this. First, the perception of an outcome as reflecting one's abilities enables a more rapid and easier appraisal of the transaction with the environment than the search and analysis for numerous external factors. Second, one's abilities and skills are more salient pieces of information than unknown and fortuitous external factors. Third, the belief that some responses can obtain the outcome may symbolically cancel the irreversibility of events ("If I would learn new skills, I could obtain the outcomes that today appear to be uncontrollable"). Fourth, the correspondence between control and self-efficacy may preserve beliefs about a just world. All these reasons may thus create a correspondence between the expectancy of self-efficacy and the expectancy of control.

The second issue concerns whether the expectancy of success is an adequate operationalization of the expectancy of control. Abramson, Seligman, and Teasdale (1978) originally noted that expectancy of success is not synonymous with expectancy of control. Although this distinction is logical, however, it is not relevant for the conceptualization of the expectancy construct within the LH paradigm. Because people in LH studies receive instructions on the skill dependence of the tasks (see Chapter 1), they would subjectively correlate success with control and failure with lack of control. Moreover, people who believe they are able to alter outcomes would expect to attain success, whereas those who doubt their ability would naturally have lower success expectancy. The expectancy of success after helplessness training may thus be considered synonymous with expectancy of control.

For these reasons, I believe that the role of the expectancy of control can also be tested by assessing self-efficacy expectancy or success expectancy. In fact, Abramson, Seligman, and Teasdale (1978) claim that the effects of the expectancy of no control would be reliably reproduced when that expectancy was derived form low outcome expectancy or low self-efficacy expectancy. In this chapter I will not deal with the accuracy of this statement, because most of the studies reviewed have incidentally induced "personal helplessness." Chapter 6 will explore the differential effects of self-efficacy versus outcome expectancy.

THE EXPECTATIONAL EFFECTS OF HELPLESSNESS TRAINING

In this section I elaborate on the path from helplessness training to expectancy. I examine the hypothesis that repeated uncontrollable failure is able to reduce the expectancy of control.

THEORETICAL STATEMENTS

The idea on the expectational effects of helplessness training is not new. It was first elaborated in the original Learned Helplessness theory (Maier & Seligman, 1976). It is also found in Seligman's successive reformulations of the theory (e.g., Abramson, Seligman, & Teasdale, 1978; Alloy & Seligman, 1979) as well as in the revisions made by other theorists (e.g., Miller & Norman, 1979; Roth, 1980; Wortman & Brehm, 1975; Zuroff, 1980). In fact, there is no theory in the LH area that has explicitly negated the expectancy chance, though some theories consider it irrelevant for explaining performance variations (e.g., Lavelle, Metalsky, & Coyne,

1979; Kuhl, 1981; Levis, 1976). In these views, expectancy change, if it occurs at all, is merely a by-product of helplessness training.

The hypothesis that the experience with recurrent lack of control generates an expectancy of no control in a new task is based on two assumptions: first, that people tend to anticipate future events congruent with present and/or past events; and second, that they tend to generalize expectancies to new tasks and situations. In the typical LH paradigm, people are exposed to prolonged, uninterrupted, and consistent objective noncontingency between responses and outcomes (failure in controlling outcomes) throughout the entire helplessness training. They may learn that they cannot control the outcome of the task, begin to anticipate a lack of control in future task attempts, and generalize their expectations to new tasks. In other words, they may come to expect having no control in both similar and dissimilar tasks.

Human beings are capable of processing and exploiting environmental information on contingencies between outcomes and responses. They seem to possess the ability to perceive these contingencies, to learn and remember them, and to form expectancies that a particular course of action will have certain consequences. Incoming information is encoded not only to bring about an immediate response, but also to foresee the future and to prepare the organism for new contingencies. Attention is focused, and cognitive resources are allocated in forming these anticipatory cognitions.

The question here is why people may rely on objective response–outcome contingencies for developing their future expectancies. First of all, these contingencies may have an informational value. They inform people about whether their responses can alter the environment, and if so, which responses are the most effective means for achieving that goal. Contingencies enable people to develop general beliefs about control as well as specific beliefs about the instrumentality of particular responses. In the helplessness training, the message that people receive is that responses are valueless and that they would fail to alter outcome occurrence in further attempts with the task regardless of the responses they emit.

In addition, response–outcome contingencies may have adaptive significance. They may tell people about the nature of the mismatch produced by failure and about the ways to cope with actual dangers and potential threats. They inform people whether instrumental actions and active fighting are useful means for altering the environment, or whether "flight" responses are more appropriate ways to deal with the current circumstances. On this basis, the learning of response–outcome contingencies may enable people to organize adaptive coping actions that fit reality constraints: active fighting under favorable contingencies, and flight responses under unfavorable ones.

HELPLESSNESS TRAINING AND FUTURE ANTICIPATION

I begin the examination of the expectational effects of helplessness training with a test of the hypothesis that people who fail to control environmental events may anticipate the same lack of control in the future. Two lines of research are reviewed: studies that focus on the formation of expectations and on the general link between past experiences and future anticipation, and studies that ask whether this link applies in the LH paradigm.

The link between past outcomes and future anticipation was first demonstrated in studies concerned with the determinants of the expectancy of success in achievement tasks. The typical strategy of these studies was to measure and/or manipulate actual performance (i.e., the attainment of success, the avoidance of failure) in an achievement task and then to ask people to estimate their chances of future success (e.g., "What score do you expect to get on the next task?" or "How confident are you of succeeding at the next task?"). Results consistently showed that once people start to work on a task, their expectancies are influenced by their actual performance: the more successful the performance, the higher the subsequent success expectancy (e.g., DeSoto, Coleman, & Putram, 1960; Diggory, 1949; Diggory & Morlock, 1964; Feather, 1961, 1963b, 1965, 1968; Schwartz, 1966). Similar findings were obtained when success and failure were manipulated at each trial of a task (Feather, 1963c), and when subjects received favorable or unfavorable feedback at the end of a task (Feather, 1966, Feather & Seville, 1967).

More recently, several studies also demonstrated that performance in a task influences the expectancy of self-efficacy. Findings reveal that self-efficacy expectancy increases after exposure to either bogus or real success feedback (e.g., Locke, Frederick, Lee, & Bolko, 1984), and decreases after failure feedback (e.g., Campbell & Hackett, 1985; Hackett & Betz, 1984; Hackett, Betz, O'Halloran, & Romac, 1990). In addition, other studies found that the expectancy is altered by vicarious experiences, such as viewing a failing/ succeeding model (e.g., Feltz, Landers, & Raeder, 1979; Gould & Weiss, 1981).

In addition to demonstrating that people tend to anticipate future outcomes congruent with present and past outcomes, a number of studies support the idea that this tendency is generalized across tasks and situations. These studies consistently demonstrated that people tend to use outcomes in a task to anticipate the same outcome in other tasks. In other words, performance feedback in a task has been found to bring about changes in expectancies for other subsequent tasks (e.g., Heath, 1961, Jessor, 1954; Rychlack, 1958). It is important to note, however, that this expectancy generalization seems to depend on the similarities of the tasks and reinforcements (Heath, 1961; Jessor, 1954) as well as on the person's causal beliefs (Alloy et al., 1984; Mikulincer, 1986a).

Research has also shown that the effects of task outcomes on expectancy are moderated by a number of task-related factors. For example, Rychlack (1958) found that performance accomplishments cause stronger expectancy changes in novel laboratory tasks than in familiar life tasks. Castaneda (1952) and Good (1957) found that the expectancy effect of success/failure feedback is an inverse function of the amount of prior experience with a task, and Bennion (1961) and Blackman (1962) found that this effect is stronger following long sequences of stable outcomes than short sequences of varying outcomes. Phares (1961, 1966) found that periods of delay interspersed between trials weaken the expectancy effects of performance feedback. Because typical helplessness training involves long uninterrupted sequences of constant outcomes in a novel task, one can confidently argue that the lack of control it induces has the power to create an expectancy of no control for the next task.

This conclusion has been empirically supported by a series of studies that assessed the expectational effects of lack of control in classic LH settings (see Table 4.1 for a summary). In these studies, subjects exposed either to helplessness training or to other control conditions were asked to estimate their expectancies for a new

TABLE 4.1. Review of Expectational Effects of Helplessness Training

Study	Manipulation	Expectancy assessment		Effect of HT
		Timing	Wording	
Prindaville & Stein (1978)	Inescapable noise	After test	Confidence in retesting	Lower confidence
Brown & Inouye (1978)	Unsolvable problem	During study	Efficacy expectancy	Lower expectancy
Willis & Blaney (1978)	Unsolvable problem	After test	Confidence in success	Lower confidence
Breen, Vulcano, & Dyck (1979)	Unsolvable problem	After test	Success expectancy	Lower expectancy
Harris & Highlen (1979)	Inescapable noise	After test	Success expectancy	Lower expectancy
Pasahow (1980)	Unsolvable problem	After test	Success expectancy	Lower expectancy
Kuhl (1981)	Unsolvable problem	Before test	Success expectancy	No effect of training
Kammer (1983)	Unsolvable problems	During study	Success expectancy	Lower expectancy
Riskind (1984)	Unsolvable problems	Before test	Success expectancy	Lower expectancy
Mikulincer (1986b)	Unsolvable problems	Before test	Success expectancy	Lower expectancy
Gerlsma & Albersnagel (1987)	Noncontingent feedback	Before test	Success expectancy	Lower expectancy
Tiggemann & Winefeld (1987)	Inescapable noise	After test	Confidence in next task	Lower confidence
Zedek & Kofta (1990)	Unsolvable problems	Before test	Success expectancy	Lower expectancy

Note: HT = helplessness training.

task. Most of the studies found that helplessness training produced a lower expectancy of control for the test task than did control conditions. This finding was also obtained after observational helplessness training (seeing another subject fail repeatedly) and after failure in social interaction. Interestingly, the experience with lack of control appears to reduce the expectancy of self-efficacy (e.g., Brown & Inouye, 1978), but there is no indication about its effects on outcome expectancy—the expectancy that the test task will be chance dependent. In general, helplessness training seems to produce unfavorable expectancies that seem to reflect the conviction that one is not able to execute the behaviors required to obtain outcomes (rather than a belief in the objective uncontrollability of the task).

THE PERSISTENCE OF EXPECTANCY CHANGE

Research has also focused on the maintainance of the expectancy of no control throughout the solvable test task—that is, whether the expectancy of no control developed from helplessness training *persists* throughout the test task despite the presence of high response–outcome contingency. In an initial attempt, Miller and Seligman (1976) and Klein and Seligman (1976) argued that the amount of change in success expectancy after failure and success in the test task (i.e., expectancy reduction after failure, expectancy increase after success) is a valid measure of the individual's belief of control. This argument was based on Rotter's studies on locus of control (e.g., James & Rotter, 1958; Phares, 1957; Rotter, Liverant, & Crowne, 1961), which demonstrated that the recognition of outcomes as objectively uncontrollable leads to relatively limited expectancy change over trials. If people perceive outcomes to be controlled by their responses, then success on a trial should increase their expectancy for future success ("I possess the required responses"), and failure should decrease it ("I do not possess the required responses"). If, however, people perceive outcomes as independent of responses (chance dependent), then success or failure should have little effect on their expectancy.

On this basis, Miller and Seligman (1976) and Klein and Seligman (1976) argued that if an expectancy of no control persists throughout the test task, people exposed to helplessness training will exhibit less expectancy change than control subjects in test tasks where the outcome is actually contingent on responses (skill tasks). In chance tasks, where response and outcome are independent, both subjects exposed to helplessness training and control subjects were predicted to show relatively small expectancy changes.

In examining these predictions, Miller and Seligman (1976) and Klein and Seligman (1976) exposed subjects to either no, escapable, or inescapable noise and asked them to perform either a chance task or a so-called skill task; in each case the subjects received experimentally controlled feedback after each trial and rated their success expectancy for the next trial. Results showed no difference in expectancy change among the various conditions in the chance task. In the skill task, though, subjects exposed to inescapable noise showed less expectancy change after both success and failure than controls. Based on these results, Seligman and his colleagues inferred that the expectancy of no control produced by helplessness training persisted throughout the test task and interfered with learning that responses may produce outcomes.

This interpretation, however, is open to question. Analyzing subjects' answers to a postexperimental questionnaire, Costello (1978) noted that although subjects exposed to helplessness training showed relatively small expectancy change, they actually believed that outcomes in the test tasks were objectively controllable. On this basis, Costello argued that the expectancy change findings did not imply that subjects perceive the test task as chance dependent.

Alloy and Seligman (1979) suggest alternatively that the limited expectancy change of subjects exposed to helplessness training may reflect a tendency to attribute outcomes to unstable causes. As research by Weiner (1979, 1986) has demonstrated, unstable attribution produces less expectancy changes than stable attribution. In addition, I believe that the expectancy change findings may reflect the effects of helplessness training on information processing. It may be that people exposed to helplessness training tend to disengage from the active processing of task-relevant information and to ignore incoming information that demands generation of new knowledge. One manifestation of this disengagement would be "helpless" people's unwillingness to revise their expectancies after feedback, because such a revision would demand active and effortful cognitive work—the rejection of prior beliefs and the generation of new hypotheses.

In response to these criticisms, researchers abandoned the assessment of expectancy changes. But although the limited expectancy change findings do not reflect the recognition of outcomes' uncontrollability, they tell something of relevance about the inability or unwillingness of people exposed to helplessness training to alter their expectancies in face of new environmental information. At least, they indicate that some portion of the unfavorable expectancy formed during helplessness training may perseverate despite the occurrence of more favorable outcomes.

A more direct method of examining the perception of control during the test task was developed by Alloy and Abramson (1979), who asked people to quantify the degree of control they believed they had over outcomes in a contingency learning problem. This problem consisted of a series of 40 trials in which subjects could make one of two possible responses (i.e., pressing or not pressing a button) and received one of two possible outcomes (a green light or no green light). At the end of the trials, subjects were asked to judge the degree of control their responses had on the outcomes.

Using this research strategy, Alloy and Abramson (1982) and Ford and Neale (1985) reasoned that if the belief in lack of control produced by helplessness training persists in the test task, it should lead to an underestimation of control in a highly contingent problem. Their findings, however, appear to contradict this reasoning. Subjects exposed to helplessness training did not carry their perceived lack of control over to the test task. Like those exposed to controllable or no noise, subjects exposed to uncontrollable noise were found to perceive accurately the presence of high contingency between responses and outcomes in a new task. That is, people exposed to helplessness training had no difficulty in learning that there were effective responses for controlling outcomes in the test task. On this basis, the authors concluded that the belief in no control dissipates with the experience of a controllable test task.

In my opinion, the above conclusion is erroneous. Integration of the expectancy change findings with findings on judged control shows that only low *outcome* expectancy, but not low *self-efficacy* expectancy, dissipates during the test task. As pointed out above, people exposed to helplessness training form an unfavorable expectancy (see Table 4.1) and are unable or unwilling to alter it despite the feedback they receive in the test task (see expectancy change findings). Because the control judgment studies show that people exposed to helplessness training accurately recognize the presence of high contingency between responses and outcomes, the expectancy findings cannot reflect a belief in the objective uncontrollability of the test task (universal helplessness). Rather, the persistent unfavorable expectancy may reflect low self-efficacy expectancy (personal helplessness). What may persist throughout the test task is the belief that one lacks the responses and abilities required for controlling what is perceived as an objectively controllable outcome.

The fact that people exposed to helplessness training recognize the objective controllability of the test task only indicates that low outcome expectancies, if they are formed at all, dissipate in face of new contingencies. It does not, however, guarantee the renewal of the expectancy of control. When people develop a sense of personal helplessness, a low self-efficacy expectancy may sustain the expectancy of no control even after they recognize that outcomes can be controlled with the right responses. As shown earlier, the typical helplessness training may raise doubts about one's self-efficacy, and these doubts may persist throughout the test task and may underlie the conviction that one is unable to control the new outcomes.

In Study 7 of the series of LH studies that I present in this book (see Table 1.1 for details), I exposed subjects to failure or no feedback in four unsolvable problems, and then all the subjects observed a confederate performing a 40-trial contingency problem similar to that used by Alloy and Abramson (1982) and Ford and Neale (1985). The objective contingency between the confederate's responses and the outcome (a green light) was high (50%). At the end of the task, all the subjects were asked about (a) the extent to which the confederate controlled the outcome, and (b) the extent to which they themselves possess the responses necessary for exerting the same level of control as that exerted by the confederate.

If both low outcome expectancy and low self-efficacy expectancy dissipate during the observational controllable task, subjects exposed to helplessness training should believe, like no-feedback subjects, that the confederate controls the outcome and that they themselves possess the response necessary for achieving the same level of control. The results, though, indicated a different pattern (see Table 4.2). Whereas "helplessness" subjects accurately judged the high control of the confeder-

TABLE 4.2. Means, Standard Deviations, and F-Ratios
of Judgments of Control for Actor and Self
According to Feedback (Study 7)

	No feedback ($N = 15$)	Failure ($N = 15$)	F
Judgments of control			
Actor			0.20
Mean	55.80	57.92	
Standard deviation	11.82	12.85	
Self			10.91[a]
Mean	57.13	44.80	
Standard deviation	8.07	11.90	

[a]$p < .01$

ate, they were less confident in the efficacy of their own responses for controlling the outcome than no-feedback subjects. The findings imply that the doubts about self-efficacy created by helplessness training persist in the test task despite subjects' recognition that the task is objectively controllable.

SUMMARY

The data are consistent with the hypothesis that experience with lack of control is able to reduce the expectancy of control. The findings also show that this effect does not reflect the formation of low outcome expectancy. People may sustain unfavorable expectancies throughout the test task despite their accurate perception of the controllability of the task. In this case, the expectancy of lack of control appears to be derived from the conviction that one does not possess the responses required to control what is perceived as a controllable outcome.

THE FORMATION OF THE EXPECTANCY OF NO CONTROL

In the view of the original formulation of the Learned Helplessness theory (Maier & Seligman, 1976; Seligman, 1975), the exposure to objective lack of control leads directly to the formation of an expectancy of no control for the test task. Accumulative findings, however, emphasize that the route from helplessness training to the expectancy of lack of control is not simple and automatic as expected. In fact, it seems to be composed of different steps and to be moderated by an array of situational and personal factors (e.g., see Abramson, Seligman, & Teasdale, 1978; Levis, 1976; Roth, 1980).

This section has two basic aims. First, it attempts to delineate which factors contribute to expectancy change. Specifically, I focus on two factors that are consistently viewed as the proximal antecedents of expectancy change after failure: the perception of control, and the causal attribution of the failure (Abramson, Seligman, & Teasdale, 1978; Alloy & Seligman, 1979). Second, it examines my hypothesis that a small amount of failure does not reduce the expectancy of control, and that only a large amount of failure does. I shall present empirical evidence on this hypothesis and then analyze how the antecedents of expectancy can determine the effects of small and large amounts of failure.

THE PERCEPTION OF CONTROL

One possible step in the formation of the expectancy of no control is the perception of lack of control. Maier and Seligman (1976) and Alloy and Seligman (1979) proposed that when people experience lack of control, they must cognitively encode it before they can form the expectancy of no control. If people are unable to perceive that they lack control in the training task, they have no reason to expect lack of control in the test task. Only after people register their failure to control outcomes could they come to expect that this would also be true in the next task.

The perception of control during helplessness training is frequently assessed in typical LH studies; it usually serves as a check for the manipulation of lack of control. More than two hundred LH studies have made this assessment during the last two decades, and though there is no uniformity in the wording, scaling, and timing (before or after the test task) of the measures, most of the studies have found that subjects are able to detect lack of control. Subjects exposed to uncontrollable outcomes judged they had less control than subjects in controllable conditions.

These findings, however, are in direct opposition to human learning and social psychology research that points to difficulty in detecting and learning response–outcome contingencies in general, and lack of control in particular. Jenkins and Ward (1965), for example, found that subjects failed to make accurate judgments of control on the basis of the degree of response–outcome contingency. Their judgments were highly related to the frequency of the outcome—the more trials on which the outcome occurred, the higher the judged control. When the outcome was frequent, even though its occurrence was independent of responses, people estimated high levels of control. This effect occurred (a) when subjects were active participants as well as when they were merely spectators, (b) under different instructional sets, and (c) when a remedial procedure was introduced (subjects received exemplars of contingent and noncontingent sequences).

The discrepant findings may be attributable to procedural differences. Whereas subjects in LH studies receive explicit feedback about their performance at the end of the training task, Jenkins and Ward's subjects received no feedback. In addition, the LH studies operationalize response–outcome contingency as an all-or-nothing affair (subjects are exposed to either complete lack of control or fully controllable outcomes), and Jenkins and Ward operationalized it in a more graduated fashion (subjects were exposed to different levels of partially controllable outcomes). Giving explicit performance feedback and inducing complete noncontingency may help subjects in LH studies to detect lack of control accurately.

In addition, the exposure to helplessness training implies not only lack of control but also failure in bringing about a desired outcome (see Chapter 1). As Jenkins and Ward themselves observed, the link between noncontingency and the low frequency of a desire outcome may also facilitate detecting lack of control. This line of reasoning was supported by Alloy and Abramson (1979), who manipulated the objective degree of response–outcome contingency and the frequency of outcome occurrence. At first sight, the results appear to corroborate the thesis that people are unable to detect lack of control: Nondepressed subjects judged control accurately for the highly contingent problems, but overestimated control in noncontingent problems. The results also show, though, that this inaccurate judgment occurred only when the frequency of the noncontingent outcome was high. When the frequency of outcome was low, people accurately judged that they had no control.

Alloy and Abramson (1979) propose another methodological explanation. They point out that Jenkins and Ward (1965) may have reached an erroneous conclusion because of how they calculated the objective contingency. Jenkins and Ward compared the probability of the outcome following one response (pressing button 1) to the probability of the outcome following another response (pressing button 2). They did not take into account the probability of outcome when subjects pressed no button. There is nothing saying that subjects did not consider this third possibility in judging control; if they did, Alloy and Abramson suspect they may have made control judgments by subtracting the probability of outcome when no response was made from some average of the probability of outcome following one of the two main responses. Because the probability of outcome after no response was always zero, this difference would be highly related to the frequency to which the outcome occurred at all. On this basis, Alloy and Abramson argued that Jenkins and Ward's subjects made accurate judgments of contingency.

Still another explanation for the discrepant findings involves the amount of training. Whereas Jenkins and Ward presented people with only one noncontingent problem, most of the LH studies presented subjects with four or five noncontingent problems. In dealing with one noncontingent problem, people could deny or ignore lack of control. Each successive noncontingent task, however, might make that denial more difficult and so facilitate the recognition of lack of control.

In support of this view, Study 1 of the series I present in this book showed that the reduction in perceived control ("the extent to which your responses were able to alter outcomes") was a positive function of the amount of helplessness training (see Figure 4.1). As compared to no feedback, one or two unsolvable problems did not produce any significant reduction in perceived control; only large amounts of training (three to five unsolvable problems) did.

Another possibility is that the perceived lack of control produced by helplessness training reflects beliefs in personal helplessness. Although people may be

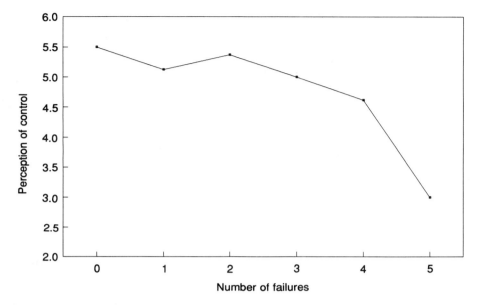

FIGURE 4.1. Means of perceived control according to number of failures.

unaware of the objective noncontingency, they may become convinced that they lack the responses required to obtain outcomes, and thus they may be prone to estimate that they *personally* have no control. In other words, the perceived lack of control evidenced after helplessness training may stem from doubts in one's self-efficacy. In support, I found in Study 7 of my series of studies that helplessness training, as compared to control conditions, reduces the perception of self-efficacy but does not lead people to perceive the task as chance dependent (see Table 4.3).

TABLE 4.3. Means, Standard Deviations, and F-Ratios of Perceived Self-Efficacy and Perceptions of Task as Chance Dependent according to Feedback

	No feedback ($N = 15$)	Failure ($N = 15$)	F
Perceived self-efficacy			7.87[a]
Mean	4.93	3.33	
Standard deviation	1.53	1.59	
Task as chance dependent			0.59
Mean	2.33	2.00	
Standard deviation	1.29	1.07	

[a]$p < .01$

No matter the explanation, the findings show that typical helplessness training enables people to perceive lack of control. This learning appears to be gradual, however, and it requires prolonged exposure to uncontrollable failure. Moreover, it may reflect doubts about one's self-efficacy rather than an accurate recognition of the objective uncontrollability of the task.

CAUSAL ATTRIBUTION

Causal attribution may be another precursor of expectancy change. In his attributional theory of achievement motivation, Weiner (1979, 1985, 1986) took the position that changes in expectancies depend not only on environmental outcomes but also on the way in which the outcomes are subjectively represented. Weiner thus proposed that when people fail in a task, they ask themselves why, and that the answers affect their expectancies.

Weiner mainly focuses on the *stability* dimension of causal attribution— whether an outcome is caused by stable factors (e.g., ability) that will persist in the future, or by unstable factors (e.g., tiredness) that need not recur. He hypothesizes that stable attribution leads people to expect that future outcomes in a task will be the same as past outcomes, whereas unstable attribution leads them to expect no such continuity. Weiner summarized his reasoning under the rubric of the "expectancy principle."

In their reformulation of the Learned Helplessness theory, Abramson, Seligman, and Teasdale (1978) adopted Weiner's reasoning and extended it to the *globality* dimension of causal attribution: the degree to which a person attributes an outcome to global factors ("I'm incompetent at everything") that will produce the same outcome in a wide variety of situations, or to specific factors ("I'm incompetent at anagrams") that will produce the outcome only in similar tasks. According to Abramson, Seligman, and Teasdale, the globality dimension moderates the generalization of expectancy to new situations. If a person decides that the lack of control is attributable to factors present in a wide range of situations, he or she will expect lack of control to recur in dissimilar settings. In contrast, if the lack of control is explained by factors specific to the training task, the expectancy tends to be restricted to that task. People who believe that the failure results from task-specific factors have no reason to expect the same outcome to persist when these factors are altered in a new task.

On this basis, one can predict that the transfer of the expectancy of no control to a new task is more likely to occur when subjects tend to attribute failure to more stable and global causes. One can also explain findings on the situational specificity of expectancy changes and their dissipation with time. In addition, one can delineate some of the factors related to causal attribution that may precede the expectational effects of helplessness training. These include situational cues that determine the choice of a particular explanation of failure (the valence of the event, its consistency over time, and its discrepancy from social norms), as well as projective inferences drawn from a person's habitual "explanatory style" when reality does not offer a clear account of the causes of failure. Several authors have addressed this attributional analysis in explaining expectancy change within LH settings (e.g., Alloy, 1982; Miller & Norman, 1979).

The introduction of causal attribution raises new questions as to whether people spontaneously make attribution, however, and if so, whether they organize these attributions along the stability and globality dimensions (Wortman & Dintzer, 1978). If people exposed to helplessness training neither spontaneously pose attributional questions to themselves nor consider the stability and globality of the failure, it would be unreasonable to argue that these dimensions are involved in the formation of the expectancy of no control.

Given this theoretical background, an empirical test of the role of causal attribution should answer to the questions originally raised by Wortman and Dintzer (1978): Do people make attributions? Is the organization of causal attribution along stability and globality dimensions adequate? Only after positively answering these questions can one evaluate whether the attributional dimensions of stability and globality affect expectancy change after helplessness training.

THE MAKING OF SPONTANEOUS ATTRIBUTION

Research show that people spontaneously engage in causal analysis when they experience failure, particularly if it is unexpected (e.g., Bohner, Bless, Schwartz, & Strack, 1988; Pittman & Pittman, 1980; Pyszczynski & Greenberg, 1981; Wong & Weiner, 1981), as occurs in the helplessness training. In contrast, one early LH study found no spontaneous attribution after failure (Hanusa & Schultz, 1977); its results indicated that "subjects did not spontaneously report attributions. . . . Typically, subjects responded to the attribution questions by repeating the outcome" (p. 608).

Moreover, LH research has found individual differences in the making of attributions. Diener and Dweck (1978), for example, found that children with a general tendency to attribute failure to lack of effort are less likely to engage in causal analysis than children with a predisposition to attribute failure to lack of ability. Brunstein and Olbrich (1985) found that children who habitually focus on action alternatives were less likely to ask why failures occurred than children who habitually focus on off-task thoughts. Although these findings do not rule out the attributional analysis, they may explain individual differences in the formation of the expectancy of no control.

THE DIMENSIONS OF CAUSAL ATTRIBUTION

Studies using factor analysis and multidimensional scaling to identify the dimensions that underlie people's causal analysis support the idea that attributions are organized along the stability dimension (see Weiner, 1985, for a detailed review). In contrast, with the exception of Van-Overwalle's (1989) study, most research has not identified a global–specific property of attribution. Nonetheless, Weiner (1985) cautions that "the argument in favor of a distinction between general and specific causes certainly cannot be faulted on grounds of face validity. . . . When personality psychologists discuss traits, both temporal aspects (consistency over time) and generalizability (consistency across situations) are considered. In a similar manner, causes can logically be construed in terms of those two characteristics. Globality therefore might be a basic property of causes" (pp. 554–555).

Other studies on the structure of attributional questionnaires have found high correlations between scores of stable and global attributions (e.g., Mikulincer, Bizman, & Aizenberg, 1989). On this basis, one can argue that globality should be subsumed to stability; that is, the dimension of stability may encompass the consistency of outcomes both over time and across situations.

THE STABILITY DIMENSION AND EXPECTANCY CHANGE

In his extensive review, Weiner (1985, 1986) reported numerous studies that have demonstrated the expectancy principle at work. Specifically, he found that (a) the more stable the attribution, the higher the increase in the expectancy of success after success and the higher the increase in the expectancy of failure after failure; and (b) the induction of stable attribution produced stronger expectancy change than the induction of unstable attribution. Weiner (1985) also presented evidence that the expectancy principle applies to a wide variety of nonachievement settings (including parole decisions, consumer behavior, and social persuasion) and that the effects of stability attribution can be isolated from other causal dimensions (i.e., internal–external attribution). In a correlational study, Weiner, Nierenberg, and Goldstein (1976) found stronger expectancy change after stable attribution—whether it was made in terms of internal (ability) or external (task difficulty) causes—than after unstable attribution (effort, luck).

Evidence for the impact of stability attribution on expectancy is also found in three of my LH studies (Mikulincer, 1986a, 1988b, 1990), in which subjects exposed to either failure or no feedback in four unsolvable problems were preselected on the basis of their habitual attributional style and/or were randomly divided according to the induction of stable–unstable attribution for the current failure. The results showed that subjects who attributed their lack of control to stable causes were more likely to expect no control for the test task than those who made an unstable attribution. This included both subjects in whom the attribution was manipulated and those in whom it was a personality feature. The results also indicated that helplessness training, as compared to no feedback, produced expectancy of no control only among subjects who made a stable attribution.

THE GLOBALITY DIMENSION AND EXPECTANCY CHANGE

The link between globality attribution and expectancy has not received extensive empirical attention; to date, only three LH studies have been designed to test it. Pasahow (1980) and Mikulincer (1986a) found that subjects encouraged to make global attributions for lack of control were more likely to expect no control in a new test task than subjects encouraged to make specific attributions. These authors also found that helplessness training, as compared to control conditions, reduced the expectancy of success/control for the test task only among subjects who were led to make global attributions. Miller and Norman (1981) reported that induction of global attribution for success produced higher success expectancy for a new task than induction of task-specific attribution. Only Miller and Norman failed to find that global attribution affected the expectancy of control.

Although the findings are in keeping with the idea that lack of control produces expectancies of no control for a new task only when it is attributed to stable and global causes, it should be noted that asking people to verbalize attributions may itself change their expectancy and performance (e.g., Campbell & Fairey, 1985; den-Boer, Meertens, Kok, & Van-Knippenberg, 1989). According to Tverski and Kahneman (1973), this makes the explained outcome available in memory and more likely to be utilized in anticipating future events. Alloy (1982) suggested that the making of attribution in helplessness training may in and of itself increase the expectancy that poor performance will recur in the test task.

THE SLOPE OF EXPECTANCY CHANGE

Neither theory nor research systematically deal with the slope of expectancy change during helplessness training. Only Wortman and Brehm (1975) and Zuroff (1980)—who predict that expectancy of control declines following large, but not small amounts of typical helplessness training—allude to this issue. To fill in this gap, I (Mikulincer, 1985) exposed subjects to either failure or no feedback in four unsolvable problems and asked them to rate the probability of their success in each. Data show that one or two failures did not produce lower expectancy than no failure, but more training (three failures) did. The one shortcoming in the experiment was that the data were obtained via a within-subject measurement of expectancy, which is a reactive procedure that can alter subsequent cognitions (Dweck & Gilliard, 1975).

In ruling out this possibility, Study 1 of the series I present in this book examined the slope of expectancy change in a between-subject design. Results (see Figure 4.2) validated my previous findings. Subjects exposed to one or two failures had expectations similar to those of subjects exposed to no failure; subjects exposed to three or more failures exhibited lower expectations. Similar slopes were found in four more of these studies, which exposed subjects to no, one, or four failures and asked them to rate their expectancies of control (see Table 4.4). A conceptually similar slope of expectancy change is found in the Baum et al. (1978) study of students who lived in dormitory rooms off of short or long corridors.

Given these findings, I turn to the question of what factors go into shaping the slope. Zuroff (1980) contends that failure may not initially reduce expectancies, because people may begin a task with favorable expectancy based on experiences in related situations, but the contribution of this generalized expectancy decreases with

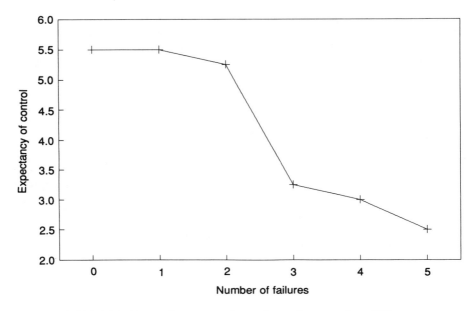

FIGURE 4.2. Means of expectancy of control according to number of failures.

experience in the task. So "repeated failure will lead to subject's specific expectancies to approach zero and . . . as the contribution of the generalized expectancies to the overall expectancies drops out over repeated trials, the overall expectancies will also become small" (Zuroff, 1980, p. 134). Unfortunately, Zuroff's explanation that the slope of expectancy change reflects an alteration in the contribution of generalized expectancies cannot be empirically tested.

Alternatively, the slope of expectancy change may be explained by the difficulty in detecting lack of control after a small amount of failure. When this occurs, it might slow down the formation of the expectancy of no control. This delay would result in a drastic reduction in the expectancy of control only after large amounts of

TABLE 4.4. Means and F-Ratios of Expectancy of Control
by Number of Failures

Study number	No failures	One failure	Four failures	F
9	5.56	5.19	3.12	14.70[a]
10	5.43	5.12	3.68	7.34[a]
11	5.62	5.31	3.50	10.97[a]
12	5.44	5.31	3.12	12.92[a]

[a]$p < .01$

helplessness training. Yet another explanation is based on Weiner's (1985) expectancy principle. The lack of expectancy change after small amounts of failure may result from an unstable attribution; the change of expectancy after larger amounts of failure may reflect the action of stable attribution. This explanation implies an initially unstable attribution of failure and a transition toward a stable attribution.

This attributional transition was documented by Meyer (1970), who found that subjects attributed initial failure to more unstable than stable factors, but repeated ones to more stable factors. Importantly, this transition was found mainly among subjects with low achievement need; those with high achievement need made unstable attribution even after five failures. Meyer's findings were complicated by some methodological problems (interdependence of attributional ratings, and repeated assessment), but I found the same transition in Study 1 of the series that I present in this book. People exposed to four or five failures made a more stable attribution than those exposed to one or two failures (see Figure 4.3).

Whether the perceptual or attributional mechanism underlies the slope of expectancy change, the question of why people initially misjudge lack of control and make unstable attributions and then alter their views remains unanswered. One factor that may be responsible for both the perceptual and attributional patterns is the expectancy people hold prior to the helplessness training.

Alloy and Tabachnik (1984) claim that the perception of control depends on both available situational information and the expectations that people bring to the

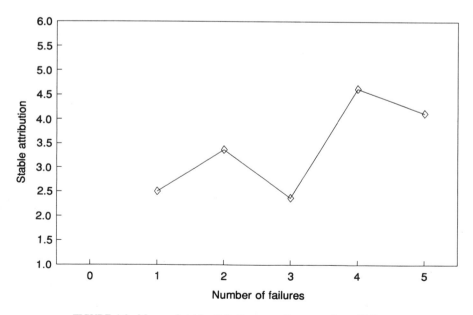

FIGURE 4.3. Means of stable attribution according to number of failures.

situation. They suggest that people make accurate judgments of control when the situational information is abundant, when they have little or no confidence in their a priori expectations, or when the situational information is congruent with expectations. People tend to misjudge control when situational information and initial expectations are incongruent; in such cases, they typically base their judgments of control on their initial beliefs and ignore the incongruent situational cues. In support of this view, Peterson (1980) found that experimental manipulations of subjects' expectations of the likelihood of noncontingency occurrence biased judgments of control in the direction of the manipulated expectation.

In analyzing the determinants of stable–unstable attribution, Valle and Frieze (1976) emphasized the impact of the consistency between outcome and prior expectancy. They argued that an outcome consistent with prior expectancy tends to be related to past accomplishments and attributed to stable factors, whereas an outcome that diverges from prior expectations tends to be perceived as fortuitous and attributed to more unstable causes. On this basis, they predicted that people who hold low success expectancy may attribute a failure to stable causes, whereas those who hold high success expectancy may attribute a failure to unstable causes. This prediction was supported by several studies (e.g., Feather, 1969; Feather & Simon, 1971; McAuley & Duncan, 1989).

Ordinary, well-functioning people tend to begin the helplessness training with a high or moderate expectancy of control based on everyday experiences with response–outcome contingencies. Because this prior expectancy is incongruent with the current experience of lack of control, it may lead people to overestimate their control and to attribute their failure to unstable factors, which in turn sustains their high expectancy of control for the next task. After successive failures, the difficulties of continuing to negate strong situational cues pointing to lack of control and of explaining consistent outcomes by unstable factors may significantly reduce control expectancy.

It thus seems that the slope of expectancy change depends on personal and situational factors. It may depend on prior expectancy of control; people holding a prior expectancy of no control would require only a single failure to believe that lack of control will recur in the next task. Or it may be affected by the situation in which the person experiences no control; for example, one-trial learning may occur in traumatic situations, where the death of a loved person is objectively irreversible or in a situation (e.g., war) so overwhelming that people immediately feel they have no response for dealing with it.

EPISTEMIC ACTIVITY AND EXPECTANCY CHANGE

In my view, the expectancy change is a product of the individual's epistemic activity, by which anticipatory cognitions are continuously formed and modified throughout the task. This occurs in a two-phase sequence in which people generate hypotheses about control of outcome, then test them using deductive reasoning and production rules, just as they do hypotheses about the task (Anderson, 1990; Kruglanski, 1989).

This epistemic activity is organized hierarchically. At the higher (molar) level, people test hypotheses as to whether their responses can alter outcome. At the lower (molecular) level, they test hypotheses about the specific responses needed to alter outcome. The testing at each of the levels bears on the testing at the other. The molecular search for responses to alter outcome is activated only when people reach the conclusion at the molar level that they can affect the outcome. At the same time, the results of the testing of the molecular hypotheses would either confirm the molar hypothesis that the outcome is controllable (if effective responses are found) or refute it (if they are not found). Every refutation of a lower-level hypothesis may raise doubts about the possibility of control until, at some point, accumulated refutations convince people that control is lost.

When the problem is solvable, some of the lower-level hypotheses will be supported by the effectiveness of the responses being tested. As more and more evidence is found for the effectiveness of a response and, conversely, for the failure to attain the outcome without that response, any uncertainty as to whether the problem can actually be solved is gradually reduced; people then become increasingly convinced that they have discovered a way of altering the outcome, and this belief in turn validates the hypothesis of control. In helplessness training, however, the evidence is inconsistent with all the lower-level hypotheses that people generate, does not allow a reduction of the initial uncertainty about the problem solution, and requires the generation of new hypotheses in the successive trials of the problem. Here hypothesis testing may be an endless, but futile activity.

In reality, the epistemic process would stop at some point. Each refutation of a lower-level hypothesis may increasingly raise doubts about the validity of the belief of control and may generate the alternative belief of lack of control. After a period of futile cognitive work in which each hypothesis is refuted, people would come to expect that the outcome is impossible to control. The generation and testing of lower-level hypotheses would be stopped when this expectancy of no control was formed, and the conviction of no control would be "frozen" (Kruglanski, 1989) for subsequent task attempts.

In this epistemic process, the strength of the prior belief of control may determine the amount of evidence that is necessary for refuting it. Like every schema, strong prior belief of control would skew perception, attention, and memory to reject contradictory data (e.g., Anderson, 1990). Only persistent and undeniable contradictory evidence would have the power to change such self-maintaining schema. Consequently the more confident people are of their ability to manipulate the environment, the more contradictory evidence they would need to undermine that belief, and the more failure trials they would require to create the expectancy of no control.

The stability and globality causal dimensions moderate the strength of refuted lower-level hypotheses for changing the belief of control. The attribution of failure to stable-global causes implies that the inefficacy of a response reflects some general and long-lasting trends in the situation, thus raising doubts about the possibility of exerting control. In contrast, the attribution of failure to unstable-specific causes means that a single failure would tell people very little about the possibility of control, and the more failures would be needed to convince them that something stable is happening.

EXPECTANCY AND COPING

The next task in evaluating the mediational role of the expectancy of control within the LH paradigm is to examine the path from expectancy to coping. I test the hypothesis that the expectancy of control determines the adoption of a particular coping orientation.

THEORETICAL STATEMENTS

In my terms, the expectancy of control plays an important role in the coping process. Specifically, expectancy is a cognitive appraisal that helps people choose among coping alternatives. It is a part of what Lazarus and Folkman (1984) call *secondary appraisal*—"an evaluation of the person's options and resources for coping with the situation and future prospects" (p. 145). Lazarus (1991) speaks of two secondary appraisal components that parallel the two components of the expectancy of control: (a) *coping potential,* the extent to which people believe they have the responses required to manage the demands of a given situation (which matches self-efficacy expectancy); and (b) *future expectancy,* the extent to which people expect to attain or not attain the goal, (which matches outcome expectancy). Both components act as a "psychological watershed" (Carver & Scheier, 1981), guiding a person in his or her choices of coping actions in a given situation.

The idea that expectancy alters coping actions is based on the concept of "cognitively generated motivation" (Bandura, 1986). People guide their actions by anticipating the probable outcomes of the latter. They consider what they can do to cope with life's adversities, and they then perform the behavior that is expected to maximize their gains and minimize their losses. Expectancy thus translates the construed future events into what is believed to be the most suitable course of action, and it motivates the person to take this course. Expectancy is a representational way of informing people what they must do to deal with a task, as well as an incentive for initiating the appropriate responses. The same reasoning was adopted by Bandura and Cervone (1983), who claim that "it is partly on the basis of self-percepts of efficacy that people choose what to do, how much effort to mobilize for given activities, and how long to persevere at them" (p. 1018).

In LH settings, people are faced with the task of coping with a mismatch. Before undertaking any further coping behavior, people process information on coping options and estimate future expectancy. This cognitive activity provides the basis for evaluating the effectiveness of coping actions and for adopting the strategy that is expected to lead to the most favorable outcomes. People may direct coping efforts toward the task when they expect their actions to have an impact on the task outcome. They may abandon problem solving and adopt off-task coping, however, when they expect to have no control over the environment. These effects of the expectancy of control are manifested in the undertaking of particular coping strategies as well as in the cognitive substrate of these strategies (mental rumination).

On the one hand, high expectancy of control may lead people to undertake problem solving and to engage in action rumination. It means that outcomes are expected to be affected by action and that the main coping task is to organize and enact adequate problem-focused strategies. The "hopeful" person with high expectancy of control is likely to assign high instrumental value to problem solving and action rumination—and to see them as fitting the appraised reality constraints—and would thus be prone to undertake an active, problem-focused approach to the task.

Expectancy of no control, on the other hand, leads people to undertake off-task coping and to engage in off-task rumination. When people believe that there is no instrumental action that can overcome the failure, they may withdraw their efforts from the task. Instead, they may make intrapsychic changes that can minimize the threatening implications of failure (Archibald, 1974; Folkman, 1984; Rothbaum et al., 1982). Rather than persevere at attempts to change what has come to be perceived as an unchangeable or uncontrollable environment, they try to avoid the failure situation and/or to change their goals. Persons with low expectancy of control would freeze any attempt to solve the problem and might attempt cognitively to avoid any direct or symbolic confrontation with the threat. Alternatively, they may attempt to reshape their mental structures to end the mismatch. In fact, people who believe they are unable to overcome failure may accept the inadequacy of their goals, which is the painful first step in working through the failure and reorganizing personal priorities.

In my terms, the expectancy of no control determines only that some kind of off-task coping will be employed; other anticipatory cognitions will determine whether the choice will be avoidance or reorganization. One such cognition is the expectancy of resolving a mismatch—that is, whether one is capable of reshaping mental structures so as to restore the disrupted equilibrium. People who believe that they have the resources and abilities needed to resolve a mismatch will tend to expect that the reshaping of structures will maximize their adaptive gains, and they will thus be likely to undertake reorganization coping. In contrast, people who believe that they lack these resources and abilities may be more prone to leave the mismatch unresolved and to avoid any direct confrontation with the threat. These people will tend to abandon any active attempt to resolve the mismatch and will direct their coping efforts only at mitigating the resulting distress.

It is important to distinguish between the expectancy of control and the expectancy of resolving a mismatch. The former seems to be a particular case of the latter. People who believe that they are able to resolve mismatches can expect either to have control over outcomes (like people who undertake problem solving), or to have no control (like people who employ reorganization). People who believe that they cannot resolve a mismatch, however, can only expect lack of control.

In addition, whereas the expectancy of control differentiates between problem solving and off-task coping, the expectancy of resolving a mismatch differentiates between avoidance and other ways of coping. People who believe that they cannot resolve a mismatch by either alloplastic or autoplastic attempts will tend to undertake avoidance coping. People who believe in their ability to end the mismatch, though, are more likely to engage in problem solving or reorganization, in accord with their expectancy of control. This does not imply that people who use problem solving to coping with a single failure will use reorganization after repeated failure. In fact, after recognizing the futility of problem solving, one is likely to engage in avoidance out of the belief that problem solving is the only available path for ending a mismatch.

Another important difference between the two types of expectancies deals with the effects of environmental outcomes. On the one hand, the expectancy of control may be changed by environmental outcomes. The efficacy of one's actions in shaping the world and the "moldability" of the world may thus influence one's ideas about the extent to which action can really alter the world. On the other hand, the expectancy of resolving a mismatch may be less sensitive to environmental outcomes. It reflects one's belief that one possesses the resources needed to transform either the world or one's own mental structures, and as such, it is likely to be based on the outcomes of one's prior experiences with mismatches.

A final comment should be made on the possibility that changes in the expectancy of control can account for the observed changes in coping responses and mental rumination in the course of helplessness training (see Chapters 2 and 3). As noted above, although a large amount of failure produces a drastic reduction in the expectancy of control, a small amount of failure is unable to change expectancies. Thus the use of problem-solving strategies and the engagement in action rumination after a small amount of failure may derive from the maintenance of high expectancy of control. The use of off-task coping and the engagement in off-task rumination after a large amount of failure may derive from the reduction in the expectancy of control.

THE EFFECTS OF EXPECTANCY ON COPING STRATEGIES

There is evidence that expectancy is related to the use of problem-solving and avoidance strategies. This evidence extends to the diverse facets of expectancy (perception of control, generalized belief of control, expectancy of success, and self-efficacy expectancy) as well as to the antecedents of expectancy changes (stability and globality attributions). In addition, my recent series of studies provides preliminary data on the contribution of expectancy to reorganization coping.

The appraisal of a stressful event as controllable has been found to be positively associated with the use of problem-focused coping (Folkman & Lazarus, 1980, 1985; Folkman et al., 1986; Torestad, Magnusson, & Olah, 1990). In addition, Folkman and Lazarus (1985) reported that avoidance coping was used more after a course examination (when obviously nothing could be done to change the grade) than before it. Folkman et al. (1986) found that the appraisal of controllability of a stressful event was positively related to the use of reappraisal and inversely related to the use of wishful thinking, social withdrawal, and distancing.

In a series of studies, Moos (1984) found that avoidance was activated mainly when the appraisal of a stressful encounter led to the perception that the personal and environmental resources for dealing with the threat were insufficient. Accordingly, Hilton (1989) found that avoidance was characteristic of women with breast cancer who perceived low control over their illness. In a developmental study, Altshuler and Ruble (1989) found that children reported having dealt with uncontrollable situations via avoidance strategies.

The generalized belief of internal locus of control has been found to promote problem solving. In a thoughtful review, Strickland (1978) concluded that this belief promotes searches for information about disease and health and the undertaking of problem-focused behaviors designed to prevent diseases. This superior use of problem solving among people with an internal locus of control was also found in dealing with business-related demands (Anderson, 1977) and in a school context (Sadowski & Blackwell, 1987). This pattern of coping, however, has been found mainly when the situation is controllable and demands problem solving (Parkes, 1984). There is also evidence that the belief that one lacks control leads to greater use of cognitive avoidance in dealing with academic failure (Cooley & Klinger, 1989), war (Solomon, Mikulincer, & Benbenishty, 1989), and chronic illness (Keller, 1988).

There is also supportive evidence as to the impact of success expectancy and self-efficacy expectancy. The generalized expectancy of success (as assessed by the Life Orientation Test, Carver et al., 1989) was positively related to problem solving and reappraisal, but inversely related to avoidance (e.g., Carver et al., 1989; Scheier et al., 1986). Accordingly, some studies found self-efficacy expectancy to be related to the use of more problem solving and less avoidance coping (e.g., Cronkite & Moos, 1984; Fleishman, 1984; Holahan & Moos, 1987). In an integrative study, Rippetoe and Rogers (1987) found that the two components of high expectancy of control (outcome and self-efficacy) activate problem solving and inhibit avoidance.

Research also shows that the proximal antecedents of expectancy changes after failure—stable-global attribution (Abramson, Seligman, & Teasdale, 1978)—are related to the use of coping strategies. In two studies, Mikulincer (1989b) and Mikulincer and Solomon (1989) found that the attribution of recalled and actual bad events to more stable-global causes was related to less frequent use of problem-focused coping and more frequent use of cognitive avoidance. Mikulincer (1989b, Study 2) also showed that these links were mediated by the reduction in the expect-

TABLE 4.5. Pearson Correlations of Expectancy of Control and Coping Scores

Study number	Problem solving	Reappraisal	Reorganization	Avoidance
1	.40[b]	.37[a]	−.51[b]	−.31[a]
8	.18	.11	−.19	−.34[a]
9	.49[b]	.16	−.34[a]	−.38[a]
10	.32[a]	.04	−.63[b]	−.51[b]
11	.30[a]	−.12	−.28	−.22
12	.19	.11	−.56[b]	−.45[b]

[a] $p < .05$
[b] $p < .01$

ancy of control. Stable-global attribution reduced expectancy of control, which inhibited problem solving and promoted avoidance.

Six of the LH studies that I present in this book went a step forward and examined the entire spectrum of the four major coping categories within classic LH settings. As can be seen in Table 4.5, Pearson correlations between the reported expectancy of control after helplessness training and scores on the four coping items supported the expectancy–coping link. Most of the studies found that the higher the expectancy of control was, the more likely was the use of problem solving, and the lower the expectancy of control was, the more prone subjects were to rely on avoidance and reorganization coping. Taken together, the findings suggest that the expectancy of control alters the type of coping response people undertake in LH settings.

THE EFFECTS OF EXPECTANCY ON MENTAL RUMINATION

Kuhl (1984) proposed two factors that may underlie the passage from action to state rumination. One is the perceived surmountability of failure: Action thoughts occur as long as the self is perceived as able to overcome the failure. If the failure is perceived as irreversible or the self as too weak to overcome it, the person may give up his or her frustrating attempts to mold the environment and engage in state rumination as a device for accommodating mental structures to the insurmountable reality constraints. The second factor is the degeneration of intentions. When one or more elements of an intention are damaged, the person engages in state rumination aimed at repairing the degenerated intention. In this case, people attempt to assess the state of the intention instead of trying to enact it.

In my terms, Kuhl's ideas reflect the underlying action of the expectancy of control. First, the perceived surmountability of failure is synonymous with the expectancy of control. Evidently, the stronger the belief that one's actions can alter outcomes, the stronger the expectancy of failure reversibility. Second, the expectancy of no control may underlie the damage of intentions. It signals that people believe that action alternatives relevant to ending failure are ineffective—one of Kuhl's definitional features of an ill-defined intention.

One may wonder why Kuhl did not explicitly mention the impact of expectancy on rumination. I believe that in reaction to the overemphasis of the Learned Helplessness theory on the expectancy of control, Kuhl (19981) virtually discarded the construct. Kuhl explained LH deficits as the direct outcome of an excessive engagement in state rumination, regardless of the expectancy of control, and obviated the possible link between state rumination and the expectancy of no control.

Correlational evidence indicates that the frequency of self-preoccupative worry reported in the Worry–Emotionality Scale was inversely related to success expectations of students taking academic exams (e.g., Doctor & Altman, 1969; Liebert & Morris, 1967; Morris & Liebert, 1970). In addition, changes in self-preoccupative worry over time were found to be a function of changes in success expectancy (Doctor & Altman, 1969). Accordingly, Heckhausen (1982) found that the frequency of state thoughts and task-irrelevant thoughts during an examination was inversely related to subjects' success expectancy. A similar result was reported by Mikulincer (1989b) and Stiensmeier-Perlster (1989) in LH studies.

Using a thought sampling method, Klinger, Barta, and Maxeiner (1980) demonstrated that the expectancy of goal attainment is positively related to the frequency of action thoughts. The time people spend thinking about goal attainment increases proportionally with the expectation of attaining the goals. Klinger et al. also found that goals perceived as attainable foster more task-relevant thoughts than goals deemed out of reach.

Another relevant line of research focused on global attribution—one of the proximal antecedents of the expectancy of no control. In two studies, Mikulincer and Nizan (1988) found that subjects who expected no control—that is, who made global attributions for failure, whether by preselection or by manipulation—reported more frequent off-task thoughts (as measured by the CIQ) after helplessness training than those who made task-specific attributions. Moreover, it was only

TABLE 4.6. Pearson Correlations of Expectancy
of Control and Rumination Scores

Study number	Action	State	Task-irrelevant
1	.42[b]	−.43[b]	−.49[b]
8	.11	−.10	−.18
9	.55[b]	−.38[a]	−.50[b]
10	.25	−.35[a]	−.28[a]
11	.41[b]	−.53[b]	−.41[b]
12	−.03	−.56[b]	−.31[a]

[a]$p < .05$
[b]$p < .01$

among the global attributors that the frequency of off-task state thoughts increased following helplessness training.

In six of the LH studies that I present in this book, I went a step further and examined the associations between expectancy and the frequencies of action, state, and task-irrelevant thoughts (as assessed by single items) after helplessness training. Table 4.6 shows that most of the studies found (a) a significant positive correlation between expectancy of control and the frequency of action thoughts, and (b) a significant inverse correlation between expectancy and the frequencies of state thoughts and task-irrelevant thoughts.

EXPECTANCY AND TASK PERFORMANCE

In this section I focus on the contribution of expectancy to LH effects. Though the findings presented in the last section could indicate that expectancy contributes to LH effects because it alters two of the antecedents of task performance (coping actions and mental rumination), we still need direct empirical findings on the expectancy–performance path. My basic assumption is that the expectancy of control is a precursor of task performance following helplessness training. Specifically, the lower the expectancy of control, the worse the subsequent task performance.

The expectancy–performance link is a reflection of the constraints that the cognitive appraisal of a mismatch imposes on the choice of coping actions. Favorable expectancies reflect an appraisal that one can remove the harm from the environment. They thus favor the allocation of coping efforts into problem solving, which in turn may improve task performance. The expectancy of no control reflects an appraisal that one cannot mold the environment in accord with one's aims and that the allocation of coping efforts into task-relevant actions can only enlarge rather than reduce the harms. The expectancy of no control thus favors the adoption of off-task coping, which in turn may be deleterious for task performance.

Some points of agreement and disagreement can be found between my reasoning and the Learned Helplessness theory, which also views the expectancy of no control as a precursor of LH deficits. The Learned Helplessness theory, which is cognitive in nature, argues that the experience of response–outcome noncontingency is not sufficient, and that for performance deficits to appear in the test task, people must come to expect that there is nothing they can do to avoid failure. In other words, they must form an expectancy of no control.

The various reformulations of the Learned Helplessness theory all maintain that the expectancy of no control is a *sufficient* antecedent of performance deficits. As noted above, these reformulations simply add the idea that causal attributions of failure may determine expectancy. Even Abramson, Seligman, and Teasdale (1978) state that "the attribution merely predicts the recurrence of the expectation of no-control but the expectation determines the occurrence of the helplessness deficits. . . . If the expectation is present then helplessness must occur" (p. 59). In other words, the expectation of no control may be stronger when stable and global attributions are made than in other cases, but it is still the expectation that produces the performance deficits.

In Seligman's terms, expectancy influences performance via its impact on the motivation to engage in task attempts. People who believe that they can solve the problem by their own actions are motivated to undertake instrumental problem-solving actions, which prevent performance deficits. People convinced that instrumental actions will be futile, however, have little incentive to do so. Their logical response is to withdraw effort and resources form problem-solving activity, which results in deterioration of performance.

Though similar predictions are derived from my reasoning and from the Learned Helplessness theory, some basic conceptual differences exist between the two accounts. First, they differ as to the explanation of the expectancy–performance link. Whereas Seligman claims that expectancy of no control impairs performance by fostering the abandonment of task attempts, I add the concomitant engagement in off-task coping. In my terms, the expectancy of no control not only causes a reduction in task-relevant activities but also leads people to adopt other off-task coping actions that impair performance. People who expect no control are passive only toward the task; they are still active in their intrapsychic attempts to cope with failure. The problem is that these attempts impair rather than improve performance.

Second, the two accounts differ in their definitions of a person's goals after helplessness training. Implicit in Seligman's ideas is the notion that the individual's goals are *to reassert control and succeed in the task,* and that an expectancy of no control leads them to disengage from these unattainable goals. In my terms, the individual's main goal in LH settings is *to restore the disrupted equilibrium with the environment* and to bring it into a better alignment with his or her goals. The reassertion of control is thus only one means for minimizing the mismatch that helplessness training creates. What the expectancy of no control does, in my view, is redirect coping efforts away from the task. An expectation of no control can reduce people's attempts to reassert control, replacing them with alternative off-task coping means. It does not, however, put an end to coping efforts.

Third, the two accounts differ with regard to the sufficiency of expectancy for explaining performance changes. Whereas Seligman sees expectancy as a sufficient antecedent, I see it as only one of the components of a network of factors that mediate LH effects. In this context, my reasoning shares some common ideas with other theories of human LH that view expectancy as an important but not sufficient antecedent of performance variations (e.g., Carver & Scheier, 1981; Roth, 1980; Wortman & Brehm, 1975; Zuroff, 1980). These theories claim that the detrimental effects of the expectancy of no control depend on other psychological processes, such as the perceived value of the training and test tasks or the individual's focus of attention.

Despite the above divergences, both my reasoning and Seligman's theory oppose theories that have tried to dismiss the expectancy–performance link completely and to replace it with other explanations for task performance, such as the arousal of inner tension (e.g., Lavelle et al., 1979), engagement in self-focused cognitions (e.g., Kuhl, 1981), or the use of self-protective devices (e.g., Frankel & Snyder, 1978). The problem with these theories is that they do not take into account the possibility that expectancy can affect performance indirectly through its associations with other factors. In addition, they fail to consider the possibility that expectancy may interact with these factors in determining LH effects.

In the coming subsections I review evidence on the expectancy–performance link. I present three sets of findings: (a) correlations between reports of the expectancy of control in a task and subsequent performance in that task; (b) the performance effects of two proximal antecedents of expectancy change, stability, and globality attributions; and (c) the performance reactions of subjects preselected on the basis of their habitual expectancy of control.

The Expectancy–Performance Correlation

Starting with the pioneering work of Tolman (1932), researchers have consistently reported a positive correlation between expectancy of success/control and performance. Almost without exception, unfavorable expectancy is said to impair temporarily otherwise normal performance in achievement, educational, organizational, and sport settings (see Eccles, 1983; Kirsch, 1986; Pintrich, 1989; Schunk, 1985; Wurtele, 1986, for reviews). This conclusion applies for expectancy of success, expectancy of control, and self-efficacy expectancy.

Multon, Brown, and Lent (1991) conducted a meta-analysis of 39 studies that assessed the impact of self-efficacy expectancy on academic performance and persistence. Results indicate a significant positive association between expectancy and performance across a wide variety of samples, designs, and assessment techniques. Overall, results from the 39 studies reviewed show that self-efficacy expectancy accounts for 14% of academic performance variance and 12% of academic persistence variance. This effect of self-efficacy expectancy is especially pronounced when pursuing a course of action involves overcoming setbacks, failures, and obstacles.

Though it provides converging evidence of the association between expectancy and task performance, the above research has a number of weaknesses. First of all, the studies used a correlational design, which cannot rule out the possibility that the decision as to how much effort to expend on a task is an antecedent rather than a consequence of expectancy (Kukla, 1972). It is also likely that prior performance feedback had affected subjects' expectancies, thereby producing the reported correlations. In addition, the studies do not consider the possibility that the measurement of expectancy is a reactive procedure that may alter subsequent performance. Dweck and Gilliard (1975) and Sherman, Skov, Hervitz, and Stock (1981) found

TABLE 4.7. Pearson Correlations of
Expectancy of Control and Accuracy

Study number	Performance accuracy
1	.63[b]
8	.37[a]
9	.46[b]
10	.39[b]
11	.22
12	.48[b]

[a]$p < .05$
[b]$p < .01$

that following an actual or hypothetical failure, only subjects who explicitly stated their expectancies exhibited subsequent performance deficits.

A number of studies have attempted to overcome the above weaknesses by using different methodological strategies. There are studies that experimentally manipulated expectancies and found that persons given favorable expectancies in a task performed more successfully than those given unfavorable expectancies (e.g., Dickstein & Kephart, 1972; Feather, 1966). Other studies demonstrated that when stable individual differences in past accomplishments or some index of ability (IQ scores) are controlled, expectancy still predicts subsequent task performance (e.g., Battle, 1966). In fact, Battle (1966) found that students with low IQ but high success expectancy for academic tasks achieved better grades than subjects with high IQ who held unfavorable expectancies.

LH literature also contains correlational evidence that supports the hypothe-sized expectancy–performance link. For example, Brown and Inouye (1978) found that the lower the expectancy of self-efficacy after helplessness training, the less the persistence in a subsequent task. A significant correlation between self-reported low expectancy of success/control following helplessness training and deficits in test task performance has been also reported in some of my published studies (Mik-ulincer, 1986a, b, 1988b, 1990) as well as in most of the studies that I present in this book (see Table 4.7). Although a number of LH studies fail to find that correlation (Kuhl, 1981; Mikulincer, 1988b, 1989a), it may be that they incorporate situational and personal factors (attentional focus, coping strategies) that sever the expectancy–performance link.

Stable–Unstable Attribution and Performance

The expectancy–performance link can also be examined by measuring and/or manipulating the attributional antecedents of expectancy change—the stability and globality dimensions. The idea is that if an expectancy of no control impairs task performance after helplessness training, its proximal antecedents should also impair performance. Therefore stable-global attributions, which reduce the expectancy of control, should produce stronger LH deficits than unstable-specific attributions. In this subsection I present pertinent data on the stability dimension; the next subsection reviews evidence on the effects of the globality dimension.

Research on the performance effects of stable–unstable attribution began with studies that preselected subjects on the basis of their attributional style and measured their performance after failure. This strategy was first implemented by Dweck and Repucci (1973), who found that by the age of about 10 years, a tendency to attribute failure to the stable cause of ability (as measured by the Intellectual Achievement Responsibility [IAR] Scale) leads children to react to failure in unsolvable block designs by giving up on subsequent solvable puzzles. In contrast, children who habitually tend to attribute failure to the modifiable quality of effort persist in the task after failure. The findings were replicated in studies on children's cognitive and social functioning (e.g., Goetz & Dweck, 1980; Johnson, 1981; Licht & Dweck, 1984).

The hypothesized effects of stable attribution on LH deficits were also found in two studies of Diener and Dweck (1978, 1980) that assessed free verbalizations and the use of hypothesis-testing strategies in solvable and unsolvable problems. In the solvable problems, stable and unstable attributors (according to the IAR) showed similar verbalizations and hypothesis testing strategies. With the onset of unsolvable problems, however, two distinct patterns rapidly emerged. First, whereas unstable attributors verbalized thoughts reflecting hope of goal attainment, stable attributors appeared to lose hope. Second, unstable attributors verbalized an increasing quantity of action and problem-solving thoughts, whereas stable attributors verbalized frequent off-task thoughts. Third, stable attributors used ineffectual strategies more often than unstable attributors and showed a progressive decrease of useful strategies across failure trials. In contrast, most of the unstable attributors showed no such decline, and some of them even showed a tendency to use increasingly sophisticated strategies. These findings led Dweck and Licht (1980) to conclude that "children who show deterioration of performance in the face of failure have a greater tendency to attribute their failures to stable factors and that those who show enhanced performance under failure tend to choose attributions to more variable factors" (p. 198).

Similar findings have been obtained in adult samples (e.g., Belgrave, Johnson, & Carey, 1985; Kistner, Osborne, & LeVerrier, 1988). Using the Attributional Style Questionnaire (ASQ), for example, C. Peterson and Barrett (1987) reported that students who explain failure with stable causes at the beginning of a school year tend to obtain poorer grades that year than unstable attributors, even when assessments of ability level are held constant. In the LH context, Seligman, Nolen-Hoeksema, Thornton, and Thornton (1990) have shown that subjects who tend to attribute bad events to stable causes (in the ASQ) performed worse after failure than unstable attributors.

The conclusion that stable–unstable attribution affects task performance has been strongly reinforced in experiments that overcome the flaws of correlational research. Instead of asking whether attribution is linked to performance (an association that can be caused by numerous uncontrolled factors), these studies attempt to show that altering attribution produces corresponding changes in performance.

Using this research strategy, Dweck (1975) identified 12 fifth graders who attributed failure to lack of ability, exposed them to recurrent success (success-only treatment) or to 20% of failure trials that were attributed by the experimenter to low effort (attribution retraining), and assessed their math performance after failure. Children encouraged to attribute failure to unstable causes had fewer performance deficits after failure than they had in their pretraining performance; 5 out of 6 actually showed superior math performance following failure than preceding it. In contrast, children in the success-only treatment showed no consistent improvement in performance but continued to display performance deficits after failure. These findings demonstrate that attributional tendencies can be altered by environmental information, that children can be taught to attribute failure to unstable causes, and most important, that attributional training has an impact on performance after failure.

Dweck's germinal study was followed by a wealth of studies which found that subjects who were convinced to make unstable attributions showed better functioning and proved more resilient to the detrimental effects of failure than subjects not so persuaded (see Forsterling, 1985, for a review). These positive effects of effort-attribution training have been found in cognitive performance (e.g., Noel, Forsyth, & Kelley, 1987; Wilson & Linville, 1982, 1985; Zoeller, Mahoney, & Weiner, 1983), task persistence (e.g., Andrews & Debus, 1978; Chapin & Dyck, 1976; Fowler & Peterson, 1981), the use of metacognitive strategies (Borkowski, Weyhing, & Carr, 1988; Reid & Borkowski, 1987), social performance (Aydin, 1988), persuasion ability (Anderson, 1983), and sport performance (Grove & Pargman, 1986). In addition, these effects have been derived not only from a persuasive experimenter's message but also from vicarious and self-instructional training (e.g., Craske, 1985). Some of the studies, however, also indicate that such individual differences as gender, locus of control, and motivation to protect self-esteem should be taken into account when analyzing the effects of the induction of unstable attribution (e.g., Craske, 1988; Lanoue & Curtis, 1985; Perry & Penner, 1990).

Some of these studies also clear the effects of attribution from alternative interpretations, such as schedule of reinforcement (Chapin & Dyck, 1976; Meyer & Dyck, 1986). In Dweck's study, the experimental groups differed not only in the attributional messages they received but also in their schedules of reinforcement. Whereas the attribution training group received an intermitent schedule of success and failure, the control group received only success feedback. Because intermittent reinforcement increases behavioral persistence (e.g., see Amsel, 1972), the relative contribution of attributional change and the intermittent schedule to performance improvement after treatment was unclear. By maintaining the schedule of reinforcement constant across the experimental groups, subsequent attribution training studies rule out the alternative interpretation and provide evidence for the unique effect of the induction of unstable attribution.

A number of problems, however, weaken the conclusions of attributional training studies. Forsterling (1985) noted that most of the studies do not examine (a) the differential effects of attribution for success and for failure, (b) the generalization of the effects of attribution training across tasks, (c) the relative effectiveness of different training techniques (e.g., persuasion versus modeling), and (d) the psychological processes by which attribution training influences behavior. In addition, Forsterling claimed that the studies cannot rule out the possibility that the results result from demand characteristics. Subjects may well have interpreted the message that their failure was caused by lack of effort as an order to try harder. Despite these criticisms, however, Forsterling concludes that "attributional retraining methods have been consistently successful in increasing persistence and performance" (p. 509).

The attribution training studies suffer two additional flaws. One is that the manipulation of ability versus effort attributions may have led to the confounding of stable–unstable attribution with other attributional dimensions (e.g., globality and internality), leaving unanswered the question of which attributional dimension was responsible for the observed performance effects. Second, most of the studies reviewed above do not provide compelling evidence for the hypothesis that stable attribution accounts for the performance effects of helplessness training. No evidence was provided as to whether attributional manipulations moderated the performance differences between helplessness training and control conditions.

To overcome these flaws, I (Mikulincer, 1988b, 1990) sought evidence for the role of stable attribution in the LH paradigm (a) by directly manipulating and/or measuring the stability dimension while holding other self-reported attributions constant, and (b) by analyzing the performance effects of helplessness training (relative to control conditions) separately for stable and unstable attributors. The results accorded with the predicted effects of stable–unstable attribution. Following helplessness training, subjects who made stable attributions, whether by preselection or induction, showed worse task performance than subjects who made unstable attributions. More important, helplessness training impaired test task performance among subjects who made stable attributions, but not among those who were believed that failure was unstable. These effects were also found when self-reports of other attributional dimensions (e.g., globality, internality) were kept constant, implying an independent performance effect of the stability dimension.

In these studies, the link between stable attribution and performance was further supported by two additional findings. First, self-reports of stable attribution of failure in helplessness training were significantly related to performance deficits.

Second, both subjects who received no attributional information and nondefined attributors actually made a stable attribution for their failure and exhibited performance deficits following unsolvable problems. Although they did not have a stable attributional style and were not encouraged to make a stable attribution, it was their spontaneous stable attribution that led to the impairment in performance.

Indirect evidence for the hypothesized effects of stable attribution was provided by a developmental LH study conducted by Rholes, Blackwell, Jordan, and Walters (1980). Rholes et al. predicted that younger children would be less susceptible than older ones to the detrimental effects of failure, because they would not yet view failure as having stable implications for future performance (Nicholls, 1978; Parsons & Ruble, 1977). The results supported this prediction and indicated that failure brought about performance deficits in a hidden-figure test among fifth graders but not among younger children. In other words, helplessness training did not impair performance until children acquired the cognitive capacity to make stable attributions.

Dweck's work on sex differences in the LH paradigm provides further indirect evidence for the effects of stable attribution (Dweck & Bush, 1976; Dweck, Davidson, Nelson, & Enna, 1978; Dweck, Goetz, & Strauss, 1980). Generally speaking, girls have been found to show stronger LH deficits than boys. So if a stable attribution of failure and an expectancy of no control underlie these deficits, one should find corresponding sex differences in attribution and expectancy variables.

In keeping with this prediction, Dweck and her colleagues, as well as Erkut (1983) and Stipeck (1984), found that girls are more likely than boys to make a stable attribution for failure and to expect less success/control for a new task after helplessness training. Moreover, some aspects of the classroom situation appear to foster a stable attribution of poor intellectual performance among girls and to inhibit the same attribution among boys. Whereas teachers tend to give diffuse negative feedback on nonintellectual aspects of boys' behavior and to attribute boys' failure to lack of effort, they tend to give clear negative feedback on intellectual features of girls' work and to attribute girls' failure to lack of intellectual ability (e.g., see Dweck et al., 1978). Whether sex differences in attribution result from socialization in achievement situations or specific features of these situations, it seems that girls who show performance deficits after helplessness training are likely to make stable attributions.

GLOBAL–SPECIFIC ATTRIBUTION AND TASK PERFORMANCE

Evidence on the effects of global attribution comes exclusively from laboratory LH experiments. Alloy et al. (1984) exposed global and specific attributors (according to ASQ scores) to either no, escapable, or inescapable noise and tested them at one of two tasks: one similar to the training task (noise escape task), and the other a dissimilar task (anagrams). Inescapable noise impaired the noise escape performance of both global and specific attributors; however, it impaired anagram performance only among global attributors. Conceptually similar findings were reported in three other LH experiments that manipulated global–specific attribution in helplessness training (Anderson, Anderson, Fleming, & Kinghorn, 1983; Mikulincer, 1986a; Pasahow, 1980). On the whole, helplessness training, as compared to no feedback, impaired performance in dissimilar tasks only among subjects who made global attributions, whether by preselection or induction.

A similar research strategy was used by Miller and Norman (1981) in assessing whether "success feedback" therapy could reverse the detrimental effects of helplessness training. Subjects previously exposed to inescapable noise received either global or specific attribution for successful performance in a social intelligence task, and then their anagram performance was assessed. As predicted, success significantly improved anagram performance only among subjects who were instructed to make global attributions, but not among those who received a task-specific attribution.

In drawing a more integrative picture of attributional effects, I (Mikulincer, 1986a, Experiment 2) assessed the interactive effects of manipulations of global and stable attributions on task performance after helplessness training. Because both attributions contribute to the formation of the expectancy of no control for the test task, it was predicted that helplessness training would impair performance only when failure was attributed to both stable and global causes. In keeping with these predictions, unsolvable problems (as compared to control conditions) impaired performance only among subjects in the global-stable condition. No performance deficit was found among subjects encouraged to attribute failure to either unstable or specific causes.

These findings enable us to formulate the following sequence of mediating events: The causal attribution that subjects make for failure affects their expectancy of control, which in turn affects subsequent performance. Subjects who make global-stable attributions expect the causes of failure to persist and expect failure to recur after a longer lapse of time and across more dissimilar settings than subjects who make specific or unstable attribution. This effect on expectancy is in turn reflected in task performance.

Disconfirming Attributional Findings

Although the induction of stable-global attribution has been consistently found to impair performance following helplessness training, some studies have found no significant correlations between self-reported attributions and performance. For example, Pasahow (1980) and Mikulincer (1986a) found only a weak correlation between subjects' self-reported global attribution for failure in helplessness training and their subsequent performance. Covington and Omerlich (1979, 1984) similarly found that self-reports of lack of ability attribution for academic failure were not correlated with subsequent performance.

Similar disconfirming findings were reported in a series of studies published in

1982 in the *Journal of Personality* that assessed the role of cognitive processes in the LH paradigm. For example, Oakes and Curtis (19982) found that although subjects exposed to helplessness training performed worse than controls, the two groups made similar attributions to ability, effort, task difficulty, and luck. Tennen, Gillen, and Drum (1982) and Tennen, Drum, et al. (1982) found that attributions of failure along the internality, stability, and globality dimensions were not correlated with task performance.

Nonetheless, these disconfirming findings pose only a limited challenge to the hypothesized expectancy–performance link. There are many fewer negative than positive findings to date, and those that are available are not all that strong. None of the *Journal of Personality* studies, for example, directly assessed the expectancy of control after helplessness training. More generally, all the disconfirming results are compromised by the use of single questions to assess attribution. The reliability and validity of these questions is unknown, and there is evidence that single-item measures tend to be unreliable (Campbell & Fiske, 1959). This problem is highlighted by the fact that reliable and valid multiple-item measures of causal attribution have yielded more supportive findings (e.g., Alloy et al., 1984; Mikulincer, 1988a, b). The findings of Covington and Omerlich (1979, 1984) and Oakes and Curtis (1982) are also compromised by the assessment of particular causes rather than causal dimensions per se.

GENERALIZED EXPECTANCY OF CONTROL

Another line of research that focuses on the expectancy–performance link examines the role of the personality dimension of internal–external locus of control (Rotter, 1966). "Internals" tend habitually to expect that they can influence outcome by their behaviors, whereas "externals" tend to regard outcome as independent of their actions. If expectancy of no control produces LH deficits, externals (who are prone to expect lack of control) should show worse performance following helplessness training than internals (who are less likely to perceive lack of control).

Three early LH studies seem to support this prediction. Hiroto (1974) exposed internals and externals (on Rotter's scale) to either no, escapable, or inescapable noise and found that the exposure to inescapable noise impaired subsequent avoidance learning only among externals, but not among internals. Cohen et al. (1976) and Albert and Geller (1978) similarly exposed internals and externals (on Rotter's scale) to success or failure in cognitive problems, and they found that the deteriorating effects of failure on performance were more pervasive among externals than internals.

All these studies, however, suffer from methodological problems that limit their conclusions. According to Gregory, Chartier, and Wright (1979), subjects in Hiroto's study were not informed as to whether they had terminated the noise by their own responses or whether it ended automatically. Consequently internal subjects, who habitually tend to perceive control over outcomes, may have thought that at least some of their responses were effective in ending the inescapable noise, and this partial reinforcement may have favored persistence in the test task. The Albert and Geller (1978) and Cohen et al. (1976) studies suffer from the absence of a no-feedback condition; they compared the effects of failure only to the effect of success. Thus their finding that externals performed better after success than after failure can be attributed to performance enhancement after success or to performance decrement after failure.

To overcome these problems, Gregory et al. (1979) replicated Hiroto's procedure and manipulations but added a response-contingency light to the training apparatus that indicated to the subjects whether or not their responses put an end to the noise. Unexpectedly, results showed that inescapable noise produced worse performance than no noise only among internals, whereas among externals, escapable noise improved performance and inescapable noise had no effect. In addition, internals performed worse than externals after helplessness training. Similar results were obtained by Benson and Kenelly (1976), who exposed internals and externals (on Levenson's scale) to either no, solvable, or unsolvable cognitive problems.

Pittman and Pittman (1979) extended the research by assessing the performance of internals and externals after either small and large amounts of helplessness training. Internals showed significant better anagram performance after two unsolvable problems than after none, and worse performance after six unsolvable problems. Externals showed weaker performance variations as a result of both small and large amounts of helplessness training. Generally speaking, internals appear to be more susceptible than externals to both the positive and detrimental effects of helplessness training.

At the first sight, these findings are at odds with those derived from studies on the performance effects of expectancy and causal attribution. Although the latter studies found the strongest detrimental effects of helplessness training among subjects who expected no control for the subsequent tasks, the locus of control studies found that internals, who are unlikely to perceive and to expect lack of control, showed the worst performance following a large amount of failure.

Analysis of postexperimental questionnaires in the locus of control studies, however, indicates that externals and internals did not differ in their estimations of the control they had in the training and test tasks. Although internals and externals were differently predisposed to perceive and expect control, both groups were convinced after helplessness training that they could not control the current outcomes. It thus appears that internals recognized the current lack of control as well as externals, but performed worse anyway. In other words, one cannot say that internals' deficits were produced without the concomitant perception of lack of control. This pattern of findings changes the questions that locus of control studies raise about the role of the expectancy. Instead of asking why performance deficits are found among subjects who do not expect lack of control (i.e., internals), they ask why it is possible that people who expect lack of control (i.e., externals) show no performance deficits after helplessness training.

The externals' resilience to the effects of helplessness training can be explained by the congruence between their prior expectancy of no control and the lack of control they experienced in the training task. Furthermore, this prior expectancy of no control may heighten their sensitivity to response–outcome noncontingency, may facilitate the recognition of the objective uncontrollability, and may create a state of universal helplessness. Internals, though, who generally believe that they can potentially control events, may find it difficult to recognize objective noncontingency and thus may tend to interpret any failure in terms of their lack of self-efficacy. These differential interpretations (of universal helplessness versus personal helplessness) may be reflected in performance variations.

This line of reasoning implies that the expectancy of no control may impair performance following helplessness training only when it reflects a sense of personal helplessness. The belief that some objective noncontingency is responsible for the experienced lack of control may mitigate the detrimental effects of helplessness training, even after the formation of the expectancy of no control. This possibility goes against Abramson, Seligman, and Teasdale's (1978) hypothesis of the sufficiency of the expectancy of no control. It may be that expectancy is an important contributor to LH effects, but that other factors—such a sense of personal helplessness—may also be involved.

Study 8 of the studies presented in this book (see Table 1.1 for details) corroborates the above reasoning and shows that generalized low expectancy of self-efficacy prior to helplessness training prones the person to LH deficits. Subjects were preselected according to their expectancies of self-efficacy in cognitive tasks, and their performance was assessed in a letter cancellation task after failure or no feedback in four unsolvable problems. Findings indicate that helplessness training produced less accurate task performance than no feedback only among low self-efficacy subjects (see Table 4.8). Persons holding favorable expectancies were impervious to LH effects and performed better after failure than those holding unfavorable expectancies.

Similar conclusions can be drawn from studies assessing self-esteem, a personality correlate of self-efficacy expectancies. These studies have consistently shown that people with high self-esteem expect to succeed more than people with low self-

TABLE 4.8. Means and Standard Deviations of Performance Accuracy by Feedback and Problem-Solving Self-Efficacy (Study 8)

| | No feedback | | Failure | |
	Low	High	Low	High
Mean	84.90	82.80	67.70	81.00
Standard deviation	6.13	8.50	12.35	8.95

esteem (e.g., McFarlin & Blascovich, 1981) and that this expectational difference is manifested in their task performance after failure (e.g., McFarlin, Baumeister, & Blascovich, 1984; Shrauger & Rosenberg, 1970; Shrauger & Sorman, 1977). Specifically, subjects holding unfavorable expectancies (low self-esteem) have been found to perform more poorly after failure than subjects with favorable expectancies (high self-esteem). In addition, the latter subjects seem to respond to failure with increased effort and persistence, even when such a response is not productive.

CONCLUSIONS

The findings reviewed throughout this chapter support the hypothesis that the expectancy of control is one of the mediators of LH effects. High control expectancy is maintained after a small amount of failure, and it seems to underlie performance facilitation. An expectancy of no control is mainly formed after a large amount of training, and it seems to underlie the observed performance deficits. Moreover, these performance effects may reflect the role of expectancy in the coping process. The expectancy of control seems to influence task performance by directing coping efforts toward or away from the task. People holding favorable expectancies are convinced that they could cope with failure by task-relevant actions; they may then be prone to undertake problem solving, which in turn may improve task performance. People holding unfavorable expectancies are convinced that they should adopt off-task coping if they want to manage the threats created by failure. Thus they may be prone to undertake avoidance or reorganization coping, which in turn would be manifested in LH deficits.

The effects of expectancy on performance have a secondary but important implication for understanding human LH: The link creates a self-exacerbating cycle of maladjustment. Poor performance in helplessness training reduces the expectancy of control for the test task, which leads to poorer performance, which further reduces the expectancy, and so on. In this way, people may develop a maladaptive pattern of mutually reinforcing poor performance and negative expectancy that can be difficult to break.

EMOTIONAL AROUSAL
AS A DISTAL MEDIATOR
OF LH EFFECTS

Chapter 4 examined the expectancy of control, the first of two hypothesized distal mediators of LH effects. This chapter focuses on the second distal mediator: emotional arousal. In my conceptualization of human LH, emotion serves to sustain and augment the effects of helplessness training on coping and task performance. Emotion is evoked by helplessness training as an adaptive device that motivates the person to undertake the coping activities cued by the expectancy of control. Emotion is an important part of the coping process: It strengthens the link between expectancy and the person's chosen coping strategies, and it indirectly contributes to task performance via the coping activities that it reinforces and sustains.

I propose three basic hypotheses on the mediating role of emotion in human LH. First, emotions are aroused following helplessness training as a response to the person–environment mismatch and the consequent threats produced by failure. Second, the particular emotion that one experiences depends on one's expectancy of control. A high expectancy of control evokes anger after failure, the emotional expression of the conviction that one can destroy the obstacles that produce a mismatch (Lazarus, 1991). A low expectancy of control evokes anxiety and depression, the emotional expressions of the conviction that one has no available response to overcome a failure and restore a loss (Lazarus, 1991). Third, emotions reinforce and sustain coping activities and thereby contribute to the performance changes that these activities produce. Anger strengthens problem solving and subsequent reactance. Anxiety and depression strengthen off-task coping and subsequent LH deficits. The current chapter is organized around these three hypotheses and develops a coherent theoretical framework that incorporates the role of emotion in human LH.

A WORKING MODEL OF THE EMOTION SYSTEM

Emotions are one of the most central aspects of human experience. They are organismic responses to personally relevant events, and they can influence the individual's motives, thoughts, and actions. Historically emotions have been conceptualized alternatively as an adaptational device (see Plutchik, 1980, for a review) and as a primary source of human problems (Arnold, 1960; Young, 1961). Some authors have thus related emotions to the adaptive organization of perception, memory, and behavior (e.g., Izard, 1977), whereas others have taken the position that emotions play a central role in the development of psychopathology (e.g., Rapaport, 1942). The romantic tradition assumes that emotion is the most important and challenging human experience, whereas the view that emotion and intellect are contradictory links emotion to psychopathology and cognitive interference.

In psychology, theoretical and empirical attempts have been made to delineate the basic features of emotion-arousing events, to understand the psychological processes that determine the intensity and quality of emotional responses, and to examine the cognitive and behavioral consequences of emotion. Attention has been focused on a wide array of antecedents of emotional arousal, such as obtained and anticipated outcomes and the interruption of activities. Studies have also been conducted on the influence of emotion on helping, judgment, decision making, and problem solving (for reviews see Isen, 1987).

Recent attempts (e.g., Lazarus, 1991) to integrate theoretical and empirical knowledge about emotion with a theory of coping suggest that emotion plays an important role in the coping process. Emotion is considered to be a compound of physiological and subjective reactions to the appraisal of the personal gains and losses implied in a person–environment transaction and to serve the function of motivating and preparing the person to cope with the transaction (e.g., to maximize benefits and to minimize losses). In other words, the entire emotional response—including physiological activity and subjective affect—is believed to be organized around the appraisal of a transaction with the environment and the need to cope with that transaction.

These ideas apply equally to "negative" and "positive" emotions. The so-called negative emotions may motivate people to remove the source of harm from the environment or to accommodate to reality constraints if the latter are seen as intractable. The so-called positive emotions may support attempts to maintain and reinforce the fit with the environment that the person has attained. They may motivate people to improve their situation and to increase their mastery and gains.

I adopt the view that emotion is a coping device, but I add that it may sometimes have a disorganizing and paralyzing effect. My approach is based on four postulates. First, emotion fulfills important functions in the service of adaptation. Second, the appraisal of the person–environment transaction organizes the emotional experience. Third, emotion embodies action tendencies that motivate the person to cope with environmental demands. Fourth, some emotions may at times fragment thought and disrupt coping actions. Each of these postulates will be considered in turn.

THE ADAPTATIONAL FUNCTION OF EMOTION

Most theorists and researchers agree that emotional arousal serves important functions in adaptation and survival (see Fridja, 1986; Lazarus, 1991; Plutchik, 1980, for reviews). From an evolutionary perspective, they hold that emotion is not an irrational and bizarre component of the human mental apparatus but, to the contrary, a functional response in the process of coping with adversity that helps people in their struggle to maintain an equilibrium between reality constraints and their personal desires. In general, they believe that emotion mediates between environmental stimuli and behavioral responses, facilitates the flexible organization of appropriate coping responses, and sustains these responses until adaptation and survival are assured (e.g., Fridja, 1986; Izard, 1977; Lazarus, 1991; Mandler, 1975).

More specifically, it can be said that emotion helps people in responding to environmental events that demand adaptive changes in behavior (see Fridja, 1986; Lazarus, 1991). This is because emotional arousal is responsive to person–environment transactions that impose urgent action demands on the organism (e.g., to fight, to flee) and functions as an auxiliary mechanism that motivates the person to undertake the required activities. According to Tomkins (1962), emotional arousal amplifies and catalyzes action demands; according to Mandler (1975), it acts as a "backward warning system" signaling that pertinent activities should continue until the demands are met or some relevant change takes place. Lazarus (1991) similarly suggests that emotion sustains the shift of attention toward the adaptational requirements of a situation and the execution of appropriate actions. According to Mandler (1975), emotional arousal is a psychological alarm bell that warns people that something of personal importance is at stake and prompts them to direct cognitive resources toward the person–environment transaction in order to determine its meaning and personal implications and to decide on the type of actions they should take to cope with that transaction. It may also ensure that people are prepared to fight or flee whenever they are required to do so, thereby keeping them in an emergency alert ready to undertake immediate coping actions if it seems that the latter may facilitate adaptation.

COGNITIVE APPRAISAL AND EMOTION

In recent years, theory and research on emotion have focused on the relations between emotion and cognitive appraisal (e.g., Fridja, 1986; Lazarus, 1991; Roseman, 1984; Scherer, 1984; Shaver, Schwartz, Kirson, & O'Connor, 1987; Smith, 1990). Scholars have proposed a causal path by which the nature and intensity of emotions depend on people's assessment of the adaptational significance of their transaction with the environment. The cognitive appraisal of the personal significance of a transaction is based on both the features and demands of the environment and the person's goals and beliefs, and it underlies the instigation of emotion. It is the "appraisal" (Arnold, 1960; Lazarus, 1991), "meaning analysis" (Fridja, 1986; Mandler, 1975), or "evaluation check" (Scherer, 1984) of the transaction rather than the objective features of the situation that give rise to and shape particular emotions.

To be sure, only those cognitions that have a direct impact on the coping process are considered precursors of emotions. Smith (1990) and Lazarus (1991) focus on two global appraisals originally proposed in Lazarus and Folkman's (1984) theory of stress and coping: primary and secondary appraisals. *Primary appraisal* is the appraisal of the relevance of a transaction to the person's endeavors, and it determines whether or not emotions are aroused. Emotions would be aroused to support relevant coping actions only when people appraise that there is something of personal importance at stake and feel the need to cope with the mismatch. *Secondary appraisal* is the appraisal of the resources and options the person has for coping with the mismatch; it would determine the type of emotions that are aroused. More specifically, the idea is that because secondary appraisal is what tells the person which coping actions are available and/or appropriate under the circumstances, it would elicit these emotions that are specialized in sustaining the chosen actions.

Lazarus (1991) went a step further and stated that each distinct emotion may reflect a distinct "core relational theme." These themes correspond to the type of personal harm or benefit implied in the person–environment transaction, each of which has different implications for the coping process. That is, the themes summarize the meaning of the transaction in terms of harms and benefits. For example, the categorical evaluation that one is facing an assault to self-esteem may produce anger, whereas the categorical evaluation that one is suffering an irrevocable loss produces sadness (Lazarus, 1991).

Emotion and Coping Actions

From an evolutionary perspective, emotions are phylogenetically and ontogenetically developed around the activation and preservation of particular types of action. Each involves distinct physiological patterns and motor programs that prepare the person to cope with the appraised environmental requirements (Fridja, 1986; Lazarus, 1991). Each emotion propels the person to respond to a transaction with the environment in a particular way—anxiety to flee or avoid, anger to attack, and so forth.

The link between emotion and coping actions seems to be mediated by what Lazarus (1991) calls "action tendencies" and Fridja (1986) calls "states of action readiness." These tendencies are components of emotion. They consist of prewired action patterns and physiological responses that underlie particular coping responses. In Fridja's terms, action tendencies characterize emotions and differentiate them from nonemotional experiences, link experience to behavior, and control action and thought.

THE DISORGANIZING EFFECTS OF EMOTION

Some emotions, as noted earlier, may sometimes fragment thought and disrupt coping activities (Lazarus, 1991). This idea is already implicit in theoretical statements that emotions may sometimes create adjustment problems (e.g., Arnold, 1960; Young, 1961) and interfere with cognitive activities (e.g., Hamilton, 1975; Sarason, 1975), in theories that view emotion as inferior to the higher mental processes of reason (Rapaport, 1942), and in theories that emphasize the uncontrollability of emotion (e.g., Arnold, 1960; Tomkins, 1962).

In their analysis of the coping process, Lazarus and Folkman (1984) combine the view that emotions are signals for initiating coping actions with the understanding that some emotions, such as anxiety, may interfere with coping. Thus they propose that emotion may either alert the person to make adaptive changes or provoke a strong physiological discharge that overwhelms the cognitive system and impedes adaptation. Mandler (1975) similarly proposes that emotion can either be adaptive—by ensuring analysis of the interruption for which appropriate actions must be taken—or lead to mental disorganization if people become convinced that they cannot end the interruption. Emotionally, this conviction is experienced as anxiety: "One becomes immobilized in a truly fundamental state of helplessness, unable to move but continuously subject to an extremely painful state of anxiety or distress which is unrelieved by any kind of organized behavior" (Mandler, 1972, p. 372).

In my terms, emotion becomes an *interfering force* when people believe that they cannot resolve a mismatch by either alloplastic or autoplastic means and decide to avoid any direct or symbolic confrontation with it. People for whom emotion acts as an internal stimulus that recalls both the unresolved mismatch and their own weaknesses and vulnerability may perceive emotion as an uninvited intruder that counteracts their avoidance coping. They may also experience their emotions as overwhelming and disorganizing forces that demand that they resolve the mismatch, which is precisely what they feel they cannot do. In this case, emotions do not facilitate adaptation and mastery but rather reflect failure of control and flooding, and they may disorganize the person's avoidance activities. Even when emotion impedes avoidance, however, it may still have a coping function: It may paradoxically propel people to restore their defense barriers and strengthen their avoidance attempts.

One can delineate the following sequences of emotional events. On the one hand, when people appraise themselves as capable of making the response needed to end the mismatch, particular emotions are evoked to reinforce and sustain alloplastic or autoplastic coping responses. These emotions would remain active until the disrupted equilibrium is restored. With the end of the mismatch, emotion loses its adaptive function and ceases. In this case, emotion is a functional device that contributes to coping and adaptation. On the other hand, when people appraise themselves as unable to resolve the mismatch, particular emotions are evoked to reinforce and sustain avoidance coping. The emotions, however, are then themselves affected by both the avoidance coping they strengthen and by the intrusion of autonomic failure-related thoughts into consciousness. Avoidance suppresses the emotion because it recalls the unresolved mismatch; the autonomic failure-related thoughts that intrude into consciousness with every recollection of the mismatch may rearouse it. Thus the rearoused emotion is now experienced as an unwanted intruder that disrupts the person's coping activities. At the same time, though, it would intensify avoidance efforts to again suppress the disrupting emotion and the autonomic thoughts until new stimuli reactivate them. In this way, a self-exacerbating cycle of avoidance and dysfunctional emotion is created that may increasingly constrict functioning and recurrently lead to mental disorganization.

THE EMOTIONAL EFFECTS OF HELPLESSNESS TRAINING

Is helplessness training an emotion-arousing event? In this section I focus on my first hypothesis: that helplessness training evokes emotions. I explain the rationale of the hypothesis, present the positions taken by a number of theories of human LH, and review pertinent evidence.

THE AROUSAL OF EMOTION

The idea that helplessness training is a precursor of emotional arousal is directly derived from the concept of emotion as a coping device. In my terms, emotions may be aroused after helplessness training as a part of the individual's attempts to cope with the uncontrollable failure. First of all, the failure's interruption of pre-established plans may evoke emotion as an auxiliary to ending that interruption. Then, as repeated failure repeatedly negates the value of actions identified as potential means of putting an end to the interruption, emotion might remain unabated throughout the helplessness training. According to Mandler (1975), emotions are typically experienced in situations wherein people's actions are interrupted, their expectations are not realized, and/or their cognitive schemas are proven inadequate. Emotion continues until either the source of the interruption is removed or a substitute response allows the completion of the interrupted action.

The cognitive discrepancies created by helplessness training between the actual course of events and the person's goals, between reality and expectations, and among diverse self-representations (see Chapter 1) may also evoke emotion. Lazarus (1991) contends that negative emotions are evoked by person–environment transactions that are discrepant with the person's goals. Abelson (1983) argues that emotion follows an expectancy–outcome discrepancy: Negative emotions are evoked when a goal-oriented plan leading to a desirable outcome is construed in imagination but the real outcome is undesirable. Accordingly, Higgins (1987) suggests that discrepancies among various aspects of the self underlie the arousal of emotions. He argues that negative emotions arise in situations that create two types of self-discrepancies: one between the actual self and the ideal self that the person wishes to be, the other between the actual self and the self that the person feels he or she should be.

Emotion in Theories of Human LH

The idea that emotions are evoked by helplessness training recurs more or less explicitly in diverse theories of human LH. This view was first advanced in Seligman's (1975) original Learned Helplessness theory. Seligman demonstrated that the behavioral effects of uncontrollable outcomes dissipate in time, suggesting the presence of a transient emotional change. Seligman (1975) proposed two stages in the emotional impact of helplessness training: Initially, lack of control heightens fear and frustration. If control returns, emotional arousal may disappear; if not, the arousal continues and may be experienced as depression.

The emotional effects of helplessness training have been also proposed by Wortman and Brehm (1975). Their main hypothesis is that different amounts of helplessness training produce different emotions. A small number of uncontrollable failures would result in frustration and anger, whereas a larger number would result in depressed affect. According to Wortman and Brehm, anger is the emotional manifestation of psychological reactance and reflects the desire to conquer and destroy the obstacles to the reassertion of control, whereas depressed affect results (as in the Learned Helplessness theory) from learning that outcomes are uncontrollable. Wortman and Brehm claim that depression follows the recognition that control is irremediably lost and that no response—even aggressive action—can restore it. They also propose that helplessness training may evoke anxiety feelings, which would increase steadily after each consecutive failure. In their terms, the arousal of anxiety reflects the tension and distress produced by the elimination of personal freedom—one of the basic features of helplessness training.

Another statement about the emotional products of helplessness training was made by Lavelle et al. (1979), who view this training as an experimenter-induced failure and contend that differences in terminology have obscured the similarities between LH research and studies on environmental stress. Both lines of research use similar experimental designs: exposure to aversive events and subsequent assessment of performance in a similar or dissimilar task. On this basis, Lavelle et al. conclude that helplessness training evokes emotions and that these emotions are the same as those evoked by other stressors. Specifically they propose that anxiety, the most prototypical response to environmental stress, is the basic emotional product of helplessness training.

EMPIRICAL EVIDENCE

A large number of LH experiments similarly suggest that helplessness training is able to evoke emotions. Table 5.1 presents a representative sample of studies that exposed subjects to helplessness training or some other control conditions and asked them to rate the extent to which they felt each of a series of negative emotions during the experiment. As can be seen, most of the studies support the hypothesis that helplessness training heightens emotions, especially anger, depression, and anxiety.

Although some of these studies are problematic because neither their wording nor timing of emotional assessment is standardized, and more important, because they use single-item measures—which, in the words of Klein, Fencil-Morse, and Seligman (1976), tend to be "at best crude indicators of mood" (p. 512)—LH studies that used standardized multiple-item affective scales have obtained similar findings. Most of the studies that administered the depression, anxiety, and hostility scales of the Multiple Affect Adjective Checklist (MAACL) before and after helplessness training found that this training increased emotionality, though they differ as to the type of emotion evoked. For example, Cole and Coyne (1977) found that helplessness training increased hostility and depression; Miller and Seligman (1975) found an increase in anxiety and hostility; and Gatchel, Paulus, and Maples (1975), Gatchel and Proctor (1976), Gatchel, McKinney, and Koebernick (1977), Pittman and Pittman (1979, 1980), and Tuffin, Hesketh, and Podd (1985) found a significant increase in anxiety, depression, and hostility. Using the Paired Anxiety and Depression Scale, Mould (1975) and Griffith (1977) also found that lack of control heightened self-reports of depression and anxiety. Only two studies that used the MAACL found no effect of helplessness training on emotion (Fox & Oakes, 1984; Oakes & Curtis, 1982). The fact that the MAACL was completed only after the training task prevented the examination of within-subject emotional changes, however, and the helplessness training was so artificial that the authors themselves were not surprised by the lack of emotional impact.

Supportive evidence is also provided by LH studies that assessed physiological manifestations of emotional arousal, such as galvanic skin response (GSR) and blood pressure. Krantz, Glass, and Snyder (1974) conducted two studies in which the GSR of subjects exposed to escapable or inescapable noise was recorded throughout the experiment. In Study 1, the helplessness training lowered phasic skin conductance in response to noise stimuli, a symptom linked to the arousal of depressive affect. In Study 2, no skin conductance difference between the experimental groups was found, but Gatchel and Proctor (1976) demonstrated that this was attributable to the method of GSR measurement employed. Two other studies that used a better GSR measurement (Gatchel & Proctor, 1976; Gatchel et al., 1977) found that helplessness training did produce physiological signs of depression (low phasic conductance) as well as a greater frequency of spontaneous conductance fluctuations during the latter training trials, a symptom tied to anxiety and distress. Glass, Reim, and Singer (1971) similarly reported that inescapable noise heightened

TABLE 5.1. Review of Emotional Effects of Helplessness Training

Study	Manipulation	Emotional assessment		Effect of HT
		Timing	Scale	
Miller & Seligman (1975)	Inescapable noise	Before noise	MAACL anger, anxiety, depression	More anger and anxiety
Roth & Kubal (1975)	Unsolvable problem	After test	SI of anger, frustration, depression, anxiety	Higher score in all the emotinoal items
Gatchel, Paulus, & Maples (1975)	Inescapable noise	Before test	MAACL anger, anxiety, depression	More anger, anxiety, and depression
Klein, Pencil-Morse, & Seligman (1976)	Unsolvable problems	After test	SI of anger, depression	More anger
Klein & Seligman (1976)	Unsolvable problems	After test	SI of anger, sadness, nervousness	No effect
Cohen, Rothbart, & Phillips (1976)	Unsolvable problems	After test	SI of stress, frustration	Higher score in the items
Hockanson & Sacco (1976)	Inescapable noise	During study	SI giving up, irritability	More giving up
Gatchel & Proctor (1976)	Inescapable noise	Before test	MAACL anger, anxiety, depression	More anger, anxiety, and depression
Tennen & Eller (1977)	Unsolvable problems	Before test	SI of anger, nervousness, sadness	More anger and sadness
Cole & Coyne (1977)	Inescapable noise	Before test	MAACL anger, anxiety, depression	More anger and depression
Griffith (1977)	Unsolvable problems	Before test	PADS anxiety, depression	More anxiety, depression
Gatchel, McKinney, & Koebernick (1977)	Inescapable noise	Before test	MAACL anger, anxiety, depression	More anger, anxiety, and depression
Frankel & Snyder (1978)	Unsolvable problem	After test	SI of poor mood	No effect
Willis & Blaney (1978)	Unsolvable problem	After test	SI of depression	More depression
Teasdale (1978)	Unsolvable problem	After test	SI anxiety, frustration, despondency	More despondency
Pittman & Pittman (1979)	Unsolvable problems	Before test	MAACL anger, anxiety, and depression	More anger, anxiety, and depression

(*continued*)

TABLE 5.1. (*Continued*)

Study	Manipulation	Emotional assessment		Effect of HT
		Timing	Scale	
Tennen & Gillen (1979)	Inescapable noise	After test	SI of anger, sadness, frustration	More anger and frustration
Brockner (1979)	Unsolvable problems	After test	SI of anxiety	More anxiety
Baucom & Danker-Brown (1979)	Unsolvable problems	Before test	DACL depression	More depression
Coyne, Metalsky, & Lavelle (1980)	Inescapable noise	Before test	SI tension, anger, frustration	More anger, frustration
Burger & Arkin (1980)	Inescapable noise	Before test	MAACL depression	More depression
Nation & Cooney (1980)	Unsolvable problems	After test	SI sadness, frustration	More sadness, frustration
Noel & Lisman (1980)	Unsolvable problems	Before test	MAACL anger, anxiety, depression	More anger, anxiety, and depression
Raps, Reinhard, & Seligman (1980)	Inescapable noise	Before test	DACL depression	More depression
Pittman & Pittman (1980)	Unsolvable problems	Before test	MAACL anger, anxiety, depression	More anger, anxiety, and depression
Tiggemann (1981)	Inescapable noise	After task	SI of negative affect	More negative affect
Orbach & Hadas (1982)	Unsolvable problem	After task	DACL depression	More depression
Oakes & Curtis (1982)	Noncontingent feedback	Before test	MAACL anger, anxiety, depression	No effect
Tennen, Gillen et al. (1982)	Inescapable noise	After test	SI of anger, frustration	More anger, frustration
Kramer & Rosellini (1982)	Noncontingent feedback	After test	DACL depression	No effect
Greer & Calhoun (1983)	Unsolvable problems	Before test	MAACL anger, anxiety, depression	More anger, anxiety, and depression
Baucom (1983)	Unsolvable problem	Before test	DACL depression	More depression
Fox & Oakes (1982)	Noncontingent feedback	Before test	MAACL anger, anxiety, depression	No effect
Baucom & Danker-Brown (1984)	Unsolvable problems	Before test	DACL depression	More depression

(*continued*)

TABLE 5.1. (*Continued*)

Study	Manipulation	Emotional assessment		Effect of HT
		Timing	Scale	
Tuffin, Hesketh, & Podd (1985)	Unsolvable problems	Before test	MAACL anger, anxiety, depression	More anger, anxiety, and depression
Wilner & Neiva (1986)	Inescapable noise	After test	SI of mood, tension, happiness	More tension
Mikulincer & Nizan (1988)	Unsolvable problems	Before test	5 negative mood items	More negative mood
Mikulincer (1988a)	Unsolvable problems	Before test	5 negative mood items	More negative mood

Notes: HT = helplessness training; SI = single item.

tonic skin conductance, a sign of inner tension and anxiety. Yet another study, by Hokanson and Sacco (1976), found that subjects exposed to inescapable noise showed lower systolic blood pressure—a symptom linked to depressed affect—than subjects exposed to no noise.

Unfortunately, the physiological data involve some interpretational problems. For example, the fact that all the findings were obtained during noise/shock exposure prevents their extrapolation to other LH inductions (e.g., unsolvable problems). Taken together, however, the findings consistently suggest that helplessness training produces both physiological and subjective signs of anxiety and depression.

SUMMARY

Theory and research support the hypothesis that people tend to react to helplessness training with heightened emotions. This emotional reaction has both subjective and physiological manifestations. It can be explained by the fact that helplessness training creates cognitive discrepancies and a threat to the person's goals and schemas.

EXPECTANCY AND EMOTION

This section deals with the hypothesis that the expectancy of control channels the emotional arousal elicited by failure into those particular emotions that prepare and motivate people to undertake the coping responses cued by that expectancy. The expectancy of control tells people what can and cannot be done to cope with failure, and then it elicits those emotions that are specialized in sustaining the chosen coping actions.

The idea that the expectancy of control elicits specific emotions appears in most cognitive accounts of emotion. It is implicit, for example, in Lazarus's (1991) contention that secondary appraisal is an emotionally relevant dimension. It is also implicit in Fridja's (1986) argument that people's emotions are shaped by anticipatory cognitions of what the situation does or does not allow them to do. In fact, Fridja's dimensions of openness (the ability to penetrate barriers that block a goal), controllability (the ability to modify an event by one's actions), and modifiability (the likelihood of the event recurring in the future) can all be seen as components of the expectancy of control. Two persons who experience the same failure may react with different emotions if they hold different beliefs on the likelihood of removing barriers, controlling outcomes, and restoring a blocked goal.

The expectancy of control is also implicit in theories that point to cognitions of "power," "potency," and "influence" in eliciting specific emotions (e.g., Roseman, 1984; Scherer, 1984). These cognitions range from the appraisal that one has power to alter the environment to the appraisal that one lacks such power. Weiner's (1979, 1985) attributional theory, which holds that the stability dimension of causal attribution—the proximal antecedent of expectancy change—is a crucial determinant of emotion refers directly to the emotional impact of expectancy. In this theory, failure attributed to stable causes may evoke different emotions from those evoked by failure attributed to unstable causes. Although the various theorists each assign different names to the appraisal components, they incorporate control expectancy in eliciting specific emotions.

In the LH context, both the Learned Helplessness theory and Wortman and Brehm's integrative model assume that the expectancy of control determines the type of the emotional reaction to helplessness training. They hypothesize that people respond to helplessness training with heightened anger when they hold a high expectancy of control for the next task, but with heightened depressed affect when helplessness training is followed by a drastic reduction in the expectancy of control.

Expectancy and Anger

A high expectancy of control implies that something can be done to overcome failure, and it tends to lead people to cope with the failure by moving toward problem-focused activities (see Chapter 4). The emotions aroused would be those that could sustain these activities. Anger may be the prototypical instrumental emotion because, as will be discussed later, it is an "attack" emotion that motivates people to remove the source of a harm.

In my view, the combination of failure with favorable expectancies of control is critical for the arousal of anger in LH settings. Helplessness training may incline people to anger because it typically implies an insult to self-identity (see Chapter 1). Lazarus (1991) claims that the core relational theme of anger is "a demeaning offense against me and mine" (p. 222). Similarly, Beck (1976) suggests that anger is provoked when a person is convinced that he or she has been wronged, and De-

Rivera (1977) emphasizes the link between anger and the violation of self-esteem. Carlson and Miller (1988) found anger to be evoked when a person's self-identity is insulted or criticized, and Averill (1978) found that most of the subjects he had asked to describe the most intense episode of anger they had experienced reported events that threatened their view of themselves as capable of attaining goals or implementing plans. Similar findings were reported by Shaver et al. (1987), who found that subjects reported anger in situations that entailed a loss of power, a violation of wishes, or physical or psychological pain.

Anger does not necessarily follow every insult to self-identity, however, but emerges mainly when people expect to be able to redress the insult (i.e., have a high expectancy of control). In other words, anger follows the appraisal that one is strong enough to fight actively against failure and remove any external obstacle to success. Roseman (1984) claims that anger results from the perception of self-strength after failure and the appraisal of "I should be able to do this." Scherer (1984) argues that anger is aroused when people believe they have the power to remove the obstructions to a blocked goal. Fridja (1986) and Izard (1977) similarly contend that anger implies the nonacceptance of an aversive event as necessary or uncontrollable. As Fridja (1986) puts it, "Anger implies hope" (p. 429). Lazarus (1991) suggests that anger follows expectations that (a) one possesses the responses required to remove the offense to the self (high self-efficacy expectancy), and (b) active fighting leads to threat removal (high outcome expectancy).

There is also empirical evidence on the association between expectancy and anger. Persons expecting to have control over outcomes have been found to respond more aggressively to attack than those expecting to have no control (Dengerink, O'Leary, & Kasner, 1975). Russell and McAuley (1986) found that people are likely to feel anger in response to failure attributed to unstable causes that would not necessarily recur in the next tasks. Fridja, Kuipers, and Ter-Schure (1989) similarly found that the more subjects appraised a bad event as modifiable by their actions, the more they adopted a reactant attitude and become angry.

Similar effects have been found when analyzing people's accounts of others' emotions. Weiner, Graham, Stern, and Lawson (1982) found that when a hypothetical teacher displayed anger toward a failing child, subjects assumed that the teacher believed the child could succeed in the future (unstable attribution). Stein and Levine (1989), who asked preschoolers, first graders, and college students to indicate which emotions a protagonist would experience in various hypothetical incidents, found that subjects were most likely to say that the protagonist was angry when the latter had high expectancy of success/control. The findings imply that people so frequently hold positive expectancies when angry that the association between anger and such expectancies becomes part of their schema of anger.

Roseman, Spindel, and Jose (1990), who found no evidence for the expectancy–anger link, attributed its absence to methodological problems: "Subjects may have appraised themselves as powerless across all negative emotions because they did not prevent the occurrence of a negative event. . . . Perhaps assessing subjects' power to respond to an event would discriminate among negative emotions. If one can respond effectively to a negative event, one may feel angry" (p. 911).

EXPECTANCY AND THE AROUSAL OF ANXIETY AND DEPRESSED AFFECTS

Strong emotions also arise when people are convinced of the irrevocability of failure and expect no control in the next tasks. But here the belief that nothing can be done to overcome failure makes anger irrelevant. The expectancy of no control would instead signal that one can cope with failure only by avoiding a direct confrontation with it or by readjusting one's mental structures. The emotions aroused would be those that would best sustain these tendencies. As will discussed later, anxiety and depressed affects appear to be the most appropriate emotions for reinforcing and sustaining avoidance and reorganization attempts.

The combination of failure with unfavorable expectancies of control is critical for the arousal of anxiety and depressed affects in LH settings. Helplessness training inclines people to anxiety because it entails an immediate threat to the person's view of the self and the world (see Chapter 1). Several theoretical frameworks (e.g., DeRivera, 1977; Kelly, 1955; Lazarus, 1991) and a number of studies (e.g., McNally, 1990; Tobacyk & Downs, 1986) emphasize that anxiety entails the recognition that one's view of the self and the world may be incorrect. One illustrative example is the prototype analysis by Shaver et al. (1987) of the emotion of fear, which found that most of the subjects reported experiencing fear in situations that threatened the self, especially when they were uncertain about the meaning of events and ways of avoiding the threat.

Helplessness training also produces personal losses (see Chapter 1), which may be directly reflected in the arousal of sadness, the most prototypical affect of depression. Lazarus (1991) proposes that sadness follows a loss that diminishes the person's identity, and Beck (1976) that it follows a loss that narrows the individual's personal domain. Lazarus (1991) emphasizes that "any major loss, especially one that is important in defining who we think we are in the world, will produce the potential for sadness" (p. 250).

Several studies have corroborated the link between loss and depressed affects. For example, Deadman, Dewey, Owens, and Leinster (1989) found that in a sample of women suffering from breast cancer, breast amputation (the loss of an important part of the self) was followed by depressed affects. Using the Cognition Checklist on psychiatric outpatients, Clark, Beck, and Brown (1989), and Clark, Beck, and Stewart (1990) found that depressed affects were linked to cognitions about personal losses. Similar findings have also been obtained in studies assessing emotional states in normal samples (e.g., Clark, 1986; Wickless & Kirsch, 1988).

Anxiety and depressed affects, however, do not necessarily follow every threat or loss. People may become anxious when their views of the self/world are threatened and they believe they are powerless to maintain them intact. Similarly, people may become sad when they experience a personal loss and believe they have no response for restoring it. In both these cases, the expectancy of no control seems to be the critical factor.

Both theory and research support the hypothesis that anxiety and depressed affects are most likely to be experienced when people hold negative and pessimistic expectancies about the future. Epstein (1972), who made an integrative summary of psychological theories of anxiety, concluded that anxiety is rooted in "response unavailability," the belief that one possesses no response to overcome failure. Epstein's "response unavailability" resembles the low self-efficacy component of the expectancy of no control. Similarly, Mandler (1980) argued that "anxious experiences arise out of the combination of the interruption of ongoing behavior and thought on the one hand and the unavailability of appropriate, situation-relevant, or task- or problem-solving actions on the other" (p. 234).

Depressed affect has also been linked to the expectancy of no control. Bibring (1953) argued that depressed affects are experienced when people become convinced that they are unable to attain important goals. From a more cognitive perspective, Bandura (1986), Mandler (1975), and Lazarus (1991) held that a key to sadness is the belief that the loss implied by failure is irrevocable because available modes of problem-focused actions are ineffective. Beck (1967, 1976) also suggests that sadness occurs when people anticipate the likelihood of negative events to be extremely high. These ideas have received considerable support from recent studies on the pattern of cognitive appraisal associated with sadness (e.g., Fridja et al., 1989; Roseman et al., 1990).

Correlational studies provide extensive support for the association between the expectancy of control and the arousal of anxiety and depressed affects (see Archibald, 1974; Bandura, 1986; Meece, Wigfield, & Eccles, 1990, for reviews). In general, the findings indicate that the lower the expectancy of control, the stronger the reported anxiety and depressed affects. These correlations are significant in a wide variety of achievement and nonachievement settings. Though these studies tell nothing about the direction of causality, more specific research into the expectancy–affect link after failure provides strong support for the prediction.

Andersen and Lyon (1987), for example, found that when subjects regarded the likelihood of an aversive event occurring after failure as certain and unavoidable, they reported relatively high anxiety and depressed affects. When they remained hopeful as to the possibility of avoiding an aversive event, they reported weaker anxiety and depressed affects. In another study, Stanley and Maddux (1986) found that the induction of low self-efficacy expectancy for a social interaction was followed by higher reports of depressed affect than the induction of high self-efficacy expectancy.

Comprehensive support for the effects of the expectancy of no control on anxiety and depressed affects is also found in studies that measured or manipulated stable-global attribution, the proximal antecedent of expectancy change after failure. This line of research includes correlational, prospective, and experimental investigations.

Dozens of studies have focused on the correlation between self-reports of causal attribution and depressed affect. Although some of the methodology may have been flawed, most of the studies suggest that people who attribute failure to stable-global causes are more likely to report depressed mood than those who attribute it to unstable-specific factors (see extensive reviews in Brewin, 1985; Peterson & Seligman, 1984; Robins, 1988; Sweeney, Anderson, & Bailey, 1986). A number of studies have also found that a stable-global attribution of failure was linked with stronger anxiety than an unstable-specific one (e.g., Ganellen, 1988). Although Riskind, Castellon, and Beck (1989) found no significant relations of anxiety to causal attribution, on a whole, the accumulated evidence strongly suggests that stable-global attribution of failure, the antecedent of the expectancy of no control, is a correlate of depressed and anxiety affects.

A more methodologically powerful line of research consists of prospective studies that measured attributional style for bad events and depressed affects at Time 1, exposed subjects to failure at Time 2, and assessed any change in depressed affects after failure. In the first of these studies, Metalsky, Abramson, Seligman, Semmel, and Peterson (1982) found that stable-global attribution contributed to depressed affects after failure and that unstable-specific attribution prevented these affects. After failing in a midterm exam, only those students who made stable-global attributions for negative events experienced enhanced depressed affects. Poor grades did not produce any increase in depressed affect among students who habitually made unstable-specific attributions.

Conceptually similar findings were reported by Metalsky, Halberstadt, and Abramson (1987), Follete and Jacobson (1987), and Hunsley (1989). In addition, the findings were replicated in other situations: for example, after childbirth (Cutrona, 1983), six months of unemployment (Rothwell & Williams, 1983), imprisonment (Peterson & Seligman, 1984), and an abortion (Major, Mueller, & Hildebrandt, 1985). With the exception of one study with children (Hammen, Adrian, & Hiroto, 1988), all the above studies converge in demonstrating that stable-global attributions for bad events increase the likelihood of depressed affects in response to these events.

A third, though sparse, line of research consists of two studies that experimentally induced causal attribution for failure (see Chapter 2 for details). Dweck (1975) found that the induction of unstable attributions for failure had no effect on test anxiety. Wilson and Linville (1982) found the opposite: Subjects who were trained to attribute failure to unstable causes reported feeling less anxiety and depressed affect after failure than subjects who received no attributional training. This discrepancy may derive from methodological differences. Whereas Wilson and Linville used a scale sensitive to mood changes (MAACL), Dweck apparently assessed anxiety via a traitlike measure unlikely to change after task-specific inductions.

In general, the findings suggest that the expectancy of no control is related to the arousal of anxiety and depressed affects. Moreover, there is some evidence that depressed affects may be heightened after failure mainly when causal attribution favors the formation of the expectancy of no control (stable-global attribution).

A Note on Anxiety and Depressed Affects

The above review does not mean that anxiety and depressed affects are the same. Though the two emotions have been consistently found to be aroused together and similar cognitions participate in their arousal, they are different emotional states. Several authors have noted basic differences between anxiety and depressed affects. For example, Garber, Miller, and Abramson (1980) claimed that depressed affects and anxiety differ in the perceived certainty of an uncontrollable failure. Whereas depressed affect is aroused when people are certain of the occurrence of an uncontrollable failure, anxiety is aroused when people believe that such an outcome is highly probable but not certain. Beck and Clark (1988) delineated the specific content of negative expectancies related to anxiety and depressed affects. In their view, whereas anxiety is linked to the anticipation of future threats, depressed affect is tied to the experience of important losses. According to Lazarus (1991), "Sadness and anxiety are . . . similar in that they both have a strong existential aspect; the difference is that in anxiety, a sense of loss (of meaning) has not yet occurred but is imminent. In sadness, the loss has already occurred and is irrevocable" (p. 250).

In addition, anxiety and depressed affects are differentially related to different expectancies of resolving the mismatch with an intractable world. Lazarus (1991) contends that depressed affects follow the expectancy that one can work through the irrevocable loss, accept it, and recommit to new goals. In this view, depressed affect would be the emotional expression of hope of being able to adapt to an intractable environment. In contrast, the arousal of anxiety follows the appraisal that one is unable to work through the irrevocable loss and that the single available coping pathway is to leave the mismatch unsolved and to avoid any confrontation with the threat. In this view, anxiety would be the emotional expression of a double hopelessness—of changing the threatening world, and of accommodating to it.

It is important to note that I deal with the affect of sadness rather than with the subjective state of depression. According to Lazarus (1991), sadness arises with one's coming to terms with a specific, irrevocable loss, whereas depression is a complex of emotions centered around the personal implications of an irrevocable loss and is a response to the failure to come to terms with that loss. Importantly, Lazarus assumes that anxiety is one of the emotions that define the subjective state of depression.

In short, one can claim that the expectancy of no control may precede both anxiety and depressed affects, but it does not explain why one person holding that expectancy reacts to loss with sadness and another does so with anxiety and a generalized state of depression. One factor that might contribute to the difference is the degree of threat the loss entails to the person's well-being: the stronger the threat, the higher the likelihood of anxiety. A more important factor is the extent to which people believe they can successfully accommodate their mental structures to the new reality. The more hopeful people are, the more likely it is that they will react with sadness rather than anxiety.

The Expectancy–Emotion Link in the LH Paradigm

Although the studies reviewed above support the hypothesized expectancy–emotion link, they do not provide any information as to whether this link applies to human LH because they do not assess emotion after helplessness training. To fill in this gap, I present three lines of research that assess the emotional effects of the expectancy of control within LH settings.

The first consists of my recent series of studies that provide correlational evidence on the expectancy–emotion link (see Table 5.2). Only one study found a positive correlation between the expectancy of control after helplessness training and the strength of anger. Most of the studies, however, found that expectancy was inversely related to the strength of anxiety and depression. In general, the findings show that the lower the expectancy, the stronger the anxiety and depression. Of course, the findings are correlational and preclude any conclusion as to the direction of the expectancy–emotion link.

Another relevant piece of information is provided by Study 8 of the same recent series (see Chapter 4). The results show an interesting pattern of emotional effects (see Table 5.3). On the one hand, low self-efficacy subjects reported stronger anxiety and depression (via single items) after four unsolvable problems than high self-efficacy subjects. Moreover, these unsolvable problems produced stronger anxiety and depression than control conditions only among subjects who habitually held low self-efficacy expectancy. That is, the arousal of anxiety and depression after helplessness training seems to be fostered by the belief that one does not possess the responses required to solve the problems.

On the other hand, the effects of helplessness training and self-efficacy on

TABLE 5.2. Pearson Correlations of Expectancy of Control and Emotion Scores

Study number	Anger	Anxiety	Depression
1	.27[a]	−.67[b]	−.48[b]
8	.03	−.68[b]	−.55[b]
9	.06	−.20	−.40[b]
10	.09	−.20	−.25
11	.04	−.34[b]	−.08
12	.11	−.46[b]	−.43[b]

[a]$p < .05$
[b]$p < .01$

TABLE 5.3. Means and Standard Deviations of Emotion Scores by Feedback and Problem-Solving Self-Efficacy (Study 8)

	No feedback		Failure	
	Low	High	Low	High
Anger				
Mean	1.40	1.50	1.30	1.60
Standard deviation	0.69	0.71	0.48	0.84
Anxiety				
Mean	1.50	1.40	3.40	1.90
Standard deviation	0.71	0.52	1.42	0.88
Depressed affect				
Mean	1.60	1.40	3.40	1.50
Standard deviation	0.69	0.52	2.01	0.71

reports of anger (via single items) were not significant. In my view, this finding may be accounted for by the fact that subjects experienced four failures, which in and by themselves could create self-doubt even among high self-efficacy subjects. Though high self-efficacy subjects might have held higher expectancies of control after helplessness training than did low self-efficacy subjects, their expectancies might have been lower than those held by high self-efficacy subjects exposed to no feedback. That is, the helplessness training might have reduced the expectancies of high self-efficacy subjects, which in turn might have inhibited the arousal of anger.

Indirect support for the hypothesized expectancy–emotion link is found in LH studies that varied the amount of failure, with the expectancy of control typically maintained after small amounts of helplessness training but drastically reduced after larger doses (see Chapter 4). Thus, if anger is produced by the persistence of an expectancy of control, it will appear after small but not large amounts of failure. Accordingly, if depression and anxiety are produced by the expectancy of no control, they will appear only after large amounts of training.

Two LH studies support the above ideas. Using the anger, anxiety, and depression scales of the MAACL, Pittman and Pittman (1980) showed that anger was highest after a small amount of helplessness training (two unsolvable problems), depression occurred mostly after larger amounts (six unsolvable problems), and anxiety was induced after both small and large amounts. Study 1 of my recent series (see Chapter 1) showed that reports of anger increased after one and two failures, then steadily decreased after each new failure; in contrast, reports of depression increased only after four and five failures. In addition, although one or two failures had no effect on reports of anxiety, such reports increased dramatically after three failures, and the higher level remained constant with each new failure (see Figure 5.1).

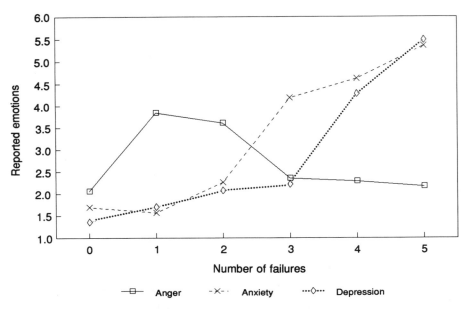

FIGURE 5.1. Means of anger, anxiety, and depressed affect according to number of failures.

SUMMARY

This review suggests that the expectancy of control is involved in the arousal of anger, anxiety, and depressed affects. On the one hand, a high expectancy of control fosters the appraisal of failure as a temporary offense to self-identity and evokes anger. On the other hand, an expectancy of no control highlights the irrevocability of the loss produced by failure and the inability of the individual to influence the threatening environment, thus favoring the arousal of anxiety and depressed affects.

Expectancy, however, is not a sufficient antecedent of these emotions. Although anxiety and depressed affects are highly correlated (e.g., Watson & Clark, 1984), some persons may react to unfavorable expectancies with anxiety, and others with depressed affects. In addition, some persons may experience no strong emotion under either favorable or unfavorable expectancies. As stated earlier, individual differences in the experience of anxiety and depressed affects can only be explained by other situational and personality factors that might moderate the impact of the expectancy of no control.

Nor is the progress between expectancy and emotion necessarily unidirectional. Though most of the findings suggest that expectancy precedes emotion, some suggest that anxiety and depressed affects may exacerbate the expectancy changes produced by failure. Bower (1981) and Blaney (1986) claimed that the arousal of depressed affect may facilitate the accessibility of memories of bad events, which in turn leads to the expectancy that these events will recur in the future. Several studies have found that the induction of depressed affect produces higher expectancy of unpleasant events and lower self-efficacy than the induction of neutral affects (e.g., Cunningham, 1988; Johnson & Tverski, 1983; Kavanagh & Bower, 1985).

Finally, anger, anxiety, and depressed affects are not the only emotional responses to failure. Other emotions (e.g., shame, guilt) may be experienced in LH settings. It is simply that anger, anxiety, and depressed affects are the most frequently reported emotional responses to lack of control (see Table 5.1), are related to control expectancy, and (as will be discussed in the next section) have an impact on performance. Other emotions may affect and be affected by lack of control, but they do not determine the basic course of the LH process or the strength of LH effects. Anger, anxiety, and depressed affects are emphasized here because they are the core emotions of human LH.

THE EMOTION–PERFORMANCE LINK

In previous sections I presented theory and research that treat emotion mainly as a dependent variable. I also assume, however, that emotion is an independent factor that may affect coping and performance. In this section I examine the hypothesis that emotions may influence LH effects by sustaining particular coping reactions.

My basic position is that emotion contributes to LH effects. Behavior derives not only from the actual experience or anticipation of lack of control but also from a person's emotional reaction to that lack. Those emotional reactions may have significant motivational and cognitive effects, which in turn may have repercussions on task performance. Motivationally, emotion may urge some immediate changes in behavior. Cognitively, emotion may alter the allocation of resources, the sort of material that is likely to be processed, and the activation of inhibitory processes. For example, an angry person may give priority to different actions, allocate resources to different cognitive activities, process different material, and hence function differently in task settings than an anxious person.

This position radically differs from the original and reformulated Learned Helplessness theories, which explicitly reject any causal link between emotion and performance. According to Seligman and his colleagues, behavior results from "cold" cognitive processes (attribution, expectation) in which there is no place for "hot" emotional processes. The expectancy of no control does not require any emotion—even depressed affect—to impair performance. Emotions may be altered by helplessness training and may correlate with functioning, but need not determine it.

The two positions may reflect different conceptualizations of emotion. On the one hand, the Learned Helplessness theory regards emotion as a mental state or a physiological reaction to environmental events that cannot explain functioning or performance. Behavior, in the view of this theory, is to be explained by other psychological constructs (e.g., activation or expectancies) that seem more scientific and free of the problems inherent to the subjectivity, complexity, and fluidity of emotional responses. On the other hand, my position stems from current personality theories (e.g., Bandura, 1986; Lazarus, 1991) that point out the complex interconnections among the emotional, cognitive, and motivational systems. In the view of these theories, emotions are not purely physiological states but enrich our cognitions and regulate our actions, and behavior is the outcome of the conjoint action of emotional, cognitive, and motivational elements.

The hypothesized emotion–performance link is based primarily on the contribution of emotion to coping. In my terms, emotion may contribute to LH effects by amplifying the effects of the expectancy of control on coping responses, motivating people to undertake the cued coping activities, and sustaining these until their ends are fulfilled. In this schema, emotion is not a direct precursor of performance changes; the coping actions are. Nor does emotion determine the choice of the particular responses used to cope with failure; the expectancy of control does. Emotion can only affect task performance after helplessness training by intensifying and sustaining the coping activities cued by the expectancy of control.

On this basis, the arousal of anger after high expectancy of control may amplify and sustain the problem-solving orientation, action rumination, and performance facilitation originally produced by this expectancy. Anger urges people to remove the source of the harm from what is perceived as a controllable environment via problem solving and action rumination, which in turn are reflected in performance improvement. The anxiety and depressed affects evoked after low expectancy of control may amplify and sustain the off-task coping orientation, off-task rumination, and performance deficits originally produced by this expectancy. Depressed affects propel people to disengage from the irrevocable loss and to change their goals via reorganization coping and state rumination. Anxiety propels people to withdraw cognitively and behaviorally from the threat via avoidance strategies and task-irrelevant rumination. Both anxiety and depressed affects support coping activities that divert attention away from the task and impair task performance.

The corollary of the above reasoning is that in the absence of emotional arousal, helplessness training should have only a mild impact on task performance. Without the emotional signal that prompts them to meet the coping demands posed by failure, people should not feel any urgent need to respond to those demands in the test task. Emotionally cool, they would be left free to undertake the new task without the compulsion to minimize the prior actual–ideal mismatch. In short, LH effects should be most likely to occur under strong emotional arousal.

EMOTIONALITY AND PERFORMANCE

The performance effects of emotional arousal within the LH paradigm were examined in Study 9 of the series I present in this book (see Table 1.1). This study assessed the contribution of the personality dimension of emotional intensity to LH effects. The dimension of emotional intensity refers to the strength of a person's responses to emotion-provoking stimuli, such as uncontrollable failure (Larsen & Diener, 1987), and distinguishes between persons who experience emotions only mildly and with only minor fluctuations and those who experience emotions strongly and are emotionally reactive and variable (Larsen & Diener, 1987). Emotional intensity has been assessed through a wide variety of measures and under a variety of rubrics, including reactivity, arousability, and excitation potential, and it was found to be linked to extraversion, productivity, and cyclothymic tendencies (see Larsen & Diener, 1987, for a review).

In my study, subjects completed the Affect Intensity Measure (Larsen & Diener, 1987); were exposed to either no, one, or four unsolvable problems; and had their performance assessed in a letter cancellation task. After the test task, subjects filled in anger, anxiety, and depression items tapping their emotions in the experimental session and my scales on mental rumination and coping strategies.

This study design made it possible to test two contradictory positions on the emotion–performance link. The prediction derived from my analysis is that LH effects would be preceded by strong emotional arousal, so that the facilitatory effects of a small amount of helplessness training and the detrimental effects of a large amount of training would both be most likely to occur among persons who react to failure with strong emotions. The prediction derived from the Learned Helplessness theory is that both the facilitatory and detrimental effects of helplessness training could occur regardless of the strength of the aroused emotions, so that LH effects would be recorded even among subjects who reacted to failure with mild emotions.

The data were in keeping with my position (see Table 5.4). Significant LH

TABLE 5.4. Means of Accuracy, Emotion, Rumination, and Coping Scores by Number of Failures and Emotional Intensity (Study 9)

	No failures		One failure		Four failures	
	Low	High	Low	High	Low	High
Performance accuracy	84.25	79.75	79.00	87.50	81.00	67.25
Anger	1.50	1.37	1.50	3.37	1.75	1.62
Anxiety	1.25	1.37	1.37	1.50	1.62	3.12
Depressed affect	1.50	1.50	1.75	1.37	1.75	3.87
Action rumination	3.75	4.00	3.62	4.62	2.37	1.87
State rumination	1.50	1.50	1.50	1.25	1.62	4.12
Task-irrelevant rumination	1.62	1.50	1.50	1.87	1.87	3.87
Problem-focused coping	4.00	4.37	4.37	5.50	2.37	2.25
Reappraisal	1.37	1.50	1.75	2.00	1.75	1.62
Reorganization	1.25	1.62	1.37	1.37	1.87	3.00
Avoidance	1.75	1.50	1.62	1.12	1.87	2.87

effects were found only among subjects who tended to have strong emotional reactions. In these emotionally reactive subjects, a small amount of helplessness training improved performance, and a large amount impaired performance. Moreover, it was only among these persons that one failure produced more anger and four failures produced more anxiety and depressed affects than among those in the no-problem condition. Persons low in emotional intensity reported no elevation of emotions and showed no performance change after failure.

In addition, the data also provide information about the hypothesized effects of emotional arousal on rumination and coping strategies (see Table 5.4). Compared to persons low in emotional intensity, emotionally reactive persons reported more action rumination and more problem-solving strategies after one unsolvable problem, and more state rumination and avoidance coping after four unsolvable problems. In fact, both small and large amounts of failure led to an elevation in rumination and coping only among emotionally reactive persons.

Putting together the findings, one can delineate the following sequence of events: Both the facilitatory and detrimental effects of helplessness training are limited by the person's emotional reaction to the failure. Initially, after a small amount of failure, the tendency to strong emotional arousal seems to be reflected in anger, which sustains action rumination, problem-focused coping, and performance facilitation. After a large dose of failure, however, it is reflected in anxiety and depressed affects, which sustain state rumination, off-task coping, and LH deficits. In the absence of strong emotional arousal, no affective, cognitive, or performance changes are observed in emotionally nonreactive persons.

THE PERFORMANCE IMPACT OF ANGER

Both theory and research suggest that anger motivates and prepares people to fight against external impediments and to overcome failure. Theoretically, anger has been consistently referred as the emotion of "fight" and "attack" (e.g., Izard, 1977). It underlies active fighting designed to conquer obstacles that block goal attainment (Averill, 1978; Plutchik, 1980; Scherer, 1984; Tomkins, 1962). It helps people to restore a lost goal by active fighting against events and objects that they perceive to be responsible for the loss (Frijda, 1986). Anger acts as a logistical support to alloplastic adaptation via problem solving.

In support of this view, Izard (1977) found that the most frequent action that college students reported having taken in anger-arousing situations was to try actively to reassert control over outcomes. Averill (1978) found that most of the subjects he studied reported that their anger was motivated by the wish to assert their authority and change the course of events. Shaver et al. (1987), summing up their findings on accounts of anger episodes, state that "the angry person reports becoming stronger (higher in potency) and more energized in order to fight or rail against the cause of danger. His or her responses seem designed to rectify injustice—to reassert power or status, to fighten the offending persons into compliance, to restore a desired state of affairs" (p. 1078). At first sight, all of these effects of anger should lead to performance improvement.

A rapid review of the literature, however, suggests that these positive effects do not include all the consequences of anger. Anger may have some negative consequences (e.g., conflict escalation, emotional distance, rehersal of grievances, loss of social respect, and deterioration of physical health) that may be reflected in performance deficits. Deffenbacher, Demm, and Brandon (1986) summarized these costs and claim that the tendency to become easily and frequently angered may contribute to physical and verbal aggression, child abuse, personal injury and property damage, ineffective problem solving, and such health problems as hypertension and coronary heart disease.

These costs of anger may be also manifested within LH settings. Anger may produce anxiety as long as the failure cannot be overcome by active fighting. As I see it, the recurrence of failure despite active efforts forces the angry person to confront his or her weakness and the uselessness of his or her assertive actions. It also makes it difficult for angry persons to break the link between failure and the self, because they cannot convince anyone—themselves included—that they did not actively strive for success. Under these circumstances, anger may intensify the threat to self-identity posed by failure and contribute to anxiety arousal after the expectancy of no control is formed.

Support for the positive and negative effects of anger is to be found in Study 10 of my recent series (see Table 1.1). In this study, subjects were preselected according to their propensity to react with anger to anger-arousing stimuli (high or low), as assessed by the Spielberger Trait Anger Scale. One week later, they were exposed to either no, one, or four unsolvable problems and performed a letter cancellation task. Finally, they completed anger, anxiety, and depression items tapping their current emotions, as well as my scales on mental rumination and coping strategies.

In line with my view of the facilitative effects of anger, high-anger subjects showed more accurate performance after one failure than low-anger subjects. They were less accurate, however, after four failures (see Table 5.5). Moreover, relative to no failure, one failure improved performance and four failures impaired performance only among subjects with a propensity to anger. In the absence of anger proneness, neither small nor large amounts of failure had any significant performance effect.

Results also point to the affective and coping substrates of the LH effects (see Table 5.5). Relative to no failure, high-anger subjects reacted to a small amount of failure with elevated anger, action rumination, and problem solving, which might have been behind their reactance. After a large amount of failure, they reacted with elevated anger, anxiety, depressed affect, state rumination, and avoidance coping, which might have been behind their LH deficits. Subjects low in their propensity to anger reacted to both amounts of failure with no heightened affect, rumination, or coping action.

On the whole, anger may contribute to the reactance effects of a small amount

TABLE 5.5. Means of Accuracy, Emotion, Rumination, and Coping Scores by Number of Failures and Trait Anger (Study 10)

	No failures		One failure		Four failures	
	Low	High	Low	High	Low	High
Performance accuracy	81.25	79.37	76.62	87.62	80.75	66.62
Anger	1.50	1.50	1.50	3.50	1.75	3.62
Anxiety	1.37	1.62	1.50	1.87	1.62	3.37
Depressed affect	1.62	1.37	1.75	1.37	1.50	3.25
Action rumination	1.62	4.62	3.87	5.12	2.87	2.62
State rumination	4.12	1.37	1.50	1.75	1.50	2.50
Task-irrelevant rumination	1.62	1.25	1.25	1.37	1.50	3.37
Problem-focused coping	4.37	5.00	3.87	5.37	3.50	3.00
Reappraisal	1.50	1.75	1.75	3.00	1.62	2.00
Reorganization	1.75	1.25	1.87	1.62	1.25	3.25
Avoidance	1.62	1.62	1.37	1.87	1.37	2.62

of helplessness training by sustaining action rumination and problem solving. People may pay a high price for their propensity to anger, however, as failure continues despite their active fighting. After repeated failures, anger proneness fosters anxiety and depressed affects, favors off-task coping, and impairs performance.

THE IMPACT OF ANXIETY AND DEPRESSED FEELINGS

Multiple reviews and theoretical analyses dating back to the 1950s converge in emphasizing the hypothesized detrimental effects of anxiety and depressed affects on task performance. They support the idea that these emotions sustain off-task rumination and coping, which move people away from the task and interfere with performance.

According to Frijda (1986) and Lazarus (1991), depressed affects prepare and motivate people to disengage from losses and failures and to reorganize their priorities (Frijda, 1986; Klinger, 1975; Lazarus, 1991). According to Lazarus (1991), "In sadness there seems to be no clear action tendency—except inaction, or withdrawal into oneself" (p. 251). Depressed affects are also hypothesized to sustain the allocation of resources in off-task coping activities and hence to reduce the capacity to allocate resources to relevant aspects of the task (e.g., Ellis & Ashbrook, 1988; Hasher & Zacks, 1979). This account originated from Kahneman's (1973) assumptions that a fixed pool of resources are available for cognitive processing and that variations in task performance result from changes in the policy of resource allocation.

In the same vein, theorists with psychoanalytic (Bibring, 1953), cognitive (Beck, 1976), and behavioral (Kanfer & Hagerman, 1981) perspectives agree that depressed affect may heighten the tendency to ruminate on personal losses as well as on the past, present, and future state of the self. Cognitive theories also emphasize the association between depression and excessive thinking about negative aspects of the self (e.g., Beck & Clark, 1988; Pyszczynski & Greenberg, 1987). In addition, studies have consistently found that depressed affects are related to high frequency of thoughts on themes of self-evaluation and hopelessness (see Beck & Clark, 1988, and Ingram, 1990, for reviews). To be sure, these theories and studies do not directly state that the state ruminations that arise from depressed affect have some adaptive function. In my terms, the state rumination and LH deficits that follow depressed affects reflect a temporary disengagement by which the person's mental structures readjust to reality and attain a new level of adaptation.

Though depressed affects follow the acceptance of a loss and are a sign of resignation, they do not mean that the working-through process has been completed and new goals have replaced the old ones. These affects imply only the recognition of the futility of problem-focused attempts and the decision to reorganize mental structures. At this juncture, depressed affects serve as a coping device that reinforces and sustains the reorganization task. As Lazarus (1991) said, "Sadness is typically a temporary state of mind until it is worked through" (p. 248).

With regard to anxiety, several authors emphasize the idea that anxiety may sustain avoidance coping, which again would impair task performance. Lazarus (1991) and Izard (1977) claim that anxiety moves people to run away from a threatening task at the price of poor performance. Similarly, Frijda (1986) contends that anxiety favors coping actions designed to inhibit task-relevant actions and to help the person avoid future threats, escape annoying transactions, and understand the nature and source of the threat. At the same time, anxiety may also lead people to pay attention to internal and external stimuli that can recall the threat. Anxiety may then contribute to LH deficits by favoring the intrusion of failure-related thoughts into consciousness that draw away resources from task-relevant activities. In addition, anxiety may be intensified by this intrusion to such extreme levels that it may begin to overwhelm the cognitive system, fragment thought, and further interfere with task performance.

In this view, the performance deficits produced by anxiety may have both functional and dysfunctional aspects. On the one hand, anxiety may impair performance by propelling people to make a trade-off between distress mitigation and task performance. It fosters avoidance coping and the sacrifice of performance for the sake of inner calm. On the other hand, anxiety may impair performance by producing autonomic thoughts. One should keep in mind, however, that even these effects of anxiety may follow from its original coping function.

Early conceptions emphasized the detrimental effects of anxiety on cognition and performance. They viewed anxiety as a learned drive that produces feelings of inadequacy, feelings of helplessness, anticipation of punishment, anticipation of loss of self-esteem, increased somatic activity, and implicit attempts to leave the task situation (e.g., Mandler & Sarason, 1952). In more recent accounts, these responses are described in attentional terms (e.g., Hamilton, 1975; Sarason, 1975; Wine, 1971). For example, Wine (1971) characterized highly anxious persons as those whose attention is focused on self and social evaluative cues, and whose thought flow is full with worries about their present and future state.

A large number of empirical studies have also corroborated these detrimental effects of anxiety (see Eysenck, 1982; Sarason, 1975; for reviews). In both paper and pencil measures and oral interviews, anxious persons were found to be self-preoccupied and self-evaluative, to spend more time worrying about how well they were performing, and to recollect memories on personal threats and dangers. Only a small number of studies failed to find any correlation between anxiety and off-task thoughts (e.g., Fulkerson, Galassi, & Galassi, 1984; Klinger, 1984).

The relationships of anxiety and depressed affect to off-task coping and rumination have been also demonstrated within the LH context. In six of the studies that I present in this book, significant correlations were found between scores on single anxiety and depression items and the reported engagement in mental rumination and coping strategies after helplessness training (see Table 5.6). Most of the studies found that the stronger the reported anxiety and depressed affects, the higher the frequency of state and task-irrelevant thoughts and the more likely the use of avoidance and reorganization strategies. Moreover, the stronger the anxiety and depressed affects, the lower the frequency of action thoughts and the less likely the adoption of problem-focused coping.

Supportive evidence is also found for the hypothesized performance effects of anxiety and depressed affect. First of all, there is ample correlational evidence that

TABLE 5.6. Associations of Anxiety and Depression to Rumination and Coping

	Study number	Action	State	Task-irrelevant	Problem solving	Reappraisal	Reorganization	Avoidance
Anxiety								
	1	−.50[b]	.59[b]	.54[b]	−.45[b]	−.32[a]	.56[b]	.49[b]
	8	−.04	.54[b]	.56[b]	−.46[b]	.10	.45[b]	.55[b]
	9	−.36[a]	.47[b]	.56[b]	−.35[a]	−.06	.27	.35[a]
	10	−.34[a]	.54[b]	.50[b]	−.26	−.10	.62[b]	.48[b]
	11	−.15	.39[b]	.37[a]	−.46[b]	−.05	.33[a]	.42[b]
	12	−.30[a]	.47[b]	.51[b]	−.39[b]	.04	.48[b]	.51[b]
Depression								
	1	−.35[c]	.48[b]	.58[b]	−.23	−.49[b]	.56[b]	.64[b]
	8	−.01	.68[b]	.38[a]	−.52[b]	.08	.64[b]	.60[b]
	9	−.40[b]	.67[b]	.57[b]	−.33[a]	.03	.36[a]	.45[b]
	10	−.43[b]	.49[b]	.45[b]	−.15	−.14	.48[b]	.56[b]
	11	−.34[a]	.47[b]	.49[b]	−.33[a]	−.15	.47[b]	.36[a]
	12	−.38[b]	.49[b]	.53[b]	−.36[b]	−.27[a]	.49[b]	.54[b]

[a]$p < .05$
[b]$p < .01$

TABLE 5.7. Pearson Correlations of
Performance Accuracy and Emotion Scores

Study number	Anxiety	Depression
1	−.53[b]	−.49[b]
8	−.36[a]	−.38[a]
9	−.21	−.29
10	−.34[a]	−.32[a]
11	−.27	−.43[b]
12	−.56[b]	−.31[a]

[a]$p < .05$
[b]$p < .01$

task performance is inversely related to the intensity of anxiety and depressed affects. Reports of anxiety and depressed affect in a variety of achievement settings have been found to be related to poor performance in cognitive, learning, perceptual, and psychomotor tasks (see reviews in Miller, 1975; Sarason, 1975; Wine, 1971), as well as to the impairment of several aspects of information processing, including problem solving, attention, memory, and categorization (see reviews in Eysenck, 1982, Geen, 1980; Hasher & Zacks, 1979; Miller, 1975).

To be sure, none of these studies assessed emotions after failure, and most of their measures include a wide variety of cognitive and motivational responses that partly confound the performance impact of anxiety and depressed affects with the impact of other LH-related factors (e.g., low control expectancy). Nonetheless, my six studies, which do not have these shortcomings (see Table 5.7), obtained similar correlations. In most of these studies, reports of anxiety and depressed affects after helplessness training were significantly correlated with performance deficits in the test phase. Because the findings are correlational, however, they support the proposition that anxiety and depressed affects derive from poor performance in the test task as much as the proposition that these emotions cause performance deficits.

Supportive evidence is also found in studies that experimentally induced depressed and anxiety affects using a variety of means, including hypnotic suggestion, self-statements, music, ego-threatening instructions, and anticipatory threats (e.g., Bower, 1981; Sarason, 1984; Sarason & Stoops, 1978; Slyker & McNally, 1991). These studies show that anxiety and depressed affect impair performance. They do not provide information, though, as to whether these emotions underlie performance deficits after failure.

Two lines of research show that these emotions underlie LH deficits. One selected subjects according to their proneness to anxiety or depressed affect, and the other manipulated experimental procedures to prevent the arousal of these emotions. If anxiety and depressed affect underlie LH deficits, helplessness training would impair performance mainly among persons who are prone to these emotions and are not exposed to any therapeutic procedure. The lack of propensity to anxiety and depressed affect or the induction of treatments that weaken these emotions would avert LH deficits. I first present findings on the propensity to anxiety and depressed affect, and then findings on therapeutic procedures.

Findings of anxiety studies since the 1950s consistently indicate that the detrimental effects of failure depend on the propensity to anxiety (see Eysenck, 1982; Sarason, 1975, for reviews). These studies measured anxiety on various scales (e.g., MAS, TAS), exposed subjects to success or failure, and assessed their performance in a wide variety of tasks (e.g., noise escape, math problems). In most of the studies, failure produced slower and less accurate performance than success only among high-anxiety subjects. Low-anxiety subjects suffered no ill effects, and in fact failure appears to have led them to perform better.

The above findings have been replicated in classic LH settings. For example, Lavelle et al. (1979) found that the performance of subjects high in trait anxiety (TAS) was impaired by helplessness training, whereas that of subjects low in the propensity to anxiety was not. Specifically, inescapable noise (as compared to escapable noise) led to elevated self-reports of anxiety during the experiment and produced higher solving latency and more mistakes in solvable anagrams only among high anxiety subjects. Similar findings were reported by Meites, Pishkin, and Bourne (1981) in a concept learning task, and by Rocklin and Thompson (1985) in a verbal task.

Findings of studies that selected people on the basis of their propensity to depression were not as consistent as those reported in the anxiety studies. On the one hand, some studies (e.g., Brockner & Guare, 1983; Kenelly, Hayslip, & Richardson, 1985) showed that failure produced worse performance than control conditions mainly among subjects who were prone to depression. On the other hand, other studies (Klein et al., 1976; Klein & Seligman, 1976; Miller & Seligman, 1975; Mikulincer et al., 1991) showed that helplessness training produced worse performance than control conditions only among subjects who did not show any propensity to depression. Subjects with a tendency to depression performed poorly whether they were exposed to failure or no feedback.

If these latter studies seem to suggest that depressed feelings do not account for LH deficits, additional findings in the same studies tell otherwise. First, helplessness training was found to evoke depressed feelings among subjects who were not prone to depression (e.g., Klein et al., 1976; Miller & Seligman, 1975). Second, these subjects reported more frequent state thoughts after failure than after no feedback (Mikulincer et al., 1991).

The findings highlight the basic methodological problem of "predisposition" LH studies. Helplessness training may evoke depressed affects among nondepressed subjects and thereby may lead them to behave similarly to those who tend to be habitually depressed. In this way, helplessness training may blur the effects of the propensity to depression. Less blurring seems to occur in the anxiety studies. Potentially, this difference might be accounted for either by the possibility that low-anxiety subjects are more resilient to the emotional impact of helplessness training than subjects without the propensity to depression, or by the possibility that helplessness training produces stronger depression than anxiety. The findings, however, suggest that the second possibility is unlikely.

Only one LH study found no effect of depressed affect on test task performance. Gerlsma and Albersnagel (1987) reported that subjects who had become depressed after helplessness training showed no subsequent performance deficit. Methodological problems, though, may have been responsible for the disconfirming finding. First, mood was assessed via single-item scales. Second, performance was assessed via a stable measure of intelligence, which may be insensitive to experimental inductions. Third, subjects also took the IQ test before the training, which may have immunized them against LH deficits.

Another line of research examines the therapeutic implications of treatment aimed at alleviating these emotions. These studies consistently suggest that anxiety and depressed affects account for LH deficits. In the first two "therapeutic" studies, Kilpatrick-Tabak and Roth (1978) and Raps, Reinhard, and Seligman (1980) found that a mood elevation procedure (reading 60 of Velten's self-statements expressing feelings of competence, efficacy, and cheerfulness) reduced reports of depressed affects and improved task performance after helplessness training. They also found that helplessness training, as compared to control conditions, impaired performance only among subjects who were not given any mood elevation procedure (who waited alone, performed a neutral task, or read 60 of Velten's neutral mood statements).

In one unpublished study, two of my students (Semel & Newman, 1991) examined the effectiveness of the Velten's mood-elation procedure in immunizing people against LH deficits. The rationale was that if the arousal of depressed affects underlies these deficits, the induction of positive mood before helplessness training may delay or counteract that arousal and help to sustain appropriate test task performance. As expected, four unsolvable problems, as compared to no problem, produced higher reported depression (as measured by a single item), more frequent state and task-irrelevant thoughts (as measured by the CIQ), and less accurate performance in a letter cancellation task only among subjects who had been previously asked to read neutral self-statements. Reports of depression and off-task thoughts were reduced, and performance was improved, by introducing the mood elevation procedure before helplessness training.

Coyne et al. (1980) found that an imaginal anxiety-alleviation task ("to think of mountain scenery") reduced the report of anxiety feelings after helplessness training and, more important, improved test task performance. Four unsolvable problems produced worse anagram performance than solvable or no problems only in a no-intervention condition, but not after the imaginal task.

These findings were replicated and extended in two studies conducted by my students. Gerby (1991) examined the effectiveness of three different anxiety-alleviation procedures (imaginal exercise, aerobic exercise, and chocolate ingestion), and Margalit and Zilberberg (1991) the effectiveness of bogus feedback on heart rate. There is evidence that aerobic exercise and eating a sweet snack both reduce the somatic and affective manifestations of anxiety (e.g., Lang & Harvey, 1988; Thayer, 1987). Moreover, Valins (1966) found that connecting subjects to a ECG and providing them with bogus heart rate feedback indicating that they were calm and serene was effective in alleviating anxiety.

Results of the two studies suggest that LH deficits depend on the arousal of anxiety. Four unsolvable problems, as compared to no feedback, produced elevated reports of anxiety and more frequent state and task-irrelevant thoughts (measured by the CIQ) during the experiment and less accurate performance in a subsequent test task (letter cancellation, logical reasoning) only in the no-intervention condition. Subjects in the imaginal task, aerobic exercise, chocolate ingestion, and bogus heart rate feedback conditions showed no elevation of anxiety or off-task thoughts and no performance deficit despite the prior lack of control.

SUMMARY

On the whole, the findings are in keeping with the hypothesis that emotion contributes to LH effects. Both the facilitatory and detrimental effects of helplessness training have been found mainly among subjects who tend to react to failure with strong emotions. In addition, the findings suggest that helplessness training impairs task performance when it induces increased anxiety and depressed affects. There is also evidence that anger contributes to reactance after a small amount of helplessness training, but impairs performance after a large amount of training.

CONCLUSIONS

An integration of the findings reviewed throughout this chapter allows us to assume that emotion acts as a distal mediator of LH effects. Whereas anger contributes to reactance affects, anxiety and depressed feelings contribute to LH deficits. On the one hand, favorable expectancies after a small amount of failure evoke anger, which support problem solving and action rumination and thereby improve performance. On the other hand, the formation of an expectancy of no control after a large amount of failure evokes anxiety and depressed affects, which support off-task coping and thoughts and thereby impair task performance. These chains of events imply that (a) emotions indirectly alter task performance via the coping activities and ruminative thoughts they reinforce and sustain, and (b) they mediate the effects of the expectancy of control on coping, rumination, and performance.

The above conclusion argues against two independent pathways leading to LH effects—one cognitive and the other emotional. Instead, it emphasizes the intricate interconnections between "cold" and "hot" processes. Though expectancy of control is a product of a "cold" rational analysis of the person–environment transaction, it tells something of affective relevance that may alter the person's emotional state. In fact, any attempt to separate so-called cold and hot processes is futile and artificial.

LH effects should be understood as the product of "hot" cognitive processes, in which the expectancy of control influences performance via an affective pathway.

The performance effects of emotional arousal, however, cannot be completely assimilated to those of the expectancy of control. Several personality and situational factors unrelated to the individual's expectancies can alter the intensity and quality of emotional arousal and thereby alter test task performance. In fact, if for any reason people react to failure with weak or no emotional arousal, weak LH effects would be recorded regardless of the expectancy of control. LH effects depend on both the individual's cognitions and emotions.

CHAPTER 6

PERCEIVED TASK VALUE AS A MODERATOR OF LH EFFECTS

Individual differences in the perceived value of failure may increase accuracy in predicting reactions to helplessness training. In a task situation, people may analyze the personal consequences of success and failure in the task—the extent to which the outcomes affect the attainment of important personal goals and the confirmation of central self-representations. This knowledge has a motivational significance: It determines the extent to which people commit themselves to a task and the amount of effort they will be willing to expend on coping actions after failure. If task outcomes are appraised as having no relevance for personal goals and self-identity, there will not be any commitment or coping activity; if outcomes are seen to be relevant, one or another coping action will be undertaken, depending on the expectancy of control.

My concept of human LH includes the perception of task value as a component of the process of coping with failure that moderates LH effects. It is a necessary step for deciding about the mobilization of coping effort after failure. This appraisal helps people to evaluate the personal implications of failure and to understand whether there is a real need to undertake coping activities. On this basis, the perception of task value may follow every experience of failure and may precede the mobilization of coping effort.

I propose three basic hypotheses about the role of perceived task value. First, perceived task value influences coping efforts: the higher the perceived value of helplessness training, the stronger the subsequent coping reactions. Second, these effects would be manifested in the strength of LH effects. Both reactance and LH deficits would be found mainly when people assign high value to the helplessness training and thus feel pressed to undertake coping responses that alter performance. Low task value would weaken LH effects by making the coping activities unnecessary. Third, perceived task value moderates the expectancy–performance link: Unfavorable expectancies produces worse performance than favorable expectancies mainly under high task value conditions. This chapter examines the hypothesized effects of two basic components of task value: the perceived importance of failure (the extent to which failure touches on personal goals), and its perceived self-relevance (the extent to which failure touches on self-identity).

THE VALUATION PROCESS

The valuation process is a cognitive activity by which people attempt to under-stand the personal implications of success and failure in a task. It underlies the goal-relevance component of Lazarus and Folkman's (1984) primary appraisal—the extent to which outcomes in a task are relevant to the person's endeavors. It consists of the assessment of the goals that can be attained or thwarted in a task, the self aspects that may be involved in task performance, and the centrality of these goals and self-aspects in the person's goal hierarchy and self-identity. Theory and research have focused on two products of the valuation process: perceived task importance and perceived task self-relevance. I shall present some theoretical statements bear-ing on each of these products in turn, and then some integrative ideas about the valuation process.

Perceived Task Importance

In the short history of modern psychology, the terms used to designate per-ceived task importance have changed several times and have included task attrac-tiveness, goal valence, reinforcement value, incentive level, and others (e.g., At-kinson & Feather, 1966; Rotter, 1954). Phenomenologically, these terms all refer to the extent to which people feel attracted by a task and attach importance to its outcomes. Theoretically, they refer to the extent to which task outcomes are ex-pected to be followed by some beneficial or harmful consequences to one's endeav-ors: whether success would be followed by the achievement of personal goals, and whether failure would be followed by the thwarting of these goals. The greater the expectancy of benefit or harm and the more important the beneficial/harmful conse-quences, the higher the importance attached to a task. In other words, high per-ceived task importance reflects the appraisal of task success as a personal benefit and the appraisal of task failure as a personal threat.

Perceived task importance evolves from a self-reflective process by which people compare the goals that can be attained or thwarted in a task with their own goal hierarchy. Each person holds a stable goal hierarchy, which is the inner repre-sentation of his or her endeavors and commitments (e.g., Carver & Scheier, 1981) and provides the basis for evaluating whether a task may have some personal beneficial or harmful consequences (Lazarus, 1991). The more that the goals in the task are seen to be relevant to one's goal hierarchy, the higher the importance that one will assign to the task. So, for example, persons with strong achievement goals and weak affiliation goals may assign higher importance to achievement tasks than to affiliation tasks, because outcomes in the former tasks touch on central aspects of their goal hierarchy. The reverse pattern may be found for persons with strong affiliation goals and weak achievement goals.

Though using different names for the relation of task outcomes to goal hierarchy (e.g., instrumentality, outcome–consequence expectancy) and emphasizing diverse consequences (e.g., need satisfaction, goal attainment), most current theories of motivation conceptualize perceived task importance in terms of the anticipated consequences associated with task outcomes (e.g., Atkinson & Feather, 1966; Heckhausen, 1977). They hold that task importance is determined not solely by objective task features but also by people's endeavors and their beliefs in the relevance of outcomes to these endeavors.

A similar conceptualization of perceived task importance was suggested by Brehm (1966), who defined it as "a direct function of the unique instrumental value which the behavior has for the satisfaction of needs multiplied by the actual or potential maximum magnitude of the need" (pp. 4–5). This definition implies that when the magnitude of a need is high, task importance will vary directly with the extent to which success satisfies the need and failure frustrates it. When task outcomes are perceived to be instrumental to need satisfaction, task importance will vary directly with the magnitude of the need. If the magnitude of the need is low or task outcomes have no relevance to need satisfaction, little importance will be given to the task.

On this basis, the effects of perceived task importance can be studied either by manipulating messages about the link between the task outcomes and the person's goals or by measuring individual differences in the magnitude of the person's needs and goals that can be affected by task outcomes. Both techniques have been employed in LH studies. Some studies have provided information about the importance of the training and/or test tasks. Other studies have preselected subjects according to two individual-differences factors that contribute to the perception of task importance in LH settings: achievement need, and the personality dimension of Type A– Type B.

Achievement need is defined as the desire to do well in competition with standards of excellence (McLelland, Atkinson, Clark, & Lowell, 1958). High-achievement-need subjects are more motivated than low-achievement-need subjects to get ahead at the ego-ideal level, to compete with a standard of excellence, and to achieve unique accomplishments (e.g., Atkinson & Feather, 1966; McLelland et al., 1958). They consider the attainment of success in skill tasks to be an important endeavor, and therefore they tend to commit themselves to any task that has the potential for achieving success. In contrast, people with low achievement needs tend not to view such tasks as potential sources of pride, and thus they are unconcerned with evaluating their performance.

It therefore appears that people high in the need for achievement would be likely to assign more importance to the training and test tasks of typical LH studies than people low in that need. These two tasks are typically presented as skill dependent, and they involve competition with a standard of excellence (see Chapter 1). Hence their outcomes are likely to bear a great deal of significance in relation to the basic goals of people who are primarily motivated by a need for achievement: Success holds the potential to satisfy their basic goals, and failure may represent an immediate threat to their endeavors. In contrast, neither success nor failure are relevant to the basic goals of people with low achievement needs; for this reason, the latter would be expected to assign a low level of importance to the LH tasks.

Type A personality is marked by forceful, speeded-up, and competitive behaviors and is tied to achievement need and desire for control (Glass, 1977). Type B personality is more relaxed, slower, less competitive, and less achievement oriented. In both laboratory and field research, Type A individuals have been found to assign high importance to success and control, Type B individuals less (e.g., Glass & Carver, 1980). Type A individuals have also been found to be less ready to relinquish control than Type B individuals, even when maintaining control was maladaptive (e.g., Miller, Lack, & Asroff, 1985; Strube & Werner, 1985).

In reviewing the literature, Glass (1977) concluded that Type A persons are motivated by an intense desire for personal control. They work hard, suppress fatigue, and perform at a rapid pace in order to assert control over potentially harmful events. This characteristic pattern of behavior comes into play especially during control deprivation. It is thus reasonable to assume that Type A–Type B personality might contribute to the perception of task importance in LH settings, with Type A individuals assigning more importance to the tasks than Type B individuals. The deprivation of control during helplessness training and its possible restoration in the test task would be much more relevant to Type A individuals, with their strong desire for control, than to Type B individuals, for whom the attainment and maintenance of control is less important.

Perceived Self-Relevance

Another product of the valuation process is the perceived self-relevance of a task. It refers to the extent to which task outcomes are expected to have an impact on a person's self-identity: whether success has beneficial implications for self-identity (confirmation of self-aspects involved in the task), and whether failure has threatening effects on self-schemas. Perceived self-relevance evolves from assessing the extent to which task outcomes affect self-representations and the centrality of these representations for one's self-identity. The stronger the impact of task outcomes on self-representations and the more central these representations for self-identity, the higher the self-relevance attached to a task.

A link between task outcomes and self-representations would be perceived depending on the attribution of outcomes to internal or external causes (e.g., Abramson, Seligman, & Teasdale, 1978; Heider, 1958; Weiner, 1985). In some task situations, people may attribute outcomes to internal factors (e.g., abilities, skills, traits) and may therefore tend to see them as touching on some of their self-schemas. Here success confirms or enhances the belief that one possesses the traits responsible for the outcomes, whereas failure threatens and raises doubts about the possession of these traits. There are other situations, however, in which task outcomes are attributed to external-contextual factors (e.g., luck, task features) and neither success nor failure are perceived as relevant to self-identity. Consistent with this hypothesis, McFarland and Ross (1982) found that positive views of the self (self-esteem) were reduced after failure in a social accuracy task only among subjects who were induced to make an internal attribution. I (Mikulincer, 1986a) similarly found a reported threat to self-esteem only after a message designed to produce internal attribution for failure.

In the LH paradigm, information about the normative difficulty of the tasks is one of the factors that determine the individual's attribution along the internal–external dimension. Tasks described as moderately easy are expected to have the most bearing on self-definition, because it is hardest to attribute failing in them to task difficulty. An external attribution would be more likely in tasks presented as very difficult; in this case, people can convince themselves or any audience that failure tells nothing about their abilities and skills ("Everyone would fail in such a very difficult task").

Perceived self-relevance may also depend on the importance of the aspects of the self that may be touched by task outcomes. According to Snyder et al. (1978), little self-relevance is assigned to a task when its outcomes are linked to unimportant self-aspects. A task is appraised as having a high level of self-relevance only when outcomes are attributed to important self-aspects.

Snyder et al. (1978) illustrated this point as follows:

> If someone plays a game and loses, threat to self-esteem depends both on attributing the failure to oneself and on believing one's failure says something negative about an important aspect of self. If one believes the game is a matter of chance and the outcome is independent of what one does, the first factor is absent and there should be no threat. Even if one believes the game depends on skill and that the blame for the loss rests squarely on one's shoulders, there is no threat if the game is perceived as irrelevant to important aspects of self. Someone may believe that losing at bridge is one's own fault but may not regard poor ability at card games as important. Skill at card games is irrelevant to this person's self-esteem (pp. 93–94).

In my view, self-relevance depends also on a third factor: the pursuit of self-evaluation in the task. That is, it depends on the extent of a person's concern with the changes that outcomes may produce on their self-views. Where it is important for people to evaluate their self-views in a task, the perceived self-relevance of the task will vary, as explained above, with the attribution of outcomes to internal factors and the centrality of these factors to self-identity. Where people are *not* interested in evaluating themselves, then the self-relevance of the task will be psychologically insignificant, regardless of the internal–external attribution. In other words, although internally attributed outcomes usually tell something of relevance about the self, people may regard these evaluative cues as irrelevant for their current concerns if they are not inclined to evaluate themselves.

Elliott and Dweck (1988) distinguish between two goals in achievement tasks: "(a) performance goals, in which individuals seek to maintain positive judgments of their ability and avoid negative judgments by seeking to prove, validate, or document their ability and not discredit it; and (b) learning goals, in which individuals seek to increase their ability or master new tasks" (p. 5). Only the pursuit of performance goals implies the desire to evaluate the self in the task situation and the appraisal of task outcome as touching on self-identity. In this case, the experience of failure may constitute a serious threat to self-identity, which in turn would lead someone to assign high self-relevance to the task. This sequence of events is all the more likely when the failure is attributed to internal factors.

GOALS AND SELF-IDENTITY

Are perceived importance and perceived self-relevance two different types of task valuation, or separate facets of a single process? Raynor (1970) postulated that they are manifestations of two different motivational systems: the behavioral system and the self system. Arousal in the behavioral system refers to the motivation to attain higher-order goals. Arousal in the self system refers to the motivation to become a particular type of person and to attain and maintain a sense of identity.

Lazarus (1991), however, presents a very different view. He suggests that the self is a motivational system that organizes the person's goal hierarchy:

> A self or ego organizes motives and attitudes into hierarchies of importance. . . . Goals are not disconnected from each other, and decisions must be made about which goal to center on and which to subordinate or suppress. Threats to any personal goal are, at bottom, threats to oneself. It makes little sense to speak of goals that are part of the self and goals that are not, because all are in some way a property of the person. Thus, the self or ego-identity is in large part a motivational concept, and goal hierarchies are organized by an executive agency of the personality, which coordinates and regulates in action what a person desires or build into a self-schema that is differentiated from the rest of the world (p. 101).

In line with Lazarus's reasoning, I think that perceived task importance and perceived self-relevance may be so closely related that it would be meaningless to speak of them as manifestations of two separate motivational systems. To begin with, the decision to pursue a goal may be based on the congruence between that goal and one's self-definition. Then the attainment or nonattainment of an important goal often has repercussions for that self-definition, which in turn may further alter the goals one pursues. In this way, a loop is created by which the self system and the behavioral system reciprocally alter each other and become interconnected in a complex network.

Take, for example, people who strive for a high level of control over the environment. Their desire for control may be congruent with their representations of the self as powerful, competent, and assertive. In addition, the satisfaction of this desire may confirm their self-representations ("I exert control, so I'm powerful"), whereas its frustration may threaten the self-schema ("I fail to exert control, so my view of the self as powerful may be wrong"). In fact, any failure of control directly thwarts their basic striving for control and threatens their sense of the self as a controlling agent. Given these interconnections, the high importance these people may assign to tasks in which they can exert control also signals the involvement of central self-aspects in the task. Of course, all these links are true only when outcomes are attributed to personal factors and when the person is concerned with self-evaluation.

In more general terms, the perception of task importance and the perception of self-relevance may occur together. In a task situation, where people compare goals that can be attained or thwarted with their goal hierarchy, they are also indirectly assessing whether these goals are relevant to their self-identity because, according to Lazarus, the goal hierarchy is a reflection of the self. Therefore the assignment of high perceived task importance implies not only that task outcomes affect central aspects of goal hierarchy but also that they may, if they are attributed to internal factors, confirm or threaten self-identity. The benefits of success in a valued task may be reflected in both the attainment of important goals and the confirmation of the aspects of self-identity that are related to these goals. The harm of failure in such a task may be reflected in the thwarting of important goals and the threat to the sense of self that underlies the pursuit of these goals.

To summarize, I see the appraisals of task importance and self-relevance as two interconnected aspects of the valuation process. For this reason, the hypotheses and rationale I present in the following sections treat the perception of task value as one integrated process.

PERCEIVED TASK VALUE AND THE COPING PROCESS

This section deals with my hypothesis that perceived task value moderates the mobilization of coping efforts after failure. This effect would be observed in the strength of the various coping devices that failure may activate: coping strategies, mental rumination, and emotional reactions. Specifically, the higher the perceived value of the tasks, the stronger the effects of failure on coping strategies, mental rumination, and emotion (see Chapters 2, 3, and 5). Any factor that reduces the perceived value of the tasks makes unnecessary the undertaking of coping strategies, the engagement in rumination, and the arousal of emotion after helplessness training.

In my terms, the assignment of high value to a task seems to create a state of personal commitment to the task, which leads to a greater investment of effort. Because important goals and central self-aspects are perceived to be involved in the task, people are likely to invest effort in order either to actualize the anticipated benefits of success or to cope with the anticipated damage of failure. Having assigned little or no value to a task, people may have no personal reason for committing themselves to it or expending efforts in achieving a valueless success or coping with a nonthreatening failure.

Modern theories of motivation argue that judgments about the importance of a task situation motivate task-related actions (e.g., Atkinson & Feather, 1966). According to Tolman (1932), for example, the tendency to perform an act depends on two factors: the expectancy that the act will lead to the attainment of a goal, and the subjective importance of that goal.

Perceived self-relevance has also been viewed as a basic motivating factor (e.g., Feather, 1969; Weiner & Sierad, 1975). In his social learning theory, Bandura (1977, 1986) states that people expend little or no effort in activities that have no personal relevance for them. Rather, it is in those areas of life affecting self-identity that motivational commitment is activated. In Bandura's terms, most people feel a sense of pride and pleasure over the accomplishments that they attribute to their own abilities and competences. Conversely, they seldom derive much satisfaction when they attribute their success to external factors. The same holds true for judgments of failure. People tend to respond self-critically to poor performance for which they view themselves responsible, but not to failure that they perceive as attributable to mitigating circumstances or other impediments.

The assignment of high value to a task transforms a transaction with the environment into one of the person's main concerns (Klinger, 1975; Lazarus, 1991). This is reflected in cognitive, emotional, and behavioral activity. At the cognitive level, people may be occupied with the task outcomes and their implications, and they will thus allocate cognitive resources to analyze any material related to the transaction. At the emotional level, they may react with strong emotions to any task outcome that implies the attainment or thwarting of personal goals. Behaviorally, they may invest substantial effort in the task situation and may find it hard to abandon even after it becomes clear that success is unlikely.

In the LH paradigm, the valuation process acquires a specific meaning. It corresponds to what Lazarus and Folkman (1984) call "threat appraisal"; it brings information about the extent to which the failure experienced in helplessness training threatens one's goal hierarchy and self-identity. The higher the value one assigns to a task, the more likely it is that a failure in that task would be appraised as a *self-relevant threat*. Such failure may threaten the attainment of important personal goals and the self-aspects that could have been confirmed by the attainment of these goals.

Importantly, threat appraisal is unrelated to the formation of an expectancy of no control. People may assign high value to a task and may appraise the failure as a threat irrespective of their control expectancies. That is, the expectancy of control does not modify the threat appraisal of failure; it can, however, modify a person's appraisal of what can be done with that threat. Under favorable expectancies, failure in high valued tasks may be perceived as a threat that can be removed by one's actions, whereas under unfavorable expectancies, the same failure may be perceived as a threat that cannot be reversed by task-relevant actions.

The valuation process also acquires a particular motivating function in human

LH. Though high perceived task value in neutral conditions may be an incentive mainly for task-relevant activities, after helplessness training it may be better described as an incentive for the entire spectrum of coping actions, including some that may even disrupt task-relevant activities. Here the knowledge generated in the valuation process is used to decide whether there is a need to invest efforts in coping with failure. The higher the perceived value of the task, the more threatening the appraised consequences of failure and, therefore, the higher the need for coping with the failure. This need would be manifested in the undertaking of coping strategies, the engagement in purposive mental rumination, and the arousal of emotions that reinforce and sustain the coping effort.

PERCEIVED TASK VALUE AND COPING STRATEGIES

There is evidence that perceived task value strengthens coping effort after failure without cueing any particular coping response. For example, it was found that the higher the self-relevance of failure is, the more likely a person is to use excuse attributions (e.g., Rosenfield & Stephan, 1978; Stevens & Jones, 1976). Inductions of high perceived task value have also been found to increase claims of self-handicaps (DeGree & Snyder, 1985; Smith, Snyder, & Handelsman, 1982; Snyder, Smith, Augelli, & Ingram, 1985) and behavioral disengaging from a task via distracting music or effort withdrawal (Pyszczynski & Greenberg, 1983; Shepperd & Arkin, 1989). In addition, I found that internal attributions strengthen the undertaking of wishful thinking and cognitive avoidance after failure (Mikulincer, 1989b).

There is also evidence that Type A individuals, to whom maintaining control is important, expend more effort in coping with lack of control than do Type B individuals, for whom failure is not self-relevant. Type A people were found to use more problem-focused coping in response to threatening events than Type B people and to adopt a more active, vigilant attitude (Glass, 1977; Strube & Lott, 1985). In addition, Type A individuals tend to use more avoidance coping than Type B individuals. There is evidence that Type A people deny and suppress feelings of discomfort (e.g., Pittner, Houston, & Spiridigliozzi, 1983), suppress attending to negative mood during performance (Strube & Lott, 1985), and choose to take performance-inhibiting drugs when faced with the prospect of failing after unsolvable problems (Weidner, 1980). It is possible that Type A individuals activate these avoidance responses when they become convinced of the futility of problem-focused coping attempts.

PERCEIVED TASK VALUE AND MENTAL RUMINATION

Perceived task value may also alter the cognitive substrate of coping responses—mental rumination. The basic idea here is that rumination, like other coping responses, may be activated after failure to the extent that something of personal significance is at stake and coping actions are needed. Mental rumination is the cognitive manifestation of a person's current concerns (Klinger, 1975), because people tend to process information primarily on topics that are perceived to be important for the realization of their goals. They tend not to invest cognitive efforts on issues that are irrelevant to their interests (Seta & Seta, 1982). In LH settings, people may thus be motivated to ruminate on the task situation only insofar as the failure is considered to be a threat to the attainment of their goals or a reflection of their identity.

These ideas emphasize the interface between motivation and cognition. Personal endeavors determine when cognitive activity will be initiated, as well as its content and duration. Moreover, rumination contains a motivational component arising not only from personality dispositions but also from transient contextual influences. From this perspective, rumination is not an automatic reaction to failure but a purposive, goal-oriented activity.

The association between current concerns and rumination has been found in an early series of studies. Using TAT stories as a measure of thought content, it was found that making achievement need one of the person's concerns (e.g., through incentives, ego-involving messages) increased the number of TAT stories that included references to achievement-related activities (e.g., McLelland et al., 1949). Other studies also found that the arousal of strong needs (e.g., hunger, thirst) increased the incidence of TAT stories that included reference to these needs (see Klinger, 1977, for a review). Although these studies suffered from methodological and conceptual problems and some of the inductions of need arousal confounded goal blockage with motivation, the findings provide some preliminary evidence on the impact of motivation on rumination.

More recent studies demonstrated that rumination while working in a task is a direct function of the importance/self-relevance of the task. Klinger et al. (1980) found that the time people spent thinking about their goals increased with the importance they attached to the latter. Morris and Fulmer (1976) found that messages of high task importance produced reports of higher self-preoccupative worry than did low-importance messages. In the LH context, Stiensmeier-Pelster (1989) found that the more important people considered a failure to be, the more they engaged in state thoughts. I (Mikulincer, 1989b) found that the frequency of both state and task-irrelevant thoughts after failure increased with the perceived self-relevance of the task.

Studies that focus on personality antecedents of perceived task value also have supported the idea that rumination is a direct function of task value. For example, Brunson and Matthews (1982) found that Type A persons engaged in more state rumination after failure than did Type B persons. Using the same research strategy, Elliott and Dweck (1988) found that free verbalizations of state thoughts increased after failure only among subjects who pursued performance goals. Among subjects who pursued learning goals, failure did not increase reports of state thoughts, even when they held unfavorable expectancy. The findings clearly imply that people engage in mental rumination only when failure touches on self-evaluation (performance goals). This conclusion was supported in a study conducted by Barkan (1991), who used the CIQ to assess the state and task-irrelevant thoughts of college students exposed to failure in a social judgment task.

Perceived Task Value and Emotional Intensity

Particular emotions are aroused in order to prepare and motivate people to undertake particular coping actions. Whether emotions will be aroused depends on the perceived value of failure, which determines the need for coping. The assignment of high value to a failure may be a prerequisite for strong emotions—either anger, anxiety, or depressed affects—because it indicates that there is a personal stake in the situation and a need for undertaking coping actions. When the failure is perceived to tell nothing of value to the person's wants and needs, his or her state may one of apathy or quiet tranquility. Here there is no real need for coping or for any logistic support.

Recent accounts of emotion emphasize the impact of the perceived value of failure. Lazarus (1991) claims that "there would be no emotion, if people did not arrive on the scene of an encounter with a desire, want, wish, need, or goal commitment that could be advanced or thwarted" (p. 94). Roseman (1984) stated that "people have emotions about events of relevance to active motives and preferences" (p. 17). Frijda (1986) included among the "core" components of emotion, which differentiate emotional from nonemotional experiences, the appraisal of the importance and self-relevance of a transaction.

Some theories of human LH have also noted the effects of the perceived value of helplessness training on the strength of the evoked emotions. Abramson, Seligman, and Teasdale (1978) suggested that the more important the lack of control, the stronger the emotional arousal. They also argued that emotional intensity increases proportionally with the perceived self-relevance of failure. Wortman and Brehm (1975) and Miller and Norman (1979) state that the strength of the emotional effects of failure is a direct function of the perceived task value.

Supportive evidence on the value–emotion link is found in several LH studies that manipulated or measured one or more of the antecedents of perceived task value. Using single-item measures of emotion, two studies (Roth & Kubal, 1975; Skinner, 1979) found that subjects in a high-task-importance condition reported higher anxiety and depressed affects after a large amount of helplessness training than subjects who received low-importance messages. In addition, the emotional effects of helplessness training were significant only in the high-importance condition.

Dyck, Vallentyne, and Breen (1979), Wortman, Panciera, Shusterman, and Hibscher (1976), and Mikulincer (1988c), using single-item measures, found that small amounts of helplessness training produced significantly higher reports of distress, anger, frustration, and sadness than did no feedback only among subjects who were convinced of the self-relevance of the task (moderate-difficulty instructions). The introduction of high-difficulty instructions, which breaks the link between failure and the self, eliminated the significant emotional effects. Mikulincer (1988c) and Dyck et al. (1979) also found, however, that messages of perceived difficulty had no effect on reports of anxiety and depression following large amounts of helplessness training.

Although certain limitations of the above studies—their use of single-item measures of questionable reliability, the failure of the manipulations of Mikulincer (1988c) and Wortman et al. (1976) to produce the differential effect of small and large amounts of helplessness training on anger and sadness, and the use by Dyck et al. (1979) of an affective state ("stress") that cannot be classified as either anger or depressed feelings—other studies obtained similar results using reliable composite scores of anger and depression. In one study, I (Mikulincer, 1988a) found that internal attributors reported more anger after one failure and more depression after four failures, as assessed by a 10-item scale, than external attributors (who did not perceive task performance as relevant to self-evaluation). In addition, relative to a no-feedback condition, one failure provoked stronger anger and four failures stronger depression only among subjects who tend to link failure to the self.

Similar findings were reported by McFarland and Ross (1982), who assigned subjects to success or failure in a social accuracy test, manipulated the causal explanation for performance (internal or external), and assessed subjects' mood via a 77-adjective scale. Reports of negative affects were highest for subjects who were induced to attribute failure to internal causes. A manipulation producing external attribution averted these negative affects.

Supportive evidence for the hypothesized link between perceived task value and emotional intensity is also found in LH studies that preselected subjects according to predispositional antecedents of task value. Winefeld and Norris (1981) found that high-achievement-need subjects, who assign high value to helplessness training, became more depressed after the training than low-achievement-need subjects. Brunson and Matthews (1982) found that Type A individuals, who see lack of control as a self-relevant threat, were more likely to spontaneously report negative emotions after helplessness training than Type B individuals. Similar findings occurred in studies that assessed reports and physiological signs of anxiety and depression following real-life uncontrollable events (e.g., Pittner & Houston, 1980). Burger and Arkin (1980) found that subjects who regarded the exertion of control as one of their central goals felt more depressed after helplessness training than did those with a low desire for control. On the whole, the reviewed studies emphasize that perceived task value increases the strength of evoked emotions and moderates the emotional impact of helplessness training.

Two additional lines of research provide indirect evidence supporting the above conclusion. The first is provided by Pittman and Pittman's (1979) research on the effects of the internal–external locus of control dimension. Using the MAACL, Pittman and Pittman found that internals—who, as shown in Chapter 4, are prone to perceive lack of control as a matter of personal inefficacy—reported more anger after one uncontrollable failure and more anxiety and depression after three failures than externals. The latter tend to perceive lack of control as reflecting the features of the task rather than of themselves, experience no self-relevant threat, and hence do not tend to react to helplessness training with strong emotion.

The second line of research focuses on the effects of motivational orientation (performance versus learning goals). If perceived self-relevance regulates emotional arousal, failure would evoke stronger anger, anxiety, and depression in performance than learning-goal conditions. In the former condition, people are focused on self-evaluation and see failure as threatening their sense of self-worth. Persons pursuing learning goals, by contrast, would not react to helplessness training with these emotions, for failure is not perceived as a personal threat but rather signals the opportunity to learn new skills (Dweck & Leggett, 1988).

This reasoning was supported by Elliott and Dweck (1988), who found that fifth-grade children's free verbalizations of depressed affect during and after failure was highest in conditions wherein a performance goal was induced. The induction of learning goals was followed by sporadic verbalizations of depressed affect, even when subjects expected to fail in the task. This finding was conceptually replicated by Barkan (1991) in a sample of undergraduate students.

The above findings, however, do not mean that subjects pursuing learning goals do not experience any emotion after helplessness training. They simply show that such subjects do not react to failure with depressed affect. One can argue that persons pursuing learning goals may react to failure with other emotions that were not assessed in the above studies. For example, they may experience challenge-related affects, because they see failure as an opportunity to increase mastery and to gain new knowledge on the self and the world.

SUMMARY

This section presents considerable evidence on the effects of perceived task value on the strength of the coping process. The appraisal of high task value intensifies the undertaking of coping strategies, the engagement in mental rumination, and the arousal of emotions after helplessness training. The above conclusions, however, do not negate the possibility of recursive influences between perceived task value and coping. Though the entire section is built upon the idea that perceived task value determines coping, it is possible that coping may change the perceived value of a task. For example, reorganization and goal substitution imply that what was previously appraised as a highly valued task does not touch on the person's new priorities.

PERCEIVED TASK VALUE AND LH EFFECTS

This section deals with my hypothesis that the perceived value of the training and test tasks moderates LH effects. Specifically, high perceived task value seems to be a prerequisite for the two basic effects of helplessness training: reactance and LH deficits. Reactance after a small amount of helplessness training and performance deficits after a large amount of training may both be more likely in high- than low-valued tasks. Any reduction in the perceived value of the training or test tasks may make people impervious to the helplessness training.

Both the reactance and LH deficits are a person's reaction to a threat to their goal hierarchy and self-identity. The more important the goals and self-aspects involved in helplessness training and the higher the attribution of failure to these self-aspects, the stronger the subsequent reactance and LH deficits. Lack of control would not alter subsequent performance when it is perceived as being caused by external conditions or when the task is appraised as unimportant to one's sense of self.

Perceived task value determines the strength of LH effects via its impact on amount of coping efforts. After helplessness training, people who perceive that nothing of personal value is at stake in the situation may feel no obligation to initiate coping actions. They will therefore perform the test task as if they had experienced no helplessness training. They will show no reactance effect because they do not try to cope with failure via enhanced problem solving. That is, they would neither redouble task attempts nor try to destroy obstacles that block the solution of problems. In addition, they will show no LH deficit because their cognitive resources are not directed toward off-task coping actions. They do not need to waste time and resources in reorganizing their self-views and priorities, for the nonvalued failure cannot harm any central inner structure, and they do not need obsessively to escape/avoid situations that recall the failure, because it does not produce any apprehension or fear of self-disintegration.

When the tasks are of high value, a major source of self-definition (Pyszczynski & Greenberg, 1987), a means for attaining important goals (Martin & Tesser, 1989), or a matter of primary commitments (Klinger, 1975), however, failure is perceived as a self-relevant threat, and people are propelled to cope with the mismatch that it creates. They may be occupied with the failure even in the new test task and see the task as either an opportunity for overcoming the failure or as an additional threat that needs to be managed. Their cognitions, emotions, and actions in the test task may be guided by the failure, and their performance may be a reflection of their coping attempts: It may be facilitated by the adoption of problem-focused coping, or it may be impaired by the adoption of off-task coping.

My ideas on the effects of perceived task value are not unique in human LH literature. The proposal that high perceived task importance intensifies both reactance and LH effects recurs in various theories, beginning with Wortman and Brehm's (1975) theory. Using different theoretical frameworks (e.g., Weiner's attributional theory, Rotter's social learning theory, neo-Hullian theory), Feinberg, Niller, Weiss, Steigleder, and Lombardo (1982), Miller and Norman (1979), and Zuroff (1980) made similar predictions. According to these authors, reactance and LH deficits are both potentiated in conditions that promote, and/or among subjects who assign, high importance to the training and test tasks.

The problem with these theories is that they fail to state explicitly which mechanisms underlie the performance effects of perceived task value. Moreover, they do not delineate the specific role of the valuation process in human LH. My theory takes us one step forward by stating that these effects are mediated by the intensity of the coping actions undertaken and by specifying that the perception of task value acts as a force that motivates these coping actions.

Only one theory of human LH makes different predictions regarding the impact of perceived task importance. Roth (1980) has argued that helplessness training impairs performance only when perceived task importance approaches zero. The assignment of high importance to the tasks enhances motivation to try hard, restores the motivation originally reduced by the expectancy of no control, and improves task performance. It thus appears that, according to this theory, high perceived task importance *inhibits* the link between the expectancy of no control and performance deficits: "When the value of successful task performance is high, either because of the a priori importance of performing well or because of the training-induced importance of performing well, the relationship between the future expectancy and consequent performance deficits will be weakened" (p. 114).

The differences in the predictions may derive from different conceptualizations of the processes by which helplessness training impairs performance. On the one hand, Roth, like Seligman, focuses solely on the reduction of the incentive to initiate instrumental actions produced by the expectancy of no control, and she claims that high perceived task importance reduces performance deficits because it motivates people to engage in these actions. This reasoning seems to be counterintuitive, however, for it implies that high perceived task importance motivates task attempts even when people believe that these attempts are useless. In contrast, my theory focuses on the engagement in off-task coping strategies, and it claims that high perceived task importance may motivate people to engage in these actions when they lose the hope that their problem-focused actions can be effective.

The idea that perceived self-relevance of the task may intensify LH effects can be found also in the egotism explanation of LH (Frankel & Snyder, 1978). But the egotism theory and my theory differ on three basic issues. First, the egotism theory does not present a prediction regarding the effects of perceived self-relevance on reactance. Second, it focuses on behavioral avoidance as the exclusive coping action that high perceived self-relevance may activate. Third, the egotism theory dismisses the interaction between perceived self-relevance and the expectancy of control. In contrast, I suggest that high perceived self-relevance may intensify both reactance and LH deficits by motivating people to undertake whatever coping activities are cued to be appropriate in the given circumstances. These may include not only behavioral avoidance but also problem-focused coping and reorganization. Finally, I consider LH effects to result from an expectancy–value interaction: The perceived value of the task determines the intensity of the LH effects, whereas the expectancy of control determines their quality (reactance or LH deficits).

As with any hypothesis, the validity of the hypothesized effects of perceived task value is determined by their consistency with available experimental evidence. Any finding showing that LH effects do not depend on the perceived importance/self-relevance of the task might cause one to question seriously the validity of the hypothesis. In the following pages, I review available evidence on the performance effects of perceived task value. Specifically, I focus on the performance effects of situational and personality antecedents of perceived importance and perceived self-relevance of tasks.

TASK IMPORTANCE INSTRUCTIONS

Evidence for the hypothesized effects of perceived task importance is found in studies that provide information about the link between task outcomes and important personal goals. This strategy was first used in an early LH experiment by Roth and Kubal (1975) that manipulated the importance of the *training* task and assessed whether it moderates the performance effects of one and three unsolvable problems. In the "important" condition, subjects were told prior to working on the task that it reflected academic abilities, a central aspect of the self-definition of undergraduate students. Subjects in the "unimportant" group performed the task without any information as to task importance.

Findings on test task performance showed a fragmented pattern. On the one hand, the findings demonstrated that high task importance strengthened LH deficits after a large amount of helplessness training. After three unsolvable problems, subjects in the high-importance condition performed worse than subjects in the unimportant condition. Moreover, three unsolvable problems produced worse performance than success or no feedback only under the high-importance (but not low-importance) condition. On the other hand, the findings provided no substantial evidence on the role of perceived task importance after a small amount of helplessness training. Though greater performance facilitation is predicted after a small amount of helplessness training under high-importance than under low-importance conditions, results showed no significant difference between the two conditions. One unsolvable problem produced better performance than success or no feedback under both high- and low-importance conditions. Thus, although training task importance *potentiated* performance deficits, it did not alter performance facilitation.

There is reason to believe, however, that the fragmented effects of task importance in Roth and Kubal's findings derive from the weak manipulation of that variable. For neither of the two questions that were designed to check on the manipulation of task importance yielded significant differences between high- and low-importance conditions. More valid manipulations of training task importance were carried out in three published LH studies (Dyck & Breen, 1978; Mikulincer, 1986b, Study 1; Skinner, 1979) and in Study 11 of the series that I present in this book (see Table 1.1). In these studies, high task importance was induced in the same way as in Roth and Kubal's study, but the induction of low importance was more explicit. Subjects received clear information that the training task was unimportant and did not measure any skill or ability.

Results of the four studies show that task importance instructions were effective in altering perceptions of training task importance. In addition, the findings replicated the performance pattern Roth and Kubal found after a large amount of helplessness training. In all four experiments, increasing the importance of the helplessness training increased subsequent performance deficits. More important, my Study 11 supported the hypothesis that perceived task importance strengthens reactance after a small amount of failure. The exposure to one failure was found to produce better performance in a letter cancellation task than no feedback—a reactance effect—only under high but not low task importance conditions (see Table 6.1).

In addition, Study 11 provides information about the effects of task importance on coping strategies, mental rumination, and emotions. After completing the test task, all the subjects filled out coping, rumination, and emotion items (see previous chapters). As can be seen in Table 6.2, messages on the high importance of helplessness training intensify whatever coping strategy, ruminative thought, and emotion state predominate after small and large amounts of failure. Problem solving, action rumination, and anger were more frequently reported after one failure than after zero or four failures. This tendency was higher among subjects who were induced to believe the task was very important. Reorganization and avoidance strategies, state rumination, and anxiety and depressed feelings were more frequently reported after four failures than after zero or one failure, and this tendency was higher still among subjects in the high-importance condition.

In one additional study, I manipulated instructions about test task importance (Mikulincer, 1988d, Study 1). Though most LH studies introduce messages about training task importance, there is no reason to expect different effects from the manipulation of the importance of the test task. Indeed, the findings were consistent with the performance effects of training task importance. They showed that test task importance moderated the LH effects: High-importance messages facilitated these effects; low-importance messages inhibited them. Only in the high-importance condition did failure in four unsolvable problems result in fewer Raven problems solved than no feedback.

Nonetheless, all of these findings—which consistently show that LH effects are mainly found under high task importance conditions—can be explained differ-

TABLE 6.1. Means and Standard Deviations of Performance Accuracy by Number of Failures and Task Importance Instructions (Study 11)

	No failures		One failure		Four failures	
	Low	High	Low	High	Low	High
Mean	83.37	81.75	80.50	88.87	80.00	68.37
Standard deviation	8.40	5.52	9.05	6.77	7.72	10.54

TABLE 6.2. Means of Emotion, Rumination, and Coping Scores by Number
of Failures and Task Importance Instructions (Study 11)

	No failures		One failure		Four failures	
	Low	High	Low	High	Low	High
Anger	1.50	1.37	1.87	3.50	1.62	2.12
Anxiety	1.37	1.62	1.87	1.75	2.00	3.50
Depressed affect	1.50	1.62	2.12	2.25	1.50	3.62
Action rumination	3.75	4.25	3.75	5.25	3.87	2.37
State rumination	1.75	1.75	1.62	2.12	2.25	3.75
Task-irrelevant rumination	1.62	1.37	1.62	1.62	1.75	3.12
Problem solving	4.00	4.25	4.50	5.37	4.25	2.00
Reappraisal	3.75	3.25	4.25	3.87	3.75	4.00
Reorganization	1.37	2.00	2.12	2.00	2.12	3.25
Avoidance	2.00	2.12	1.87	1.37	2.12	3.00

ently by the instructions used in the studies. By explicitly asserting that the task is a
measure of cognitive skills, the instructions would seen to forge an association
between failure and intellectual level, thereby confounding the importance of the
task with its self-relevance. Manipulating task importance by more extrinsic means
(e.g., money) that bear no relation to the person's character or ability might have led
to different results. In fact, there is some evidence indicating that monetary reward
inhibits the detrimental effects of helplessness training (Miller & Hom, 1990).

ACHIEVEMENT NEED

Evidence for the effects of perceived task value is also found in LH studies that
assess the reactions of individuals differing in their achievement need. If perceived
task value moderates LH effects, individual differences in achievement need would
be reflected in the strength of these effects. High-achievement-need persons, who
assign high value to the tasks, may react with strong reactance to a small amount of
failure and with strong LH deficits to a large amount of failure. Low-achievement-
need persons will be impervious to both the positive and negative effects of failure.

This reasoning receives strong support in a series of studies conducted by
Winefeld and his colleagues. Jardine and Winefeld (1981) found that the strength of
reactance effects after a small amount of helplessness training is a positive function
of achievement need. In two experiments, high-achievement-need subjects (classified according to Smith's Achievement test and Mehrabian's test) showed a significant reactance effect; they performed better in an anagram task (more anagrams
solved in less time) following the exposure to noncontingent outcomes in ten trials
of Hudson's Uses of Objects test than following no or contingent training. For the
low-achievement-need subjects, the difference among the three conditions did not
reach significance.

Winefeld and Jardine (1982) extended these findings to the LH deficits produced by a large amount of helplessness training. For this purpose, they replicated the procedure used by Jardine and Winefeld (1981), only instead of exposing all subjects to ten trials of the Hudson test, they classified them into two subgroups according to the amount of helplessness training they received, with 10 trials a small amount and 20 trials a large amount. High-achievement-need subjects showed better performance after a small amount of helplessness training and worse performance after a large amount of training than after no or contingent training. Low-achievement-need subjects showed no performance effect of either amount of helplessness training.

The impact of achievement need was also demonstrated by Barber and Winefeld (1987). Using the Personal Interests Questionnaire, which measures the motivation to do well on tasks similar to those employed in LH research, the authors found that performance deficits following helplessness training were recorded only among high-motivation subjects: "This finding leads to the conclusion that unless individuals possess a certain minimum level of motivation to begin with, noncontingency training will not affect them" (Barber and Winefeld, p. 28).

Two experiments of Jardine and Winefeld (1984), however, suggest some limits to the effects of achievement need. In the first experiment, only high-achievement-need subjects who could not predict how much of a reward they would receive showed performance facilitation after a small amount of helplessness training. The anticipation of the amount of the reward inhibited the reactance effect. Jardine and Winefeld argue that knowing the amount of reward gave subjects some sort of perceived control that might have prevented the reactance effect. Whether this post hoc explanation is correct or not, the findings suggest that as long as perceived control is threatened, only high-achievement-need subjects are responsive to helplessness training.

The second experiment indicated that neither high- nor low-achievement-need subjects showed performance change following helplessness training when the reinforcement was negative (noncontingent loss of money after making a response in the Hudson test). It may be that such a procedure in and of itself reduces the perceived task importance, even in high-achievement-need subjects. In the first study, the motivation to acquire money might have been compounded by the motivation to achieve success in what people believed was a scholastic aptitude task. In the second study, the giving of money to avoid thinking might have eliminated the perception of the task as an indication of aptitude and left the desire to gain small sums of money (which might have been insufficient to promote performance changes) as the single motivating factor.

TYPE A PERSONALITY

Additional evidence on the performance effects of perceived task value is provided by a series of LH studies that focus on Type A–Type B personalities. The high value Type A persons attach to control may strengthen both the facilitatory and detrimental effects of helplessness training. When Type A individuals encounter lack of control, they initially react with increasing efforts aimed at restoring control, which in turn lead to performance facilitation. But if their efforts meet with failure and they begin to expect no control, as is the case after a large amount of helplessness training, they exhibit performance deficits. Though Glass (1977) also made similar predictions, he did not explicitly propose some mechanism for the LH deficits of Type A people. In my terms, these LH deficits reflect the intense allocation of effort in off-task coping activities after instrumental actions are revealed as ineffective.

Several studies have investigated the responses of Type A individuals to lack of control, but only five of them provide valid evidence. Some of them have focused exclusively on physiological rather than performance reactions (see Glass & Carver, 1980, for a review). Others have made sui generis operationalizations of lack of control that cannot be considered valid instances of the helplessness phenomenon (e.g., Contrada et al., 1982). Still other studies, which have been conducted in classic LH settings, have included extremely disturbing elements (e.g., the exposure to lack of control in different tasks, an uncommon measure of Type A personality) that prevent a clear interpretation of the findings (Lovallo & Pishkin, 1980).

Two studies reported by Glass (1977) examined the impact of Type A personality on reactions to a small amount of helplessness training. In one study, Type A individuals performed better in a reaction time task after 12 bursts of inescapable noise than after escapable noise. In a second study, Type A persons performed better in a test task that required subjects to wait a fixed time before responding following two unsolvable than they did following two solvable problems. In the two experiments, no performance difference was found among Type B individuals. The findings are in keeping with the prediction that Type A subjects would show stronger reactance than Type B subjects after small amounts of control deprivation.

Krantz et al. (1974) assessed the effects of Type A personality on performance following a large amount of helplessness training. Type A and Type B individuals were exposed to 35 bursts of either loud (105 decibels) or moderate (78 decibels) noise, which was either escapable or inescapable (Krantz et al.'s 35 bursts of noise constituted a larger amount of training than Glass and Carver's 12 bursts). Results showed that inescapable noise impaired test task performance (more trials required to end noise bursts) only among Type A subjects who had been exposed to loud noise. Performance deficits were found neither under moderate noise nor among Type B subjects.

The findings suggest that Type B persons, who generally do not see the exertion of control as an important goal, are not vulnerable to the detrimental effects of lack of control. In addition, they indicate that under certain conditions Type A people, who attach importance to controlling environmental events, are susceptible to performance deficits after large amounts of helplessness training. This is particularly true when situational cues signal high task importance. It is reasonable to assume that the unpleasantness of the loud noise in the Krantz et al. (1974) study had something to do with the importance Type A subjects attached to stopping it: the louder the noise, the more important it may have been to control it, the higher the frustration after failure, and thus the stronger the LH deficits shown by Type A subjects.

Evidence also supports the idea that Type A individuals exhibit performance deficits after helplessness training only when they recognize the uncontrollability of the event. Brunson and Matthews (1981) exposed Type A and Type B subjects to four unsolvable problems and assessed their performance during or after that exposure. (Again, the four problems represent an increase in amount of training over the two problems in Glass's experiment.) The study also manipulated the salience of the contingency between responses and outcomes by asking half the subjects to keep detailed records of whether their answers were correct. Results indicated that unsolvable problems produced worse performance than solvable problems only among Type A subjects for whom the response–outcome contingency was highly salient. No performance change was found among Type B subjects or in conditions of low salient contingency.

The findings suggest that to have a detrimental impact on Type A individuals, a large amount of helplessness training must take place under conditions that facilitate the perception and expectancy of no control. Helplessness training impaired the performance of Type A subjects only when lack of control was so salient that it may have generated the expectancy of no control. Any condition that helps maintain hope of asserting control may delay Type A individuals' deficits.

The behavioral reactions of Type A people are similar to those exhibited by high-achievement-need persons. Both regard the failure situation as highly important and relevant to their high-order goals and may direct all their cognitions and actions to cope with it. They at first may redouble their task-relevant efforts to overcome failure and show reactance. As they become convinced that the failure is irreversible, they may adopt off-task coping and show performance deficits.

Along this reasoning, studies on the desire for control (Burger & Cooper, 1979) have shown that subjects with strong wishes for control performed better after a single failure than subjects with little desire for control (Burger, 1987), and worse after a large amount of training with inescapable noise (Burger & Arkin, 1980). Like Type A and high-achievement-need persons, people who show a strong desire of control may assign high value to the training and test task, and they thereby may be reactive to the effects of lack of control.

TASK DIFFICULTY INSTRUCTIONS

Evidence on the effects of perceived self-relevance is found in LH studies that manipulate the normative difficulty of the tasks. If perceived self-relevance contributes to LH effects, messages on task difficulty would produce performance changes after helplessness training. Presenting the task as moderately difficult, which links failure to the self, may lead people to react with strong reactance to a small amount of helplessness training and with strong LH deficits to a large amount of training. Messages on the high difficulty of the tasks may make subjects impervious to both the facilitatory and detrimental effects of helplessness training.

The first relevant piece of evidence comes from early research on persons who are chronically anxious about failing in a task (e.g., Feather, 1961, 1963a). It was found that these subjects improved their performance when the task was described as highly difficult—that is, people who expect to fail in a task and worry about that possibility perform better when difficulty messages weaken the self-relevance of poor performance.

More supportive evidence has been provided by several LH studies that examined whether information about *training* task difficulty moderates LH deficits. Douglas and Anisman (1975) exposed subjects to either success or failure in problems that were either very easy or very difficult to solve. Burger and Cooper (1979) exposed subjects to uncontrollable aversive noise blasts and informed half the subjects before they embarked in the task that it would be impossible for them to put an end to the noise. Tennen and Eller (1977) exposed subjects to three unsolvable cognitive problems and informed them that the problems would become progressively easier or harder. Dyck et al. (1979), Harris and Tryon (1983), and Polaino and Villamisar (1984) exposed subjects to unsolvable problems and provided bogus information on the performance by other subjects ("Most of the subjects performed well/poorly on the task"). Klein et al. (1976) and Mikulincer (1988c) provided normative information about the probability of success in the training task.

Seven out of these eight studies demonstrated that low-difficulty instructions produced stronger performance deficits after a large amount of failure than did high-difficulty ones. In addition, these instructions moderated the detrimental effects of helplessness training. As compared to control conditions, helplessness training impaired performance only when subjects were told that the task was easy (internal attribution of failure). It had no significant effect when the failure was said to stem from high task difficulty.

Somewhat discrepant findings were reported by Klein et al. (1976), who showed that nondepressed subjects exposed to helplessness training performed worse than controls under both low- and high-difficulty instructions. They also found, however, that telling depressed subjects exposed to helplessness training that the task was extremely difficult improved their performance relative to other depressed subjects who had received moderate-difficulty messages or no difficulty instructions at all.

In exploring the egotism hypothesis, Frankel and Snyder (1978) found that the high self-relevance of the test task was also a prerequisite for LH deficits. As compared to success subjects, subjects exposed to repeated failures displayed performance impairment when the test task was said to be of moderate difficulty; the impairment was absent when the task was said to be very difficult. These findings were replicated by Hagan and Medway (1989) in sixth- and seventh-grade children and by Miller (1985, 1986) in 11-year-old boys who had a mature conception of ability and effort. Miller failed, though, to replicate these findings among girls. Miller (1986) explained the discrepancy by gender differences in motivational orientation: Whereas boys may pursue self-evaluation goals and attempt to protect their self-identity from potential threats, girls may be more directed by the intrinsic goal of learning new skills. If this post hoc reasoning is correct, it points to the importance of including the pursuit of self-evaluation for understanding the impact of task difficulty.

Snyder, Smoller, Strenta, and Frankel (1981) also demonstrated that performance effects of perceived self-relevance by telling some subjects preexposed to helplessness training that they would do the test task with background music that could distract them and impede performance. Evidently, this message led subjects to perceive the test task as highly difficult and to attribute any potential failure to task characteristics (distractive music). The results showed that only subjects who did the test task with no background music showed LH deficits; the "debilitating music" instructions prevented these deficits. This effect of distracting stimuli was also found by Leary (1986) in his research on the interpersonal behavior of socially anxious persons.

Snyder et al. (1981) explored an alternative interpretation of the findings: negativity. They suggested that helplessness training might produce hostility toward the experimenter. This hostility, they proposed, might lead either to a reduction of effort and poor performance as a means of disobeying the experimenter's request to do the test task, or to increased effort and improved performance when the experimenter suggests performance will be poor (as in the case when the test task is said to be difficult or the music distracting). To test this explanation, Snyder et al. told some subjects that the music would facilitate performance. But contrary to the negativity thesis, in which such instruction should lead to poor performance, subjects in the facilitatory-music condition showed no LH deficits and performed better than those given no music.

Other LH studies have investigated the performance impact of task difficulty instructions on reactance effects. The findings, however, are inconclusive. On the one hand, I (Mikulincer, 1988c) found that a small amount of helplessness training, relative to no feedback, improved performance only when subjects were convinced that the training task was moderately easy. The induction of external attribution (high difficulty) prevented these facilitatory effects. On the other hand, Dyck et al. (1979) and Wortman et al. (1976) found just the opposite: A small amount of helplessness training produced no performance effect in the easy condition, but did in the difficult condition. Surprisingly, subjects who were led to attribute failure to high task difficulty showed worse test task performance than controls.

The last two studies suffer from a methodological problem, however, in that loud noise was introduced in the training phase but eliminated in the test phase. Miller and Norman (1979) suggest that subjects in the easy condition may have attributed failure to the difficulty of solving problems with background noise. When the noise was ended, they may have concluded that they could succeed and were motivated to do well.

Yet although task difficulty findings on the whole show that high perceived self-relevance intensifies both reactance and LH deficits, some methodological and theoretical reservations must be noted. Methodologically, task difficulty instructions confound internal–external attribution with other attributional dimensions, such as stability and globality. For example, telling people that a task is very difficult fosters the attribution of failure to an external cause that is also stable over time and specific to the task. This confusion is particularly illustrated in the study by Hanusa and Schultz (1977) on the effects of ability, effort, and task difficulty attributions.

Theoretically, the performance effects of task difficulty can be accounted for by psychological processes other than internal–external attribution. For example, Douglas and Anisman (1975) explained the performance effects of training task difficulty in terms of expectancy–outcome congruence. When people perceive the training task to be moderately easy, failure impairs task performance by undercutting that perception. In training tasks described as very difficult or impossible, failure is congruent with the induced belief, so it need not lead to a performance deficit.

The beneficial effects of high task difficulty instructions can also be ascribed to the advantages of predictability (Burger & Arkin, 1980). It has been shown that (a) people prefer predictable aversive events to unpredictable aversive events (e.g., Monat, Averill, & Lazarus, 1972); (b) predictable aversive events provoke a less severe physiological reaction than unpredictable aversive events (e.g., Averill, O'Brien, & DeWitt, 1977); and (c) a predictable aversive event is appraised as less threatening than an unpredictable aversive event (e.g., Mills & Krantz, 1979). On this basis, it may be argued that people react better to failure in a very difficult task than to failure in a moderately easy task because they are better able to anticipate the former.

Nonetheless, these alternative explanations tell nothing about the intensification of reactance produced by moderate task difficulty messages. Moreover, they are confined to the effects of training task difficulty. If unpredictability and expectation–outcome incongruence also underlie the effects of test task difficulty instructions, LH deficits should have been recorded among subjects who perceived the test task as highly difficult. But although these subjects made faulty anticipations of failure in what was a solvable task, findings showed no performance decrements among them.

INTERNAL–EXTERNAL ATTRIBUTION

LH studies have dealt with the problems inherent in task difficulty inductions by providing explicit messages about the internality dimension of causality. These messages have been designed to alter beliefs about the link between failure and the self directly without giving any cue as to the stability or globality of the failure.

This research strategy was adopted by six studies that examine the effectiveness of "debriefing" procedures (Eisenberg, Kaplan, & Singer, 1974; Koller & Kaplan, 1978; Lavelle et al., 1979; Mikulincer, 1989d, Study 1; Miller & Klein, 1989; Tennen & Gillen, 1979). Prior to the test task, subjects in these studies were either informed or not that their prior failure did not reflect any self-attribute. Generally, those so informed were told that the experimenter had controlled the solutions to the problems in the task. Findings in the six studies demonstrated that helplessness training, relative to control conditions, impaired performance only among nondebriefed subjects. Telling subjects that lack of control had nothing to do with their selves weakened the effects of helplessness training. The recognition of no control that was implicit in the debriefing instructions frees the subjects of personal responsibility, weakens the self-relevant threats and the need for coping actions, and inhibits LH effects.

The possibility that the debriefing led to unstable and specific attribution, and that these were responsible for the performance effects, was ruled out by a detailed examination of the wording of the debriefing messages. These contained no information about the stability or globality of the prior failure, so debriefed subjects could still expect the next task to be controlled by the experimenter.

Another interpretation of the debriefing findings offered by Tennen and Gillen (1979) can also be refuted. Tennen and Gillen suggest that helplessness training causes the subject to feel that he or she is being deceived, and that the debriefing procedure may lend credibility to the test task by confirming these suspicions, thus preventing LH deficits. "Debriefed subjects, whose faith in the experimenter is bolstered through verification of their preexisting perceptions regarding the uncontrollability of the noise task, seem to redouble their efforts on the anagram task" (p. 639). The question here, though, is what guarantee the subjects have concluded that the deception is not repeated in the test task.

In a recent study, Ramirez, Maldonado, and Martos (1992) also reported that internal attribution made people more vulnerable to the debilitating effects of helplessness training. Specifically, noise escape performance after four unsolvable problems was worse among subjects instructed to make internal attributions than among those instructed to make external attributions (Experiments 2 and 3). These findings, however, should be taken with caution; Ramirez et al. confounded the globality and internality dimensions in their measurement of attributional style and in their instructions. In addition, Experiments 2 and 3 did not include any control condition for comparing the performance effects of helplessness training. On this basis, we do not know whether there was a real LH effect at all.

A more clear and complete assessment of the effects of internal–external attribution was conducted in one of my LH experiments (Mikulincer, 1988a), which employed the strategy of preselecting subjects according to their habitual attributional style (in the ASQ) and exposing them to either no, one, or four unsolvable problems. The results demonstrated that a single failure improved performance and four failures impaired it only among internal attributors. Among external attributors, neither one nor four failures affected performance. The performance impact of internal–external attributional style remained unchanged when both the ASQ and task-specific stability and globality attributions were used as covariates. These findings imply that people who link failure to the self are susceptible to both reactance and LH deficits, whereas those who do not appear to be impervious to them.

Only one LH study (Kofta & Sedek, 1989) appears to dismiss the role of perceived self-relevance. In this study, unsolvable cognitive problems produced worse performance in a noise avoidance task than did solvable problems in both internal and external attribution conditions. This finding, however, may have derived from ambiguous induction of external attribution. Although the message explicitly pointed to external causation ("The results in this task depend in part on the construction of the apparatus"), it also explicitly maintained the possibility of internal causation ("However, the final results depend to some degree on a correct inference from your attempts to eliminate unpleasant noise in the preceding trials . . . the solution partially depends on the efficiency of action"). These hybrid instructions may have lead to some kind of mixed attribution that may have sustained the self-relevance of outcomes and thereby enabled performance deficits. Kofta and Sedek lamentably did not check on the effectiveness of their manipulation.

GOAL ORIENTATION

Relevant findings on the impact of perceived self-relevance is provided by LH studies that look at the extent to which the individual's goal orientation reflects the pursuit of self-evaluation. For persons pursuing performance goals, a failure may constitute a serious threat to self-identity, which in turn mobilizes coping efforts that may end in LH effects. For people committed to learning goals, failure may not threaten any important self-representation and thus may fail to mobilize coping efforts and to produce LH effects.

This reasoning was supported by Boggiano and Barrett (1985), who assessed LH effects in "extrinsic" and "intrinsic" chidren (according to scores on the Scale of Intrinsic Versus Extrinsic Orientation in the Classroom). Extrinsics were defined as those who habitually pursued performance goals, such as approval, grades, and the avoidance of criticism; intrinsics were those who habitually sought the pleasure inherent in learning. Results showed that failure in unsolvable problems caused worse performance than success or no feedback only among children who pursued performance goals. Those who pursued learning goals did not evince any performance deterioration after failure. In addition, extrinsics were found behaviorally to avoid tasks similar to the original helplessness task, whereas intrinsics showed a clear preference for tasks identical or similar to the training task. In other words, children who pursued learning goals showed no effort withdrawal from activities related to the helplessness training; those who pursued performance goals did.

Although the goals pursued can explain Boggiano and Barrett's findings, extrinsic–intrinsic orientation can also alter performance by other paths. Boggiano and Barrett argued that extrinsics show performance deficits after failure because they habitually have low self-efficacy expectancy and see outcomes as beyond their personal control. Boggiano and Barrett also suggested that the high self-efficacy expectancy of intrinsics, derived from their reliance on internal criteria for self-evaluation, may underlie their resilience to lack of control.

Even if this explanation is correct, however, it need not negate the underlying role of self-relevance. If, as this explanation suggests, extrinsics begin a task with doubts about their self-efficacy, any outcome confirming their initial self-doubts would be linked to the self (internal attribution), would exacerbate these doubts, and would increase self-relevant threats. The same lack of control would not so threaten the self-identity of intrinsics, who have little doubts about their efficacy to begin with.

Another piece of indirect, but supportive evidence was reported by Miller and Hom (1990), who manipulated subjects' motivation to attain an incentive (monetary reward) that had nothing to do with self-evaluation. The results indicated that helplessness training produced worse anagram performance only when moderate-difficulty instructions were introduced for the test task and no monetary reward was promised. Either the introduction of high-difficulty instructions or the presence of a monetary reward prevented performance deficits.

Miller and Hom explained these findings by suggesting that the introduction of a monetary reward may have reduced the centrality of self-evaluation. People promised money may have convinced themselves that they were expending effort to obtain material gain rather than to confirm self-identity, and they may have attributed their failure to the characteristics of the reward ("There was so little reward that I did not expend effort at the task") rather than to personal inability. It is this weakening of self-relevance that prevented performance deficits following helplessness training.

SELF-IDENTITY CONFIRMATION

Studies that introduce messages confirming self-identity after helplessness training also provide evidence of the hypothesized effects of perceived self-relevance. If reactance and LH deficits do in fact result from the threat to self-identity that is produced by an internally attributed failure, then any procedure that could weaken that threat should lower these effects. Communicating messages that confirm central aspects of self-identity may be one means of achieving this. Such messages may counteract the threat implied by failure and may thereby reduce the need for coping actions that alter performance.

This research strategy was first employed by Orbach and Hadas (1982). Psychology students were exposed to controllable, uncontrollable, or no feedback on a task presented as allegedly measuring their ability to reduce the anxiety of another person. Following this, their performance on a word recognition task was assessed.

Subjects in each training group were divided into a self-enhancing condition, wherein they were given a message confirming some traits that are highly valued by psychology students ("You are able to express concern and respect for others, to make people confide in you, to establish good rapport with others"), and a non-self-enhancing condition, wherein they did not receive any self-relevant feedback. Helplessness training produced worse test task performance than control conditions only in the non-self-enhancing condition. There was no significant difference between the training groups in the self-enhancing condition; that is, the confirmation of important aspects of self-identity appears to have alleviated self-relevant threats and thereby to have weakened the LH effects.

Orbach and Hadas themselves, however, noted two basic caveats regarding the interpretation of these findings. First, they did not assess changes in self-esteem, so they could not be sure that a self-enhancing message had really affected the subjects' sense of self. Second, the self-aspects that were threatened by failure (the ability to reduce another person's anxiety) were similar to those aspects for which subjects received self-enhancing messages (the ability to make another person confide in them). This similarity may have not only confirmed global self-identity but also restored the expectancy of control undermined by failure.

These two problems were overcome in a recent study conducted by two of my students (Shefet & Eilam, 1991) that exposed subjects to zero, one, or four failures in unsolvable problems, asked them to complete a 9-item scale tapping their self-esteem in the experiment, and provided messages that confirmed either the dimension of the self that was threatened by failure or some other aspect of the global self-definition of psychology students. The results corroborated and extended those of Orbach and Hadas. They showed that both reactance and LH deficits depend on the occurrence of a self-relevant threat. A small amount of failure produced better performance than no failure, and a large amount of failure produced worse performance only among subjects who received no self-enhancing message. The introduction of self-enhancing messages (either task-specific or global) eliminated both positive and negative LH effects. In addition, reports of self-esteem were enhanced by both the global and specific self-enhancing messages, demonstrating the effectiveness of these messages for alleviating the threat.

The fact that not only specific but also global self-enhancing messages weakened LH effects implies that the threat produced by failure can be mitigated by confirming other central aspects of self-identity. The findings also imply that the threat produced by failure determines the intensity but not the quality of LH effects; that is, it seems to contribute to both reactance and LH effects. What determines the quality of the LH effects are the person's expectancies and the way he or she copes with the threat. The threat to self-identity determines only that people will engage in some form of coping activities.

Supportive findings were also reported by another student of mine (Gilat, 1992), who assessed LH effects after either the provision of a message indicating that the test task was highly difficult (external attribution) or the completion of

Rokeach's value scale, which afforded subjects an opportunity to endorse and affirm their most important values (self-enhancing induction; Liu & Steele, 1986). Results revealed that, compared to no feedback, four unsolvable problems produced less accurate performance in a letter cancellation task only among subjects who received no attributional message or no self-enhancing induction. The introduction of external attribution or the possibility of confirming self-identity lessened the LH effects. Like the other studies reviewed above, this study demonstrates that helplessness training alters performance only when it has a threatening impact on the person's self-identity. Any event or message that can prevent or revert the threatening implications of failure for self-identity is likely to weaken the LH effects.

SELF-RELEVANCE AND PERCEIVED TASK IMPORTANCE

The studies reviewed above focused on either perceived task importance or self-relevance without considering the possible links between them. There is evidence that they are at least moderately correlated (Feather, 1967, 1968, 1969), though, with tasks whose outcomes are attributed to personal causes being perceived as more attractive than those whose outcomes are externally attributed.

In fact, two LH studies have found that performance following helplessness training is an interactive function of task importance and self-relevance. In one, Winefeld and Norris (1981) assessed the interactive effects of achievement need and task difficulty instructions on performance after a small amount of helplessness training (ten trials in the Hudson test). Anagram data (solving time) indicated that high-achievement-need subjects exposed to helplessness training performed better than controls only under the moderate-difficulty condition. No effect of helplessness training was recorded among high achievers in the high-difficulty condition or among low-achievement-need subjects in the moderate-difficulty condition. These findings imply that the performance facilitation of helplessness training is a function of both a strong motive to achieve and the self-relevance of failure brought about by the perception of moderate difficulty.

In the other study, I (Mikulincer, 1989d, Study 2) manipulated the external–internal attribution for failure along with the perceived importance of the test task (low or high). Results showed that a large amount of helplessness training, as compared to no feedback, impaired performance when subjects received both internal attributions for failure and high-importance instructions for the test task. No deficit was found in either the low importance–internal attribution condition or in the high importance–external attribution condition.

SUMMARY

Most of the LH studies reviewed above suggest that both the LH deficits produced by a large amount of helplessness training and the reactance produced by a small amount of helplessness training are mainly found when helplessness training threatens the attainment of personal goals and the confirmation of self-identity. Human LH makes sense only when those things that the person wants, needs, or cares about are at stake in the helplessness training. If nothing the person cares about is at stake, then little or no LH effects are found.

THE EXPECTANCY–VALUE INTERACTION

Another hypothesis derived from my coping conceptualization of human LH is that perceived task value may moderate the effects of the expectancy of control on test task performance following helplessness training. Although the expectancy of control may direct coping efforts toward problem solving or off-task coping and hence determine the quality of LH effects (reactance or LH deficits), the perceived task value may determine the intensity of the coping efforts and the resulting performar.ce effects. Expectancy may alter performance when people attach high value to a task and are motivated to undertake the coping actions cued as the most appropriate in the given situation. These performance effects may be inhibited, however, by the assignment of low value to the tasks, because this may preclude any kind of coping attempt.

It may be argued that even though an expectancy of no control may not lead to off-task coping under low value conditions, it may still produce performance deficits by reducing the incentive for instrumental action in the test task (e.g., Atkinson & Feather, 1966; Maier & Seligman, 1976). This is likely to be the case, however, only if we assume that the expectancy of no control will always generalize and persevere throughout the test task. It is my contention that this is not the case and that the generalization and perseverance of the low control expectancy depends on the perception of high task value. A failure that is perceived to have little or no personal significance (e.g., an externally attributed failure) may be expected to recur only in similar tasks, so a change in task characteristics may prevent the transfer of the no-control expectancy in these cases. Moreover, findings presented in Chapter 4 suggest that when the expectancy of no control is derived from the learning of task features rather from a belief in personal inefficacy, it seems to evaporate throughout the test task. In fact, the expectancy of control formed in the helplessness training may persist and shape behavior during a new test task only when it is linked to the belief that failure affects self-identity.

On this basis, LH effects seem to reflect the interaction of the expectancy of control and perceived task value. If there is a low perceived task value, the expectancy of control has no impact on the coping process and task performance. Whether the expectancy is favorable or not, people do not feel any need to undertake coping strategies or engage in rumination, they do not experience any emotion, and they therefore show no performance changes. High task value changes the rules of the game and activates the effects of the expectancy of control: High control expectancy will enhance problem solving, action rumination, anger, and reactance, whereas an expectancy of no control will foster off-task coping and rumination, anxiety and depressed affects, and LH deficits.

This reasoning argues against Seligman's hypotheses that (a) the expectancy of no control is sufficient to explain LH deficits, and (b) the perception of task importance influences emotional reactions but does not affect performance. Instead I suggest that the expectancy of no control is not sufficient to produce LH effects. Where people attach low value to the training or test tasks, expectancy of control will not produce LH deficits, and neither will the high expectancy of control produce reactance.

Evidence for the above expectancy–value interaction has been provided by several LH studies. Two studies of mine (Mikulincer, 1986b, Studies 2 and 3) manipulated the importance of helplessness training and the expectancy of control for the test task (explicit messages on the probability of success after failing in the training task; messages on the stability of failure). Findings demonstrated that high perceived task importance strengthens both reactance and LH deficits, and that its specific effects depend on the expectancy of control. When the expectancy of no control after four unsolvable problems was formed by an explicit message or stable attribution, high-importance instructions produced worse performance in a Raven task than low-importance messages. The expectancy of success in the test task and the belief in the unstability of failure led to a reversed pattern of performance differences. Here, high-importance messages produced better performance than low-importance messages.

The findings also show that high task importance is a *prerequisite* for the detrimental effects of the expectancy of no control. As compared to no feedback, the induction of unfavorable expectancy after helplessness training impaired performance only under the high-importance condition. Subjects who were led to perceive low task importance showed no LH deficit, even when they expected failure to recur in the test task. This pattern implies that the expectancy of no control is apparently not sufficient to impair performance, but requires the perception of high task value.

There is also extensive evidence that the expectancy of no control impairs performance after helplessness training only under high self-relevance conditions. In a series of five experiments, I (Mikulincer, 1985; 1986b, Study 3) exposed subjects to no feedback or failure in four unsolvable problems, and I manipulated either the success expectancy for the test task or the stability-globality attributions for failure along with one of two antecedents of the self-relevance of helplessness training: task difficulty and explicit internal–external attribution of failure. The induction of the expectancy of no control (low success expectancy, stable-global attribution) led to worse performance in a Raven task than the induction of a more positive expectancy (high success expectancy, unstable-specific attribution) only under high self-relevance conditions (moderate task difficulty, explicit internal attribution). Davis and Yates (1982) similarly found performance deficits only when subjects were led to believe that they had a low probability of success and the failure was attributed to internal causes.

Brewin and Shapiro (1985) described a similar interaction between stable-global attribution and internal attribution. In the first phase of the study, all subjects were exposed to four unsolvable problems and asked to make attributional ratings for the failure. The second phase involved an anagram task. Then all subjects were told that the initial failures were under the experimenter's control, a procedure designed to induce subjects who had made internal attributions to reattribute their failure to external causes. After this was done, subjects solved ten additional anagrams. Results indicate that subjects who expected no control (self-reported stable-global attribution) and believed in the high self-relevance of failure (internal attribution) showed the *strongest* deficits after failure and the highest performance improvement after the debriefing procedure.

The interactive effects of expectancy and self-relevance were also reported by Elliott and Dweck (1988) in their study of goal orientation (performance, learning) among fifth-grade children. Under performance-goal conditions, children who were led to expect failure showed stronger deterioration in problem-solving strategies during and after unsolvable problems than children who were led to expect success. Under learning-goal conditions, no difference was found between the favorable and unfavorable expectancy groups. Both groups displayed adequate performance during and after unsolvable problems.

Relevant data are also provided by studies that separate the two components of the expectancy of control—outcome and self-efficacy—and examine their unique contributions to behavior. If expectancies alter performance only under high self-relevance conditions, self-efficacy but not outcome expectancy would be responsible for performance changes. Outcome expectancy pertains to the objective characteristics of a task and does not convey any direct information about the self. In contrast, self-efficacy expectancy relates to self-identity; it signals that one possesses or lacks the skills and abilities needed to control an outcome.

Most studies have found that variations in self-efficacy expectancy explain most of the variation in performance (e.g., Green, 1985; Manning & Wright, 1983; Shell, Murphy, & Bruning, 1989). Moreover, some of the studies have found that although outcome expectancy can influence behavior, its effect is mediated almost entirely by changes in self-efficacy expectancy. When variations in self-efficacy expectancy are partialed out, outcome expectancy independently contributes very little to variance in behavior (e.g., Green, 1985; Shell, Murphy, & Bruning, 1989). This result implies that, contrary to Seligman's hypothesis, the expectancy of no control is not sufficient to explain LH deficits. Rather, it requires the creation of a sense of self-inefficacy—the appraisal that the anticipated failure tells something of relevance for self-identity.

HELPLESSNESS TRAINING AND PERCEIVED TASK VALUE

The studies reviewed above clearly indicate that the valuation of the tasks moderates the performance effects of helplessness training. No one of these studies, however, provides evidence for the possible impact of uncontrollable failure on the valuation process. That would require assessing changes in the perception of task value throughout the helplessness training. Such an assessment may be an additional step in delineating the role of the subjective task value in human LH.

Though the assignment of high value to a task is determined prior to task performance, recurrent failure may further increase the perceived task value. The idea here is that for people perceiving task outcomes to be related to valued goals and self-aspects, each failure makes their loss more palpable and more salient. So, with every failure, these persons might find it increasingly difficult to deny the negative implications of failure for their self-identity. Poor task performance would be perceived as increasingly threatening, and coping with the failure as increasingly challenging. Each failure would strengthen the appraisal that something of importance is really at stake, highlight the importance and self-relevance of the task, and thereby increase the originally high perceived task value.

Failure may increase the perception of task value by concretizing the threat to self-identity and creating pressures for the immediate undertaking of coping actions. The assignment of high value to a task prior to performing it means that important personal goals are at stake and that the person's self-identity is potentially endangered if the goals are not attained. What failure does is to actualize that threat; it raises a danger flag and rings an alarm bell. Now important goals are not only involved in the task but really thwarted by failure.

Theory and research on human motivation suggest that failure in a task may increase the perceived value of the frustrating activity. Lewin (1936) and Atkinson and Cartwright (1964) claimed that when goal attainment is blocked in a task, the task is perceived as increasingly more attractive. According to Weiner (1972), this heightened attractiveness results from "inertial tendencies," the carryover motivational effects of failure. He argued that failure to obtain a goal leaves a residual "inertial tendency" that persists until the goal is attained and potentiates the magnitude of the unsatisfied need. This tendency should thus add to the value people assign to task performance and augment their motivation to succeed in it. Similar ideas were suggested by Atkinson and Birch (1970) in what they call the "immediate-motivational effect" of failure.

The motivational effect of failure is manifested in findings by Zeigarnick (1927) and Mahler (1933) that people recall more and tend to return more to tasks they failed than tasks that they successfully completed. It is also manifested in the increase of perceived task value following goal blockage, as evidenced in self-report scales (Brehm, 1972; Feather, 1963a; Mischel & Masters, 1966) and in other indirect behavioral measures, such as looking time and overestimation of size (Knott, Nunally, & Duchnowski, 1967).

In the context of LH research, studies that have assessed subjects' self-reports on the perceived value of the tasks after helplessness training yielded inconsistent findings; Table 6.3 presents their procedural details and results. Some of the studies found a lower perceived value of the task after helplessness training than after control conditions, some others found a reverse pattern, and still some others found

TABLE 6.3. Review of Effects of Helplessness Training on Perceived Task Value

		Task value assessment		
Study	Manipulation	Timing	Wording	Effect of HT
Roth & Kuball (1975)	Unsolvable problem	After test	Interest in task	Lower-rated interest
Gregory, Chartier, & Wight (1979)	Inescapable noise	After test	Level of motivation	No effect
Breen, Vulcano, & Dyck (1979)	Unsolvable problem	After test	Task importance	No effect
Pasahow (1980)	Unsolvable problem	After test	Task importance	No effect
Foushee, Davis, Stephan, & Bernstein (1980)	Inescapable noise	After test	Task importance	Lower-rated importance
Kuhl (1981)	Unsolvable problem	After test	Task importance	Higher-rated importance
Jardine & Winefeld (1981)	Noncontingent feedback	After test	Task importance	No effect
Carlson & Feld (1981)	Noncontingent feedback	After test	Task importance	Lower-rated importance
Winefeld & Norris (1981)	Noncontingent feedback	After test	Task importance	Lower-rated importance
Winefeld & Jardine (1982)	Noncontingent feedback	After test	Task importance	No effect
Alloy & Abramson (1982)	Inescapable noise	After test	Level of motivation	Lower-rated motivation
Winefeld & Fay (1982)	Noncontingent feedback	After test	Task importance	Lower-rated importance
Tennen, Gillen, & Drum (1982)	Inescapable noise	After test	Interest in ending noise	No effect
Danker-Brown & Baucom (1982)	Unsolvable problems	Before test	Task importance	Lower-rated importance
Winefeld (1983)	Noncontingent feedback	After test	Task importance	Lower-rated importance
Rosenbaum & Jaffe (1983)	Inescapable noise	After test	Level of motivation	Lower-rated motivation
Jardine & Winefeld (1984)	Noncontingent feedback	After test	Task importance	No effect
Carlson & Cassisi (1985)	Failure feedback	After test	Task importance	No effect
Barber & Winefeld (1986)	Inescapable noise	After test	Task importance	No effect
Tiggemann & Winefeld (1987)	Inescapable noise	Before test	Interest in ending noise	No effect
Miller & Hom (1990)	Unsolvable problem	After test	Interest in problems	Lower-rated interest

Note: HT = helplessness training.

no significant difference. These inconsistencies may have resulted from the facts that (a) most of the studies assessed perceived task value after rather than before the test task, and (b) no study controlled for test task performance. Miller and Seligman (1975) have already observed that subjects exposed to helplessness training "looked like [they were] trying very hard to solve a difficult problem" (p. 236) at the beginning of the test task but reduced their strivings when confronted with their poor performance. This observation suggests that (a) helplessness training may be followed by some carryover motivational tendencies, and (b) perceived task value is lowered after poor performance in the test task itself.

Two of my studies measured the perception of task value before subjects performed the test task. In one of these studies (Mikulincer, 1985), success and failure subjects did not differ in the value they assigned to the first training task. Failure subjects, however, assigned higher value than success subjects to the second, third, and fourth tasks. Study 1 of the series that I present in this book indicated that the perceived value of the test task steadily increased from zero to three failures, and that this increased value remained constant after four and five failures (see Figure 6.1).

In general, the findings reviewed throughout this chapter suggest that when people assign low value to the tasks, they may feel no need for coping and may be impervious to LH effects. In contrast, when they assign high value to the tasks, they may appraise the failure as a threat, undertake coping actions, and thereby show reactance or LH deficits. Moreover, their perception of task value may increase after each failure, intensifying the resulting LH effects.

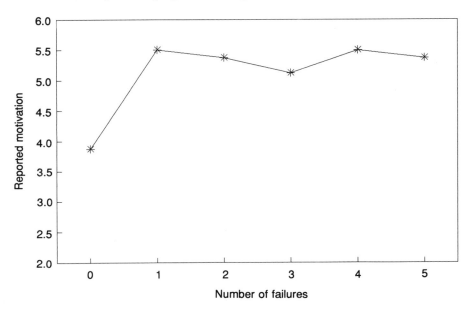

FIGURE 6.1. Means of reported motivation according to number of failures.

CHAPTER 7

SELF-FOCUSED ATTENTION AS A MODERATOR OF LH EFFECTS

With the introduction of cognitive concepts to social and clinical psychology, theorists and researchers have begun to suggest that the individual's focus of attention may be a critical element in the shaping of cognition, emotion, and behavior (e.g., Carver & Scheier, 1981; Duval & Wicklund, 1972; Gibbons, 1990). They borrow from cognitive psychology the idea that attention selects information for further processing (Anderson, 1990) and suggest that the act of directing attention toward the self (self-focus) may facilitate the processing of the particular types of information needed for translation of intentions into actions. Self-focus helps to decipher the personal meaning of a transaction and enables people to adjust their behavior so that it will promote attainment of their goals.

The effects of self-focus cut across cognition, emotion, and behavior, and they seem to be implicated in the processes of self-regulation, self-evaluation, and coping with undesirable events. Self-focus has been shown to influence a variety of psychological phenomena, including attitude or behavior consistency, accessibility of self-relevant information, affect intensity, causal attribution of outcomes and behaviors, self-disclosure, and behavioral reactions to threatening situations (for reviews, see Gibbons, 1990; Scheier & Carver, 1988). In addition, self-focus is involved in such diverse psychological disorders as anxiety, depression, paranoia, and alcoholism (see Ingram, 1990, for a review).

In my conceptualization of human LH, self-focus is another component of the process of coping with failure that moderates LH effects. Specifically, I hypothesize that self-focus acts on the various components of the coping process. It may facilitate the valuation process, detection of self-relevant threats, assessment of the probability of control, experience of emotions, engagement in mental rumination, and the undertaking of coping actions. I also hypothesize that self-focus may be a precondition for the effects of helplessness training on coping and performance. In fact, it strengthens each of the performance changes that have been observed following failure. On the whole, I view self-focus as an integral part of the coping process; it is an adaptive device that catalyzes the cognitive, emotional, and behavioral reactions to failure and aids in managing the person–environment mismatch. This chapter delineates the role of self-focus in human LH and explores whether and how self-focus takes part in the process of coping with failure.

SELF-FOCUS DEFINED

The systematic study of self-focus begun with Duval and Wicklund's (1972) theory of self-awareness, and it was stimulated by Carver and Scheier's (1981) cybernetic model of self-regulation. These theories, though differing somewhat in their focus of attention, have guided most of the research during the last 20 years. According to them, attention is bidirectional, and it may be focused on the self or the environment. Focusing attention on the self makes people aware of momentarily salient self-representations, which become the object of cognitive processing and self-assessment and a guideline for decisions and actions. These representations may be the to-be-attained goals, the self-aspects involved in the task, or the emotions evoked by interruptions and cognitive discrepancies.

Carver (1979) defined self-focus as follows:

> When attention is self-directed, it sometimes takes the form of focus on internal perceptual events, that is, information from those sensory receptors that react to changes in bodily activity. Self-focus may also take the form of an enhanced awareness of one's present or past physical behavior, that is, a heightened cognizance of what one is doing or what one is like. Alternatively, self-attention can be an awareness of the more or less permanently encoded bits of information that comprise, for example, one's attitudes (p. 1255).

In a similar vein, Gibbons (1990) states that

> the self-focused person is one who becomes more careful in deliberating his or her own behavior and its consequences and who is more concerned about the self than about others. Perhaps the psychological state of self-focus is best defined in contrast with mindless behavior discussed by Langer (1975) or the "top of the head" response pattern described in Taylor and Fiske (1978). In those instances, focus of attention is the immediate environment and people show relatively little concern for the meaning or consequences of their actions. In short, they do what the environment dictates. In contrast, the self-focused person is more concerned about what pattern of action is most appropriate— what should be done in the particular situation (p. 262).

In these definitions, self-focus does not mean an introspective in-depth examination of general aspects of the self, nor does it imply that the person is consciously aware of the cognitive procedures that underlie their decisions and actions. Instead, it refers to the momentary shifting of attention to the relevant aspects of the self that are involved in a transaction with the environment, such as aspirations, goals, abilities, skills, and intended actions. Self-focus only means that people are aware of the state of their strivings and actions and the personal benefits and harms that may follow from a transaction.

The cornerstone of both Duval and Wicklund's (1972) theory and Carver and Scheier's (1981) formulation is that self-focus accomplishes adaptive functions. First of all, self-focus makes up part of the self-regulatory efforts that try to produce a change in the environment in order to bring it closer in line with one's goals. That is, it auxiliates the proceeding of self-regulatory processes, such as the test-operate-test-exit (TOTE) sequence (Carver & Scheier, 1981), and the consequent activation of problem-focused, task-relevant actions. When people strive for a goal, they may experience a discrepancy between their actual state and the ideal state they want to reach. In this condition, a TOTE sequence may be activated by which people compare the consequences of their actions to the ideal state and activate task-relevant actions in order to minimize the discrepancy. This behavioral activation is followed by further comparisons with the standard and further attempts to reduce the discrepancy. Then, through successive comparisons and operations, the TOTE sequence enables a better person–environment alignment.

According to Carver and Scheier (1981), the TOTE sequence is not an automatic response to person–environment discrepancies. Rather, it depends on the tendency to direct attention inward. Though nonhuman control devices can regulate a system's action without any particular attentional focus, human self-regulatory cycles require the focusing of attention on the self. As Carver and Scheier put it, people can reflect on their goals, compare them with their current state, and process the self-relevant information needed for the reduction of person–environment discrepancies only if they direct attention to the self.

In addition, self-focus may play a role in accommodating mental structures to reality constraints (Pyszczynski & Greenberg, 1987). Working through an irrevocable loss, assessing the damaged parts of one's goal hierarchy or self-identity, and molding self-views and priorities to match reality constraints better are all self-reflective activities that draw attention to one's self-representations. In these activities, self-focus serves a more reflective, self-evaluative function by highlighting the state of one's goal hierarchy and self-identity.

An in-depth analysis of the self-evaluation process reveals the crucial role of self-focus. The process of self-evaluation may begin with a review of the abilities, skills, and traits that may be reflected in one's task performance. This is followed by an assessment of the state of these personal characteristics following the success/failure feedback. The process culminates in either maintainance or change of the self-representations. The retrieval of self-schemas from long-term memory, their admittance into working memory, and the entire assessment process that follows can all be carried out only by devoting attention to the pertinent self-representations. Self-focus facilitates the activation of self-schemas and makes them accessible for information processing, whereas the diversion of attention away from the self may impede the processing of self-representations (Gibbons, 1990; Hull & Levy, 1979).

This reasoning suggests that self-focus may facilitate both alloplastic and autoplastic adaptation. In my view, these two functions of self-focus are not mutually exclusive. Rather, they may represent two different ways by which self-focus may serve as a catalyst for coping with a person–environment mismatch. On the one hand, acting as a self-regulatory device, self-focus helps people to activate appropriate problem-focused strategies designed to remove a source of threat from the environment. On the other hand, by increasing the availability of the mental structures damaged by failure, self-focus may help one to make adaptive intrapsychic changes. That is, self-focus may equally facilitate both the molding of the environment to one's goals and the molding of one's goals to reality constraints. Either way, self-focus contributes to coping with the person–environment mismatch and helps one adapt to life's adversities.

SELF-FOCUS AND THE COPING PROCESS

This section deals with my hypothesis that self-focus serves as a catalyst of the coping process; that is, it may influence the diverse components of the process of coping with uncontrollable failure. When people fail to realize their strivings (e.g., in helplessness training), the heightening of self-focus facilitates the comparison of their states to the salient goal, the appraisal of the personal implications of failure, the assessment of coping resources and options, the arousal of emotions, and the taking of some coping steps in accordance with their expectancies of goal attainment. Without self-focus, people may experience no self-relevant threat and no emotional pressure for undertaking coping actions, and they may react to failure as if nothing of personal importance had happened.

Focusing attention on the self helps one to access stored material about the physical, cognitive, emotional, dispositional, and evaluative characteristics of the self, thereby allowing faster retrieval and processing of self-referent information (Hull & Levy, 1979; Nasby, 1985). Just as attending to an external object activates the schema of this object (Taylor & Fiske, 1978) and enables its assessment, so paying attention to the self activates the self-schema. It makes people more cognizant of themselves and more capable of making self-assessments. In the LH context, self-focus is like a light beam that selectively illuminates three basic facets of the self-schema: (a) ideal aspects of the self (goals, aspirations), (b) current affective state, and (c) personal abilities and responses that can help to cope with failure. These aspects of the self may become accessible either sequentially or simultaneously. They all contribute to the person's decision how best to cope with the threat of failure.

First of all, self-focus seems to allow people to compare their actual achievements to the ideal state that they strive to reach: It helps them to become aware of the cognitive discrepancies implied by failure. Because the comparison process is self-reflective in nature, it can operate only when certain attentional requirements are met. People have to be aware of the personal goals that guide their current behavior. They must also think about that behavior and about the gap between their achievements and their goals. Logically, these requirements can be met only when the person directs attention to the self. Self-focus precedes both one's awareness of personal goals and reflection on the actual state of the self. Indeed, research has demonstrated that a high level of self-focus increases the frequency of comparisons between present and ideal states and also promotes a close correspondence between behavior and goals (for reviews, see Gibbons, 1990; Scheier & Carver, 1988).

Second, self-focus may increase attentiveness and responsiveness to the personal threats produced by a self-relevant failure. The shifting of attention inward may facilitate the activation of the person's goal hierarchy and self-schemas and may help gain access to stored material on the specific goals and self-aspects involved in a given task (Gibbons, 1990; Hull & Levy, 1979). This increased availability may in turn help people to reflect on their aspirations and self-identity and to assess the implications that a failure may have for these self-representations. In this way, self-focus may increase awareness to any personal threat that failure may produce.

Third, self-focus may increase awareness of emotions and engagement in the action tendencies motivated by these emotions. The shifting of attention inward makes people aware of their inner experience, attentive to any changes in their physiological and psychological states, and reactive to such emotion-arousing stimuli as interruptions of goal-oriented plans and cognitive discrepancies (Carver & Scheier, 1981; Duval & Wicklund, 1972; Gibbons, 1990). In this way, self-focus leads to an awareness of any emotional changes produced by failure and thereby elicits behavior that is in accordance with the evoked emotions.

Fourth, self-focus may affect the expectancy process. To reassess the likelihood of goal attainment after failure, people must first compare their actual state against their goals and recognize that the discrepancy has widened rather than narrowed. To estimate the probability of control, people must evaluate whether they possess the skills and abilities needed to control the current outcomes. Again, both of these requirements can be met only when people direct attention inward. Self-focus allows people to be aware of the mismatch that has been enlarged by failure. Furthermore, it facilitates the self-reflective assessment of abilities and skills.

Fifth, self-focus may facilitate the organization of coping actions by directing attention toward the material needed to organize problem-solving plans and/or substitute goals. Self-focus makes procedural problem-focused rules and declarative knowledge on problem-solving settings available, and it thereby sets the basis for the construction of a cognitive context (via action rumination) that may facilitate the organization of problem-focused plans. Accordingly, it may make available self-schemas and personal projects and goals, thereby setting the basis of the construction of a cognitive context that may facilitate reorganization coping.

In the next parts of this section I review studies that have documented the above hypothesized effects of self-focus. Some studies induced self-focus by exposing subjects to manipulations reminding them of themselves (e.g., an audience of observers, a mirror, a TV camera). Other studies examined the effects of self-focus by measuring subjects' predispositions to self-focus via the Self-Consciousness

Scale (Fenigstein, Scheier, & Buss, 1975). These latter studies concentrate on the private factor of self-consciousness—the habitual tendency to focus on private aspects of the self (one's own cognitions, attitudes, feelings, values). A large number of studies have proven that the private factor of the Self-Consciousness Scale taps the same psychological state as that produced by the various situational inductions of self-focus (Carver & Scheier, 1981).

SELF-FOCUS AND COPING STRATEGIES

The contribution of self-focus to the strength of coping efforts has been documented in a number of recent studies. In a study that exposed high and low self-conscious subjects to success or failure in a cognitive task, then measured the amount of alcohol they consumed in a subsequent wine taste, Hull and Young (1983) showed that failure produced more alcohol consumption than success only among the high self-conscious subjects. According to the authors, this finding reveals the tendency of self-focused persons to cope with the distress created by failure. For such subjects, alcohol may function to decrease awareness of self-relevant threats by inhibiting encoding and memory processes, or as a self-handicapping excuse. Whatever explanation applies, Hull and Young's findings show that high self-focused persons are more likely to undertake avoidance coping than their low self-focused counterparts.

In Study 12 of my recent series (see Chapter 1), I assessed self-reports of coping activities (via my 4-item scale) following zero, one, or four failures in unsolvable problems under the presence of either self-focusing stimuli (mirror and video camera) or instructions encouraging people to divert their attention away from themselves. Results showed that a small amount of failure produced higher reports of problem-focused coping than did no feedback, and a large amount of failure produced higher reports of reorganization and avoidance strategies only among high self-focused persons (see Table 7.1). Persons in this low self-focus condition showed no significant elevation of problem-solving, avoidance, or reorganization coping under any of the failure conditions, and they were less likely to undertake these coping actions in response to failure than persons in the high self-focus

TABLE 7.1. Means of Coping Scores by Number of Failures and Induced Self-Focus (Study 12)

	No failures		One failure		Four failures	
	Low	High	Low	High	Low	High
Problem solving	4.25	4.12	3.87	5.25	3.75	2.25
Reappraisal	1.37	1.50	3.62	3.75	4.25	1.50
Reorganization	1.37	1.87	1.50	1.75	1.50	2.50
Avoidance	1.37	1.37	1.50	1.87	1.87	2.62

condition. In general, self-focus appears to intensify the strength of whatever type of coping efforts predominate after helplessness training.

After a large amount of helplessness training, however, subjects in the low self-focus condition reported using more reappraisal strategies than high self-focused subjects. That is, self-focus seemed to inhibit the use of reappraisal. Interestingly, this conclusion is in keeping with the finding by Mikulincer and Marshand (1991, Study 2) that the presence of a mirror inhibited excuse making. Failure subjects who made attributions in front of a mirror did not attribute performance more to external/specific causes than did no-feedback subjects; attribution was used in an excuselike manner only in a no-mirror condition. Similar findings were obtained by one of my students (Weinberg, 1990) in her study on private self-consciousness.

Why does self-focus inhibit excuse making after repeated failure? Self-focus may make people aware of the likelihood of goal attainment and prevent any interpretation that does not accord with that awareness. When their expectancies are favorable, self-focused persons can try to redefine the failure situation positively, as this reappraisal accords with their hopeful attitude. When expectancies are unfavorable (e.g., after repeated failure), however, their awareness of the irreversibility of the failure would impede any excuse making, because the latter can no longer remedy matters.

Alternatively, Snyder and Higgins (1988) proposed that excuse making requires a reduction of self-focus. Awareness of excuse making transforms it into a "bad act." . . . "Not only has the person failed, but he or she is caught in the pejorative excuse making process" (Mehlman & Snyder, 1985, p. 1000). The reluctance to be caught in a self-deceptive act may lead people to avoid making excuses and to accept the painful reality. Self-focus thus prevents any rationalization of failure because it minimizes self-deception opportunities.

SELF-FOCUS AND MENTAL RUMINATION

Self-focus may also be essential for purposive mental rumination, the cognitive substrate of coping responses. Almost by definition, it is impossible to ruminate without self-focus. Rumination is a self-reflective activity requiring that attention be directed on information regarding one's actions and their implications. To ruminate, people must divert their attention away from external sources, concentrate fully on the processing of stored material, and become intensely aware of what they are doing and what they are like. All of these requirements may be met only when the person is focused on the self.

A series of studies with clinically depressed patients demonstrated that an experimental reduction of self-focus weakened state rumination (Fenell & Teasdale, 1984; Fenell, Teasdale, Jones, & Damle, 1987; Teasdale & Rezin, 1978). All the studies found that depressed persons, who habitually tend to direct attention inward and to engage in state rumination, reported less state thoughts after being asked to

TABLE 7.2. Means of Rumination Scores by Number of Failures
and Induced Self-Focus (Study 12)

	No failures		One failure		Four failures	
	Low	High	Low	High	Low	High
Action rumination	3.87	4.12	3.37	5.37	3.25	2.62
State rumination	1.75	1.62	1.25	1.75	1.87	2.75
Task-irrelevant rumination	1.37	2.12	1.75	1.12	1.87	2.87

direct their attention to a series of slides on outdoor scenes. This effect was found only among nonendogenous depressed patients, however, implying that the state thoughts of endogenous patients may be so strong that manipulations of self-focus cannot influence it.

There is also evidence that the propensity to self-focus affects cognitive reactions to failure (Ingram, Johnson, Bernet, & Dombeck, 1992, Study 1). Although persons who were not self-focused showed few cognitive changes after failure, chronically self-focused persons reacted to failure with an increase in failure-oriented thoughts, as assessed by the Automatic Thought Questionnaire. This finding was replicated in a naturalistic study that assessed cognitive reactions to stressful events over a 10-week period (Ingram et al., 1992, Study 2). Ingram et al. concluded that self-focused individuals are prone to react to failures and obstacles with heightened ruminative thoughts.

This conclusion was supported in Study 12 of my recent series (see Table 1.1), which manipulated the number of unsolvable problems (zero, one, four) and self-focus. This study showed that persons in a self-focus condition (mirror and video) reported more frequent action thoughts after one failure and more frequent state thoughts after repeated failures, as assessed by my 3-item scale, than persons who received instructions encouraging them to reduce self-focus (see Table 7.2). That is, the presence of a self-focusing stimulus increased the frequency of action thoughts after one failure and the frequency of state thoughts after repeated failures.

SELF-FOCUS AND EXPECTANCY

The effects of self-focus on the expectancy process should be most clearly manifested in the accuracy of self assessments. Self-focus may allow people to process material on their abilities and skills, to reflect on their efficacy for altering outcomes, and then to generate anticipatory cognitions in accordance with the sense of self-efficacy they hold in a given situation. In general, the literature supports the idea that the induction of self-focus promotes more accurate self-assessments (see Carver & Scheier, 1981; Gibbons, 1990, for reviews). For example, Pryor, Gibbons, Wicklund, Fazio, and Hood (1977) found that subjects' self-reports of sociability were more consistent with their behavior when they were made in front of a mirror. Gibbons et al. (1985) found that a mirror increased the accuracy with which psychiatric patients reported on their emotional problems. Similar findings were obtained by Scheier (1980) and Scheier, Buss, and Buss (1978) in their studies of self-consciousness.

In the LH paradigm, the heightened accuracy of self-assessment produced by self-focus may be manifested in an accurate perception of lack of control. The allocation of resources in the assessment of one's responses repertoire and the intensive information processing concerning one's self-efficacy may facilitate the recognition that no response could control outcomes in the helplessness training. Moreover, self-focus may increase people's awareness of the fallacious basis of the beliefs they held prior to failure ("I could control the outcomes") and may induce them to rectify their misconceptions by matching their beliefs to a more veridical standard.

A study of mine (Mikulincer, Gerber, & Weisenberg, 1990) seems to corroborate this suggestion. Regardless of the presence or absence of a mirror, nondepressed persons made accurate judgments of control for a controllable problem (identical to that used by Alloy & Abramson, 1979). Variations in self-focus, however, determined the accuracy of judgments of an uncontrollable problem. Under the no-mirror condition, nondepressed persons were unable to recognize the lack of control but maintained the classic illusion of control (Langer, 1975). Under the mirror condition, they made accurate judgments and recognized the uncontrollability of the outcomes; that is, the presence of a self-focusing stimuli facilitated the learning of uncontrollability.

These findings imply that self-focused attention increases the accuracy of self-assessments. Alternatively, the findings can be explained in terms of the effects of self-focus on "illusory cognitions" (Snyder & Higgins, 1988). According to Snyder and Higgins (1988) a mirror minimizes self-deception opportunities and prevents illusory cognitions, such as the belief of control in uncontrollable situations. Either way, self-focus may increase awareness to one's low self-efficacy and enable the recognition of no control.

Depressed subjects, interestingly, made accurate judgments of no control with or without a mirror, but accurate judgments of controllable problems only under the no-mirror condition. This pattern may be explained by the chronic propensity of depressed subjects for self-focus (e.g., Ingram, 1984, 1990), which may produce depressogenic self-schemas ("I'm incompetent"), and/or heightened depressed affects, resulting in the underestimation of control. In any case, the findings regarding depressed persons do not detract from the point that under normal circumstances self-focus improves perception of no control.

Another related issue that has received some empirical attention concerns the effects of self-focus on the generalization of expectancies to new tasks (Davies, 1982). In a study of belief perseverance, Davies (1982) exposed subjects to bogus success or failure feedback in a suicide-judgment task, debriefed them about the false nature of the feedback on one of four groups according to the presence or absence of a mirror before or after the debriefing, and assessed their ratings of their actual performance. Results indicated that the presence of a self-focusing stimuli before the debriefing increased belief perseverance after the debriefing, in that subjects did not take into account the messages on the false nature of feedback. (That is, subjects exposed to failure erroneously continued to evaluate their performance to be poorer than did subjects exposed to success.) In contrast, the presence of self-focusing stimuli after the debriefing prevented belief perseverance—subjects did not take into account the prior feedback in evaluating their performance.

The findings suggest that the effects of self-focus on the transfer of expectancy of no control from helplessness training to a new test task may depend on the timing of self-focus. During helplessness training, self-focus may result in the increased processing of failure-relevant information (e.g., stored data on prior failure experiences and negative self-evaluations) that reinforces the validity of beliefs on low self-efficacy and facilitates their generalization to new tasks. Also, self-focus may augment the probability of internal attribution for the failure (Duval & Wicklund, 1973), which in turn contributes to belief perseverance (Fleming & Arrowood, 1979). In the test task, however, self-focus may prevent the perseverance of the beliefs engendered by failure and enable persons to make more accurate judgments of control. Here self-focus strengthens people's attempts to match their assessments to a valid performance standard and helps them realize that the impressions derived from the failure task are invalid.

The effects of self-focus in the test task, however, may be tempered by the fact that subjects in the LH paradigm are never debriefed before performing the task. In fact, they can revise the expectancies of no control they form during the helplessness training only by actually learning that the test task is different and that they can control its outcomes through instrumental actions. In other words, in the LH setting, self-focus cannot prevent subjects from erroneously believing that the new task is uncontrollable unless they actually do it. Furthermore, once they form the expectancy of no control during helplessness training and generalize it to the test task, self-focused persons would regard the instrumental actions necessary to control outcomes as futile and be reluctant to undertake them. This deficit would in turn impede their learning that outcomes in the test task are controllable and thus prevent revision of their expectancies.

On this basis, one can delineate the following effects of self-focus. First of all, self-focus during helplessness training may facilitate the perception and expectancy of no control and their generalization to the next task. Second, self-focus in the test task may facilitate the revision of the negative expectancy only after people make instrumental responses. Third, the withdrawal of task efforts may temper the corrective action of self-focus.

Self-Focus and Emotional Experience

There is extensive evidence that self-focus increases the awareness of the most salient emotions, just as it does to any other prevailing cognitive self-dimension.

This heightened awareness increases the intensity of emotions and makes self-focused persons more responsive to their emotional states and more accurate in reporting their inner emotional experience.

Research has consistently found that the reports of an affective state originally induced by some experimental manipulations are enhanced by self-focus. For example, subjects who had been angered by a provocation exhibited more angry aggression (retaliatory responses) when their attention was self-focused by a mirror that when it was not (Scheier, 1976). The report of depressed affect in conditions designed to induce this sort of affect (e.g., Velten mood-induction procedure) was higher among persons who were self-focused, either by predisposition or induction, than among persons who were not self-focused (Brockner, Hjelle, & Plant, 1985; Scheier & Carver, 1977). In addition, the induction of self-focus increased the reports of fear, anxiety, and worry among subjects who were exposed to threatening situations (e.g., Scheier, Carver, & Gibbons, 1981). Similar effects of self-focus were found with regard to the enhancement of emotional distress following the exposure to chronic stress (Frone & McFarlin, 1989) and to the enhancement of positive affects following a humorous stimulus (Porterfield, Mayer, Dougherty, & Kredich, 1988).

Research has also found that persons who are self-focused, either by disposition or induction, are more aware of their physiological arousal than non-self-focused persons (e.g., Gibbons, Carver, Scheier, & Hormuth, 1979; Hansen, Hansen, & Crano, 1989; Scheier, Carver, & Matthews, 1982). There is also evidence that self-consciousness enhances the intensity of prevailing chronic affective states (Flett, Boase, McAndrews, & Blankstein, 1986) and the reporting of higher levels of pain among chronic pain patients (Ahles, Pecora, & Riley, 1987). Accordingly, several studies found positive correlations between self-focus and the strength of test anxiety (Deffenbacher & Deitz, 1978; Deffenbacher & Hazaleus, 1985; Flett, Blankstein, & Boase, 1987) and social anxiety (e.g., Hope & Heimberg, 1988).

Self-focus has also been found to have implications for the intensity of depressive states. In a seminal study, Smith and Greenberg (1981) found a positive correlation between depression and the dispositional tendency to be highly self-focused (as measured by Fenigstein's Self-Consciousness Scale) in a college sample. This finding has been replicated using different measures of self-consciousness and depression, and among clinically depressed people (e.g., Ingram & Smith, 1984; Ingram, Lumry, Cruet, & Sieber, 1987). In addition, Smith, Ingram, and Roth (1985), Gibbons et al. (1985), and Ingram, Cruet, Johnson, and Wisnicki (1988) found that the level of depressive affects among depressed persons was positively related to their dispositional and situational tendency to self-focus.

Some studies, however, have found no link between the intensity of anxiety and depressive affects and the tendency to self-focus (e.g., Carver & Glass, 1976; Exner, 1973; Turner, Scheier, Carver, & Ickes, 1978). Ingram (1990) reviewed these studies and concluded that "because all of these studies used unselected samples of college students, there is no reason to believe that both subjects' anxiety

TABLE 7.3. Means of Emotion Scores by Number of Failures
and Induced Self-Focus (Study 12)

	No failures		One failure		Four failures	
	Low	High	Low	High	Low	High
Anger	1.62	1.50	1.50	2.75	1.62	1.75
Anxiety	1.12	1.37	1.50	1.75	1.62	2.50
Depression	1.25	1.50	1.12	1.50	1.37	2.37

and heightened self-focused attention had been activated by any emotion-provoking situation" (p. 160). That is, self-focus may only increase the intensity of anxiety and depression originally provoked by emotion-arousing stimuli. It cannot by itself evoke emotions when there is no reason to react to a situation with strong emotions.

In the LH context, self-focus has been found to intensify the individual's emotional reactions to failure. Hull and Young (1983) found that high self-consciousness persons reported greater negative affect in the MAACL after failure than low self-consciousness persons. Accordingly, Ingram (1988) found that whereas low self-consciousness persons were not affected by a failure–success manipulation, high self-consciousness persons reported more negative affects after failure than after success. In Study 12 of my recent series, self-focusing stimuli (mirror and video) were found to produce stronger reports of anger after a small amount of failure and stronger reports of anxiety and depressed affects (as measured by single items) after repeated failures than instructions that reduced self-focus (see Table 7.3). In fact, failure produced stronger emotions than no feedback only among subjects under high self-focus. Instructions encouraging people to divert attention away from the self prevented any elevation of anger, anxiety, or depressed affects after either a small or a large amount of failure.

SELF-FOCUS AND THE VALUATION PROCESS

From the beginning of the research in self-focus, authors have suggested that the act of directing attention toward the self may alter a person's valuation of a task (e.g., Duval & Wicklund, 1972). In their original theory of self-awareness, Duval and Wicklund (1972) claimed that self-focus increases the self-relevance of a task. In support of this view, several studies have found that situational inductions of self-focus consistently increase the tendency to make internal attributions and hence to link outcomes to the self (e.g., Duval & Wicklund, 1973; Fenigstein & Carver, 1978; Fenigstein & Levine, 1984). In addition, Buss and Scheier (1976) found that high self-consciousness persons accepted more personal responsibility for hypothetical and real outcomes, either positive or negative, than did low self-consciousness persons.

Duval and Wicklund (1972) explained the attributional bias of self-focused persons in terms of the phenomenological salience of the self as a "causal agent." Increasing the perceptual salience or the cognitive availability of any object increases the extent to which the object influences perceptions and cognitions (Tverski & Kahneman, 1973) and the extent to which it is perceived as a causal agent. It has been consistently shown that the amount of causal responsibility assigned to a particular stimulus covaries with the salience of that stimulus (Taylor & Fiske, 1978). Because self-focus increases the salience of the self, it would also increase the perception of the self as a causal agent, biasing attribution to more internal causes.

Evidence of the link between self-focus and internal attribution, however, has not gone entirely unchallenged. In fact, some researchers have failed to replicate the positive association between self-focus and internal attribution (Franzoi & Sweeney, 1986; Nadler, 1983). In addition, other studies have found that self-focus may interact with outcome (success or failure) in determining attribution, with self-focus increasing internal attribution for success but decreasing the acceptance of personal responsibility for failure (Cohen, Dowling, Bishop, & Maney, 1985; Federoff & Harvey, 1976).

In clarifying the relationship between self-focus and internal attribution, Gibbons (1983, 1990) claimed that self-focus increases the self-relevance of an outcome only when there are some cues linking the outcome to the self. In his terms, self-focus fosters a careful consideration of the antecedents and consequences of behavior, and thus it increases the accuracy with which people assess their own contribution to an outcome. This accurate analysis is reflected in more internal attributions when the self is the actual causal agent of the outcomes, but more external attributions when environmental features produce the outcome. In support of this view, individuals who are self-focused, either by induction or disposition, have been found to be less likely than non-self-focused persons to accept responsibility for a group activity and for a change in a partner's behavior for which they were not responsible, and to be more accurate in making internal attributions for emotional problems (Ellis & Holmes, 1982; Stephenson & Wicklund, 1983).

Another related hypothesis on the relationship between self-focus and internal attribution was proposed by Brown (1988). In his terms, self-focus does not necessarily increase internal attribution, but rather intensifies whether causal judgment may be dominant at the time. The reasoning is that self-focus makes accessible the cognitive material that is salient at a given moment (Carver & Scheier, 1981). Self-focus may increase internal attribution when the acceptance of personal responsibility is the prevailing judgment, but it may reduce that attribution when the person puts emphasis on external causation.

On this basis, Brown (1988) hypothesized that self-focus may intensify the person's habitual tendency to make internal attributions for outcomes that are consistent with expectations. Research has found that persons who anticipate success tend to attribute positive outcomes to the self but deny responsibility for unexpected failure, whereas persons who anticipate failure are more inclined to accept responsibility for failure but deny credit for success (e.g., Fitch, 1970). If this is correct, self-focus may increase internal attribution for failure only among subjects who expect to fail and have a tendency to take personal responsibility for the failure. Using self-esteem as an index of prior expectations, Brown (1988) provides some support for these hypotheses.

Brown's proposal has important implications. Because a large amount of helplessness training may reduce the expectancy of control, people would be biased to take responsibility for the expected next failure. According to Brown's reasoning, self-focus may intensify that tendency and may thus strengthen the link between the failure and the self. In support of this view, two of my students (Budner, 1991; Weinberg, 1990) found that high self-focus, either by induction or disposition, increased internal attribution for uncontrollable failures.

On the whole, self-focus seems to contribute to the perceived self-relevance of failure. All the authors agree that the perceived self-relevance of failure originally induced by some personality and/or situational factors (e.g., attributional style, instructional set, expectancies) is enhanced by self focus; that is, self-focus seems to increase the perception of the link existing between the failure and the self. It allows the person to reflect on the personal implications of a self-relevant failure and highlight the threats implied by that failure. This effect of self-focus, however, seems to be confined to situations in which there is some basis for assigning high self-relevance to a failure. When personality and situational factors break the link between failure and the self, there is no certainty that self-focus can lead by itself to internal attribution.

SUMMARY

The studies reviewed here illustrate the effects of self-focus on the coping process. Self-focus seems to act on the various components of the process of coping with uncontrollable failures. It intensifies the undertaking of coping actions, the engagement in purposive rumination, the emotional reactions to failure, and the attribution of failure to internal causes, and it facilitates the perception and learning of lack of control. The psychological state of self-focus can be defined by the concern with the meaning of a person–environment transaction, the awareness of inner experience, the careful deliberation of the pattern of action that may be most appropriate for dealing with a failure, and the undertaking of the cued coping actions. Taken together, the findings support the idea that self-focus is a catalyst of the coping process.

It is important to note that the above conclusions do not mean that self-focus can determine in and by itself the course of the coping process. For example, the proposition that self-focus allows people to assess whether failure threatens the self does not mean that this assessment may be necessarily followed by the detection of personal threats. In fact, a self-focused person may evaluate the failure and reach the conclusion that it means nothing of importance to his or her goals. Accordingly, the proposition that self-focus heightens the person's responsivity to emotional experiences and his or her proneness to undertake coping actions do not mean that it can evoke emotion and coping action in the absence of the proper instigating stimuli. If for any situational or personality reason failure does not evoke any emotion or call for any coping action, there would be no emotion or action even among highly self-focused persons. High self-focus only intensifies the emotions and coping actions that a failure may elicit. Finally, self-focus cannot determine the type of coping strategy a person undertakes in a situation; the expectancy of control does. Self-focus only intensifies the undertaking of the chosen strategy.

SELF-FOCUS AND LH EFFECTS

This section deals with the hypothesis that self-focus intensifies reactance and LH deficits—that is, variations in the direction of attention toward or away the self during or after helplessness training will be reflected in the strength of subsequent LH effects. Reactance after a small amount of helplessness training and LH deficits after a large amount of training are presumed to increase as a direct function of the direction of attention toward the self. Any reduction in self-focus may weaken the LH effects.

The above hypothesis is directly derived from the concept of self-focus as a catalyst of the coping process. Self-focus may contribute to LH effects by activating the various components of the coping process after helplessness training; it is the coping activities that are subsequently reflected in performance changes. Without self-focus, the mechanisms that underlie reactance and helplessness effects cannot be set in motion: The person will not be aware of the threat and will thus not experience the need to cope. For this reason, people who do not focus their attention inward may perform the test task similarly to those who have not experienced any lack of control.

As stated in previous chapters, the recognition of personal threat and the subsequent arousal of emotions motivate people to engage in some kind of behavior to cope with the failure, and this in turn alters test task performance. Self-focus enhances the person's awareness of self-relevant threats and provokes emotional reactions, which tend to increase the person's motivation to initiate coping activities and the likelihood of subsequent performance changes. No matter what coping strategies are chosen (e.g., problem solving or off-task), they are reflected in strong performance changes.

In addition, as stated in Chapter 4, expectancies determine the type of approach that a person takes in coping with a failure (problem-solving or off-task strategies), and they thus shape the quality (positive or negative) of the resulting LH effects. Self-focus may facilitate the assessment of the likelihood of control, make people aware of their expectancies, and thus influence them to take the most appropriate course of action: problem focused for favorable expectancies, and off-task coping for unfavorable expectancies. Self-focus may thus be considered a precondition for

LH effects. It makes a person aware of the need for behavioral change to dealing with the uncontrollable failure, it facilitates these changes, and it ties them to expectancies.

My reasoning can be schematized as follows. People in the LH paradigm encounter a failure that can thwart their goals and damage their self-identity. If self-focus is low, self-relevant threats are not detected, coping actions are inhibited, and neither type of performance change (reactance or helplessness) is observed. People who are not self-focused may thus be impervious to the effects of helplessness training. When self-focus is high, however, people will detect the threat, be aware of their emotions, and initiate coping activities in accordance with their expectancies of control. When expectancies are favorable, the self-focused person redoubles task efforts and continues to organize and perform problem-solving activities, all of which tends to culminate in improved performance. When expectancies are unfavorable, the self-focused person will withdraw from the task and/or allocate cognitive resources to the reorganization of self-views and priorities, which will eventually lead to performance deficits.

Two conclusions may be deduced from the above reasoning. First, self-focus has no directional effect; it is not exclusively associated with either reactance or LH deficits. Self-focus improves performance under favorable expectancy and impairs performance under unfavorable expectancy. Self-focus does not determine the type of performance changes observed after helplessness training. It only intensifies whatever performance change is induced by the failure.

Second, the performance effects of expectancy of control, perceived task value, and emotional arousal may depend on the direction of attention toward or away from the self. High self-focus will facilitate conscious accessing of appraisals, expectancies, and emotions, and it may increase their power to alter coping activities and thereby task performance. Self-focused people are able to consider their evaluations of task importance/self-relevance, their expectancies, and their emotional experiences in deciding what to do in the current situation, and they will tend to behave accordingly. Without self-focus, these cognitive and emotional products are inaccessible to consciousness and therefore have no impact on task performance.

THE PERFORMANCE EFFECTS OF SELF-FOCUS

The contribution of self-focus to LH effects has been documented in several studies. Using the Self-Consciousness Scale, three investigations showed that high self-focus was a precondition for LH effects. The earliest study was by Scheier and Carver (1982), which found that failure in a variant of Gottschaldt's Concealed Figures Test produced lower persistence in a subsequent cognitive-perceptual task than success only among highly self-conscious subjects, and it did not affect the persistence of low self-consciousness subjects. Moreover, high self-consciousness subjects showed less persistence after failure than low self-consciousness subjects.

Another experiment was conducted by two of my students (Carmon & Dona-ghi, 1991), who intended in part to eliminate some of Scheier and Carver's methodological problems. Scheier and Carver (1982) compared failure with success rather than with no feedback, creating confusion about whether failure undermines performance or success invigorates it. Also, their use of persistence as the parameter of performance quality made it difficult to compare their findings with those of other LH studies, most of which used performance quality in solvable tasks as the dependent variable. The results of the Carmon and Donaghi (1991) study accorded with Scheier and Carver's findings. Relative to no feedback, failure in four unsolvable problems produced less accurate performance in a letter cancellation task only among high self-consciousness persons, who exhibited worse performance after helplessness training than low self-consciousness subjects. That is, the classic LH deficit was found only among self-focused persons.

Similar results were reported by Heaton and Sigall (1991), who asked high and low self-consciousness subjects to perform a psychomotor task alone or in front of either a supportive or nonsupportive audience and gave them failure or success feedbacks. Interestingly, these authors also found that although the performance of low self-consciousness subjects was not influenced by failure–success manipulation, it was affected by the supportiveness of an audience—they performed worse in front of a nonsupportive than a supportive audience. This finding led Heaton and Sigall (1991) to conclude that "persons low and high in self-consciousness may experience different types of performance pressures resulting from differing self-presentational motives. Relative to individuals high in self-consciousness, individuals low in self-consciousness choked when disappointing the audience was likely; persons high in self-consciousness were more likely to choke when negative self-construction was imminent" (p. 185).

Heaton and Sigall made a step forward and suggested an alternative explanation of the effects of self-consciousness based on the self-presentation hypothesis of Baumeister (1982, 1986). Baumeister argued that task performance can be influenced by two different self-presentational concerns—pleasing the audience, and adapting one's actual self to become congruent with one's ideal self. On the one hand, persons low in self-consciousness may be guided by the desire to please an audience and hence may be responsive to the supportiveness of the audience. On the other hand, the inward focus of attention characteristic of individuals high in self-consciousness may reduce the attention they pay to the audience and increase the salience of internal standards (e.g., ideal self) and the consequent desire for positive self-construction. This self-presentational concern may underlie the responsiveness of high self-consciousness persons to stimuli that threaten positive self-construction, such as failure.

Baumeister's explanation raises questions about the mechanism underlying the effects of self-focus. Whereas Baumeister sees these effects as reflecting motivational tendencies, I see them as reflecting structural differences in cognitive processing. In Baumeister's terms, only highly self-focused persons are motivated to cope with a mismatch and thereby do exhibit performance changes after failure. In my terms, both low and high self-focus persons are motivated to cope with a mismatch, but only highly self-focused persons are well equipped to engage in the coping task. Though the three studies reviewed above do not provide information on the validity of the two accounts, they consistently suggest that the propensity to self-focus intensifies the detrimental impact of failure.

Relevant evidence is also provided by studies that experimentally manipulated self-focus. Although the earliest research—by Duval, Wicklund, and Fine (1972), Gibbons and Wicklund (1976), and Archer, Hormuth, and Berg (1979)—did not examine whether induced self-focus moderates LH effects, at least these authors showed that the manipulation of self-focus alters performance after failure. All of their subjects received bogus failure feedback either in the presence or absence of self-focusing stimuli (mirror, camera), and their subsequent behavioral persistence (e.g., the time subjects spent waiting for the experimenter) was assessed. Results showed that the high self-focus subjects exhibited less behavioral persistence (waited less time) after failure than low self-focus subjects.

Several years later, Carver and Scheier (1982) extended these findings by adding a control condition (success) to examine whether self-focus intensifies the performance effects of failure, and a less diffuse dependent variable to measure task performance. Carver and Scheier (1982) found that failure in three mazes produced worse task performance in subsequent mazes than success only when a mirror was introduced; no significant effect of failure was found in the absence of a mirror. In addition, failure subjects performed worse when the mirror was present than when it was absent, whereas success subjects performed better when the mirror was present than when it was absent. The findings imply that self-focus undermines performance after failure, but improves it after success. More important, "subjects' performance was uninfluenced by their prior outcomes unless their level of self-focus was relatively high" (Carver & Scheier, 1982, p. 195). The findings were conceptually replicated in a study of Strack, Blaney, Ganellen, and Coyne (1985, Study 2) that measured performance quality in an anagram task.

Beyond the above findings that link self-focus with LH deficits, a study by McDonald (1980) suggests that self-focus also contributes to performance facilitation after failure. In the presence of a mirror, failure on a creativity task led people to write more in response to a TAT picture than did success (a reactance effect). The absence of a mirror weakened whatever effect failure might have produced. In fact, an analysis of the number of words written after failure showed that subjects wrote more in the mirror than the no-mirror condition.

These findings may also suggest that self-focus acts together with favorable expectancies in facilitating performance. Scheier and Carver (1982) argued that subjects in McDonald's failure condition might have maintained positive expectancies because the training and tests were presented as very different tasks and subjects were told that writing a large number of words was an appropriate strategy for succeeding in the task. If this analysis is valid, the observed reactance effect

TABLE 7.4. Means and Standard Deviation of Performance Accuracy by Number of Failures and Induced Self-Focus (Study 12)

	No failures		One failure		Four failures	
	Low	High	Low	High	Low	High
Mean	81.25	80.25	82.62	89.12	76.50	63.12
Standard deviation	7.08	7.64	6.88	6.55	11.01	12.35

may reflect the underlying conjoint action of favorable expectancies and high self-focus. To validate this contention properly, however, requires the measurement or manipulation of the individual's expectancies and the examination of their interaction with self-focus.

A more complete picture of the performance effects of self-focus in LH settings is provided by Study 12 of the series I present in this book. In this study, subjects were exposed to zero, one, or four failures in unsolvable cognitive problems, and their performance accuracy was assessed in a subsequent letter cancellation task. Half of the subjects in each feedback condition performed the training and test tasks under self-focusing stimuli (mirror and video). The other half of the subjects received instructions that encouraged them to divert attention away from the self. Results showed that one failure produced more accurate test task performance than no failure, and four failures produced less accurate performance than no failure only among subjects in the high self-focus condition (see Table 7.4). Subjects who received instructions encouraging the reduction of self-focus showed neither reactance after one failure nor performance deficits after four failures. In other words, the experimental reduction of self-focus made people impervious to both the positive and negative effects of helplessness training.

Though the effects of the mirror induction in the studies reviewed consistently suggest that high self-focus is a prerequisite for the performance effects of failure, they can be explained by alternative interpretations. For example, Carver and Scheier (1981) themselves suggest that a mirror may alter performance by increasing physiological arousal or by enabling subjects to access their own facial expression after failure, to infer their inner state of helplessness, and to behave in accordance with that inference. Because the disposition to self-focus produces similar effects to those obtained by the introduction of a mirror, however, these explanations cannot obviate the role of self-focus in human LH.

SELF-FOCUS AND THE EXPECTANCY–PERFORMANCE LINK

The basic idea here is that high self-focus amplifies the classic expectancy–performance link. Favorable expectancies may be most likely to lead to higher task efforts and better performance than unfavorable expectancies when people are self-focused. The diversion of attention away from the self may make expectancies, whether by induction or by disposition, irrelevant in determining performance.

The first relevant study on the contribution of self-focus to the expectancy–performance link was conducted by Carver, Blaney, and Scheier (1979a). The task was to reach into a cage and pick up a boa constrictor; all the subjects were moderately fearful of snakes. On the basis of a pretest questionnaire, subjects were divided into those who doubted their ability to perform the task (unfavorable expectancy) and those who were at least moderately confident of their ability to perform it (favorable expectancy). Then subjects performed the snake approach task—half of them in front of a mirror, the other half without self-focusing stimuli.

The authors reasoned that the mirror would make subjects who habitually held unfavorable expectancies become aware of their feelings of inadequacy and so behave in accordance with them. In this case, the mirror would amplify the tendency to withdraw from the task and the difficulties in completing it. For subjects who held favorable expectancies, a self-focusing stimuli might enhance their awareness to their confidence in attaining the goal, thus amplifying their tendency to complete the task. On this basis, Carver et al. expected that variations in expectancy would determine task persistence mainly when high self-focus was induced.

The results supported this reasoning: Subjects holding unfavorable expectancies stopped their actions earlier in the approach sequence than those holding favorable expectancies only when self-focus was high. The absence of self-focus prevented expectancy from producing behavioral changes. Similar effects were found by Carver, Blaney, and Scheier (1979b), Steenbarger and Aderman (1979), and Burgio, Merluzzi, and Pryor (1986), who extended the findings to the induction of expectancy, to other performance measures (e.g., persistence in problem-solving tasks), and to social settings.

Analysis of the postexperimental questionnaire data indicates that the presence of the mirror changed the subjective states of both doubtful and confident subjects. Among doubtful subjects, the mirror increased anxiety, inadequacy feelings, awareness of chronic fearfulness, and physiological arousal. Among confident subjects, the mirror increased their awareness not only of their fear but also of the goal state. It seems that the mirror led subjects who held unfavorable expectancies to focus on factors that impeded their completion of the task, but led subjects with favorable expectancies to focus on goal attainment.

The contribution of self-focus to the expectancy–performance link was also demonstrated in field settings. Although being correlational and posing problems of interpretation, field studies are important for assessing the ecological validity of laboratory findings. In one of these studies, Hollenbeck (1989) found that reports of success expectancy in work assignments predicted organizational commitment (acceptance of organizational goals, willingness to exert effort on behalf of the organization) and behavioral withdrawal (quitting from the jobs within a year) only among salespersons who tended to focus on private aspects of their selves. In those not so predisposed, expectancy was not related to organizational commitment or behavioral withdrawal. Hollenbeck (1989) noted that "what might appear to be the logical or rational reaction to poor future prospects in one's job may only be forthcoming from individuals whose primary focus of attention is the self" (p. 423).

Another relevant series of studies was conducted by Brockner on the effects of self-esteem, a predispositional correlate of expectancy. Brockner reasoned that the performance deficits observed among low self-esteem subjects may be attributable to their tendency to direct attention inward, and that a reduction in self-focus might eliminate these deficits. In other words, performance differences between low and high self-esteem subjects may depend on the individual's self-focus.

In the first study of this series, Brockner and Hulton (1978) asked low and high self-esteem subjects to perform a concept formation task under one of three conditions: alone, in front of an audience and a mirror (self-focusing stimuli), or with instructions encouraging them to concentrate on the task ("I cannot emphasize strongly enough just how important it is that you keep your complete and undivided attention on the task at all times"). Results indicated that subjects with unfavorable expectancies (low self-esteem) performed worse than those with more favorable expectancies (high self-esteem) only when their self-focus was situationally increased, but not when they performed all the task alone. In addition, the induction of task focus led low self-esteem persons to outperform high self-esteem persons. These findings were replicated in two studies by Brockner (1979a) that used a video camera and/or a mirror as self-focusing stimuli and assessed the propensity for self-consciousness.

Another study by Brockner (1979b) extended the above findings and suggests that self-focus amplifies the link between expectancy and LH effects. Failure in a social insight task was found to produce worse performance than success only among subjects who held unfavorable expectancies (low self-esteem) and had high self-focus, either through induction or disposition. When self-focus was low, no difference was found in the performance of low and high self-esteem persons after either success or failure. Brockner's results suggest that the impact of expectancy on LH effects depends on self-focus. Although habitual expectancies (e.g., self-esteem) may make the person prone to persist or withdraw from the test task after helplessness training, it is insufficient to translate this proneness into behavioral changes. For these changes to occur, people should direct their attention inward and be aware to their ability to perform well. Only in these cases will people tend to behave in accordance with the expectancies they hold.

In two more recent studies, Brockner et al. (1983) intended to examine whether the facilitatory effects of a small amount of helplessness training and the detrimental effects of a large amount of training depend on the conjoint action of self-esteem and self-consciousness. The results were so inconsistent that no clear conclusion can be reached. Although one study found that the disposition to self-focus, at least as reflected in self-consciousness, moderated the invigorating effects of a small amount of helplessness training, the other study found no significant effect of self-consciousness. Whereas the first study yielded no significant contribution of self-esteem, the second found that the facilitatory and detrimental effects of small and large amounts of failure were found among low self-esteem subjects. In general, self-focus seemed to overshadow the effects of self-esteem in the first study and self-esteem seemed to obliterate the effects of self-focus in the second. The single clear conclusion is that helplessness training has both facilitatory and detrimental effects and that individual differences in self-consciousness and self-esteem may moderate these effects, though the particular way they do it is not clear.

In my view, the inconsistent results may result from the assessment rather than the manipulation of expectancy and self-focus. First of all, an uncontrolled "third variable," related to self-esteem and/or self-consciousness, may have affected task performance. In addition, the correlation between self-consciousness and self-esteem may have complicated the results and created some interpretational problems. Brockner et al. (1983) noted that "the effect of private self-consciousness in study 2 was likely weakened by the relative absence of low self-esteem subjects who were also low in private self-consciousness" (p. 206). If the authors had independently manipulated expectancy and self-focus, more consistent findings may have emerged.

SELF-FOCUS AND THE IMPACT OF EMOTION

In contrast to the state of affairs with the expectancy–performance link, there is no extensive and systematic work on the contribution of self-focus to the performance impact of emotions. There is some sparse evidence, however, of the detrimental effects of anxiety. Included in this is a study conducted by Carver, Peterson, Follansbee, and Scheier (1983) who found that self-focus is a precondition for the detrimental effects of a predisposition to anxiety. High anxiety produced worse performance and less persistence in anagram tasks than low anxiety only (a) under a mirror condition, or (b) among highly self-conscious subjects. The absence of situational conditions or habitual tendencies that fostered self-focus eliminated the negative effect of anxiety on performance. These findings were later replicated and extended by Rich and Woolever (1988), who found that the detrimental effects of anxiety on task performance after failure were significant only under high self-focus.

An intriguing set of findings was presented by Slapion and Carver (1981). In their study, high-anxiety subjects did not perform worse on a relatively straightforward personnel classification test than their low-anxiety counterparts. In fact, they performed better, but only when a high self-focusing stimuli (a mirror) was present. In short, experimentally induced self-focus was found to facilitate the performance of highly anxious persons. Slapion and Carver interpreted this surprising finding by explaining that the task was performed in a nonevaluative setting, which might have produced a moderate success expectancy and improved the performance of the anxious subjects.

Taken together, the findings of the studies reviewed above suggest that human actions are not always blindly driven by emotion. Rather, there are cases in which people are aware of their ongoing levels of physiological arousal and their emotional changes, and they cognitively appraise the personal meanings and implications of these so as to behave in accord. This conclusion, however, does not imply that emotions influence behavior *only* via cognitive mediation. Nor does it takes a position on the theoretical disputes regarding the link between cognition and emotion and the effects of awareness on affective responding. It implies only that, although emotions may influence *some* behaviors without people being aware of their inner experiences, performance changes do tend to require this awareness. The decision to persist in a task may be more complex and require deeper cognitive processing than the types of judgments (such as liking ratings) that have generally been shown to be influenced automatically by emotion. Emotion will contribute to task persistence only if it is accessible to consciousness and ready to be processed along with other relevant pieces of information.

SELF-FOCUS AND THE IMPACT OF PERCEIVED TASK VALUE

The idea that self-focus may amplify the performance effects of perceived task value has been investigated in three studies. After exposing subjects to failure in unsolvable mazes, Kernis, Zuckerman, Cohen, and Spadofora (1982) found that messages on the self-relevance of a design problem task influenced the amount of persistence only under a high self-focus condition (a mirror). Under this condition, a message threatening self-identity (internally attributed failure) led to less persistence than the provision of an external reason to failure. The authors concluded that non-self-focused persons do not evaluate their behavior against a self-relevant standard and are not responsive to self-relevant information. A further study by Kernis, Zuckerman, and McVay (1988) indicated that the above findings were significant only after failure, but not after success.

Another relevant piece of evidence is provided by Study 13 of my recent series, which manipulated feedback in four unsolvable problems (no feedback, failure), messages on task importance (low, high), and self-focus (mirror/video, instructions encouraging reduction of self-focus), and assessed performance accuracy in a subsequent letter cancellation task. In line with the findings of Kernis et al. (1982), messages on the importance of failure altered the individual's reactions to failure only under a mirror condition (see Table 7.5). Following failure, high-importance messages produced less accurate performance than low-importance messages only in a mirror condition. Instructions encouraging the diversion of attention away from

TABLE 7.5. Means and Standard Deviations of Performance Accuracy According to Feedback, Induced Self-Focus and Task Importance Messages (Study 13)

	Low focus		High focus	
	Low importance	High importance	Low importance	High importance
No feedback				
Mean	81.12	79.62	83.87	84.87
Standard deviation	6.42	7.03	5.71	8.01
Failure				
Mean	82.12	77.25	80.87	70.75
Standard deviation	6.38	11.41	10.30	11.08

the self weakened the effects of task importance messages. In addition, the results suggest that LH deficits depend on the conjoint action of high task importance and high self-focus. Failure produced worse performance than no feedback only when people received high importance messages under self-focusing stimuli.

The findings emphasize the importance of awareness to the threats produced by failure. Although messages on the value of failure may contribute to LH effects by increasing the threat to self-identity, they seem to do it only when the person is aware of this threat. Inaccessibility to self-relevant contents and lack of attention to inner feelings and beliefs may make people unable to see that the failure implies something of importance about their selves, thereby preventing any pressure to mobilize coping effort and thus any performance change.

Summary

All the diverse lines of research point out the important role of self-focus within the LH paradigm. They suggest that one cannot explain LH effects without taking into account variations in self-focus. They consistently support the hypothesis that self-focus intensifies LH effects, as well as the performance effects of other LH-related factors. They also refine the conclusions of previous chapters on the effects of perceived task value, expectancy, and emotion. These factors alter task performance and contribute to LH effects mainly when people are prone to shift attention to the self.

SELF-FOCUS: A COMPONENT OF THE PROCESS OF COPING WITH FAILURE

The introduction of self-focus as an antecedent of LH effects raises questions as to the position of self-focus within human LH. Is it an exogenous factor that moderates the performance effects of helplessness training? Or is it an endogenous factor that is part of the cognitive changes produced by the training? These questions deal with the process of shifting attention inward. In the studies reviewed above, this process is set in motion by either personality predisposition or experimental inductions of self-focusing stimuli (e.g., a mirror). None of these studies, however, attempts to understand the features of the person–environment transaction and the psychological processes that may precede self-focus. They mainly treat self-focus as an independent variable that may influence emotion, cognition, and behavior, and they put little theoretical and empirical effort into delineating its antecedents. In this section I treat self-focus as a dependent variable and asks whether failure and other LH-related factors may alter the tendency to shift attention inward.

FAILURE AND SELF-FOCUS

The literature suggests that failure has an impact on self-focus, though exactly what kind of impact is uncertain. Statements of the self-awareness theory by Duval and Wicklund (1972) point out that failure reduces self-focus because it makes people aware that they have fallen short of their standards and intensifies the negative emotions produced by failure. According to these authors, people tend to reduce self-focus after failure in order to avoid the resulting emotions; most people may prefer to remain unaware of the actual–ideal discrepancy so as to maintain positive affect and a positive view of themselves. Consistent with this position, research has shown that after failure people tend to avoid self-focus-enhancing stimuli, such as mirrors and tape recordings of their voices (Gibbons & Wicklund, 1976; Greenberg & Musham, 1981; Pyszczynski & Greenberg, 1985, 1986).

If Duval and Wicklund's contentions are correct, a person should desist from coping attempts whenever the latter are discomforting, and these attempts would be set in motion only when self-focus is unavoidable. Taking these implications a step further, we should expect a person to avoid self-focus and withdraw spontaneously from coping attempts with the perception of a single failure. Reality, however, suggests that the opposite is usually the case. People do not tend to give up immediately after one failure but persist even after a large number of failures (Janoff-Bulman & Brickman, 1982). Most people can stand some negative affect and delay immediate gratification, and it is generally accepted that they do invest efforts in trying to overcome failure.

In addition, Duval and Wicklund's hypothesis contradicts the concept of self-focus as a coping device. In this view, failure may enhance rather than reduce self-focus. To the extent that failure disrupts the smooth flow of behavior, creates a person–environment mismatch, and damages central aspects of self-identity, heightened self-focus is essential. The detection of a person–environment mismatch produced by failure may lead people to direct their attention inward in order to facilitate the solution of the problem or the reorganization of mental structures.

Either way, people may tend to be self-focused after failure as part of their coping attempts.

By this reasoning, the aversiveness of self-focus after failure may be compensated for by its facilitatory effects on the coping process. As elaborated earlier, self-focus is an auxiliary of the coping attempts that may end the threats by bringing the person and the environment into a better alignment. Thus what appears to be maladaptive—self-focus and the intensification of negative emotions—may have adaptive consequences at the long run. This position goes away from a simple hedonistic perspective in which people abandon self-focus at the first sight of distress. Instead, it argues that people may prefer to heighten self-focus and tolerate some distress in order to remove the sources of the negative affect.

Similar ideas are found in statements by Pyszczynski and Greenberg (1987), who emphasize the coping demands imposed by failure feedback and the consequent enhancing of self-focus:

> We here proposed that any feedback concerning one's performance in an ego-relevant task is somewhat self-focusing but that failure feedback is particularly self-focusing because it makes a discrepancy between current and desired state salient. We agree that this leads to an assessment of whether and how the discrepancy can be reduced but also argue that this effect on self-regulation necessarily involves high self-focus. In the absence of failure feedback or other obstacles to achieving one's standards, there is no self-regulatory need for such elevation in self-focus (pp. 125–126).

The view that failure reduced self-focus can also be questioned at an empirical level. Greenberg and Pyszczynski (1986), for example, point out that Duval and Wicklund's studies assessed preference for self-focus-enhancing stimuli (e.g., a mirror) rather than the subjects' actual self-focusing. When Greenberg and Pyszczynski (1986, Experiment 1) exposed subjects to success or failure on an anagram task and assessed their subsequent spontaneous self-focusing by using Exner's sentence completion test, they found that subjects were more self-focused after failure than after success (e.g., subjects exposed to failure made more self-references in completing Exner's sentences than subjects exposed to success).

To resolve the apparent contradiction between these results and the earlier findings that failure reduces the preference for self-focus enhancing stimuli, Greenberg and Pyszczynski (1986) explain that

> stimuli that encourages even further elevations of self-focus may increase this affect (negative affect) beyond a tolerable and useful level. Thus, nondepressed persons may avoid self-focus enhancing stimuli immediately after failure to avoid the increased negative affect resulting from such excessive self-focus. Nonetheless, they may still spontaneously self-focus after failure and tolerate the resulting small amounts of negative affect in order to facilitate their efforts at discrepancy reduction (p. 1041).

The question here is whether the observed focus of attention is an automatic response to failure or whether it depends on other moderating factors. In my view, the heightening of self-focus after failure is not as simple as it is portrayed above. First of all, it may depend on personality predispositions and the presence of self-focusing stimuli (e.g., a mirror). In addition, factors that underlie the need for coping may play an intervening role. In the LH context, every factor that may affect the appraisal of the failure and its personal implications may also qualify the variations in self-focus after failure. In the following section I deal with two of these factors: the perception of task value, and the arousal of emotion.

PERCEIVED TASK VALUE AND SELF-FOCUS

One factor that may determine the variations in self-focus after failure is the perceived value of the task. The assignment of high importance/self-relevance to a task means that failure thwarts important goals, raises the need to take coping steps, and thus may encourage people to direct attention inward. When people assign little or no value to a task, they do not feel any personal threat after failure—and hence no need to invest efforts in coping attempts and to direct attention to painful aspects of the self. From this perspective, the enhancement of self-focus after failure is an adaptive response to the threat of self-identity.

If the above reasoning is correct, perceived task value may affect self-focus under both favorable and unfavorable expectancies. As Pyszczynski and Greenberg (1987) state, "When the goal or standard is too central or valuable to let go of, the person may persist in self-focusing, even through objectively there is no way the discrepancy can be reduced" (p. 126).

Integrating the above reasoning with findings reviewed earlier on the effects of self-focus on the valuation process, one can propose a recursive cycle of perceived task value and self-focus. After failure, the direction of attention inward may facilitate the valuation process and the detection of any self-relevant threat that the failure may imply. When no threat is detected, self-focus may cease, and then the valuation process may be inhibited. The recognition of the high importance/self-relevance of a task and the detection of self-relevant threats may increase the tendency to direct attention inward, however, which in turn may exacerbate the perceived self-relevance of failure, and so on. In this way, the person is caught up in a cycle of self-focus and perceived threat, which may intensify the undertaking of coping actions and the resulting LH effects.

AFFECT AND SELF-FOCUS

Another factor that appears to be involved in the shaping of attentional focus is emotional arousal. There is accumulating evidence that emotional arousal may lead the person to shift attention toward the self. For example, Wegner and Giuliano (1980, 1983) manipulated the level of subjects' physiological arousal (e.g., running in place, climbing a hill) and then measured their self-focused attention via the number of self-references made in Exner's sentence completion task. The authors found that the higher the level of arousal, the greater the self-focused attention. Wood, Saltzberg, and Goldsamt (1990) found that various inductions of negative affects (imagination task, musical affect induction) produced higher scores in several measures of self-focused attention (sentence completion, free-response thought sampling) than did neutral affect inductions. These findings were replicated in a correlational study that assessed emotions and self-focused attention every day for 30 days (Wood, Saltzberg, Neale, Stone, & Rachmiel, 1990). Again, it was found that the more intense the negative emotion, the greater the self-focus.

These effects of emotional arousal on self-focus can be explained in several ways. First of all, Wood et al. (1990) proposed that emotional arousal may be a phenomenologically salient event that may capture the individual's attention and direct it inward. In their terms, the unpredictability and suddeness of emotional arousal raise the salience of emotional arousal and the consequent self-focus.

According to Wegner and Guiliano (1980), emotional arousal may promote a meaning analysis of the person–environment transaction (Mandler, 1975). People may be prone to process self-relevant information, such as the personal threats related to the evoked emotions and memories of past emotional episodes, which can help them to understand the nature of the arousal. Like other self-reflective processes, this meaning analysis requires a shifting of attention inward, mainly when people do not understand the cause of the emotional arousal. On this basis, Wegner and Giuliano (1980) argue that emotions enhance self-focus as an auxiliary means for the meaning analysis.

The impact of emotional arousal on self-focus is also explained in coping terms. According to Wood et al. (1990), "Affect may warn that something is wrong and that one must attend to the self in order to surmount the failure or to adjust one's standards" (p. 900). They also propose that emotional arousal may prompt affect-repair strategies that may also demand self-focus.

In any case, the fact that emotions heighten self-focus refutes the basic assumption of Duval and Wicklund (1972, 1973). The arousal of negative emotions, according to Duval and Wicklund, should be followed by a reduction in self-focus in order to make the distress inaccessible to consciousness. In reality, however, people do not distance themselves from the distress, and they may even direct attention to it. Again, a simple hedonistic perspective is insufficient to explain variations in self-focus. Rather, more sophisticated structural and functional concepts of self-focus may be needed for explaining the spontaneous self-focus after the arousal of emotions.

Interestingly, the findings point in the direction of yet another recursive cycle. After failure, the self-focused attention facilitates the arousal of emotion and the attentiveness and responsiveness to the evoked emotions. If for any personal or situational reason emotions are not aroused, self-focus may be reduced, and then the awareness to emotional states may be interrupted. Any arousal of emotions may intensify self-focus, however, which in turn may exacerbate the intensity of the evoked emotions. This recursive cycle of emotional intensification and self-focus maintainance may contribute to both reactance and LH deficits. It may also sustain self-focus after the formation of the expectancy of no control and may be among the mechanisms that foster the experience of overwhelming emotions.

SUMMARY

The studies reviewed above suggest that self-focus appears to be instigated by failure. They also suggest that the intensity of self-focus after failure is a function of the perceived task value and the resulting emotional arousal. As a consequence, variations in self-focus cannot be separated from the helplessness process. Rather, self-focus can be considered another intervening link in the chain of events going from helplessness training to LH effects.

Of course, this reasoning does not mean to imply that self-focus is only heightened after failure. In fact, it may be active in other types of transactions. For example, Gibbons (1990) states that self-focus may occur in situations that demand the inhibition of standard-inconsistent actions (e.g., lying, stealing). In general terms, every situation that demand self-regulation, self-evaluation, the assessment of the transaction with the environment, and/or the making of changes in self-structures may trigger self-focus. Self-relevant failure may make some of these demands and thus may heighten self-focus.

A COPING PERSPECTIVE OF HUMAN LEARNED HELPLESSNESS

In this chapter I attempt to integrate the ideas presented in previous chapters into a coping conceptualization of human LH. First I elaborate on the coping process that underlies LH effects, the direct and indirect antecedents of these effects, and the mediational sequences that go from helplessness training to performance changes. Then I deal with the psychological meanings of reactance and LH deficits and elaborate on their functional and dysfunctional aspects as well as on their generalization over time and across situations.

THE COPING PROCESS AND HUMAN LEARNED HELPLESSNESS

BASIC PREMISES

From a coping perspective, performance changes after helplessness training, whether positive or negative, result from the person's attempts to cope with the person–environment mismatch created by uncontrollable failure. This view is based on two main premises. First, helplessness training creates a disequilibrium between the environment and the person's mental structures (goals, schemas), with which the individual may expend efforts to cope. Second, coping actions may favor or interfere with the allocation of cognitive resources in task-relevant activities, which may thereby alter subsequent performance in solvable test task.

With regard to the first premise, the person–environment mismatch produced by helplessness training derives from the fact that the uncontrollable failure cannot be easily assimilated into stored cognitive schemas ("I can do the task well"). The failure interrupts goal-oriented actions, violates preplanned actions, and blocks goal attainment. It also may be at odds with self-schemas ("I'm a competent person"), and it weakens the person's sense of self-worth. In general, helplessness training may produce the loss of a person's current goals, harm some of his or her schemas, and threaten other mental structures that are related to these goals and schemas.

The state of disequilibrium produced by helpless training may fill people with negative cognitions and emotions and may elicit tension and distress. The disequilibrium implies that the world is a dangerous place in which unpredictable and uncontrollable events may endanger one's well-being, that one is unable to attain what one wants, and that one's conceptions of the self and the world are incorrect. More important, it implies that one's mental structures are not appropriate to reality and that some action should be taken to protect one's interest and well-being. That is, it implies that either the world or one's mental structures are wrong, and that they should be corrected in order to restore the disrupted equilibrium.

Helplessness training may thus impel people to undertake coping actions to bring the events and their mental structures into better alignment or at least to mitigate the distress that the mismatch causes. The restoration of the disrupted equilibrium becomes people's main goal, whether this goal is consistent or discrepant with the goal of performing well in the task. People's judgments, thoughts, and actions become centered around the loss produced by the failure, the threats the failure entails to their mental structures and well-being, and the ways of managing these threats. Accordingly, the actions people take are chosen on the basis of their expected efficacy in restoring the equilibrium that had been disrupted.

In more general terms, the exposure to uncontrollable failure may strengthen the concern with the problematic transaction. This concern is an hypothetical psychological state: a construct that heuristically intends to tap the interface between motivation and coping. *Concern* refers to the state of a person between the point at which he or she decides to pursue the goal of restoring the disrupted equilibrium and the point at which he or she ends the mismatch or disengages from coping activities. This concern is manifested in the organization of behavior. Everything the person does in the transaction with the environment occurs in an organized sequence that forms a single, coherent whole. No action in the sequence occurs at random; every response is instrumental to restoring the disrupted equilibrium. The person's behavior is not simply a reaction to the environment but a meaningful, purposive proposition designed to cope with losses and threats.

With regard to the second premise—that coping actions may favor or interfere with the allocation of resources to task-relevant activities—there are various ways of coping with a failure. Problem-focused and reappraisal strategies are alloplastic avenues of adaptation that mold the environment in accord to one's wants. They emerge from the conviction that the world is wrong and that equilibrium can be restored by changing the world. They are conservative coping strategies in that they fit the new to the old and assimilate the discrepant information into existing mental structures. The difference between problem solving and reappraisal resides in the way the assimilation is carried out: Whereas problem solving is designed to overcome failure and restore the loss, reappraisal is designed to shape the subjective construction of the failure.

Reorganization coping is an autoplastic avenue of adaptation by which existing schemas and goals are accommodated to reality, adding new experiences to the mental structures. This coping strategy emerges from the acceptance that one's goals and schemas are wrong and that equilibrium can be restored by changing these mental structures. Though reorganization is a painful process that entails working through the failure, it means personal growth and the attainment of a new level of adaptation.

Avoidance coping is a third avenue of change. It reflects an escapist attitude and the attempt to cut off the current experience from awareness. Though avoidance coping does not resolve a mismatch, it enables the person to believe that the resolution has taken place. Avoidance emerges from the conviction that the world is wrong and that existing mental structures should be maintained intact, but that one currently is powerless to change the world. Through avoidance, people deny both the existence and significance of the mismatch, escape from direct confrontation with it, and remove it from consciousness. In this way, awareness of the mismatch and the tension and distress that it causes are temporarily reduced. Whatever coping strategy is chosen produces some change in the relationship between the person and the environment.

The coping process may also have cognitive, emotional, and behavioral consequences. Successful coping (which restores the disrupted equilibrium) may reduce tension and distress, facilitate the attainment of personal goals and the accomplishment of personal plans, promote a sense of mastery and self-worth, and restore the view of the world as a predictable and controllable place. In contrast, unsuccessful coping may increase tension, distress, and self-doubts, which may overwhelm the cognitive system and interfere with adaptation. These consequences are not the main effects of the various coping strategies, however, but by-products that serve as incentives for or sources of interference with further coping attempts.

In these terms, what Lazarus and Folkman call the "multiple functions of coping" may reflect either different avenues of adaptation or different side effects. The reshaping of the environment, the reappraisal or denial of a mismatch, or the reorganization of mental structures are simply different avenues for carrying out the same coping task: the management of a mismatch. The solution of a problem or the reduction of the tension and distress caused by that problem are only side effects of the management of the mismatch. Every coping strategy—whether problem or emotion focused, autoplastic or alloplastic, confrontational or escapatory—is designed to manage a mismatch between the person and the environment.

Coping may also affect the individual's mental and behavioral activities. People may expend effort on the cognitive and behavioral activities that further the coping task while withdrawing effort from activities that compete for resources with the work of coping. The resource allocation would be manifested in task performance: The amount of effort expended on the task would depend on the extent to which that effort accords with the person's current coping strategy. Task performance would be improved when the person's coping strategy is congruent with the demands of the task and leads to the allocation of cognitive resources to task-relevant activities. Task performance would be impaired when the person's coping strategy competes for resources with task-relevant activities and leads to the withdrawal of resources from the task.

Finally, avoidance coping may affect the person's mode of cognitive functioning. On the one hand, it blunts the person's awareness of the failure and leads to the intrusion into consciousness of autonomic failure-related thoughts and affects. On the other hand, it leads to a state of chronic alertness in which the person monitors all internal or external stimuli that could recall the prior failure and expends new coping efforts every time failure-related thoughts intrude into consciousness. What happens here is that the mismatch, which seems to be ended by avoidance coping, is not really resolved but continues to elicit coping efforts and to influence the person's cognitive and behavioral activities.

A MEDIATIONAL SEQUENCE OF LH EFFECTS

The coping process is more complex than the above portrayal. First, the mobilization of coping effort is not an automatic response to uncontrollable failure. Rather, it follows a person's appraisals of the meaning and implications of the failure and may be moderated by personal and situational factors that shape these appraisals. Second. there is more than one way of coping with failure. There is a wide array of available coping strategies, from which people select those they believe are the most appropriate in the given circumstances. This selection entails effortful cognitive activity, including the assessment of what one can do and what the environment allows one to do to cope with failure. Third, coping strategies are not autonomous activities that run until completion. Rather, they are carefully organized, adapted to circumstances, evaluated against any change in the person or the environment, and sustained in face of competing motivational tendencies or blocking external forces.

On this basis, a coping analysis of LH effects should take into account not only the way coping actions alter task performance but also the cognitions and emotions that affect the mobilization of coping effort, the selection of particular coping strategies, and the organization and implementation of those strategies after helplessness training. These coping-related cognitions and emotions form an organized sequence that mediates between helplessness training and test task performance. Figure 8.1 presents a flowchart of the steps leading from the exposure to uncontrollable failure to LH effects.

1. The first step following the exposure to helplessness training is the *decision whether to mobilize effort* to cope with the failure. This step is extremely important, because a negative decision stops the coping process and prevents any change in test task performance. People who choose not to undertake coping actions would be impervious to both the positive and negative effects of helplessness training. Only those who react to failure with strong coping actions would show signs of reactance or LH deficits (see Chapter 6).

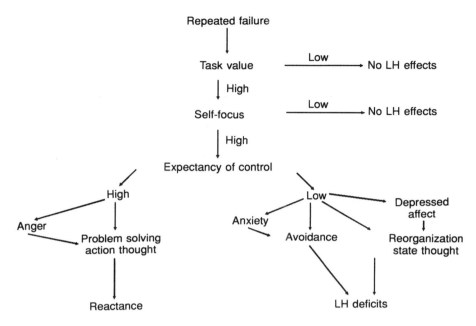

FIGURE 8.1. From helplessness training to performance changes: A coping flowchart.

The decision to mobilize coping effort depends on the person's subjective construction of the current transaction with the environment. This subjective interpretation, according to Lazarus (1991), emerges into a relational meaning, which summarizes the personal benefits and harm of a person–environment relationship from the standpoint of well-being and adaptation. It involves the appreciation of what a person with particular values and concerns believes he or she can gain or lose in a transaction. It reflects the appraisal of the positive and negative consequences of acting on the environment and the evaluation of the personal benefits and damage that the environment can produce.

In interpreting the meaning of a transaction with the environment, people assess the extent to which environmental events suit or do not suit their mental structures. These assessments make up part of what Lazarus (1991) calls the "primary appraisal" and consist of the appraisals of *goal congruence* (the extent to which a transaction is consistent or inconsistent with what a person wants in the transaction) and *goal relevance* (the extent to which this congruence or incongruence affects a person's goal hierarchy and self-identity).

In appraising the goal congruence of a transaction with the environment, people monitor the transaction, process incoming information, and activate the schemas and goals that may be affected by the transaction. Then they compare the incoming information to the activated mental structures and assess the extent to which these are consistent or discrepant. In helplessness training, people may monitor the outcomes they obtain in the task and compare them to their expectations and goals—that is, they assess whether the current outcomes confirm or disconfirm their expectations and whether the outcomes promote or block the attainment of their goals. This assessment may make people aware of any actual or potential disequilibrium with the environment, and the discovery of such a state after helplessness training may encourage them to activate the coping process.

The appraisal of the goal relevance of the failure is what I called the *valuation process* (see Chapter 6). The valuation process consists of the identification of the goals lost and the schemas damaged through the failure, followed by the assessment of the centrality of these goals and schemas to the person's goal hierarchy and self-definition. In other words, people compare the lost goals and damaged self-schemas with their basic commitments—what is important and meaningful for them. This comparison allows people to evaluate the harm that the failure may do and the importance of that damage to their well-being. The more relevant the lost goals and damaged schemas are appraised to be to the person's commitments, the greater the importance assigned to the failure and the personal harm expected from it.

The information generated in the valuation process is used to decide whether to invest effort to cope with the failure. The greater the appraised goal relevance of the failure, the more threatening its expected consequences are, and the greater the need to undertake coping actions. In fact, coping efforts are mobilized only when a failure is appraised as a threat to the person's basic commitments. If no commitment is at stake, no coping effort would be mobilized, and no performance change (either positive or negative) would be shown in the test task. The meaning of the statement that coping acts in the service of well-being lies in the ability of coping to restore the equilibrium that would protect the valued goals and schemas.

Two clusters of factors would thus contribute to the mobilization of coping effort. The first consists of the goals that a failure can thwart and the schemas that it can violate; the second consists of the commitments that the person brings to the transaction, such as his or her own goals, self-schemas, worldviews, values, and so on. A person would be prone to invest energy in coping attempts only when he or she appraises that the threatened goals and schemas affect his or her basic commitments (see Chapter 6).

2. Once the decision to mobilize coping effort is taken, the next step in the coping process entails a general change in the person's *focus of attention*. To channel the coping effort that they have decided to mobilize into new alternative coping actions that suit the reality constraints, people adopt a more attentive mind state. They may become more careful in thinking through their behavior and its consequences for their well-being and more aware of what they are doing, what they want, and what they are like. Concomitantly, they become concerned about which pattern of coping action is most appropriate (i.e., what can be done in the given circumstances). The restoration of the equilibrium disrupted by failure cannot be accomplished by automatic action in accord to what the environment seems to

dictate; rather, it requires the careful processing and analysis of both the coping actions available and the reality constraints.

This change in the person's orientation to the failure situation is reflected mainly in the direction of attention toward the self-relevant information needed to cope with it—that is, in self-focus. Focusing attention upon the self helps people to access stored self-referent material, allows faster retrieval and processing of this material, and makes them more cognizant of themselves and more capable of making self-assessments (see Chapter 7). In the LH context, self-focus may make accessible the person's goals and aspirations, his or her ongoing affective state, and his or her available coping resources. The information could then be used to assess the meaning and implications of the threat implicit in the failure and to decide how to cope with that threat. Without self-focus people could find it difficult to discover the personal meaning of their failure and to adjust their goals and behavior to the new reality constraints.

As discussed in Chapter 7, self-focus is a catalyst of the coping process, facilitating the diverse steps in the sequence leading to LH effects. First of all, by strengthening the perception of the goal relevance of the failure and the person's awareness of the detected self-relevant threat, heightened self-focus after helplessness training may increase the need to cope and the allocation of resources to the coping task. Second, by facilitating people's assessment of the likelihood of control and their awareness to their expectations, self-focus encourages people to take the course of action most appropriate to their expectations. Third, by making people more aware of the emotional arousal produced by failure, self-focus also makes them more apt to behave in accordance with the evoked emotions. Finally, self-focus makes available the stored knowledge over which a cognitive context for the organization of coping actions can be constructed. In short, the direction of attention inward after failure is an adaptive device that makes a person aware of the need to undertake coping activities, links these activities to their expectations, and facilitates their organization and implementation.

3. Once the cognitive system is focused on the self-referent information needed to cope with the failure, the next step is the *selection of coping strategies*. The choice of a coping strategy is based on a cost-benefit analysis of the strategies available. People anticipate the utility of each coping strategy in ending the mismatch or mitigating the distress it causes, and they also weight the anticipated costs of each strategy, including the effort expenditure it demands and the psychological pain it may cause. In short, people will chose those actions that are expected to be more effective in coping with the failure and to involve the lowest costs.

In the selection of coping strategies, the aspect that will have strong repercussions on the quality of the LH effects is the target of the coping effort: the environment or the person. The choice is between a focus on the task situation, with the intent of actively overcoming the failure (problem solving) or reshaping the failure's subjective representation (reappraisal), or a focus on the state of one's mental structures, with the intent of accommodating them to reality constraints (reorganization) or isolating them from the threat (avoidance). The expectancy of control is the critical factor in this choice (see Chapter 4). This expectancy acts as a "psychological watershed"(Carver & Scheier, 1981), helping people to decide whether to direct coping efforts toward problem-focused attempts or off-task activities.

The selection of a particular coping orientation is based on what Carver and Scheier (1981) call the "expectancy-assessment" process and what Lazarus and Folkman (1984) call the "secondary appraisal." With their increased self-focus after failure, people can assess their coping options and resources and form an expectancy of control. They gauge both whether they have the responses required to shape the environment to their wants (self-efficacy expectancy) and whether the environment in fact can be shaped by their responses (outcome expectancy). They estimate the probability of overcoming the failure and restoring the loss and thus compare the relative utility of alloplastic actions and intrapsychic actions, either autoplastic or escapist. This self-reflective assessment serves as the basis for the selection of the most suitable coping action.

A favorable expectancy of control—the belief that one can overcome a failure and restore the loss by one's actions—favors the adoption of problem-focused and reappraisal strategies that attempt to mold or assimilate the environment to one's wants (see Chapter 4). "Hopeful" persons would allocate cognitive resources to the processing of task-relevant information and put effort into overcoming the obstacles that caused the failure. Assigning high instrumental value to problem solving and seeing it as suitable to reality constraints, such persons would be prone to adopt an active, alloplastic coping orientation.

Unfavorable expectancies—which reflect the belief that one can do nothing to overcome a failure and that the loss is irrevocable—would favor the abandonment of alloplastic attempts and highlight the benefits of making some intrapsychic changes, either escapist or autoplastic (see Chapter 4). Rather than persevere at attempts to change what is perceived as an unchangeable environment, people will try to avoid the failure situation and/or to change their goals. These individuals will freeze any active attempt to solve the problem and put their efforts into cognitively avoiding any direct or symbolic confrontation with the failure, or they might become convinced that they should attempt to reshape their mental structures rather than the intractable environment.

After choosing the target of the coping effort, the person will choose between problem-focused actions and reappraisal or between reorganization and avoidance. The choice between problem-focused action and reappraisal is not so crucial, because these strategies may work in cooperation and have been found to activate each the other. In fact, reappraisal strategies seem to be activated whenever people have a problem-focused orientation, and they in turn seem to support problem solving by fostering an optimistic attitude and reducing the distress that can disrupt problem solving.

In contrast, the choice between reorganization and avoidance will have strong repercussions on the person's psychological state. First of all, these strategies seem to conflict with and inhibit one another: Avoiding confrontation with failure may impede the painful reorganization of mental structures, while working through failure may interfere with attempts to distance from it. In addition, these strategies seem to entail different types of cognitions and emotions and to have different effects on the mode of cognitive functions (see Chapters 3 and 5). Finally, though both reorganization and avoidance may produce LH deficits, they differ as to the chronicity of these deficits (see Chapter 2).

As pointed out in Chapter 4, we have no solid evidence on what determines the choice between reorganization and avoidance. We can only speculate that this choice, too, may be based on a cost-benefit analysis of each strategy. One factor, for example, may be the expected outcome of reorganization coping. People who are sure that their reorganization will have a positive outcome may be prepared to suffer some immediate pain and to delay gratification. People who are not so sure of such an outcome might adopt avoidance coping to protect their mental structures from the threat of self-annihilation. Another factor may be the psychological pain that the accommodation of mental structures may produce. The stronger the actual or expected pain and distress is, the more likely a person would be to abandon reorganization coping and undertake avoidance coping.

4. After the selection of a coping strategy, the next step in the process is the *initiation and sustenance* of this strategy. At this step, emotional arousal plays a crucial role: It motivates and prepares the person to allocate effort to coping actions and sustains those actions until the equilibrium with the environment is restored (see Chapter 5). As discussed earlier, uncontrollable failure may evoke tension and distress; these emotions in turn make the meaning and negative implications of the failure phenomenologically salient and transform what may be a "cold" cognitive mismatch into a "hot" and demanding aversive experience. Emotion acts both as a warning signal that some valued commitments are at stake and as an amplifier of the need to do something to end the mismatch. In this way, the arousal of aversive emotions intensifies the motivation to cope with failure.

Emotions also mediate between the expectancy of control and the undertaking of coping actions. Because the expectancy of control merely indicates which actions are to be preferred, another mechanism is needed to start up and sustain these actions until their ends are attained. Emotions are that mechanism; they seem to be an alarm that mobilizes particular action tendencies and provides the fuel for their completion. The expectancy of control may itself evoke particular emotions, which in turn may give "control preference"(Frijda, 1986) to the coping strategies that are appraised to be appropriate in the given circumstances.

Different expectancies of control evoke different emotional states that reinforce and sustain particular ways of coping with failure (see Chapter 5). A favorable expectancy of control evokes anger after helplessness training; this is the emotional expression of the desire to remove the obstacles from the environment. Anger leads the person to attempt to overcome the failure and reinforces and sustains problem-focused coping. Unfavorable expectancies of control evoke anxiety and depressed affects, which express the person's desire to escape a threat or to accept the painful reality. Depressed affects move the person toward the acceptance of a loss and the accommodation of mental structures to reality constraints, thereby reinforcing and sustaining reorganization coping. Anxiety moves the person away from the problematic situation and leads him or her to try to reduce tension and distress by avoidance coping.

Conversely, emotions may sometimes interfere with the coping task (see Chapter 5). After repeated failure to end a mismatch, accumulated distress may reach levels that overwhelm the cognitive system and disorganize rather than facilitate the coping task. This occurs if the mismatch is persistent, intensive, and impervious to coping action and steadily increases tension and distress. In this case, the emotion that originally serves as an incentive for the coping process may become an interfering force that paralyzes coping attempts and leads to a more or less permanent state of maladjustment.

This is the usual course of avoidance coping and anxiety. Avoidance coping may temporarily mitigate the distress caused by a mismatch while leaving this mismatch unsolved. At the same time, though, avoidance coping favors the intrusion of autonomic failure-related thoughts every time external or internal stimuli directly or symbolically recall the failure. This intrusion renews the person's awareness of the mismatch, appraisal of the threat related to the mismatch, and sense of powerlessness and vulnerability, thereby exacerbating anxiety that in turn strengthens and sustains the avoidance attempts. The person is caught in a self-exacerbating cycle of anxiety–avoidance coping–intrusion of autonomic failure-related thoughts that fragments thinking and disorganize coping actions while transforming anxiety into an overwhelming, dysfunctional emotional state.

In general, emotion may have two different implications in the coping process. Typically emotion may facilitate the accomplishment of the coping task. This function of emotion is emphasized in several contemporary psychological theories (e.g., Frijda, 1986; Lazarus, 1991). But emotion (mainly anxiety) may also be a mechanism of disintegration, leading to the dismantling of the coping process and maladjustment. This idea is found in theories that focus on the disorganizing and interfering nature of emotions (e.g., Hebb, 1949). Nonetheless, initially emotion is an adaptive mechanism that allows the person to respond rapidly to mismatches and to organize coping actions. Only after repeated failure to cope with a mismatch do emotions sometimes lead to disintegration.

5. The next step in the coping process is the *organization of coping strategies*. Such organization is facilitated by effortful cognitive activity, especially mental rumination. People actively search for information, encode situational cues, and retrieve memories that could be relevant to adapting the chosen coping action in the given circumstances. People analyze stored and incoming information in depth and develop anticipatory cognitions and behavioral plans based on that analysis. They also elaborate and ruminate on the encoded and retrieved pieces of information and use them in making their judgments and decisions. The central processing space of

their working memory is filled with ideations about the mismatch, and new associative pathways are created among these ideations.

The literature deals with three main types of mental ruminations: action rumination (task-relevant thoughts about problem-solving actions), state rumination (thoughts about the state of the actor performing the task) and task-irrelevant rumination (thoughts on issues that are unrelated to the task situation). The common denominator of these ruminations is that they are all cognitive tools of the coping process; they provide the cognitive context over which particular coping strategies are constructed. They are the key methods of searching for and organizing the information needed to execute a chosen coping strategy.

In my terms, the activation of a coping strategy is immediately followed by engagement in the type of rumination that can help achieve the objectives of that strategy (see Chapter 3). Problem-focused and reappraisal strategies would activate action rumination, because these strategies require a systematic analysis of the problem and the retrieval of knowledge about problem-solving situations and strategies. Reorganization coping would activate state rumination, because this way of coping requires the processing of relevant mental structures, the evaluation of personal damage, and the formulation of hypotheses about the most suitable rearrangement of these structures. All these requirements may be fulfilled by ruminating on the past, present, and future state of one's mental structures. Finally, avoidance coping would activate task-irrelevant rumination, for people would think about irrelevant, distracting issues to distance themselves from a threat.

Along with the controlled cognitive activity that facilitates the organization of coping strategies, some other, unwanted thoughts intrude into consciousness (see Chapter 3). Although these thoughts are focused on the failure situation, they do not serve any coping function, are hard to suppress, and may compete for resources with more organized and purposive cognitive activity. They absorb attention and resources that could otherwise be invested in coping with the failure and may augment anxiety by making salient the painful implications of the failure.

These autonomic failure-related thoughts may be a side effect of the purposive attempt to cope with failure via avoidance strategies. As discussed in Chapter 3, cutting off the failure from awareness does not mean that it no longer influences the person's cognitions. Rather, the suppressed failure experience remains active in the individual's memory and could autonomically intrude into consciousness every time an external or internal stimuli recalls it.

6. The last step of the coping process involves the *impact of coping attempts on task performance*. The undertaking of problem-focused and reappraisal strategies and the consequent engagement in action rumination would improve performance following helplessness training and lead to reactance (see Chapter 2). Reactance reflects the direction of cognitive resources toward task-relevant activities designed to overcome failure and the person's full concentration on the problem at hand. The positive effects of reappraisal, however, are limited to cases in which it is accompanied by problem solving (see Chapter 2). In fact, the critical factor for perfor-

mance improvement after helplessness training is the undertaking of problem-focused coping.

LH deficits may result from two different coping constellations (see Chapter 2), both of which reflect the abandonment of problem solving but differ in their orientation toward the resolution of the mismatch. In one constellation, LH deficits result from avoidance coping and the consequent engagement in task-irrelevant rumination. In the other, LH deficits result from reorganization coping and the consequent engagement in state rumination. These effects reflect the direction of cognitive resources away from task-relevant activities: toward distracting activities in avoidance coping, or toward self-schemas and personal priorities in reorganization coping. In the case of avoidance coping, the LH deficits also reflect the impact of a recursive cycle of anxiety, avoidant actions, and autonomic failure-related thoughts that overwhelm the cognitive system, constrict functioning, and paralyze action.

On this basis, one can delineate the mediational sequence that underlies reactance and LH deficits. *Reactance* following helplessness training is a direct reflection of the undertaking of problem-focused coping and the consequent allocation of resources in task-relevant activities. It is the end product of a sequence of (a) high perceived task value that mobilizes coping effort, (b) high self-focus that channels the coping effort into coping actions, (c) high expectancy of control that favors the undertaking of problem-focused coping, (d) feelings of anger that strengthen the problem-solving orientation, and (e) reappraisal coping and action rumination that support problem-focused coping.

LH deficits can be an end product of two somewhat different mediational sequences. These two sequences have in common the adoption of intrapsychic coping strategies and the engagement in cognitive activities that move people away from the test task. They both also entail (a) high perceived task value that mobilizes coping effort, (b) high self-focus that channels coping effort into coping actions, and (c) low expectancy of control that favors the abandonment of problem solving and the adoption of autoplastic or escapist ways of coping. They differ, however, in the particular coping orientation. LH deficits may reflect the undertaking of reorganization coping, the engagement in state rumination that support this coping orientation, and the experience of depressed affect that reinforces and sustains it. LH deficits may also reflect the undertaking of avoidance coping, the occurrence of task-irrelevant thoughts that support this coping, the experience of anxiety that reinforces and sustains it, and the intrusion of autonomic thoughts (one of the dysfunctional consequences of avoidance coping).

DIRECT AND INDIRECT ANTECEDENTS OF LH EFFECTS

The above mediational sequence allows us to delineate the direct and indirect antecedents of LH effects. The most direct precursors of LH effects are the coping strategies and mental rumination people undertake after helplessness training. Findings reviewed in Chapter 3 show that rumination on action alternatives and problem-solving plans is positively related to performance following helplessness training, whereas rumination on the state of the self or on other task-irrelevant subjects is negatively related to task performance. Findings reviewed in Chapter 2 show that problem-focused and reappraisal coping strategies make a positive contribution to task performance after helplessness training, that reorganization leads to temporary performance deficits, and that avoidance strategies lead to more chronic deficits.

The expectancy of control after helplessness training also has an effect on task performance. It only alters task performance indirectly, however, via the coping actions it produces. A high expectancy of control leads to reactance by favoring the undertaking of alloplastic activities, such as problem solving and action rumination, that attempt to solve the problem at hand. A low expectancy of control leads to LH deficits by favoring the abandonment of problem-focused actions and engagement in coping actions that draw resources away from task performance, such as reorganization and avoidance. Findings reviewed in Chapter 4 support these statements.

My theory differs radically from Seligman's Learned Helplessness theory. Whereas Seligman considered expectancy the direct antecedent of LH effects, I claim that expectancy has only an indirect effect via coping strategies. To Seligman's claims that an expectancy of no control impairs performance by fostering the abandonment of task attempts, I add the concomitant engagement in off-task coping. Finally, whereas Seligman sees expectancy as a sufficient antecedent, I see it as only one of the components of a network of coping-related factors that mediate LH effects. In my terms, the expectancy of control cannot be a sufficient antecedent of performance changes because any personality or situational factors that prevent the undertaking of coping actions could break the mediational chain, leaving the person without the mechanism that translates favorable and unfavorable expectancies into performance changes. It is also important to reiterate that expectancy loses its impact under conditions of low self-focus and low perceived task value, when people feel little if any pressure to cope with the failure.

The emotional reactions to helplessness training also make an indirect contribution to LH effects. Anger strengthens reactance by sustaining the problem-solving orientation originally elicited by favorable expectancies of control. Anxiety and depression intensify LH deficits by sustaining the off-task coping strategies originally fostered by unfavorable expectancies of control. In this way, emotions are not direct precursors of performance changes; the coping actions are. The role of emotions is to intensify and sustain the individual's coping attempts. Moreover, emotion cannot by itself determine whether coping strategies are activated, or the selection of the most appropriate coping strategy. Rather, it is the cognitive appraisal of the situation that seems to determine the need for coping and the choice of coping strategies. Emotion can only sustain the strategies that have been cued by the individual's cognitions. Findings reviewed in Chapter 5 consistently support the above statements.

Self-focus after helplessness training also makes an indirect contribution to LH effects. It seems to determine the strength of both reactance and LH deficits by catalyzing the coping process; that is, self-focus has a nondirectional effect on task performance via its impact on the expectancy of control, emotional responses, mental rumination, and coping actions. Findings reviewed in Chapter 6 support these ideas: the higher the self-focus, the stronger the LH effects (either reactance or LH deficits). Moreover, findings show that self-focus energizes the performance effects of the other cognitive and emotional precursors of performance change after helplessness training (see Chapter 7).

Finally perceived task value also makes indirect contributions to LH effects. It contributes to determining whether coping effort is mobilized, and thus also to the intensity of the coping actions, mental rumination, and emotional reactions, which may be reflected in either reactance or LH deficits. In other words, perceived task value is the factor that determines whether helplessness training produces any performance change at all. This contention is supported by findings reviewed in Chapter 6. High perceived task value augments both the facilitatory and detrimental effects of helplessness training; low perceived task value inhibits these performance changes.

The various factors that go into the valuation process have the same impact. These include the two components of perceived task value—the importance and self-relevance of a task—and the situational (e.g., instructional set, type and amount of incentive) and personality (e.g., achievement need, goal orientation) antecedents of task value. Moreover, findings show that high perceived task value is positively related to the strength of self-focus, coping actions, rumination, and emotional arousal, without cueing any particular cognition, emotion, or action.

FROM HELPLESSNESS TRAINING TO LH EFFECTS

The findings reviewed in this book consistently show that the typical reactance observed after a small amount of helplessness training and the LH deficits observed after a large amount can be explained by the mediational sequence presented above. The findings show that appraisal, emotions, ruminative thoughts, and coping strategies all change with the recurrence of failure. The pattern of cognitions, emotions, and actions observed after the first failure is completely different from the pattern observed after repeated failures; that is, people react differently to small and large amounts of failure. These findings are consistent with a process conceptualization of coping in which coping-related cognitions, emotions, and actions change with the evolution of the person–environment transaction. It is possible that the initial encounter with failure may typically prompt particular emotions, cognitions, and coping actions that with the recurrent failure may be recognized as inadequate and thus altered.

The typical response to a small amount of failure is an active attempt to overcome the failure. People hold favorable expectancies of control (see Chapter 4) and react to failure with feelings of anger (see Chapter 5), problem-focused and reappraisal strategies (see Chapter 2), and action rumination (see Chapter 3). The typical response to a large amount of failure is the abandonment of alloplastic adaptive attempts. People come to hold an unfavorable expectancy of control, and their cognitions, emotions, and coping strategies are organized around the damage that the failure may do to their mental structures. They experience anxiety and depression affects (see Chapter 5), undertake avoidance or reorganization strategies (see Chapter 2), and ruminate on off-task issues, either state or task-irrelevant (see Chapter 3). In addition, they may evince some signs of cognitive autonomy: the inability to suppress autonomic failure-related thoughts and affects (see Chapter 3).

On this basis, one can delineate the mediational sequences going from a small amount of failure to reactance and from a large amount of failure to LH deficits. Typically, a small amount of helplessness training does not drastically reduce the expectancy of control; that is, the person still maintains an optimistic attitude toward the restoration of the loss. This maintainance of positive expectancies is explained as follows: First, the initial failure is inconsistent with the moderate control expectancy people generally hold prior to the training task. Second, an incongruent failure tends to be attributed to unstable causes. Third, an unstable attribution of failure tends to maintain the moderate control expectancy.

This favorable expectancy of control may lead people to adopt an alloplastic orientation—undertaking problem-focused and reappraisal strategies and engaging in action rumination, which in turn may facilitate performance in solvable tasks. Moreover, this expectancy evokes anger, which reinforces and sustains alloplastic attempts and the consequent performance improvement. Thus a small amount of helplessness training leads to reactance via the maintenance of high expectancy of control and the resulting alloplastic coping orientation.

A large amount of helplessness seems to reduce the expectancy of control drastically, and the person becomes pessimistic as to the possibility of overcoming failure and restoring the loss. The formation of the expectancy of no control is explained as follows: First a failure becomes perceived as a stable outcome in the chain of recurrent failures. Second, people thus tend to attribute the failure to stable causes. Third, stable attribution of failure drastically reduces control expectancy (see Chapter 4).

The expectancy of no control leads to the abandonment of problem-solving attempts and instead to an autoplastic or escapist orientation, which in turn may impair performance in a solvable task. The autoplastic orientation is manifested in reorganization coping, engagement in state rumination, and depressed affects. The escapist orientation is manifested in avoidance coping, engagement in task-irrelevant rumination, and anxiety. The escapist orientation may also lead to the intrusion of autonomic failure-related thoughts, which further interfere with task performance. A large amount of helplessness training may thus lead to LH deficits via two different pathways—autoplastic or escapist—that seem to reflect alternative ways of coping with what is believed to be an irrevocable loss.

Of course, these mediational sequences from small and large amounts of helplessness training do not mean that helplessness training is a sufficient antecedent of LH effects. First of all, these mediational sequences are constrained by the person's focus of attention and the appraisal of the failure as a threat to one's basic commitments. As stated earlier, the diversion of attention from the self or the assignment of low value to the task may prevent threat appraisal and the activation of the coping process. In consequence, a small amount of helplessness training would not lead people to alloplastic attempts, and thereby it would not improve task performance; similarly, a large amount of helplessness would not lead people to undertake either autoplastic or escapist attempts, and thus it would not impair task performance.

Second, these mediational sequences are constrained by personality and situational factors that directly act on the components of the coping process. Every personal or situational factor that may impede the expenditure of coping effort or render such effort unnecessary would prevent performance changes and make people impervious to both the detrimental and positive effects of helplessness training. Moreover, every factor that changes the person's coping orientation and moves him or her toward or away from the test task would determine whether helplessness training would produce reactance of LH deficits.

Expectancies, emotions, ruminative thoughts, and coping actions are not induced solely by the helplessness training but depend on an array of personal and situational factors that have nothing to do with it. For example, people who are habitually reluctant to experience strong emotions or to engage in mental rumination lack the mechanisms that produce reactance and LH deficits and thus would be more impervious to the effects of failure. In addition, people who are habitually pessimistic, depressed, anxious, or prone to engaging in off-task coping and rumination would show LH deficits even after a single failure.

Third, helplessness training cannot explain why some people react to repeated failure with reorganization coping and show temporary deficits, whereas others react with avoidance coping and show more chronic deficits. In fact, the reduction of the expectancy of control following a large amount of helplessness training may lead equally to reorganization or avoidance coping. The decision to undertake one of these intrapsychic strategies may be based on predispositions that people bring to the helplessness training, such as their resources to cope with an intractable environment and to accommodate their mental structures with minimal pain.

On this basis I can refine the schema presented in Chapter 1 (see Figure 1.2). Expectancy of control, emotions, rumination, and coping strategies seem to mediate between helplessness training and performance changes. They are altered by helplessness training, alter task performance, and contribute to reactance and LH deficits. Moreover, these mediating factors form an organized sequence: The expectancy of control determines people's cognitive, behavioral, and emotional reactions to failure; emotions reinforce and sustain the cued cognitions and actions, and rumination and coping strategies are the direct precursors of performance changes. The LH effects are moderated by self-focus and the perceived task value, which determine the extent to which helplessness training activates a coping sequence and produces any performance change (either positive or negative) in the test task. Other personality and situational factors also appear to act on the diverse steps of the coping sequence and to moderate the consequent LH effects. Finally some factors seem to intervene in the choice between reorganization and avoidance coping and thus to moderate the type of LH deficits (whether short-term or chronic) produced by a large amount of helplessness training.

THE NATURE OF HUMAN LEARNED HELPLESSNESS

In this section I deal with the psychological states that underlie reactance and LH deficits: the mechanisms that create these effects, make them functional or dysfunctional, and cause them to be generalized over time and across situations. My working hypotheses are as follows:

1. The psychological state underlying LH deficits is a strong concern with an irrevocable loss, whereas the state underlying reactance is a strong concern with a revocable loss.
2. LH deficits reflect cognitive interference and/or defensive effort withdrawal. Reactance reflects the allocation of cognitive resources in the solution of the problem at hand.
3. LH effects have both functional and dysfunctional aspects. First of all, both reactance and LH deficits are by-products of the person's functional responses to the adaptational requirements of failure. Reactance in an uncontrollable situation may be somewhat dysfunctional, however, because it increases the likelihood of LH deficits upon the formation of the expectancy of no control. Accordingly, the LH deficits caused by avoidance coping and autonomic failure-related thoughts may reflect a dysfunctional, structural failure of the cognitive system.
4. The strong concern with the loss produced by failure underlies the generalization of LH effects. A self-exacerbating cycle of anxiety, avoidance coping, and autonomic failure-related thoughts seems to generalize LH deficits over time.

The Helplessness State

An analysis of the antecedents of LH deficits suggests that the psychological state underlying these deficits ("helplessness state") is a strong concern with an irrevocable loss. As stated earlier, the typical helplessness training creates a person–environment mismatch that results in the loss of personal goals and damage to schemas of the self and the world. The helplessness state emerges when (a) people recognize that the loss is irrevocable, and (b) they are strongly concerned with that loss. The helplessness state is a psychological trap in which people cannot immediately detach themselves from a personal loss even though they know that they can do nothing to restore the lost object. They are so occupied and preoccupied with the loss and its implications that they are unable or unwilling to commit themselves to new goals and to expend effort in new tasks. The state ceases when the loss is worked through, the mental structures are accommodated to the new reality constraints, and the lost goals are replaced with others. Until this inner reorganization is completed, the helplessness state continues to influence the person's behavior and to produce LH deficits.

The hypothesis that the recognition of an irrevocable loss constitutes part of the helplessness state is based on findings that a stable attribution of failure and the expectancy of no control following helplessness training contribute to performance deficits. These two cognitive factors clearly signify that the person recognizes the irreversibility of the failure and the impossibility of restoring what was lost. The person believes that the failure will recur in subsequent tasks and that his or her personal responses cannot change this; consequently he or she sees no point in instrumental activities aimed at overcoming the failure and restoring the loss.

The hypothesis that strong concern is a component of the helplessness state is based on findings that the assignment of high value to the helplessness training contributes to subsequent performance deficits. High perceived task value signals that the failure has personal significance for the person and that it threatens his or her basic commitments. High perceived task value makes it difficult for people to free themselves from the failure situation even after appraising it as irrevocable, because the disengagement from that situation without coping with the mismatch entails serious personal damage. People will remain involved in the failure situation and mobilize coping efforts until the equilibrium is restored and the personal damage reduced to a minimum.

The strong concern is also manifested in the emotional, cognitive, and behavioral reactions to failure. People who show LH deficits react to failure with strong emotional arousal, and their emotional experience is patterned around the failure. They are also preoccupied with the failure and allocate cognitive resources in processing information about it. Moreover, they organize their actions around the failure and expend effort in coping with it. As discussed earlier, all these emotional, cognitive, and behavioral manifestations are a sign of strong concern with a mismatch.

More important, the particular emotions, cognitions, and coping actions of persons who show LH deficits seem to reflect the conjunction of strong concern and the appraisal of an irrevocable loss. First of all, these persons have been found to react to failure with heightened depression and anxiety. Whereas depression is consistently viewed as the emotional expression of the appraisal of an irrevocable loss, anxiety is viewed as the emotional expression of the appraisal that the loss threatens goals and schemas to which a person is highly committed (e.g., Lazarus, 1991). Together, these two emotions reflect the person's strong concern with an irrevocable loss and its implications for his or her well-being. Moreover, they reflect the recognition that one has no available responses to undo the harm or restore the loss and that only intrapsychic change could protect one's commitments.

The adoption of reorganization coping, another antecedent of LH deficits, also seems to be a direct reflection of a strong concern with an irrevocable loss. The adoption of reorganization coping rather than problem-focused coping directly implies that a person recognizes the impossibility of overcoming the failure and restoring what has been lost, and that the disrupted equilibrium with the environment can be restored only by coming in terms with the loss. This conviction underlies every step of the reorganization task. It is implicit in the acceptance of the loss and the disengagement from futile attempts to restore it. It is also present in the working-through process by which old and cherished goals and schemas are accommodated to the intractable environment and alternative goals more appropriate to the new life conditions are adopted.

The same strong concern is reflected in the engagement in state rumination, the cognitive tool for reorganization coping and another antecedent of LH deficits. People invest energy in deliberately thinking about the failure. Their thought flow is replete with failure-relevant ideations, attention is directed toward failure-relevant stimuli, and the cognitive system is occupied with the loss. This thinking, however, is not aimed at organizing instrumental actions to overcome the failure. Rather it is focused on the implications of the failure for one's personal goals and schemas, and it aims to facilitate the working through of an irrevocable loss. It creates a cognitive context over which mental structures can be accommodated and substitute goals constructed.

Adoption of avoidance coping and consequent engagement in task-irrelevant thoughts, two other antecedents of LH deficits, also seem to reflect a strong concern with an irrevocable loss. Avoidance coping follows the recognition that one cannot restore the loss by one's actions and that is better to cope with it by escaping the failure rather than by actively fighting it. Here the strong concern is evidenced in the person's decision to expend effort in trying to distance himself or herself actively from the failure situation and to suppress all thoughts and affects related to the irrevocable loss.

Though avoidance at first seems to indicate a disengagement from a loss, the failure and the images and ideas with which it is associated remain active in memory and continue to exert autonomous control over cognitions, affects, and actions (e.g., Horowitz, 1979; Lazarus & Folkman, 1984). This control is evidenced in the intermittent intrusion of autonomic failure-related thoughts and affects into consciousness every time internal or external stimuli recall the failure. It is also evident in the scope of the activities the person avoids—namely, any activity directly or symbolically linked to the failure experience that may bring back failure-related memories. Thus, although the person is not consciously concerned with the failure, the intrusion of autonomic failure-related thoughts and the avoidance of failure-related activities together indicate that he or she is still "stuck" with the irrevocable loss and that the failure experience is mentally alive.

To summarize, the helplessness state reflects a strong concern with an irrevocable loss. This strong concern is manifested in arousal of anxiety and depressed affects, undertaking of reorganization or avoidance strategies, and engagement in state or task-irrelevant ruminations, all of which are mediators of LH deficits.

The Reactance State

Analysis of the antecedents of performance facilitation following helplessness training (see Figure 8.1) suggests that the psychological state underlying this improvement (the "reactance state") consists of a strong concern with a *revocable* loss. The reactance state emerges when (a) people recognize that they can restore the loss produced by helplessness training, and (b) they are strongly concerned with that loss. The reactance state is a reflection of the motivation to end a mismatch and restore a loss that threatens basic commitments. People are occupied with overcoming the failure and restoring what they lost, and their cognitive resources are allocated in removing obstacles form the environment. The state ceaces when the loss is restored or is seen as irrevocable. Until then, the reactance state exerts influence on the person's behavior and improves performance in a solvable task.

The hypothesis that the recognition of the revocability of a loss is the basis of the reactance state is based on findings that an unstable attribution of failure and high expectancy of control following helplessness training contribute to performance facilitation. The hypothesis that strong concern is a component of the reactance state is based on findings that the assignment of high value to the failure as well as strong emotional arousal, mental rumination, and coping efforts all contribute to performance facilitation.

The conjunction of strong concern and the appraisal of the revocability of the loss is manifested in the particular emotional, cognitive, and behavioral mediators of performance facilitation. People who show reactance after helplessness training tend to react to failure with anger, which is the emotional expression of the appraisal of a temporary, reversible blow to the person's basic commitments. In addition, persons who show reactance tend to engage in action rumination and problem-focused coping, both of which imply that the failure experience is alive in the person's mind and that his or her cognitions and behaviors are organized around overcoming it. The person deliberately thinks about ways of overcoming the failure and generates problem-solving plans to that end. The thought flow is replete with ideations about restoring the loss, attention is directed toward every stimulus that could help to remove the obstacles from the environment, and the cognitive system is occupied with the organization of problem-solving plans.

Evidently, a person's decision to engage in action rumination and problem-focused coping implies that he or she is highly concerned with the failure experience and is willing to pay some price (effort expenditure) to cope with it. In addition, such a decision implies the conviction that the failure can be overcome by one's actions. Only people who believe that their actions can be effective in overcoming a failure would invest energy in finding action alternatives and organizing problem-solving plans, as well as withdraw attention from stimuli that could interfere with the problem-solving attempts.

As can be seen, the above analysis suggests that a reactance state reflects a strong concern with a revocable loss. This subjective state is manifested in anger, action rumination, and problem-focused coping, all of which are mediators of reactance.

THE TRANSLATION OF THE HELPLESSNESS STATE INTO PERFORMANCE DEFICITS

Findings suggest that LH deficits are produced throughout two alternative ways of coping with an irrevocable loss: (a) reorganization coping and state rumination, and (b) avoidance coping and task-irrelevant rumination. Although both ways of coping may be effective for dealing with an irrevocable loss, they impair task performance by flooding the cognitive system with off-task ideations and/or by defensively withdrawing effort from task activities. The resulting performance deficits reflect both cognitive interference and defensive effort withdrawal. In other words, they reflect people's *inability* to concentrate on the task at hand because of the cognitive interference produced by off-task thoughts (either state or task-irrelevant), and/or their *unwillingness* to expend effort on tasks reminiscent of their previous failure.

The *cognitive interference* nature of LH deficits is illustrated by the effects of state rumination and task-irrelevant ruminations. State rumination directs resources toward introspective, self-evaluative issues; people ruminate on the past, present, and future state of the self and process self-relevant information in order to evaluate the damage the failure has done to their mental structures and to adjust these structures to reality. Task-irrelevant rumination directs resources toward matters that have nothing to do with the irrevocable loss. It is used as a cognitive maneuver to distance oneself from the loss and actively to suppress painful thoughts about it. In both cases, working memory and the thought flow are filled with off-task thoughts, and the cognitive system is occupied with off-task issues rather than with the problem at hand. Because cognitive resources and memory space are limited, attention cannot be directed toward task-relevant stimuli, cognitive resources and space cannot be allocated to the organization and execution of problem-solving plans, and task performance is thus impaired.

The intrusion of autonomic failure-related thoughts into consciousness that may follow avoidance coping creates an additional source of cognitive interference. These autonomic off-task thoughts also absorb attention, occupy limited working memory space, overwhelm the cognitive system, and distract the person from the problem at hand, leaving him or her with insufficient resources and working memory space to organize and execute the task-relevant actions necessary to performance. This cognitive interference, however, should be differentiated from that produced

by state and task-irrelevant ruminations. While the former results from unintention-
al, intrusive cognitive activity, the later results from the person's policy of resource
allocation.

The *defensive effort withdrawal* nature of LH deficits is illustrated by the effects
of avoidance coping. As pointed out earlier, the adoption of avoidance coping
includes the expenditure of effort in trying to distance from an irrevocable loss and to
prevent the intrusion of failure-related thoughts and affects. The person thus engages
in defensive withdrawal strategies, such as avoiding any task-relevant activity that
could directly or symbolically recall the prior failure experience; escaping/avoiding
any task-related challenge because the possibility of failure could activate memories
on the prior loss; and withdrawing effort from task performance and creating impediments to it so as to prevent any possible failure from undermining one's sense of self-
worth. In all these instances and others, defensive withdrawal strategies may help
people to distance from the irrevocable loss at the price of impaired performance.

The Translation of the Reactance State into Performance Facilitation

The performance facilitation observed following helplessness training is directly produced by engagement in action rumination and problem-focused coping. They
activate recollections of prior problem-solving transactions and the processing of
information bearing on the features of the current task and on alternative plans for
overcoming failure. They include the search through existing cognitive structures,
the retrieval of stored material that facilitates solving the problem at hand, and
conscious deliberation on problem-focused action alternatives. They also control the
type of cognitive material that is activated and the type that is inhibited: activating
cognitive material that helps the person to understand the current problem and to
find and carry out problem-solving strategies, and reducing the accessibility to
conscious thinking of material that is irrelevant to or disruptive of the search for
instrumental actions.

Because action rumination and problem-focused coping are designed to solve
the problem at hand, their adequate use may improve performance in a solvable
task. Attention is directed to task-relevant features, working memory preempted
with task-relevant ideations, and cognitive resources fully allocated in task-relevant
cognitive activities. Moreover, attention is purposely drawn away from task-
irrelevant features and cognitions, and relatively few cognitive resources and little
working memory space are available for processing task-irrelevant cognitive material. These cognitive changes converge in full concentration on the problem at hand
and in performance improvement in a solvable task.

Functional and Dysfunctional Aspects of LH Effects

Is human LH functional or dysfunctional? Theories disagree. Some emphasize
its dysfunctionality; for example, the original and reformulated Learned Helpless-

ness theories see LH deficits as maladaptive responses that reflect the overgeneraliz-ation of beliefs and the inability/unwillingness to discriminate between uncontrolla-ble and controllable situations. Lavelle et al. (1979) view LH deficits as the product of cognitive interference produced by the overwhelming, unwanted intrusion of anxiety and task-irrelevant thoughts.

Other theories see human LH as a functional response to an uncontrollable situation. For example, Klinger (1975) suggests that the passivity and giving up that are observed following failure reflect an adaptive retreat from the task at hand to gain time to assimilate the failure and to mobilize effort to deal with subsequent adaptational requirements. According to Frankel and Snyder (1978), LH deficits result from the person's deliberate attempt to protect his or her sense of self-worth from the threatening implications of failure. Kuhl (1981) states that LH deficits result from intentional engagement in state rumination in order to protect one's interests.

In my view, LH effects include both functional and dysfunctional features. Originally, a person's reactions to the helplessness training may be functional. First of all, the undertaking of coping strategies is a means for dealing with the mismatch produced by failure. In addition, the direction of attention toward the self following failure may help the individual adapt to the transaction by making available stored self-relevant information (see Chapter 7). The assessment of the probability of control helps the individual to select those coping actions that he or she appraises to be appropriate in the given circumstances (see Chapter 4). Emotional arousal may be a means of intensifying and sustaining coping efforts (see Chapter 5), and engagement in mental rumination may help the individual to organize appropriate coping actions (see Chapter 3).

What begins as a controlled attempt to bring the person and the environment into better alignment, however, may end in a failure to adapt. Specifically, what is adaptive in the uncontrollable phase of the LH paradigm may become maladaptive in the controllable test phase. Some of the responses may incidentally facilitate other maladaptive processes, which may impair performance without any alterna-tive benefit and may enlarge rather than reduce the mismatch with the environ-ment.

As elaborated earlier, the improvement of test task performance following helplessness training is the result of the person's own decision to cope with what he or she perceives as a revocable loss by means of task-relevant, problem-focused actions. All the emotions, cognitions, and actions that mediate the reactance ef-fects are intentionally controlled and are functional means for restoring the dis-rupted person–environment equilibrium. The emotions, cognitions, and actions each have their own function—anger strengthens and sustains problem-focused coping, action rumination creates a suitable cognitive context for the organization of problem-solving plans, reappraisal maintains an optimistic attitude and reduces distress that can disrupt problem solving, and problem-focused strategies attempt to actually mold the environment—on which the resulting reactance may depend. In these terms, reactance is a product of the individual's intentional coping actions and a side effect of his or her adaptive, alloplastic efforts to restore a disrupted equilibrium.

Reactance may be dysfunctional, however, during the original helplessness training. As shown throughout this book, performance deficits following the formation of the expectancy of no control are more likely to occur under conditions that produce strong reactance during the helplessness training than under conditions that weaken psychological reactance. When the problems are unsolvable, problem-focused efforts only provoke frustration and make salient the person's powerlessness. Stronger reactance means a greater threat to one's commitments after the recurrence of failure despite one's task efforts, and it makes cognitive interference and defensive effort withdrawal more likely to follow the formation of the expectancy of no control.

The dysfunctional side of reactance can be viewed as a particular instance of what Janoff-Bulman and Brickman (1982) call the "pathology of high expectation" and what Baumeister and Scher (1988) call "counterproductive perseveration." Baumeister and Scher (1988) observe that people persisting at an unsolvable problem become trapped by the feeling that they already have put time and effort into the task and that quitting means wasting their investment. So they keep trying even harder, which further augments the threat of the failure and the need for alternative ways of off-task coping.

The two direct antecedents of LH deficits, reorganization coping and avoidance coping, can be seen as functional responses to the adaptational requirements of what is perceived as an irrevocable loss. Here the person deliberately directs attention to and works through the failure so as to accommodate his or her mental structures to reality constraints, or he or she stops thinking about the failure and avoids task-oriented activities so as to reduce distress and prevent the intrusion of painful thoughts and affects. The problem with these coping responses is that they draw resources away from task-relevant actions and impair task performance when the loss is not irrevocable. LH deficits thus are the price people pay for trying to end a mismatch or to reduce the distress it produces.

As Baumeister and Scher (1988) notes, one can view LH deficits as functional trade-offs—that is, as the sacrifice of the chance for immediate success in exchange for adaptive benefits. A person who undertakes reorganization coping sacrifices task performance by directing cognitive resources to autoplastic efforts; a person who engages in avoidance coping sacrifices task performance by defensively withdrawing effort from task attempts in order to obtain inner calm. Interestingly, the adoption of avoidance coping reflects an additional trade-off: the attainment of inner calm at the price of the interruption of the working-through process, the fragmentation of mental structures, and the maintainance of a disequilibrium with the environment.

Avoidance coping, though, can also lead to dysfunctional cognitive activities. As shown earlier, avoidance may promote autonomic, unwanted thoughts and affects that absorb attention and interfere with performance without serving any coping function. Moreover, the intrusion of these thoughts into consciousness renews the threats implied by failure, increases the resulting anxiety, and strengthens the individual's avoidant responses, which in turn increase the likelihood of a further intrusion of autonomic thoughts and performance deficits. In this way, a self-exacerbating cycle of anxiety, avoidance, and autonomic thoughts is created that may overwhelm the cognitive system, fragment thought, and disorganize action. The performance deficits produced by intrusive autonomic thoughts have no functional side but reflect a *structural failure* that "sticks" the person with the failure without concomitant short- or long-term adaptational advantages.

On this basis, I divide the detrimental effects of helplessness training into functional and structural deficits and argue that each reflects a different stage in the LH process. In the first case, people who are strongly concerned about what they appraise as an irrevocable loss may make functional trade-offs in which they sacrifice task performance to mold their mental structures to reality constraints or to mitigate inner pain and distress. The resulting performance deficits can be regarded as a functional product of off-task coping. In the second case, avoidance coping may foster the intrusion of autonomic failure-related thoughts that may overwhelm the cognitive system, disrupt inner controls, and interfere with task performance. The resulting performance deficits can be regarded as a structural deficit that reflects the failure of the cognitive system to inhibit and repress the intrusion of disturbing material.

THE GENERALIZATION OF LH EFFECTS

One basic issue that every theory of human LH should address is the generalization of LH effects. That is, which factors underlie the generalization of the performance changes observed following helplessness training? This issue is of vital importance because the transfer of LH effects to a new controllable task is an essential aspect of their definition.

In my view, a strong concern with the failure situation is what underlies the generalization of LH effects. It propels people to cope with the threats implied by the helplessness training even after the training has ended and the features and demands of the task have been altered. It pushes them to persevere without doubt or delay in whatever coping actions were put into motion with the helplessness training. It discourages cool analysis of the test task and biases people to view it as a natural continuation of the helplessness training and a new opportunity to cope with failure. In this way, the person is "stuck" with the helplessness training throughout the test phase, and the performance changes that originated with this training are generalized to the new task.

On the one hand, people who show a strong concern with the failure situation continue to be occupied or preoccupied with the failure in the test task. They are unable to commit themselves to any new goal in the test task, and the meanings they attach to that task and the emotional, cognitive, and behavioral reactions to it remain shaped by the prior failure. The helplessness situation stays mentally alive throughout the test task, and it continues to control the individual's reactions. People continue to ruminate on action alternatives, the state of their mental structures, or other distracting matters, and they continue to rely on the coping strategies that they originally used to deal with failure in helplessness training. The failure experienced in helplessness training continues to affect the person's psychological state and functioning in dissimilar test tasks, with either facilitatory or detrimental effects on performance.

On the other hand, people who are not involved with the failure situation will not be occupied or preoccupied with it during the test task; they are free to commit themselves to new goals and activities. Consequently, the meanings they attach to the test task and their cognitive, emotional, and behavioral reactions to it are shaped by the new task. They are able to take time out to consider alternative courses of action, as well as to analyze the new task and differentiate it from the previous one. They are free to undertake task-relevant actions without the compulsion to cope with the previous failure. As a result, they can carry out the test task without sequelae from the prior failure.

The generalization of LH deficits is intensified by reliance in avoidance coping and the consequent intrusion of autonomic failure-related thoughts. As shown in Chapter 2, avoidance may contribute to the inappropriate transfer of the beliefs developed during helplessness training to the new test task. By defensively withdrawing efforts from task activities that recall the previous failure, avoidance coping also suppresses thoughts about the new task situation and inhibits the analysis of its features and demands. In this way, avoidance coping may interfere with discrimination between the training and test tasks and the recognition of the controllability of the test task. Moreover, because avoidance coping is activated whenever any external or internal cue evokes memories of the failure, people would redouble avoidance efforts and inhibit problem solving even in situations highly dissimilar to the helplessness training if these situations contain some minimal association with the failure. In some cases, not even an external cue that reactivates the repressed memories, but only some momentary mental associations, may be required for the person to avoid the task situation.

The intrusion of autonomic state thoughts may also contribute to the wide generalization of LH deficits. These thoughts may intrude into consciousness and interfere with task performance regardless of the features and demands of the new task situation. Because these intrusive thoughts can be activated by ideations linked to the failure, they may occur equally in situations that are directly related to the helplessness training and in situations that are only remotely associated with it. In either case they absorb attention, overwhelm the cognitive system, and produce performance deficits; in addition, they may intensify avoidance coping. All this prevents an objective evaluation of the new situation and leads to increasing constriction of functioning over a broad range of situations.

Reliance in avoidance coping and the intrusion of autonomic state thoughts may also generalize LH deficits *over time*. Reliance in avoidance coping has no natural end. Because the failure continues to be active in memory and the person–environment mismatch is left unsolved, the threats to the person's commitments continue to control his or her cognitions and actions ad infinitum. Nor does the intrusion of autonomic state thoughts end, because, without any functional role, they can be easily activated by any mental association or situational cue at any place or time. Moreover, both avoidance coping and the intrusion of autonomic thoughts prevent the deliberate replacement of the lost goal, which would put an end to the helplessness state.

One can draw two scenarios of the temporal range of LH deficits. In one, people who engage in reorganization coping and state rumination are willing and able to complete the working-through process without being overwhelmed by autonomic thoughts and without interrupting it via avoidance strategies. In this case, although the efforts to accommodate their mental structures draw resources away from task-relevant activities and interfere with task performance, the deficits are short-lived and disappear once the person finishes working through the failure and restores the disrupted equilibrium. Once people incorporate the failure into their mental structures and reorganize the latter in such a way that the failure does not threaten their commitments, they can disengage from reorganization coping and freely engage in new task activities without any further cognitive interference or defensive effort withdrawal.

In the other scenario, reorganization coping and purposive state rumination are cut off by avoidance coping and/or the intrusion of autonomic state thoughts. This course of events transforms the failure into unfinished business, impedes the restoration of the disrupted equilibrium, and thus perpetuates off-task coping and the resulting performance deficits. The failure is not integrated into mental structures; it continues to be active in memory and to exert autonomous control over the person's behavior; and the best means for ending a mismatch is aborted. More important, autonomic failure-related thoughts may intrude into consciousness intermittently, interfering with task performance and impelling people to adopt stronger avoidance measures, which in turn exacerbate the deficits and the likelihood of a further intrusion of autonomic thoughts. In this way, the short-lived deficits originally created by reorganization coping may be perpetuated and exacerbated by a repetitive avoidance–intrusion sequence.

In general, the generalization of LH deficits results from strong concern with an irrevocable loss. This concern presses people to engage in reorganization coping and purposive state rumination during the test phase. This may result in generalized, short-lived LH deficits. Alternatively, people may adopt avoidance coping and experience intrusion of failure-related autonomic thoughts, which, in turn, may make LH deficits dysfunctional and chronic.

SOME DERIVATES OF A COPING PERSPECTIVE OF HUMAN LEARNED HELPLESSNESS

In this section I elaborate on three derivates of a coping perspective of human LH. First, I delineate the personality traits that may make people likely to experience helplessness following uncontrollable failure. Second, I offer some ideas about the association between human LH and psychopathology. Third, I specify the criteria for extrapolating human LH to explain real-life adaptational problems.

THE HELPLESSNESS-PRONE PERSONALITY

From a coping perspective of human LH, two sets of individual difference factors may make people prone to LH deficits: high reactivity and the inadequacy of inner resources.

One dimension of this helplessness-prone personality is the individual's reactivity to a mismatch with the environment. This personality dimension is defined at one pole by persons who react to a mismatch with only mild reactions, and at the other pole by persons who are strongly sensitive and reactive to a mismatch. Rothbart and Derryberry (1981) call this temperament dimension "negative reactivity" and define it as the arousability of multiple physiological and behavioral systems of the organism in response to a distressing situation. They suggest that reactivity is manifested in heightened autonomic neural and endocrine activity, as well as in heightened cognitive awareness and activity during the distressing episode. According to Rothbart and Derryberry, a highly reactive person may be susceptible to distress but also prone to undertake the self-regulatory steps needed to cope with it.

Findings consistently show that highly reactive persons are sensitive to weak stimulation, have a low optimum level of stimulation and arousal, are distractible, and lack "functional endurance"—adaptation to increasingly intense, prolonged, or repetitive stimulation (e.g., Klonowicz, 1987; Strelau, 1983). Klonowicz (1987) also found that reactivity accounts for the intensity of performance changes in response to distressing environmental conditions. Highly reactive persons showed stronger changes in task performance following stress manipulation than less reactive persons. In addition, there are findings that highly reactive persons mobilize more coping actions in response to stress and that these actions sometimes prevail over basic task activities (e.g., Strelau, 1983).

On this basis, I suggest that the dimension of reactivity plays an important role in the process of coping with failure as well as in determining the intensity of LH effects. Low-reactiveness persons may react to uncontrollable failure with mild emotions and coping actions. As a consequence, they may be impervious to both the positive and negative effects of helplessness training on task performance. In contrast, high-reactiveness persons may react to uncontrollable failure with strong emotions, cognitions, and actions, which in turn would be reflected in subsequent performance changes. They will show reactance after a small amount of helplessness training and LH deficits after a larger amount of training.

Another personality factor that may make people prone to LH deficits is the inadequacy of their resources for dealing with person–environment mismatches. Resources are defined as those psychological and sociological factors that serve as a means for attainment of one's commitments (Hobfoll, 1989). They buffer the detrimental impact of stressful situations, help people in struggling positively with life adversities, and promote well-being and adaptation. According to Hobfoll (1989), every personal trait and skill that generally aids stress resistance can be considered as an internal resource.

In human LH, inner resources may contribute to LH effects by directly acting on the selection of coping strategies. On the one hand, persons with inadequate resources may choose coping strategies that lead to dysfunctional LH deficits. These persons may appraise themselves as unable to overcome failure (low expectancy of control), and/or they may lack the cognitive skills needed to reappraise the failure situation positively. Therefore they may relinquish problem solving and adopt off-task coping. Moreover, they may hold unfavorable expectancies about their ability to transform mental structures and/or lack the cognitive skills needed to integrate their wants with the discrepant reality constraints. Therefore they may be more prone to undertake avoidance rather than reorganization coping. In this way, persons with poor resources would show overgeneralized LH deficits attributable to the experience of a self-exacerbating cycle of avoidance and autonomic intrusion of failure-related thoughts.

On the other hand, persons with adequate resources may choose coping strategies that lead to either reactance or temporary, functional LH deficits. These persons are optimistic as to the probability of overcoming failure and possess the cognitive skills required to carry out alloplastic adaptation. Therefore they would adopt problem-focused coping, which would lead to reactance. In addition, when these persons receive information indicating that failure cannot be overcome by their actions, they may temporarily sacrifice task performance in exchange for adaptation. They may be secure as to the positive outcomes of the working-through process and may not feel any need to avoid the threat. In this way, these persons may take advantage of any uncontrollable situation in order to reach new levels of inner integration and adaptation, and they may be shielded against overgeneralized LH deficits.

Some support for the above ideas is found in studies reporting that the possession of inner resources seems to prevent performance deficits following helplessness training. One of these studies was conducted by Altmaier and Happ (1985), who taught subjects coping aids and gave them practice trials in solvable problems as a means to increase their inner resources in dealing with subsequent helplessness training. Results showed that unsolvable problems produced worse anagram performance than solvable- and no-problem conditions only among subjects who received no coping skill training. The learning of coping skills thus was effective in preventing LH deficits. One problem with the finding, though, is that the absence of performance deficits may have resulted from the experience of success in the practice trials (i.e., immunization).

Studies on resourcefulness (Rosenbaum & Jaffe, 1983)—the learned repertoire of behaviors and skills by which people self-regulate their distress—also documented the positive effects of inner resources. Rosenbaum and Jaffe (1983) found that inescapable noise produced worse anagram performance than escapable and no noise only among low-resourcefulness subjects. The possession of a rich and flexible repertoire of coping responses and the ability to negotiate with reality made high-resourcefulness subjects resistant to the detrimental impact of helplessness training. Similar results were obtained in two LH experiments conducted by Rosenbaum and Ben-Ari (1985) in which subjects were exposed to solvable or unsolvable problems and their persistence in unsolvable puzzles (Experiment 1) and performance in solvable anagrams (Experiment 2) were assessed.

On this basis, one can contend that inadequacy of resources may be a component of the helplessness-prone personality. Among adequately functioning people, however, inadequacy of resources is a necessary but not sufficient factor for dysfunctional LH deficits. A deficiency in resources would make a person vulnerable to these deficits only when failure threatens his or her basic commitments. Moreover, these deficits would be mainly shown among reactive persons, who habitually tend to react to failure with strong emotions and coping actions.

HUMAN LH AND PSYCHOPATHOLOGY

From the beginning of human LH research, the association between human LH and psychopathology captivated the attention of researchers and theorists. In the original Learned Helplessness theory, Seligman (1975) suggested that human LH is a prototypical exemplar of the development of reactive depression. Specifically, the exposure to uncontrollable failure should produce what Miller (1975) called the "psychological deficit" of depression. This psychological deficit describes the difficulties of depressive patients in functioning and in adapting to reality constraints that follow bad events, particularly those that people judge to be uncontrollable.

The above assumption was based on findings that depressed patients and nondepressed people exposed to uncontrollable failures show similar cognitive and behavioral reactions (e.g., Miller & Seligman, 1975; Price, Tryon, & Raps, 1978; Smolen, 1978; Willis & Blaney, 1978). There were a number of studies, however, that failed to find these similarities (e.g., Abramson, Garber, Edwards, & Seligman, 1978; O'Leary, Donovan, Krueger, & Cysewski, 1978). In addition, a number of authors criticized on both methodological and conceptual bases Seligman's conclusion that the exposure to uncontrollable outcomes is an antecedent of depression (Costello, 1978; Coyne & Gotlib, 1983; Depue & Monroe, 1978).

These criticisms led to a number of reformulations, each of which introduced attributional concepts as mediators between the exposure to uncontrollable failure and depression (e.g., Abramson, Seligman, & Teasdale, 1978; Peterson & Seligman, 1984). These reformulations, though, still see human LH as an explanation of depression. They only point out that the exposure to uncontrollable failure is an insufficient antecedent of depression; other, higher cognitive processes should be also taken into account in order to delineate the conditions in which helplessness training leads to depression.

In my terms, the association between LH deficits and depression is not absolute. From my coping perspective, LH deficits should not be always viewed as a sign of depression. As discussed previously, LH deficits may sometimes reflect a functional trade-off by which people sacrifice performance in exchange for adaptation and long-term well-being. Moreover, this sacrifice is only temporary and may end when the reorganization task is completed. Even the sadness that accompanies inner reorganization cannot be taken as a sign of pathological depression, because it is an adaptive device that supports the restoration of the equilibrium with the environment.

LH deficits may be a sign of psychopathology only when the expectancy of no control leads to avoidance coping. In my terms, the adoption of avoidance coping is a first step in the pathway that transforms what originally begins as a defensive disengagement from task-relevant activities into dysfunctional, chronic deficits. Intensive and prolonged avoidance coping may be followed by the intrusion of failure-related thoughts that disorganize action and overwhelm the cognitive system without accomplishing any adaptive function. In this case, the resulting LH deficits do not reflect functional trade-off but a structural fragmentation of thought and disorganization of action.

Even in the case that LH deficits are dysfunctional, however, they can be a sign of psychopathological reactions other than depression. Overwhelming anxiety, the appraisal of a threat to basic commitments, the intrusion of autonomic thoughts, and the undertaking of intensive, but unsuccessful cognitive and/or behavioral avoidant strategies all may be part of depressive, paranoid, and panic reactions, as well as of obsessive-compulsive and posttraumatic disorders. What may lead to the development of a particular syndrome are personal and situational factors that determine the content of the available cognitive schemas and operations.

One of my students (Budner, 1991), following the above reasoning, suggested that exposure to a large amount of helplessness training may alternatively contribute to depressive reactions or paranoid reactions. He claimed that people can attribute a personal failure directly to themselves (internal attribution) or to some external factor that prevents them personally—though not necessarily others—from controlling the outcomes (personal-external attribution). These two attributions would lead to LH deficits, because the failure implies something important about the self ("I lack intellectual ability," or "The teacher is picking on me because some of my traits") and it demands off-task coping upon unfavorable expectancies of control. Internal and personal-external attributions of failure, however, may have differing repercussions or the individual's affective state. When people attribute failure to an internal cause, they may develop depressive symptoms (Abramson, Garber et al., 1978). But when they make a personal-external attribution, no such symptoms are expected because essential ingredients (personal responsibility for failure, and the consequent blow to one's self-esteem) are missing.

Yet although personal-external attribution may avert the formation of depression, it may increase the distress stemming from failure. A person may obsess about the obstructive factor and worry about being picked on ("Why is he doing this to me?"). In addition, the person may feel anger toward the obstructive factor—anger that stems not from frustration but from a sense of personal injury. Other reactions that may derive from a personal-external attribution for failure include distrust and suspicion of the obstructive agent, fear of what it may do in the future, and even feelings of being persecuted by it. On this basis, Budner (1991) assumed that personal-external attribution of failure may lead to paranoid responses.

Budner's next step was to ask which factors may underlie the direction of the attribution and the subsequent emotional reactions. He concentrated on the extent to which the individual's attention is absorbed by self-representations or by the persons that threaten the self. Taylor and Fiske (1978) found that when attention is focused on an external stimulus, the individual tends to regard that stimulus as the cause of events, whereas when attention is focused on the self, the individual tends to regard himself or herself as the cause. Moreover, theorists suggest that paranoidlike reactions may follow the direction of attention toward a personally threatening agent (e.g., Cameron, 1967), whereas depression may follow the direction of attention toward the self (Ingram, 1984, 1990; Pyszczynski & Greenberg, 1987). This idea is supported in several studies (e.g., Locascio & Snyder, 1975; Smith et al., 1985; Ingram et al., 1987).

In examining the above reasoning, Budner (1991) conducted a series of five LH experiments in which two main factors were manipulated: feedback in four unsolvable problems (no failure, universal failure, or personal failure) and the focus of attention on the self or the threatening agent (the experimenter). Subjects in the personal-failure condition performed worse in a letter cancellation task than subjects in the universal-failure and no-failure conditions. They did not, however, necessarily show depressive reactions; rather, they sometimes showed cognitive and emotional signs of paranoid reactions. What determined the sort of reaction was the induced focus of attention. When attention was directed toward the self, subjects in the personal-failure condition reported more intense depressive feelings, had more frequent off-task depressive-related thoughts, and showed higher availability of depressive self-schemas and depressive biographical memories than subjects in the universal- or no-failure conditions. When attention was directed toward the experimenter, subjects in the personal-failure condition reported more intense paranoid feelings, had more frequent off-task paranoid thoughts, and showed higher availability of paranoid self-schemas, paranoid schemas of significant others, and paranoid biographical memories than subjects in the universal- or no-failure conditions.

Budner's findings should be viewed as an additional step in separating human LH from depression. The findings reinforce the view that the experience of lack of control may be a nonspecific component of psychopathological states. It creates a disequilibrium between the person and the environment, raises distress, endangers the person's basic commitments, and may lead to dysfunctional shifts in the cognitive, emotional, and behavioral systems as well as to a fragmentation of thought and a constriction of functioning—all of which are common features of several psychopathological states. What theorists and researchers should examine are the particular cognitive and emotional features of the dysfunctional shift that may define the type of the evolving psychopathology state. Specifically, they should focus on the manner in which information is internally organized, the particular schemas that currently dominate the cognitive system, the particular distorsions of cognitive operations, and the sort of thoughts and images that are easily accessible to awareness.

One should also recall, however, that human LH cannot be entirely tied to psychopathology. Instead, it should be viewed as a crossroads from which people can direct themselves toward inner growth and adjustment or toward maladjustment and psychopathology. What the experience of lack of control does is disrupt preestablished plans and beliefs, as well as demand a change in the relationship with the environment. At this critical point, people can see the disruption as a personal challenge and as an opportunity to reorganize their beliefs and priorities, or as an imminent threat that should be avoided at the expense of inner integration and adaptation.

APPLICATIONS OF HUMAN LEARNED HELPLESSNESS

Human LH has been frequently extrapolated from laboratory settings to explain adaptational failures in a wide variety of achievement and nonachievement settings. The best-known application of human LH is to school settings and to the explanation of problems in school achievements (Dweck, 1975). In Dweck's view, problems in school achievement shown by "helpless" children can be explained by the same mechanisms that produce LH deficits in the laboratory: a history of (academic) failure, unfavorable expectancies of control, excessive arousal of anxiety and depressed affects, engagement in off-task rumination, and adoption of coping strategies that compete for resources with task-relevant activities.

The performance deficits produced by crowding similarly have been explained by the lack of control involved in crowded spaces and by the development of unfavorable expectancies of control and the adoption of off-task coping strategies (Baum et al., 1978; Baum & Gatchel, 1981). Several theorists also apply concepts from human LH to explain some of the psychological deficiencies associated with old age (Rodin, 1986; Schultz, 1980). These deficiencies are viewed as LH deficits that result from the increasing experience with lack of control and the negative appraisals and expectancies that characterize aging.

Peterson and Seligman (1983) suggested that learned helplessness also may be involved in the phenomenon of battered women (i.e., women who stay with husbands or lovers who beat them). The authors claim that the decision to stay in an abusive relationship is a passive response that reflects the women's expectancies of lack of control and the abandonment of problem-focused coping, two of the definitional components of LH deficits. In addition, the psychological effects of institutionalization have been viewed as analogous to LH deficits in the laboratory. In both cases, events are perceived to be noncontingent on one's actions, some negative appraisals and expectancies are developed, and impairments in task performance and morale are recorded (e.g., Winefeld & Fay, 1982).

Human LH has been also applied to explain other human problems that seem to follow the exposure to uncontrollable events. For example, a mother's reactions to infant crying has been explained as resulting from prior response–outcome contingencies (Donovan, 1981). Weisz (1979) related the experience of lack of control to the passivity and deficiencies showed by mentally retarded persons, and Rolnick and Lubow (1991) viewed exposure to uncontrollable events as an antecedent of motion sickness.

As can be seen, several human problems have been viewed as real-life examples of laboratory LH deficits. The various authors emphasize the similarities between the targeted problem and LH deficits and suggest that each are caused by similar psychological processes. Most of these assumptions, however, suffer from both lack of theoretical precision and empirical validity. First of all, any attempt to extrapolate LH deficits to other human problems should be based on the precise analysis of the criteria that define LH deficits and the evaluation of the application of these criteria to the targeted problem. In addition, systematic research should be conducted in which the psychological factors that contribute to LH deficits are manipulated and/or assessed and their impact on the targeted problem is examined.

In my view, six criteria should be used to recognize LH deficits in other human problems:

1. LH deficits are present when a person displays problems in functioning and task performance, failing to meet the demands of a task situation.
2. LH deficits follow exposure to uncontrollable bad events that disrupt the equilibrium between the person and the environment.
3. LH deficits occur mainly when the uncontrollable bad event is appraised to be an imminent threat to one's basic commitments.
4. LH deficits occur mainly when exposure to uncontrollable bad events leads to the heightening of self-focused attention.
5. LH deficits are distally mediated by the acquisition of unfavorable expectancies of control during exposure to uncontrollable bad events and the generalization of these expectancies to new situations.
6. LH deficits are proximally mediated by the adoption of off-task coping.

Any application of human LH should take into account the above six criteria. Authors should empirically verify whether people showing the targeted problem have a history of uncontrollable bad events that they appraise to be important and relevant to their basic commitments. They should also check whether people react to the uncontrollable bad events with enhanced self-focus and strong emotions, learn from these events that they are unable to mold the environment in accord to their wants, and react to new challenges and difficulties with off-task ways of coping.

Take, for example, the functional problems that may follow prolonged hospitalization. Before claiming that these problems are an example of LH deficits, research should demonstrate that hospitalized people showing these problems—as compared to hospitalized people who do not show these problems—are exposed to uncontrollable events during their hospitalization, appraise these events as a personal loss and a threat to their goal hierarchy and self-identity, tend to direct attention inward during their stay in the hospital, become pessimistic, experience strong anxiety and/or depressed affects, engage in rumination about their personal state or about other distracting matters, and adopt coping strategies that interfere with problem-solving attempts.

REFERENCES

Abelson, R. P. (1983). Whatever became of consistency theory? *Personality and Social Psychology Bulletin, 9,* 37–54.

Abraham, K. (1911). Notes of psychoanalytic research and therapy of manic depressive disorders. In *Selected papers of Karl Abraham.* London: Hogarth.

Abramson, L. Y., Garber, J., Edwards, N. B., & Seligman, M. E. P. (1978). Expectancy changes in depression and schizophrenia. *Journal of Abnormal Psychology, 87,* 102–109.

Abramson, L. Y., Seligman, M. E. P., & Teasdale, J. D. (1978). Learned helplessness in humans: Critique and reformulation. *Journal of Abnormal Psychology, 87,* 49–74.

Affleck, G., Tennen, H., Pfeiffer, C., & Fifield, J. (1988). Social comparisons in rheumatoid arthritis. *Journal of Social and Clinical Psychology, 6,* 219–234.

Ahles, T. A., Pecora, J., & Riley, S. (1987). Self-focused attention, psychiatric symptoms, and chronic pain: An hypothesis. *Southern Psychologist, 3,* 25–28.

Albert, M., & Geller, E. S. (1978). Perceived control as a mediator of learned helplessness. *American Journal of Psychology, 91,* 389–400.

Aldwin, C., Folkman, S., Schaefer, C., Coyne, J. C., & Lazarus, R. S. (1980). *Ways of coping: A process measure.* Paper presented at meetings of American Psychological Association, Montreal.

Aldwin, C. M., & Revenson, T. A. (1987). Does coping help? A reexamination of the relation between coping and mental health. *Journal of Personality and Social Psychology, 53,* 337–348.

Alloy, L. B. (1982). The role of perceptions and attributions for response-outcome noncontingency in learned helplessness: A commentary and discussion. *Journal of Personality, 50,* 443–479.

Alloy, L. B., & Abramson, L. Y. (1979). Judgment of contingency in depressed and nondepressed students: Sadder but wiser? *Journal of Experimental Psychology: General, 108,* 441–485.

Alloy, L. B., & Abramson, L. Y. (1982). Learned helplessness, depression, and the illusion of control. *Journal of Personality and Social Psychology, 42,* 1114–1126.

Alloy, L. B., Peterson, C., Abramson, L. Y., & Seligman, M. E. P. (1984). Attributional style and the generality of learned helplessness. *Journal of Personality and Social Psychology, 46,* 681–687.

Alloy, L. B., & Seligman, M. E. P. (1979). On the cognitive component of learned helplessness and depression. In G. H. Bower (Ed.), *The psychology of learning and motivation* (Vol. 13). New York: Academic Press.

Alloy, L. B., & Tabachnik, N. (1984). Assessment of covariation by humans and animals: The joint influence of prior expectations and current situational information. *Psychological Review, 91,* 112–149.

275

Altmaier, E. M., & Happ, D. A. (1985). Coping skill training's immunization effects against learned helplessness. *Journal of Social and Clinical Psychology, 3,* 181–189.

Altshuler, J. L., & Ruble, D. N. (1989). Developmental changes in children's awareness of strategies for coping with uncontrollable stress. *Child Development, 60,* 1337–1349.

Amirkhan, J. H. (1991). A factor analytically derived measure of coping: The Coping Strategy Indicator. *Journal of Personality and Social Psychology, 59,* 1066–1074.

Amsel, A. (1972). Behavioral habituation, counterconditioning, and a general theory of persistence. In A. H. Back & W. F. Prokasy (Eds.), *Classical conditioning, vol. 2: Current research and theory.* New York: Appleton-Century-Croft.

Andersen, S. M., & Lyon, J. E. (1987). Anticipating undesired outcomes: The role of outcome certainty in the onset of depressive affect. *Journal of Experimental Social Psychology, 23,* 428–443.

Anderson, C. A. (1983). Motivational and performance deficits in interpersonal settings: The effects of attributional style. *Journal of Personality and Social Psychology, 45,* 1136–1141.

Anderson, C. R. (1977). Locus of control, coping behaviors, and performance in a stress setting: A longitudinal study. *Journal of Applied Psychology, 62,* 446–451.

Anderson, J. R. (1990). *Cognitive psychology.* New York: Academic Press.

Anderson, J. R., & Bower, G. H. (1973). *Human associative memory.* Washington, DC: Winston.

Anderson, R. H., Anderson, K., Fleming, D. E., & Kinghorn, E. (1984). A multidimensional test of the attributional reformulation of learned helplessness. *Bulletin of the Psychonomic Society, 22,* 211–213.

Andrews, G. R., & Debus, R. L. (1978). Persistence and the causal perception of failure: Modifying cognitive attributions. *Journal of Educational Psychology, 70,* 154–166.

Andrews, G. R., Tennant, C., Hewson, D. M., & Vaillant, G. E. (1978). Life event stress, social support, coping style, and risk of psychological impairment. *Journal of Nervous and Mental Disease, 166,* 307–316.

Anisman, H., DeCatanzaro, I., & Remington, G. (1978). Escape performance following exposure to inescapable shock: Deficits in motor response maintenance. *Journal of Experimental Psychology: Animal Behavior Processes, 4,* 197–218.

Anisman, H., & Waller, T. G. (1973). Effects of inescapable shock on subsequent avoidance performance: Role of response repertoire changes. *Behavioral Biology, 9,* 331–355.

Archer, R. L., Hormuth, S. E., & Berg, J. H. (1979). *Self-disclosure under conditions of self-awareness.* Paper presented at the annual meeting of the American Psychological Association, New York.

Archibald, W. P. (1974). Alternative explanations for self-fulfilling prophecy. *Psychological Bulletin, 81,* 74–84.

Arkin, R. M., & Baumgardner, A. H. (1985). Self-handicapping. In J. H. Harvey & G. Weary (Eds.), *Basic issues in attribution theory and research* (pp. 169–202). New York: Academic Press.

Arnold, M. B. (1960). *Emotion and personality.* New York: Columbia University Press.

Ashford, S. J. (1988). Individual strategies for coping with stress during organizational transitions. *Journal of Applied Behavioral Science, 24,* 19–36.

Atkinson, J. W., & Birch, D. (1970). *The dynamics of action.* New York: Wiley.

Atkinson, J. W., & Cartwright, D. (1964). Some neglected variables in contemporary conceptions of decision and performance. *Psychological Reports, 14,* 575–590.

Atkinson, J. W., & Feather, N. T. (Eds.). (1966). *A theory of achievement motivation.* New York: Wiley.

Averill, J. R. (1978). Anger. *Nebraska Symposium on Motivation, 26,* 1–80.

Averill, J. R., O'Brien, L., & DeWitt, G. W. (1977). The influence of response effectiveness on the preference for warning and on psychophysiological stress reactions. *Journal of Personality, 45,* 395–418.

Aydin, G. (1988). The remediation of children's helpless explanatory style and related unpopularity. *Cognitive Therapy and Research, 12,* 155–165.

Ayeroff, F., & Abelson, R. P. (1976). ESP and ESB: Belief in personal success at mental telepathy. *Journal of Personality and Social Psychology, 34,* 240–247.

Baddeley, A. D., & Hitch, G. (1974). Working memory. In G. H. Bower (Ed.), *The psychology of learning and motivation*. New York: Academic Press.

Bandura, A. (1977). Self efficacy: Toward a unifying theory of behavioral change. *Psychological Review, 84*, 191–215.

Bandura, A. (1986). *Social foundations of thought and action: A social cognitive theory*. Englewood Cliffs, NJ: Prentice-Hall.

Bandura, A., & Cervone, D. (1983). Self-evaluative and self-efficacy mechanisms governing the motivational effects of goal systems. *Journal of Personality and Social Psychology, 45*, 1017–1028.

Barber, J. G. (1989). A parametric study of learned helplessness in humans. *Quarterly Journal of Experimental Psychology, 41*, 339–354.

Barber, J. G., & Winefeld, A. H. (1986). Learned helplessness as conditioned inattention to the target stimulus. *Journal of Experimental Psychology: General, 115*, 236–246.

Barber, J. G., & Winefeld, A. H. (1987). The influence of stimulus intensity and motivational differences on learned helplessness deficits. *Personality and Individual Differences, 8*, 25–32.

Barkan, R. (1991). *Perceived self-efficacy, latent theories of abilities, and affective-cognitive reactions to failure*. Unpublished master's thesis, Bar-Ilan University, Israel.

Baron, R., & Rodin, J. (1978). Personal control and crowding stress: Processes mediating the impact of spatial and social density. In A. Baum, J. Singer, & S. Valins (Eds.), *Advances in environmental psychology* (Vol. 1). Hillsdale, NJ: Erlbaum.

Battle, E. S. (1966). Motivational determinants of academic competence. *Journal of Personality and Social Psychology, 4*, 634–642.

Baucom, D. H. (1983). Sex-role identity and the decision to regain control among women: A learned helplessness investigation. *Journal of Personality and Social Psychology, 44*, 334–343.

Baucom, D. H., & Danker-Brown, P. (1979). Influence of sex roles on the development of learned helplessness. *Journal of Consulting and Clinical Psychology, 47*, 928–936.

Baucom, D. H., & Danker-Brown, P. (1984). Sex-role identity and sex-stereotyped tasks in the development of learned helplessness in women. *Journal of Personality and Social Psychology, 46*, 422–430.

Baum, A., Aiello, J., & Calesnick, L. (1978). Crowding and personal control: Social density and the development of learned helplessness. *Journal of Personality and Social Psychology, 36*, 1000–1011.

Baum, A., & Gatchel, R. J. (1981). Cognitive determinants of reaction to uncontrollable events: Development of reactance and learned helplessness. *Journal of Personality and Social Psychology, 40*, 1078–1089.

Baum, A., & Valins, S. (1979). Architectural mediation of residential density and control: Crowding and the regulation of social contact. In E. Berkowitz (Ed.), *Advances in experimental social psychology* (Vol. 12, pp. 131–175). New York: Academic Press.

Baumeister, R. F. (1982). A self-presentational view of social phenomena. *Psychological Bulletin, 91*, 3–26.

Baumeister, R. F. (1986). *Public and private self*. New York: Springer-Verlag.

Baumeister, R. F., & Jones, E. E. (1978). When self-presentation is constrained by the target's prior knowledge: Consistency and compensation. *Journal of Personality and Social Psychology, 36*, 608–618.

Baumeister, R. F., & Scher, S. J. (1988). Self-defeating behavior patterns among normal individuals: Review and analysis of common self-destructive tendencies. *Psychological Bulletin, 104*, 3–22.

Baumgardner, A. H., & Levy, P. E. (1988). Role of self-esteem in perception of ability and effort: Illogic or insight? *Personality and Social Psychology Bulletin, 14*, 429–438.

Beck, A. T. (1967). *Depression: Clinical, experimental, and theoretical aspects*. New York: Hoeber.

Beck, A. T. (1976). *Cognitive therapy and emotional disorders*. New York: International University Press.

Beck, A. T., & Clark, D. A. (1988). Anxiety and depression: An information processing perspective. *Anxiety Research, 1,* 23–36.

Belgrave, F. Z., Johnson, R. S., & Carey, C. (1985). Attributional style and its relationship to self-esteem and academic performance in black students. *Journal of Black Psychology, 11,* 49–56.

Bennett, D. H., & Holmes, D. S. (1975). Influence of denial (situation redefinition) and projection on anxiety associated with a threat to self-esteem. *Journal of Personality and Social Psychology, 32,* 915–921.

Bennion, R. C. (1961). *Task, trial by trial score variability, and individual differences as affecting perception of internal vs. external locus of control.* Doctoral dissertation, Ohio State University.

Benson, J. S., & Kenelly, K. J. (1976). Learned helplessness: The result of uncontrollable reinforcements or uncontrollable aversive stimuli? *Journal of Personality and Social Psychology, 34,* 138–145.

Bibring, E. (1953). The mechanisms of depression. In P. Greenacre (Ed.), *Affective disorders.* New York: International University Press.

Billings, A. G., & Moos, R. H. (1981). The role of coping responses and social resources in attenuating the stress of life events. *Journal of Behavioral Medicine, 4,* 139–157.

Billings, A. G., & Moos, R. H. (1984). Coping, stress, and social resources among adults with unipolar depression. *Journal of Personality and Social Psychology, 46,* 877–891.

Blackman, S. (1962). Some factors affecting the perception of events as chance determined. *Journal of Psychology, 54,* 197–202.

Blaney, P. H. (1986). Affect and memory: A review. *Psychological Bulletin, 99,* 229–246.

Boggiano, A. K., & Barrett, M. (1985). Performance and motivational deficits of helplessness: The role of motivational orientations. *Journal of Personality and Social Psychology, 49,* 1753–1761.

Bohner, G., Bless, H., Schwartz, N., & Strack, F. (1988). What triggers causal attributions? The impact of valence and subjective probability. *European Journal of Social Psychology, 18,* 335–345.

Borkowski, J. G., Weyhing, R. S., & Carr, M. (1988). Effects of attributional retraining on strategy-based reading comprehension in learning-disabled students. *Journal of Educational Psychology, 80,* 46–53.

Bower, G. H. (1981). Mood and memory. *American Psychologist, 36,* 129–148.

Boyd, T. L. (1982). Learned helplessness in humans: A frustration-produced response pattern. *Journal of Personality and Social Psychology, 42,* 738–752.

Bracewell, R. J., & Black, A. H. (1974). The effects of restraint and noncontingent pre-shock on subsequent escape learning in the rat. *Learning and Motivation, 5,* 53–69.

Bradley, G. (1978). Self-serving biases in the attribution process: A re-examination of the fact or fiction question. *Journal of Personality and Social Psychology, 36,* 56–71.

Breen, L. J., Vulcano, B., & Dyck, D. G. (1979). Observational learning and sex roles in learned helplessness. *Psychological Reports, 44,* 135–144.

Brehm, J. W. (1966). *A theory of psychological reactance.* New York: Academic Press.

Brehm, J. W. (1972). *Responses to loss of freedom: A theory of psychological reactance.* Morristown, NJ: General Learning Press.

Brewin, C. R. (1985). Depression and causal attributions: What is their relation? *Psychological Bulletin, 98,* 297–309.

Brewin, C. R., & Shapiro, D. A. (1985). Selective impact of reattribution of failure on task performance. *British Journal of Social Psychology, 24,* 37–46.

Brockner, J. (1979a). Self-esteem, self consciousness, and task performance: Replications, extensions, and possible explanations. *Journal of Personality and Social Psychology, 37,* 447–461.

Brockner, J. (1979b). The effects of self-esteem, success-failure, and self-consciousness on task performance. *Journal of Personality and Social Psychology, 37,* 1732–1741.

Brockner, J., Gardner, M., Bierman, J., Mahan, T., Thomas, B., Weiss, W., Winters, L., & Mitchell, A. (1983). The roles of self-esteem and self-consciousness in the Wortman-Brehm model of reactance and learned helplessness. *Journal of Personality and Social Psychology, 45,* 199–209.

Brockner, J., & Guare, J. (1983). Improving the performance of low self-esteem individuals: An attributional approach. *Academy of Management Journal, 26,* 642–656.

Brockner, J., Hjelle, L., & Plant, R. (1985). Self-focused attention, self-esteem and the experience of state depression. *Journal of Personality, 50,* 425–434.

Brockner, J., & Hulton, A. J. B. (1978). How to reverse the vicious circle of low self-esteem: The importance of attentional focus. *Journal of Experimental Social Psychology, 14,* 564–578.

Brown, G. K., & Nicassio, P. M. (1987). Development of a questionnaire for the assessment of active and passive coping strategies in chronic pain patients. *Pain, 31,* 53–64.

Brown, I., & Inouye, D. K. (1978). Learned helplessness through modeling: The role of perceived similarity in competence. *Journal of Personality and Social Psychology, 36,* 900–908.

Brown, J. D. (1988). Self-directed attention, self-esteem, and causal attributions for valenced outcomes. *Personality and Social Psychology Bulletin, 14,* 252–263.

Brunson, B. I., & Matthews, K. A. (1981). The type A coronary-prone behavior pattern and reactions to uncontrollable stress: An analysis of performance strategies, affect, and attributions during failure. *Journal of Personality and Social Psychology, 40,* 906–918.

Brunstein, J. C. (1989). Action-oriented vs. state-oriented reactions to experimentally-induced failure. *Zeitschrift fur Experimentelle und Angewandte Psychologie, 36,* 349–367.

Brunstein, J. C., & Olbrich, E. (1985). Personal helplessness and action control: Analysis of achievement-related cognitions, self-assessment, and performance. *Journal of Personality and Social Psychology, 48,* 1540–1551.

Budner, E. (1991). *Personal learned helplessness and the formation of paranoid-like and depressive-like reactions: The role of attentional focus.* Unpublished doctoral dissertation, Bar-Ilan University, Israel.

Buchwald, A. M., Coyne, J. C., & Cole, C. S. (1978). A critical evaluation of the learned helplessness model of depression. *Journal of Abnormal Psychology, 87,* 180–193.

Burger, J. M. (1987). Effects of desire for control on attributions and task performance. *Basic and Applied Social Psychology, 8,* 309–320.

Burger, J. M., & Arkin, R. M. (1980). Prediction, control, and learned helplessness. *Journal of Personality and Social Psychology, 38,* 482–491.

Burger, J. M., & Cooper, H. M. (1979). The desirability of control. *Motivation and Emotion, 3,* 381–393.

Burgio, K. L., Merluzzi, T. V., & Pryor, J. B. (1986). Effects of performance expectancy and self-focused attention on social interaction. *Journal of Personality and Social Psychology, 50,* 1216–1221.

Burish, T. G., & Houston, B. K. (1979). Causal projection, similarity projection, and coping with threat to self-esteem. *Journal of Personality, 47,* 57–70.

Burstein, S., & Meichenbaum, D. (1979). The work of worrying in children undergoing surgery. *Journal of Abnormal Child Psychology, 7,* 121–132.

Buss, D. M., & Scheier, M. F. (1976). Self-consciousness, self-awareness, and self-attribution. *Journal of Research in Personality, 10,* 463–468.

Buys, N. J., & Winefeld, A. H. (1982). Learned helplessness in high school students following experience of noncontingent rewards. *Journal of Research in Personality, 16,* 118–127.

Cameron, N. (1967). Paranoid reactions. In A. M. Freedman & H. I. Kaplan (Eds.), *Comprehensive textbook of psychiatry* (pp. 665–675). Baltimore: Williams & Wilkins.

Campbell, D. T., & Fiske, D. W. (1959). Convergent and discriminant validation by the multitrait–multimethod matrix. *Psychological Bulletin, 56,* 81–105.

Campbell, J. D., & Fairey, P. (1985). Effects of self-esteem, hypothetical explanations, and verbalization of expectancies on future performance. *Journal of Personality and Social Psychology, 48,* 1097–1111.

Campbell, N. K., & Hackett, G. (1985). *The effects of mathematics task performance on math self-efficacy and task interest.* Paper presented at the meeting of the American Psychological Association.

Carlson, J. G., & Cassisi, J. E. (1985). Prior task failure as a determinant of biofeedback and cognitive task performance. *Motivation and Emotion, 9,* 331–343.

Carlson, J. G., & Feld, J. L. (1981). Expectancies of reinforcement control in biofeedback and cognitive performance. *Biofeedback and Self-Regulation, 6,* 79–91.

Carlson, M., & Miller, N. (1988). Bad experiences and aggression. *Sociology and Social Research, 72,* 155–158.

Carmon, Z., & Donaghi, S. (1991). *The emotional components of learned helplessness.* Unpublished manuscript, Bar-Ilan University, Israel.

Carver, C. S. (1979). A cybernetic model of self-attention processes. *Journal of Personality and Social Psychology, 37,* 1251–1281.

Carver, C. S., Blaney, P. H., & Scheier, M. F. (1979a). Focus of attention, chronic expectancy, and responses to a feared stimulus. *Journal of Personality and Social Psychology, 37,* 1186–1195.

Carver, C. S., Blaney, P. H., & Scheier, M. F. (1979b). Reassertion and giving up: The interactive role of self-directed attention and outcome expectancy. *Journal of Personality and Social Psychology, 37,* 1859–1870.

Carver, C. S., & Glass, D. (1976). The Self-Consciousness Scale: A discriminant validity study. *Journal of Personality Assessment, 40,* 169–172.

Carver, C. S., Peterson, L. M., Follansbee, D. J., & Scheier, M. F. (1983). Effects of self-directed attention among persons high and low in test anxiety. *Cognitive Therapy and Research, 7,* 333–354.

Carver, C. S., & Scheier, M. F. (1981). *Attention and self-regulation: A control theory approach to human behavior.* New York: Springer-Verlag.

Carver, C. S., & Scheier, M. F. (1982). Outcome expectancy, locus of attribution for expectancy, and self-directed attention as determinants of evaluation and performance. *Journal of Experimental Social Psychology, 18,* 184–200.

Carver, C. S., Scheier, M. F., & Weintraub, J. K. (1989). Assessing coping strategies: A theoretically based approach. *Journal of Personality and Social Psychology, 56,* 267–283.

Castaneda, A. (1952). *A systematic investigation of the concept expectancy as conceived within Rotter's social learning theory of personality.* Unpublished doctoral dissertation, Ohio State University.

Chanowitz, B., & Langer, E. (1980). Knowing more (or less) than you can show: Understanding control through the mindlessness–mindfulness distinction. In J. Garber & M. E. P. Seligman (Eds.), *Human helplessness.* New York: Academic Press.

Chapin, M., & Dyck, D. G. (1976). Persistence in children's reading behavior as a function of N length and attribution retraining. *Journal of Abnormal Psychology, 85,* 511–515.

Chartier, G. M., & Friedlander, S. (1981). Vicariously and directly learned helplessness and effectiveness. *Journal of Personality, 49,* 257–270.

Chodoff, P., Friedman, S. B., & Hamburg, P. A. (1964). Stress defenses and coping behavior. *American Journal of Psychiatry, 120,* 433–439.

Clark, D. A. (1986). Cognitive-affective interaction: A test of the "specificity" and "generality" hypotheses. *Cognitive Therapy and Research, 10,* 607–623.

Clark, D. A., Beck, A. T., & Brown, G. (1989). Cognitive mediation in general psychiatric outpatients: A test of the content-specificity hypothesis. *Journal of Personality and Social Psychology, 56,* 958–964.

Clark, D. A., Beck, A. T., & Stewart, B. L. (1990). Cognitive specificity and positive–negative affectivity: Complementary or contradictory views on anxiety and depression? *Journal of Abnormal Psychology, 99,* 148–155.

Clark, M. S., & Isen, A. M. (1982). Toward understanding the relationship between feeling states and social behavior. In A. H. Hastorf & A. M. Isen (Eds.), *Cognitive social psychology* (pp. 73–108). New York: Elsevier.

Cohen, J. L., Dowling, N., Bishop, B., & Maney, W. (1985). Causal attributions: Effects of self-focused attention and self-esteem feedback. *Personality and Social Psychology Bulletin, 11,* 369–378.

Cohen, S., Rothbart, M., & Phillips, S. (1976). Locus of control and the generality of learned helplessness in humans. *Journal of Personality and Social Psychology, 34,* 1049–1056.

Cole, C. S., & Coyne, J. C. (1977). Situational specificity of laboratory-induced learned helplessness. *Journal of Abnormal Psychology, 86,* 615–623.

Collins, D. L., Baum, A., & Singer, J. E. (1983). Coping with chronic stress at Three Mile Island: Psychological and biochemical evidence. *Health Psychology, 2,* 149–166.

Compas, B. E., Malcarne, V. L., & Fondacaro, K. M. (1988). Coping with stressful events in older children and young adolescents. *Journal of Consulting and Clinical Psychology, 56,* 405–411.

Contrada, R. J., Glass, D. C., Krakoff, D. S., Krantz, D. S., Kehoe, K., Isecke, W., Collins, C., & Elting, E. (1982). Effects of control over aversive stimulation and Type A behavior on cardiovascular and plasma catecholamine responses. *Psychophysiology, 19,* 408–419.

Conway, M., Howell, A., & Giannopoulus, C. (1991). Dysphoria and thought suppression. *Cognitive Therapy and Research, 15,* 153–166.

Cooley, E. C., & Klinger, C. R. (1988). Academic attributions and coping with tests. *Journal of Social and Clinical Psychology, 8,* 359–367.

Cornwell, J., Nurcombe, B., & Stevens, L. (1977). Family response to loss of a child by Sudden Infant Death Syndrome. *Medical Journal of Australia, 1,* 656–658.

Costello, C. G. (1978). A critical review of Seligman's laboratory experiments on learned helplessness and depression in humans. *Journal of Abnormal Psychology, 87,* 21–31.

Covington, M. V., & Omerlich, C. L. (1979). Are causal attributions causal? A path analysis of the cognitive model of achievement motivation. *Journal of Personality and Social Psychology, 37,* 1487–1504.

Covington, M. V., & Omerlich, C. L. (1984). An empirical examination of Weiner's critique of attribution research. *Journal of Educational Psychology, 76,* 1214–1225.

Coyne, J. C., & Gotlib, I. H. (1983). The role of cognition in depression: A critical appraisal. *Psychological Bulletin, 94,* 472–505.

Coyne, J. C., Metalsky, G. I., & Lavelle, T. L. (1980). Learned helplessness as experimenter-induced failure and its alleviation with attentional redeployment. *Journal of Abnormal Psychology, 89,* 350–357.

Craske, M. L. (1985). Improving persistence through observational learning and attribution retraining. *British Journal of Educational Psychology, 55,* 138–147.

Craske, M. L. (1988). Learned helplessness, self-worth motivation, and attribution retraining for primary school children. *British Journal of Educational Psychology, 58,* 152–164.

Cronkite, R. C., & Moos, R. H. (1984). The role of predisposing and moderating factors in the stress–illness relationship. *Journal of Health and Social Behavior, 25,* 372–393.

Cunningham, M. R. (1988). What do you do when you are happy or blue? Mood, expectancies, and behavioral interest. *Motivation and Emotion, 12,* 309–331.

Cutrona, C. E. (1983). Causal attributions and perinatal depression. *Journal of Abnormal Psychology, 92,* 161–172.

Danker-Brown, P., & Baucom, D. H. (1982). Cognitive influences on the development of learned helplessness. *Journal of Personality and Social Psychology, 43,* 793–801.

Davies, M. F. (1982). Self-focused attention and belief perseverance. *Journal of Experimental Social Psychology, 18,* 595–605.

Davis, F. W., & Yates, B. T. (1982). Self-efficacy expectancies versus outcome expectancies as determinants of performance deficits and depressive affect. *Cognitive Therapy and Research, 6,* 23–25.

Deadman, J. M., Dewey, M. J., Owens, R. G., & Leinster, S. J. (1989). Threat and loss in breast cancer. *Psychological Medicine, 19,* 677–681.

Deffenbacher, J. L. (1980). Worry and emotionality in test anxiety. In I. G. Sarason (Ed.), *Test anxiety: Theory, research, and applications* (pp. 111–128). Hillsdale, NJ: Erlbaum.

Deffenbacher, J. L., & Deitz, S. R. (1978). Effects of test anxiety on performance, worry, and emotionality in naturally occurring exams. *Psychology in the Schools, 15,* 446–450.

Deffenbacher, J. L., Demm, P. M., & Brandon, A. D. (1986). High general anger: Correlates and treatment. *Behavior Research and Therapy, 24,* 481–489.

Deffenbacher, J. L., & Hazaleus, S. L. (1985). Cognitive, emotional, and physiological components of test anxiety. *Cognitive Therapy and Research, 9,* 169–180.

DeGree, C. E., & Snyder, C. R. (1985). Adler's psychology (of use) today: Personal history of traumatic life events as a self-handicapping strategy. *Journal of Personality and Social Psychology, 48,* 1512–1519.

Dekel, A. (1993). *The learned helplessness phenomenon: Information processing in an exhausted cognitive system.* Unpublished master's thesis, Bar-Ilan University, Israel.

Den-Boer, D. J., Meertens, R., Kok, G., & Van-Knippenberg, A. (1989). Measurement effects in reattribution research. *European Journal of Social Psychology, 19,* 553–559.

Dengerink, H. A., O'Leary, M. R., & Kasner, K. H. (1975). Individual differences in aggressive responses to attack: Internal–external locus of control and field dependence–independence. *Journal of Research in Personality, 9,* 191–199.

Depue, R. G., & Monroe, S. M. (1978). Learned helplessness in the perspective of the depressive disorders: Conceptual and definitional issues. *Journal of Abnormal Psychology, 87,* 3–20.

DeRivera, J. (1977). A structural theory of emotions. *Psychological Issues, 10*(Monograph 40).

DeSoto, C. B., Coleman, E. B., & Putnam, P. L. (1960). Predictions of sequences of successes and failures. *Journal of Experimental Psychology, 59,* 41–46.

DeVellis, R. F., DeVellis, B. M., & McCauley, C. (1978). Vicarious acquisition of learned helplessness. *Journal of Personality and Social Psychology, 36,* 894–899.

Dickstein, L. S., & Kephart, J. L. (1972). Effect of explicit examiner expectancy on WAIS performance. *Psychological Reports, 30,* 207–212.

Diener, C. I., & Dweck, C. S. (1978). An analysis of learned helplessness: Continuous changes in performance strategy, and achievement cognitions following failure. *Journal of Personality and Social Psychology, 36,* 451–462.

Diener, C. I., & Dweck, C. S. (1980). An analysis of learned helplessness: II. The processing of success. *Journal of Personality and Social Psychology, 39,* 940–952.

Diggory, J. C. (1949). Responses to experimentally induced failure. *American Journal of Psychology, 62,* 48–61.

Diggory, J. C., & Morlock, H. C. (1964). Level of aspiration, or probability of success? *Journal of Abnormal and Social Psychology, 69,* 282–289.

Doctor, R. M., & Altman, F. (1969). Worry and emotionality as components of test anxiety: Replication and further data. *Psychological Reports, 24,* 563–568.

Donovan, W. L. (1981). Maternal learned helplessness and physiologic responses to infant crying. *Journal of Personality and Social Psychology, 40,* 919–926.

Douglas, D., & Anisman, H. (1975). Helplessness or expectation incongruency: Effects of aversive stimulation on subsequent performance. *Journal of Experimental Psychology: Human Perception and Performance, 1,* 411–417.

Duval, S., & Wicklund, R. A. (1972). *A theory of objective self-awareness.* New York: Academic Press.

Duval, S., & Wicklund, R. A. (1973). Effects of objective self-awareness on attribution of causality. *Journal of Experimental Social Psychology, 9,* 17–31.

Duval, S., Wicklund, R. A., & Fine, R. L. (1972). Avoidance of objective self-awareness under conditions of high and low intra-self discrepancy. In S. Duval and R. A. Wicklund, *A theory of objective self-awareness.* New York: Academic Press.

Dweck, C. (1975). The role of expectation and attribution in the alleviation of learned helplessness. *Journal of Personality and Social Psychology, 31,* 674–685.

Dweck, C., & Bush, E. (1976). Sex differences in learned helplessness: I. Differential debilitation with peer and adult evaluators. *Developmental Psychology, 12,* 147–156.

Dweck, C., Davidson, W., Nelson, S., & Enna, B. (1978). Sex differences in learned helplessness: II. The contingencies of evaluative feedback in the classroom, and III. An experimental analysis. *Developmental Psychology, 14,* 268–276.

Dweck, C., & Gilliard, D. (1975). Expectancy statements as determinants of reactions to failure: Sex differences in persistence and expectancy change. *Journal of Personality and Social Psychology, 32,* 1077–1084.

Dweck, C., Goetz, T. E., & Strauss, N. L. (1980). Sex differences in learned helplessness: IV. An experimental and naturalistic study of failure generalization and its mediators. *Journal of Personality and Social Psychology, 38,* 441–452.

Dweck, C. S., & Leggett, E. L. (1988). A social-cognitive approach to motivation and personality. *Psychological Review, 95,* 256–273.

Dweck, C., & Licht, B. G. (1980). Learned helplessness and intellectual achievement. In M. E. P. Seligman & J. Garber (Eds.), *Human helplessness: Theory and application.* New York: Academic Press.

Dweck, C. S., & Repucci, N. D. (1973). Learned helplessness and reinforcement responsibility in children. *Journal of Personality and Social Psychology, 25,* 109–116.

Dyck, D. G., & Green, L. J. (1978). Learned helplessness, immunization, and importance of tasks in humans. *Psychological Reports, 43,* 315–321.

Dyck, D. G., Vallentyne, S., & Breen, L. J. (1979). Duration of failure, causal attributions for failure, and subsequent reactions. *Journal of Experimental Social Psychology, 15,* 122–132.

Easterbrook, J. A. (1959). The effect of emotion on cue utilization and the organization of behavior. *Psychological Review, 66,* 183–201.

Eccles, J. P. (1983). Expectancies, values, and academic behaviors. In J. T. Spence (Ed.), *Achievement and achievement motives* (pp. 75–146). San Francisco: Freeman.

Eckelman, J. D., & Dyck, D. G. (1979). Task- and setting-related cues in immunization against learned helplessness. *American Journal of Psychology, 92,* 653–667.

Eisenberg, R., Kaplan, R. M., & Singer, R. D. (1974). Decremental and nondecremental effects of noncontingent social approval. *Journal of Personality and Social Psychology, 30,* 716–722.

Eisenberg, R., Park, D. C., & Frank, M. (1976). Learned industriousness and social reinforcement. *Journal of Personality and Social Psychology, 33,* 227–232.

Elliott, E. S., & Dweck, C. S. (1988). Goals: An approach to motivation and achievement. *Journal of Personality and Social Psychology, 54,* 5–12.

Ellis, H. C., & Ashbrook, P. W. (1989). The "state" of mood and memory research: A selective review. *Journal of Social Behavior and Personality, 4,* 1–21.

Ellis, R. J., & Holmes, J. G. (1982). Focus of attention and self-evaluation in social interaction. *Journal of Personality and Social Psychology, 43,* 67–77.

Endler, N. S., & Parker, J. D. (1990). Multidimensional assessment of coping: A critical evaluation. *Journal of Personality and Social Psychology, 58,* 844–854.

Epstein, S. (1972). The nature of anxiety with emphasis upon its relationship to expectancy. In C. Speilberger (Ed.), *Anxiety* (Vol. 2, pp. 292–338). New York: Academic Press.

Epstein, S., & Meier, P. (1989). Constructive thinking: A broad coping variable with specific components. *Journal of Personality and Social Psychology, 57,* 332–350.

Erkut, S. (1983). Exploring sex differences in expectancy, attribution, and academic performance. *Sex Roles, 9,* 217–231.

Erwin, T. D., & Marcus-Mendoza, S. (1987). *Action control and academic problems.* Unpublished manuscript, Texas A & M University.

Exner, J. E. (1973). The self-focus sentence completion: A study of egocentricity. *Journal of Personality Assessment, 37,* 860–870.

Eysenck, M. W. (1982). *Attention and arousal: Cognition and performance.* Berlin: Springer.

Feather, N. T. (1961). The relationship of persistence at a task to expectation of success and achievement-related motives. *Journal of Abnormal and Social Psychology, 63,* 552–561.

Feather, N. T. (1963a). Persistence at a difficult task with alternative task of immediate difficulty. *Journal of Abnormal and Social Psychology, 66,* 604–609.

Feather, N. T. (1963b). The relationship of expectation of success to reported probability, task structure, and achievement-related motivation. *Journal of Abnormal and Social Psychology, 66,* 231–238.

Feather, N. T. (1963c). The effect of differential failure on expectation of success, reported anxiety, and response uncertainty. *Journal of Personality, 31,* 289–312.

Feather, N. T. (1965). Performance at a difficult task in relation to initial expectation of success, test anxiety, and need achievement. *Journal of Personality, 33*, 200–217.

Feather, N. T. (1966). Effects of prior success and failure on expectation of success and subsequent performance. *Journal of Personality and Social Psychology, 3*, 287–298.

Feather, N. T. (1967). Valence of outcome and expectations of success in relation to task difficulty and perceived locus of control. *Journal of Personality and Social Psychology, 7*, 552–561.

Feather, N. T. (1968). Change in confidence following success or failure as a predictor of subsequent performance. *Journal of Personality and Social Psychology, 9*, 38–46.

Feather, N. T. (1969). Attribution of responsibility and valence of success and failure in relation to initial confidence and task performance. *Journal of Personality and Social Psychology, 13*, 129–144.

Feather, N. T. (1982). Actions in relation to expected consequences. In N. T. Feather (Ed.), *Expectations and actions*. Hillsdale, NJ: Erlbaum.

Feather, N. T., & Seville, M. R. (1967). Effects of amount of prior success and failure on expectations of success and subsequent task performance. *Journal of Personality and Social Psychology, 5*, 226–232.

Feather, N. T., & Simon, J. G. (1971). Causal attribution for success and failure in relation to expectations of success. *Journal of Personality, 39*, 527–544.

Federoff, N. A., & Harvey, J. H. (1976). Focus of attention, self-esteem, and the attribution of causality. *Journal of Research in Personality, 10*, 336–345.

Feinberg, R. A., Miller, F. G., Weiss, R. F., Steigleder, M. K., & Lombardo, J. P. (1982). Motivational aspects of learned helplessness. *Journal of General Psychology, 106*, 273–311.

Felton, B. S., & Revenson, T. A. (1984). Coping with chronic illness: A study of illness controllability and the influence of coping strategies on psychological adjustment. *Journal of Consulting and Clinical Psychology, 52*, 343–353.

Feltz, D. L., Landers, D. M., & Raeder, V. (1979). Enhancing self-efficacy in high avoidance motor tasks. *Journal of Sport Psychology, 1*, 112–122.

Fenell, M. J., & Teasdale, J. D. (1984). Effects of distraction on thinking and affect in depressed patients. *British Journal of Clinical Psychology, 23*, 65–66.

Fenell, M. J., Teasdale, J. D., Jones, S., & Damle, A. (1987). Distraction in neurotic and endogenous depression: An investigation of negative thinking in major depressive disorder. *Psychological Medicine, 17*, 441–452.

Fenigstein, A., & Carver, C. S. (1978). Self-focusing effects of false heartheat feedback. *Journal of Personality and Social Psychology, 36*, 1241–1250.

Fenigstein, A., & Levine, M. P. (1984). Self-attention, concept activation, and the causal self. *Journal of Experimental Social Psychology, 20*, 231–245.

Fenigstein, A., Scheier, M. F., & Buss, A. (1975). Public and private self-consciousness: Assessment and theory. *Journal of Consulting and Clinical Psychology, 43*, 522–527.

Fitch, G. (1970). Effects of self-esteem, perceived performance, and choice on causal attribution. *Journal of Personality and Social Psychology, 16*, 311–315.

Fleishman, J. A. (1984). Personality characteristics and coping patterns. *Journal of Health and Social Behavior, 25*, 372–393.

Fleming, J., & Arrowood, A. J. (1979). Information processing and the perseverance of discredited self-perceptions. *Personality and Social Psychology Bulletin, 5*, 201–205.

Flett, G. L., Blankstein, K. R., & Boase, P. (1987). Self-focused attention in test anxiety and depression. *Journal of Social Behavior and Personality, 2*, 259–266.

Flett, G. L., Boase, P., McAndrews, M. P., & Blankstein, K. R. (1986). Affect intensity and self-consciousness in college students. *Psychological Reports, 58*, 148–150.

Foa, E. B., & Kozak, M. S. (1986). Emotional processing of fear: Exposure to corrective information. *Psychological Bulletin, 99*, 20–35.

Folkman, S. (1984). Personal control and stress and coping processes: A theoretical analysis. *Journal of Personality and Social Psychology, 46*, 839–852.

Folkman, S., & Lazarus, R. S. (1980). An analysis of coping in a middle-aged community sample. *Journal of Health and Social Behavior, 21*, 219–239.

Folkman, S., & Lazarus, R. S. (1985). If it changes it must be a process: Study of emotion and coping during three stages of a colleague examination. *Journal of Personality and Social Psychology, 48*, 150–170.

Folkman, S., & Lazarus, R. S. (1988). Coping as a mediator of emotion. *Journal of Personality and Social Psychology, 54*, 466–475.

Folkman, S., Lazarus, R. S., Dunkel-Schetter, C., DeLongis, A., & Gruen, R. J. (1986). Dynamics of stressful encounter: Cognitive appraisal, coping, and encounter outcomes. *Journal of Personality and Social Psychology, 50*, 992–1003.

Follete, V. M., & Jacobson, N. S. (1987). Importance of attributions as a predictor of how people cope with failure. *Journal of Personality and Social Psychology, 52*, 1205–1211.

Ford, C. E., & Neale, J. M. (1985). Learned helplessness and judgments of control. *Journal of Personality and Social Psychology, 49*, 1330–1336.

Forsterling, F. (1985). Attributional retraining: A review. *Psychological Bulletin, 98*, 495–512.

Forsythe, C. J., & Compas, B. E. (1987). Interaction of cognitive appraisals of stressful events and coping: Testing the goodness of fit hypothesis. *Cognitive Therapy and Research, 11*, 473–485.

Foushee, H. C., Davis, M. H., Stephan, W. G., & Bernstein, W. M. (1980). The effects of cognitive and behavioral control on post-stress performance. *Journal of Human Stress, 6*, 41–48.

Fowler, J. W., & Peterson, P. L. (1981). Increasing reading persistence and altering attributional style of learned helpless children. *Journal of Educational Psychology, 73*, 251–260.

Fox, P. E., & Oakes, W. F. (1984). Learned helplessness: Noncontingent reinforcement in video game performance produces a decrement in performance on a lexical decision task. *Bulletin of the Psychonomic Society, 22*, 113–116.

Frankel, A., & Snyder, M. L. (1978). Poor performance following unsolvable problems: Learned helplessness or egotism? *Journal of Personality and Social Psychology, 36*, 1415–1423.

Franzoi, S. L., & Sweeney, P. D. (1986). Another look at the relation between private self-consciousness and self-attribution. *Journal of Research in Personality, 20*, 187–206.

Freud, S. (1957). Repression. In J. Strachey (Ed. and Trans.), *The standard edition of the complete psychological works of Sigmund Freud* (Vol. 14, pp. 146–158). London: Hogarth. (Original work published in 1914)

Frijda, N. H. (1986). *The emotions.* New York: Cambridge University Press.

Frijda, N. H., Kuipers, P., & Ter-Schure, E. (1989). Relations among emotion, appraisal, and emotional action readiness. *Journal of Personality and Social Psychology, 57*, 212–228.

Frone, M. R., & McFarlin, D. B. (1989). Chronic occupational stressors, self-focused attention, and well-being: Testing a cybernetic model of stress. *Journal of Applied Psychology, 74*, 876–883.

Fulkerson, K. F., Galassi, J. P., & Galassi, M. D. (1984). Relation between cognitions and performance in math anxious students: A failure of cognitive theory. *Journal of Counseling Psychology, 31*, 376–382.

Ganellen, R. J. (1988). Specificity of attributions and overgeneralization in depression and anxiety. *Journal of Abnormal Psychology, 97*, 83–86.

Garber, J., Miller, S. M., & Abramson, L. Y. (1980). On the distinction between anxiety and depression: Perceived control, certainty, and probability of goal attainment. In J. Garber & M. E. P. Seligman (Eds.), *Human helplessness: Theory and applications.* New York: Academic Press.

Gatchel, R. J., McKinney, M. E., & Koebernick, L. F. (1977). Learned helplessness, depression, and physiological responding. *Psychophysiology, 14*, 25–31.

Gatchel, R. J., Paulus, P. R., & Maples, C. W. (1975). Learned helplessness and self-reported affect. *Journal of Abnormal Psychology, 84*, 732–734.

Gatchel, R. J., & Proctor, J. P. (1976). Physiological correlates of learned helplessness in man. *Journal of Abnormal Psychology, 85*, 27–34.

Geen, R. G. (1980). Test anxiety and cue utilization. In I. G. Sarason (Ed.), *Test anxiety: Theory, research, and applications* (pp. 43–61). Hillsdale, NJ: Erlbaum.

Geen, R. G. (1987). Test anxiety and behavioral avoidance. *Journal of Research in Personality, 21*, 481–488.

Gentry, W. D., & Kobasa, S. C. (1984). Social and psychological resources mediating stress–illness relationships in humans. In W. D. Gentry (Ed.), *Handbook of behavioral medicine* (pp. 87–116). New York: Guilford.

Gerby, Y. (1991). *Practice of aerobic exercise and eating a sugar snack as means of reducing the learned helplessness reaction.* Unpublished master's thesis, Bar-Ilan University, Israel.

Gerlsma, C., & Albersnagel, F. A. (1987). Effects of (non-)contingency in a learned helplessness experiment: A re-analysis based on mood changes. *Behavior Research and Therapy, 25,* 329–340.

Gibbons, F. X. (1983). Self-attention and self-report: The "veridicality" hypothesis. *Journal of Personality, 51,* 517–542.

Gibbons, F. X. (1990). Self-attention and behavior: A review and theoretical update. In L. Berkowitz (Ed.), *Advances in experimental social psychology* (Vol. 23, pp. 249–303). New York: Academic Press.

Gibbons, F. X., Carver, C. S., Scheier, M. F., & Hormuth, S. E. (1979). Self-focused attention and the placebo effect: Fooling some of the people some of the time. *Journal of Experimental Social Psychology, 15,* 263–274.

Gibbons, F. X., & Gerrard, M. (1989). Effects of upward and downward social comparison on mood states. *Journal of Social and Clinical Psychology, 8,* 14–31.

Gibbons, F. X., & McCoy, S. B. (1991). Self-esteem, similarity, and reactions to active versus passive downward comparison. *Journal of Personality and Social Psychology, 60,* 414–424.

Gibbons, F. X., Smith, T. W., Ingram, R. E., Pearce, K., Brehm, S. S., & Schroeder, D. J. (1985). Self-awareness and self-confrontation: Effects of self-focused attention on members of a clinical population. *Journal of Personality and Social Psychology, 48,* 662–675.

Gibbons, F. X., & Wicklund, R. A. (1976). Selective exposure to self. *Journal of Research in Personality, 10,* 98–106.

Gilat, E. (1992). *Self complexity, excuse making, and learned helplessness.* Unpublished master's thesis, Bar-Ilan University, Israel.

Glass, D. C. (1977). *Behavior patterns, stress, and coronary disease.* Hillsdale, NJ: Erlbaum.

Glass, D. C., & Carver, C. S. (1980). Helplessness and the coronary-prone personality. In J. Garber & M. E. P. Seligman (Eds.), *Human helplessness: Theory and applications.* New York: Academic Press.

Glass, D. C., Reim, B., & Singer, J. R. (1971). Behavioral consequences of adaptation to controllable and uncontrollable noise. *Journal of Experimental Social Psychology, 7,* 244–257.

Glass, D. C., & Singer, J. E. (1972). *Urban stress: Experiments on noise and social stressors.* New York: Academic Press.

Goetz, T. E., & Dweck, C. S. (1980). Learned helplessness in social situations. *Journal of Personality and Social Psychology, 39,* 246–255.

Good, R. A. (1957). *The potentiality for change of an expectancy as a function of experience.* Unpublished doctoral dissertation, Ohio State University.

Goodkind, F. (1976). Rats learn the relationship between responding and environmental events: An expansion of the learned helplessness hypothesis. *Learning and Motivation, 7,* 382–393.

Gould, D., & Weiss, M. (1981). Effect of model similarity and model self-talk on self-efficacy in muscular endurance. *Journal of Sport Psychology, 3,* 17–29.

Green, J. C. (1985). Relationships among learning and attribution theory motivational variables. *American Educational Research Journal, 22,* 65–78.

Greenberg, J., & Musham, C. (1981). Avoiding and seeking self-focused attention. *Journal of Research in Personality, 15,* 191–200.

Greenberg, J., & Pyszczynski, T. (1985). Compensatory self-inflation: A response to the threat to self-regard of public failure. *Journal of Personality and Social Psychology, 49,* 273–280.

Greenberg, J., & Pyszczynski, T. (1986). Persistent high self-focus after failure and low self-focus after success: The depressive self-focusing style. *Journal of Personality and Social Psychology, 50,* 1039–1044.

Greer, S. E., & Calhoun, J. F. (1983). Learned helplessness and depression in acutely distressed community residents. *Cognitive Therapy and Research, 7*, 205–223.

Gregory, W. L., Chartier, G. M., & Wright, J. H. (1979). Learned helplessness and learned effectiveness: Effects of explicit response cues on individual differing in personal control expectancies. *Journal of Personality and Social Psychology, 37*, 1982–1992.

Griffith, M. (1977). Effects of noncontingent success and failure on mood and performance. *Journal of Personality, 45*, 442–457.

Grove, J. R., & Pargman, D. (1986). Attributions and performance during competition. *Journal of Sport Psychology, 8*, 129–134.

Haan, N. (1977). *Coping and defending.* New York: Academic Press.

Hackett, G., & Betz, N. E. (1984). *Gender differences in the effects of relevant and irrelevant task failure on mathematics self-efficacy expectations.* Paper presented at the annual meeting of the American Educational Research Association, New Orleans.

Hackett, G., Betz, N. E., O'Halloran, M. S., & Romac, D. S. (1990). Effects of verbal and mathematics task performance on task- and career self-efficacy and interest. *Journal of Counseling Psychology, 37*, 169–177.

Hagan, M. L., & Medway, F. J. (1989). Learned helplessness versus egotism in females: A developmental comparison. *Journal of Educational Research, 82*, 178–186.

Hamilton, V. (1975). Socialization anxiety and information processing: A capacity model of anxiety-induced performance deficits. In I. G. Saranson & C. D. Spielberger (Eds.), *Stress and anxiety* (Vol. 2). New York: Wiley.

Hammen, C., Adrian, C., & Hiroto, D. (1988). A longitudinal test of the attributional vulnerability model in children at risk for depression. *British Journal of Clinical Psychology, 27*, 37–46.

Hansen, R. D., Hansen, C. H., & Crano, W. D. (1989). Sympathetic arousal and self-attention: The accessibility of interoceptive and exteroceptive arousal cues. *Journal of Experimental Social Psychology, 25*, 437–449.

Hanson, C. L., Cigrang, J. A., Harris, M. A., & Carle, D. L. (1989). Coping styles in youths with insulin-dependent diabetes mellitus. *Journal of Consulting and Clinical Psychology, 57*, 644–651.

Hanusa, B. H., & Schultz, R. (1977). Attributional mediators of learned helplessness. *Journal of Personality and Social Psychology, 35*, 602–611.

Harris, F. A., & Tryon, W. W. (1983). Some necessary and sufficient conditions for the experimental induction of learned helplessness. *Journal of Social and Clinical Psychology, 1*, 15–26.

Harris, R. M., & Highlen, P. S. (1979). Conceptual complexity and susceptibility to learned helplessness. *Social Behavior and Personality, 10*, 183–188.

Hartmann, H. (1939). *Ego psychology and the problem of adaptation.* New York: International Universities Press.

Hasher, L., & Zacks, R. T. (1979). Automatic and effortful processes in memory. *Journal of Experimental Psychology, 108*, 356–388.

Headey, B. W., & Wearing, A. J. (1990). Subjective well-being and coping with adversity. *Social Indicators Research, 22*, 327–349.

Heath, D. (1961). Instructional sets as determinants of expectancy generalization. *Journal of General Psychology, 64*, 285–295.

Heaton, A. W., & Sigall, H. (1991). Self-consciousness, self-presentation, and performance under pressure: Who chokes, and when? *Journal of Applied Social Psychology, 21*, 175–188.

Hebb, D. O. (1949). *The organization of behavior.* New York: Wiley.

Heckhausen, H. (1977). Achievement motivation and its constructs: A cognitive model. *Motivation and Emotion, 1*, 283–330.

Heckhausen, H. (1982). Task-irrelevant cognitions during an exam: Incidence and effects. In H. Khrone & L. Laux (Eds.), *Achievement, stress, and anxiety* (pp. 247–274). Washington, DC: Hemisphere.

Heider, F. (1958). *The psychology of interpersonal relations.* New York: Wiley.

Helmrath, T. A., & Steinitz, E. M. (1978). Death of an infant: Parental grieving and the failure of social support. *Journal of Family Practice*, 785–790.

Herbert, P. (1990). *The influence of learned helplessness on the categorization process*. Unpublished master's thesis, Bar-Ilan University, Israel.

Higgins, E. T. (1987). Self-discrepancy: A theory relating self and affect. *Psychological Review*, 94, 319–340.

Hilton, B. A. (1989). The relationship of uncertainty, control, commitment, and threat of recurrence to coping strategies used by women diagnosed with breast cancer. *Journal of Behavioral Medicine*, 12, 39–54.

Hiroto, D. S. (1974). Locus of control and learned helplessness. *Journal of Experimental Psychology*, 102, 187–193.

Hiroto, D. S., & Seligman, M. E. P. (1975). Generality of learned helplessness in man. *Journal of Personality and Social Psychology*, 31, 311–322.

Hobfoll, S. E. (1989). Conservation of resources: A new attempt at conceptualizing stress. *American Psychologist*, 44, 513–524.

Hokanson, J. E., & Sacco, W. (1976). Subjective feelings and vascular responses in reaction to reduced control over aversiveness. *Perceptual and Motor Skills*, 43, 451–458.

Holahan, C. J., & Moos, R. H. (1987). Personal and contextual determinants of coping strategies. *Journal of Personality and Social Psychology*, 52, 946–955.

Holahan, C. J., & Moos, R. H. (1990). Life stressors, resistance factors, and improved psychological functioning: An extension of the stress resistance paradigm. *Journal of Personality and Social Psychology*, 58, 909–917.

Hollenbeck, J. R. (1989). Control theory and the perception of work environments: The effects of focus of attention on affective and behavioral reactions to work. *Organizational Behavior and Human Decision Processes*, 43, 406–430.

Hope, D. A., & Heimberg, R. G. (1988). Public and private self-consciousness and social phobia. *Journal of Personality Assessment*, 52, 626–639.

Horowitz, M. (1979). Psychological response to serious life events. In V. Hamilton & D. M. Warburton (Eds.), *Human stress and cognition: An information processing approach* (pp. 237–265). Chichester, England: Wiley.

Horowitz, M. (1982). Psychological processes induced by illness, injury, and loss. In T. Millon, C. Green, & R. Meagher (Eds.), *Handbook of clinical health psychology*. New York: Plenum.

Hull, J. G., & Levy, A. S. (1979). The organizational functions of the self: An alternative to Duval and Wicklund's model of self-awareness. *Journal of Personality and Social Psychology*, 37, 756–768.

Hull, J. G., & Young, R. D. (1983). Self-consciousness, self-esteem, and success–failure as determinants of alcohol consumption in male social drinkers. *Journal of Personality and Social Psychology*, 44, 1097–1109.

Hunsley, J. (1989). Vulnerability to depressive mood: An examination of the temporal consistency of the reformulated learned helplessness model. *Cognitive Therapy and Research*, 13, 599–608.

Ingram, R. E. (1984). Toward an information processing analysis of depression. *Cognitive Therapy and Research*, 8, 443–478.

Ingram, R. E. (1988). *Chronic internal attention as a risk factor for emotional distress*. Paper presented at the 96th annual meeting of the American Psychological Association, Atlanta, GA.

Ingram, R. E. (1990). Self-focused attention in clinical disorders: Review and a conceptual model. *Psychological Bulletin*, 103.

Ingram, R. E., Cruet, D., Johnson, B. R., & Wisnicki, K. S. (1988). Self-focused attention, gender, gender role, and vulnerability to negative affect. *Journal of Personality and Social Psychology*, 55, 967–978.

Ingram, R. E., Johnson, B. R., Bernet, C. Z., & Dombeck, M. (1992). Vulnerability to distress: Cognitive and emotional reactivity in chronically self-focused individuals. *Cognitive Therapy and Research*, 16, 451–472.

Ingram, R. E., Lumry, A. E., Cruet, D., & Sieber, W. (1987). Attentional processes in depressive disorders. *Cognitive Therapy and Research, 11*, 351–360.

Ingram, R. E., & Smith, T. W. (1984). Depression and internal versus external focus of attention. *Cognitive Therapy and Research, 8*, 139–152.

Isen, A. M. (1984). Toward understanding the role of affect in cognition. In R. S. Wyer & T. K. Srull (Eds.), *Handbook of social cognition* (Vol. 3, pp. 179–236). Hillsdale, NJ: Erlbaum.

Isen, A. M. (1987). Positive affect, cognitive processes, and social behavior. In L. Berkowitz (Ed.), *Advances in experimental social psychology* (Vol. 20, pp. 203–253). New York: Academic Press.

Izard, C. E. (1977). *Human emotions.* New York: Plenum.

Jackson, R. L., & Minor, T. R. (1988). Effects of signaling inescapable shock on subsequent escape learning: Implications for theories of coping and learned helplessness. *Journal of Experimental Psychology: Animal Behavior Processes, 14*, 390–400.

Jagacinski, C. M., & Nicholls, J. G. (1990). Reducing effort to protect perceived ability: "They'd do it but I wouldn't." *Journal of Educational Psychology, 82*, 15–21.

James, W. H., & Rotter, J. B. (1958). Partial and one hundred percent reinforcement under chance and skill conditions. *Journal of Experimental Psychology, 55*, 397–403.

Janis, I. L. (1958). *Psychological stress.* New York: Wiley.

Janoff-Bulman, R., & Brickman, P. (1982). Expectations and what people learn from failure. In N. T. Feather (Ed.), *Expectations and actions: Expectancy-value models in psychology.* Hillsdale, NJ: Erlbaum.

Jardine, E., & Winefeld, A. H. (1981). Achievement motivation, psychological reactance, and learned helplessness. *Motivation and Emotion, 5*, 99–113.

Jardine, E., & Winefeld, A. H. (1984). Performance differences following exposure to predictable and unpredictable noncontingent outcomes in high and low achievers. *Journal of Research in Personality, 18*, 508–521.

Jenkins, H. M., & Ward, W. C. (1965). Judgment of contingency between responses and outcomes. *Psychological Monographs: General and Applied, 79*, 1–17.

Jessor, R. (1954). The generalization of expectancies. *Journal of Abnormal and Social Psychology, 49*, 196–200.

Johnson, D. S. (1981). Naturally acquired learned helplessness: The relationship of school failure to achievement behavior, attribution, and self-concept. *Journal of Educational Psychology, 73*, 174–180.

Johnson, E. J., & Tverski, A. (1983). Affect, generalization, and the perception of risk. *Journal of Personality and Social Psychology, 45*, 20–31.

Jones, E. E., & Berglas, S. (1978). Control of attribution about the self through self-handicapping strategies: The appeal of alcohol and the role of underachievement. *Personality and Social Psychology Bulletin, 4*, 200–206.

Jones, S. L., Nation, J. R., & Massad, P. (1977). Immunization against learned helplessness in man. *Journal of Abnormal Psychology, 86*, 75–83.

Kahneman, D. (1973). *Attention and effort.* Englewood Cliffs, NJ: Prentice-Hall.

Kaloupek, D. G., & Stoupakis, T. (1985). Coping with a stressful medical procedure: Further investigation with volunteer blood donors. *Journal of Behavioral Medicine, 8*, 131–148.

Kaloupek, D. G., White, H., & Wong, M. (1984). Multiple assessment of coping strategies used by volunteer blood donors. *Journal of Behavioral Medicine, 7*, 35–60.

Kammer, D. (1983). Depression, attributional style, and failure generalization. *Cognitive Therapy and Research, 7*, 413–424.

Kanfer, F. H., & Hagerman, S. (1981). The role of self-regulation. In L. P. Rehm (Ed.), *Behavior therapy for depression.* New York: Academic Press.

Kavanagh, D. J., & Bower, G. H. (1985). Mood and self-efficacy: Impact of joy and sadness on perceived capabilities. *Cognitive Therapy and Research, 9*, 507–525.

Keller, C. (1988). Psychological and physical variables as predictors of coping strategies. *Perceptual and Motor Skills, 67*, 95–100.

Kelly, G. A. (1955). *The psychology of personal constructs* (Vol. 1). New York: Norton.

Kennelly, K. J., Hayslip, B., & Richardson, S. K. (1985). Depression and helplessness-induced cognitive deficits in the aged. *Experimental Aging Research, 11,* 169–173.

Kernis, M. H., Zuckerman, M., Cohen, A., & Spadofora, S. (1982). Persistence following failure: The interactive role of self-awareness and attributional bias for negative expectancies. *Journal of Personality and Social Psychology, 43,* 1184–1191.

Kernis, M. H., Zuckerman, M., & McVay, E. (1988). Motivational factors affecting performance: The impact of perceived locus of causality. *Personality and Social Psychology Bulletin, 14,* 524–535.

Kilpatrick-Tabak, B., & Roth, S. (1978). An attempt to reverse performance deficits associated with depression and experimentally induced helplessness. *Journal of Abnormal Psychology, 87,* 141–154.

Kirsch, I. (1986). Early research on self-efficacy: What we already know without knowing we knew. *Journal of Social and Clinical Psychology, 4,* 339–358.

Kistner, J. A., Osborne, M., & Le-Verrier, L. (1988). Causal attributions of learning-disabled children: Developmental patterns and relation to academic progress. *Journal of Educational Psychology, 80,* 82–89.

Klein, D. C., Fencil-Morse, E., & Seligman, M. E. P. (1976). Depression, learned helplessness, and the attribution of failure. *Journal of Personality and Social Psychology, 33,* 508–516.

Klein, D. C., & Seligman, M. E. P. (1976). Reversal of performance deficits and perceptual deficits in learned helplessness and depression. *Journal of Abnormal Psychology, 85,* 11–26.

Klinger, E. (1975). Consequences of commitment to and disengagement from incentives. *Psychological Review, 82,* 1–25.

Klinger, E. (1977). *Meaning and void: Inner experience and the incentives in people's lives.* Minneapolis: University of Minnesota Press.

Klinger, E. (1984). A consciousness sampling analysis of test anxiety and performance. *Journal of Personality and Social Psychology, 46,* 1376–1390.

Klinger, E., Barta, S. G., & Maxeiner, M. E. (1980). Motivational correlates of thought content frequency and commitment. *Journal of Personality and Social Psychology, 39,* 1222–1237.

Klonowicz, T. (1987). Reactivity and the control of arousal. In J. Strelau & H. J. Eysenck (Eds.), *Personality dimensions and arousal.* New York: Plenum.

Knott, P. D., Nunally, J. C., & Duchnowski, A. J. (1967). Effects of frustration on primary and conditioned incentive value. *Journal of Experimental Research in Personality, 2,* 140–149.

Kobasa, S. C. (1982). Commitment and coping in stress resistance among lawyers. *Journal of Personality and Social Psychology, 42,* 707–717.

Kofta, M., & Sedek, G. (1989). Repeated failure: A source of helplessness or a factor irrelevant to its emergence? *Journal of Experimental Psychology: General, 118,* 3–12.

Koller, P. S., & Kaplan, R. M. (1978). A two-process theory of learned helplessness. *Journal of Personality and Social Psychology, 36,* 1177–1183.

Kramer, M. E., & Rosellini, R. A. (1982). Universal and personal helplessness: A test of the reformulated model. *Psychological Record, 32,* 329–336.

Krantz, D. S., Glass, D. C., & Snyder, M. L. (1974). Helplessness, stress level, and the coronary-prone behavior pattern. *Journal of Experimental Social Psychology, 10,* 284–300.

Kruglanski, A. (1989). *Lay epistemics and human knowledge: Cognitive and motivational bases.* New York: Plenum.

Kruglanski, A., & Freund, T. (1983). The freezing and unfreezing of lay-inferences: Effects on impressional primacy, ethnic stereotyping, and numerical anchoring. *Journal of Experimental Social Psychology, 19,* 448–468.

Kuhl, J. (1981). Motivational and functional helplessness: The moderating effect of state versus action orientation. *Journal of Personality and Social Psychology, 40,* 155–170.

Kuhl, J. (1982). The expectancy-value approach in the theory of social motivation: Elaborations, extensions, critique. In N. T. Feather (Ed.), *Expectations and actions: Expectancy-value models in psychology*. Hillsdale, NJ: Erlbaum.

Kuhl, J. (1984). Volitional aspects of achievement motivation and learned helplessness: Towards a comprehensive theory of action control. In B. Maher (Ed.), *Progress in experimental personality research* (Vol. 13, pp. 99–171). New York: Academic Press.

Kuhl, J. (1985). Volitional mediators of cognition-behavior consistency: Self-regulatory processes and action versus state orientation. In J. Kuhl & D. Beckmann (Eds.), *Action control: From cognition to behavior* (pp. 101–128). New York: Springer-Verlag.

Kuhl, J., & Eisenbeiser, T. (1986). Mediating versus meditating cognitions in human motivation: Action control, inertial tendencies, and the alienation effect. In J. Kuhl & J. W. Atkinson (Eds.), *Motivation, thought, and action*. New York: Praeger.

Kuhl, J., & Wassiljew, I. (1983). *Intrinsic task involvement, coping with failure, and problem solving: Motivational and emotional determinants of the complexity of action plans*. Unpublished manuscript, Max Planck Institute, Munich.

Kuhl, J., & Weiss, G. (1983). *Performance deficits following uncontrollable failure: Impaired action control or global attributions and generalized expectancy deficits*. Unpublished manuscript, Max Planck Institute, Munich.

Kuiper, N. A., Olinger, L. J., & Air, P. A. (1989). Stressful events, dysfunctional attitudes, coping styles, and depression. *Personality and Individual Differences, 10*, 229–237.

Kukla, A. (1972). Attributional determinants of achievement related behavior. *Journal of Personality and Social Psychology, 21*, 166–174.

Lamb, D. G., Davis, S. F., Tramill, J. L., & Kleinhammer-Tramill, P. J. (1987). Noncontingent reward induced learned helplessness in humans. *Psychological Reports, 61*, 559–564.

Langer, E. (1975). The illusion of control. *Journal of Personality and Social Psychology, 32*, 311–328.

Lanoue, J. B., & Curtis, R. C. (1985). Improving women's performance in mixed-sex situations by effort attributions. *Psychology of Women Quarterly, 9*, 337–356.

Larsen, R. J., & Diener, E. (1987). Affect intensity as an individual difference characteristic: A review. *Journal of Research in Personality, 21*, 1–39.

Lavelle, T. L., Metalsky, G. I., & Coyne, J. C. (1979). Learned helplessness, test anxiety, and acknowledgment of contingencies. *Journal of Abnormal Psychology, 88*, 381–387.

Lazarus, R. S. (1983). The costs and benefits of denial. In S. Breznitz (Ed.), *The denial of stress* (pp. 1–30). New York: International Universities Press.

Lazarus, R. S. (1991). *Emotion and adaptation*. New York: Oxford University Press.

Lazarus, R. S., & Folkman, S. (1984). *Stress, appraisal, and coping*. New York: Springer.

Leary, M. R. (1986). The impact of interactional impediments on social anxiety and self-presentation. *Journal of Experimental Social Psychology, 22*, 122–135.

Leary, M. R., & Shepperd, J. A. (1986). Behavioral self-handicaps versus self-reported handicaps: A conceptual note. *Journal of Personality and Social Psychology, 51*, 1265–1268.

Lee, R. K., & Maier, S. F. (1988). Inescapable shock and attention to internal versus external cues in a water discrimination escape task. *Journal of Experimental Psychology: Animal Behavior Processes, 14*, 302–310.

Levis, D. J. (1976). Learned helplessness: A reply and an alternative S–R interpretation, *Journal of Experimental Psychology: General, 105*, 47–65.

Lewin, K. (1936). *Principles of topological psychology*. New York: McGraw-Hill.

Licht, B. G., & Dweck, C. S. (1984). Determinants of academic achievement: The interaction of children's achievement orientations with skill area. *Developmental Psychology, 20*, 628–636.

Liebert, R. M., & Morris, L. W. (1967). Cognitive and emotional components of test anxiety: A distinction and some initial data. *Psychological Reports, 20*, 975–978.

Lindemann, E. (1944). Symptomatology and management of acute grief. *American Journal of Psychiatry, 101*.

Liu, T. J., & Steele, C. M. (1986). Attributional analysis as self-affirmation. *Journal of Personality and Social Psychology, 51*, 531–540.

Locascio, J. J., & Snyder, C. R. (1975). Selective attention to threatening stimuli and field independence as factors in etiology of paranoid behavior. *Journal of Abnormal Psychology, 84*, 637–643.

Locke, E. A., Frederick, E., Lee, C., & Bolko, P. (1984). Effects of self-efficacy, goals, and task strategies on task performance. *Journal of Applied Psychology, 69*, 241–251.

Logan, G. D. (1989). Automaticity and cognitive control. In J. S. Uleman & J. A. Bargh (Eds.), *Unintended thought*. New York: Guilford.

Long, B. C., & Haney, C. J. (1988). Coping strategies for working women: Aerobic exercise and relaxation interventions. *Behavior Therapy, 19*, 75–83.

Lovallo, W. R., & Pishkin, V. (1980). Performance of Type A (coronary prone) men during and after exposure to uncontrollable noise and task failure. *Journal of Personality and Social Psychology, 38*, 963–971.

Lubow, R. E., Rosemblat, R., & Weiner, I. (1981). Confounding of controllability in the triadic design for demonstrating learned helplessness. *Journal of Personality and Social Psychology, 41*, 458–469.

Mages, N. L., & Mendelsohn, G. A. (1979). Effects of cancer on patients' lives: A personological approach. In C. C. Stone, F. Cohen, & N. E. Adler (Eds.), *Health psychology: A handbook*. San Francisco: Jossey-Bass.

Mahler, S. (1933). Eisatzhandliger werschiedener realitatgrade. *Psychologishen Forsh, 18*, 27–82.

Maier, S. F., & Jackson, R. L. (1979). Learned helplessness: All of us were right (and wrong): Inescapable shock has multiple effects. In G. H. Bower (Ed.), *The psychology of learning and motivation* (Vol. 13, pp. 155–218). New York: Academic Press.

Maier, S. F., & Seligman, M. E. P. (1976). Learned helplessness: Theory and evidence. *Journal of Experimental Psychology: General, 105*, 3–46.

Major, B., Mueller, P., & Hildebrandt, K. (1985). Attributions, expectations, and coping with abortion. *Journal of Personality and Social Psychology, 48*, 585–599.

Mandler, G. (1972). Helplessness: Theory and research in anxiety. In C. D. Spielberger (Ed.), *Anxiety: Current trends in theory and research* (Vol. 2). New York: Academic Press.

Mandler, G. (1975). *Mind and emotion*. New York: Wiley.

Mandler, G. (1980). The generation of emotion: A psychological theory. In R. Plutchik & H. Kellerman (Eds.), *Emotion: Theory, research, and experience* (Vol. 1). New York: Academic Press.

Mandler, G., & Sarason, S. B. (1952). A study of anxiety and learning. *Journal of Abnormal and Social Psychology, 47*, 166–173.

Manning, M. M., & Wright, T. L. (1983). Self-efficacy expectancies, outcome expectancies, and the persistence of pain control in childbirth. *Journal of Personality and Social Psychology, 45*, 421–431.

Margalit, N., & Zilberberg, E. (1991). *Misattribution and learned helplessness*. Unpublished manuscript, Bar-Ilan University, Israel.

Marris, P. (1974). *Loss and change*. New York: Pantheon.

Martelli, M. F., Auerbach, S. M., Alexander, J., & Mercuri, L. G. (1987). Stress management in the health care setting: Matching interventions with patient coping styles. *Journal of Consulting and Clinical Psychology, 55*, 201–207.

Martin, L. L., & Tesser, A. (1989). Toward a motivational and structural theory of ruminative thought. In J. S. Uleman & J. A. Bargh (Eds.), *Unintended thought*. New York: Guilford.

Mattlin, J. A., Wethington, E., & Kessler, R. C. (1990). Situational determinants of coping and coping effectiveness. *Journal of Health and Social Behavior, 31*, 103–122.

McAuley, E., & Duncan, T. E. (1989). Causal attributions and affective reactions to disconfirming outcomes in motor performance. *Journal of Sport and Exercise Psychology, 11*, 187–200.

McCrae, R. R. (1984). Situational determinants of coping responses: Loss, threat, and challenge. *Journal of Personality and Social Psychology, 46*, 918–928.

McCrae, R. R., & Costa, R. T. (1986). Personality, coping, and coping effectiveness in an adult sample. *Journal of Personality, 54*, 385–405.

McDonald, P. J. (1980). Reactions to objective self-awareness. *Journal of Research in Personality, 14,* 250–260.

McFarland, C., & Ross, M. (1982). Impact of causal attribution on affective reactions to success and failure. *Journal of Personality and Social Psychology, 43,* 937–946.

McFarlin, D. B., Baumeister, R. F., & Blascovich, J. (1984). On knowing when to quit: Task failure, self-esteem, advice, and nonproductive persistence. *Journal of Personality, 52,* 138–155.

McFarlin, D. B., & Blascovich, J. (1981). Effects of self-esteem and performance feedback on future affective preferences and cognitive expectations. *Journal of Personality and Social Psychology, 40,* 521–531.

McLelland, D. C., Atkinson, J. W., Clark, R. A., & Lowell, E. L. (1953). *The achievement motive.* New York: Irvington.

McNally, R. J. (1990). Psychological approaches to panic disorder: A review. *Psychological Bulletin, 108,* 403–419.

McReynolds, W. T. (1980). Learned helplessness as a schedule shift effect. *Journal of Research in Personality, 14,* 139–157.

Mechanic, D. (1977). Illness behavior, social adaptation, and the management of illness. *Journal of Nervous and Mental Disease, 165,* 79–87.

Meece, J. L., Wigfield, A., & Eccles, J. S. (1990). Predictors of math anxiety and its influence on young adolescents' course enrollment intentions and performance in mathematics. *Journal of Educational Psychology, 82,* 60–70.

Mehlman, R. C., & Snyder, C. R. (1985). Excuse theory: A test of the self-protective role of attributions. *Journal of Personality and Social Psychology, 49,* 994–1001.

Meites, K., Pishkin, V., & Bourne, L. E. (1981). Anxiety and failure in concept identification. *Bulletin of the Psychonomic Society, 18,* 293–295.

Menaghan, E. (1982). Measuring coping effectiveness: A panel analysis of marital problems and coping efforts. *Journal of Health and Social Behavior, 23,* 220–234.

Metalsky, G. I., Abramson, L. Y., Seligman, M. E. P., Semmel, A., & Peterson, C. (1982). Attributional styles and life events in the classroom: Vulnerability and invulnerability to depressive mood reactions. *Journal of Personality and Social Psychology, 43,* 612–617.

Metalsky, G. I., Halberstadt, L. J., & Abramson, L. Y. (1987). Vulnerability to depressive mood reactions: Toward a more powerful test of the diathesis–stress and causal mediation components of the reformulated theory of depression. *Journal of Personality and Social Psychology, 52,* 386–393.

Metzger, R. L., Miller, M., Sofka, M., Cohen, M., & Pennock, M. (1983). *Information processing and worrying.* Paper presented at meeting of the Association for the Advancement of Behavior Therapy.

Meyer, N. E., & Dyck, D. G. (1986). Effects of reward-schedule parameters and attribution retraining on children's attributions and reading persistence. *Bulletin of the Psychonomic Society, 24,* 65–68.

Meyer, W. U. (1970). *Selbstanwortlichkeit und Leistungsmotivation.* Unpublished doctoral dissertation, Ruhr Universitat, Bochum, Germany.

Mikulincer, M. (1985). *A reformulation of human learned helplessness.* Doctoral dissertation, Bar-Ilan University.

Mikulincer, M. (1986a). Attributional processes in the learned helplessness paradigm: The behavioral effects of globality attributions. *Journal of Personality and Social Psychology, 51,* 1248–1256.

Mikulincer, M. (1986b). Motivational involvement and learned helplessness: The behavioral effects of the importance of uncontrollable events. *Journal of Social and Clinical Psychology, 4,* 402–422.

Mikulincer, M. (1988a). Reactance and helplessness following exposure to unsolvable problems: The effects of attributional style. *Journal of Personality and Social Psychology, 54,* 679–686.

Mikulincer, M. (1988b). The relation between stable/unstable attribution and learned helplessness, *British Journal of Social Psychology, 27,* 470–478.

Mikulincer, M. (1988c). A case study of three theories of learned helplessness: The role of test importance. *Motivation and Emotion, 12,* 371–383.

Mikulincer, M. (1988d). The relationship of probability of success and performance following unsolvable problems: Reactance and helplessness effects. *Motivation and Emotion, 12,* 139–153.

Mikulincer, M. (1989a). Cognitive interference and learned helplessness: The effects of off-task cognitions on performance following unsolvable problems. *Journal of Personality and Social Psychology,* 57, 129–135.

Mikulincer, M. (1989b). Causal attribution, coping strategies, and learned helplessness. *Cognitive Therapy and Research,* 13, 565–582.

Mikulincer, M. (1989c). Coping and learned helplessness: Effects of coping strategies on performance following unsolvable problems. *European Journal of Personality,* 3, 181–194.

Mikulincer, M. (1989d). Learned helplessness and egotism: Effects of internal/external attribution on performance following unsolvable problems. *British Journal of Social Psychology,* 28, 17–29.

Mikulincer, M. (1990). Joint influence of prior beliefs and current situational information on stable and unstable attributions. *Journal of Social Psychology,* 130, 739–753.

Mikulincer, M., & Ben-Artzi, E. (1990). *Lay theories of emotion.* Unpublished manuscript, Bar-Ilan University.

Mikulincer, M., Bizman, A., & Aizenberg, R. (1989). An attributional analysis of social-comparison jealousy. *Motivation and Emotion,* 13, 235–258.

Mikulincer, M., & Caspy, T. (1986). The conceptualization of helplessness: I. A phenomenological-structural analysis. *Motivation and Emotion,* 10, 263–278.

Mikulincer, M., Gerber, H., & Weisenberg, M. (1990). Judgment of control and depression: The role of self-esteem threat and self-focused attention. *Cognitive Therapy and Research,* 14, 589–608.

Mikulincer, M., Glaubman, H., Ben-Artzi, E., & Grossman, S. (1991). The cognitive specificity of learned helplessness and depression deficits: The role of self-focused cognitions. *Anxiety Research,* 3, 273–290.

Mikulincer, M., Kedem, P., & Zilcha-Segal, H. (1989). Learned helplessness, reactance, and cue utilization. *Journal of Research in Personality,* 23, 235–247.

Mikulincer, M., & Marshand, O. (1991). An excuse perspective of the learned helplessness paradigm: The self-protective role of causal attribution. *Journal of Social and Clinical Psychology,* 10, 134–151.

Mikulincer, M., & Nizan, B. (1988). Causal attribution, cognitive interference, and the generalization of learned helplessness. *Journal of Personality and Social Psychology,* 55, 470–478.

Mikulincer, M., & Solomon, Z. (1989). Causal attribution, coping strategies, and combat-related post-traumatic stress disorder. *European Journal of Personality,* 3, 269–284.

Miller, A. (1985). A developmental study of the cognitive basis of performance impairment after failure. *Journal of Personality and Social Psychology,* 49, 529–538.

Miller, A. (1986). Performance impairment after failure: Mechanism and sex differences. *Journal of Educational Psychology,* 78, 486–491.

Miller, A., & Hom, H. L. (1990). Influence of extrinsic and ego incentive value on persistence after failure and continuing motivation. *Journal of Educational Psychology,* 82, 539–545.

Miller, A., & Klein, J. S. (1989). Individual differences in ego value of academic performance and persistence after failure. *Contemporary Educational Psychology,* 14, 124–132.

Miller, I. W., & Norman, W. H. (1979). Learned helplessness in humans: A review and attribution theory model. *Psychological Bulletin,* 86, 93–118.

Miller, I. W., & Norman, W. H. (1981). Effects of attributions for success on the alleviation of learned helplessness and depression. *Journal of Abnormal Psychology,* 90, 113–124.

Miller, R. T. (1976). Ego involvement and attribution for success and failure. *Journal of Personality and Social Psychology,* 34, 901–906.

Miller, S. (1980). When is a little knowledge a dangerous thing? Coping with stressful events by monitoring vs. blunting. In S. Levine & H. Ursin (Eds.), *Coping and health.* New York: Plenum.

Miller, S. M., Lack, E. R., & Asroff, S. (1985). Preference for control and the coronary-prone behavioral pattern: "I'd rather do it myself." *Journal of Personality and Social Psychology,* 49, 492–499.

Miller, W. R. (1975). Psychological deficit in depression. *Psychological Bulletin,* 82, 238–260.

Miller, W. R., & Seligman, M. E. P. (1975). Depression and learned helplessness in man. *Journal of Abnormal Psychology, 84,* 228–238.

Miller, W. R., & Seligman, M. E. P. (1976). Learned helplessness, depression and the perception of reinforcement. *Behavior Research and Therapy, 14,* 7–17.

Mills, R. T., & Krantz, D. S. (1979). Information, choice and reaction to stress: A field experiment in a blood bank and laboratory analogue. *Journal of Personality and Social Psychology, 37,* 608–620.

Minor, T. R., Trauner, M. A., Lee, C., & Dees, N. K. (1990). Modeling signal features of escape response: Effects of cessation conditioning in "learned helplessness" paradigm. *Journal of Experimental Psychology: Animal Behavior Processes, 16,* 123–136.

Mischel, W., & Masters, J. C. (1966). Effects of probability of reward attainment on responses to frustration. *Journal of Personality and Social Psychology, 3,* 390–396.

Monat, A., Averill, J. R., & Lazarus, R. S. (1972). Anticipatory stress and coping reactions under various conditions of uncertainty. *Journal of Personality and Social Psychology, 24,* 237–253.

Moos, R. H. (1984). Context and coping: Toward a unifying conceptual framework. *American Journal of Community Psychology, 12,* 5–25.

Moos, R. H., Brennan, P. L., Fondacaro, M. R., & Moos, B. S. (1990). Approach and avoidance coping responses among older problem and nonproblem drinkers. *Psychology and Aging, 5,* 31–40.

Morris, L. W., Davis, M. A., & Hutchings, C. H. (1981). Cognitive and emotional components of anxiety: Literature review and a revised Worry–Emotionality Scale. *Journal of Educational Psychology, 73,* 541–555.

Morris, L. W., & Fulmer, R. S. (1976). Test anxiety (worry and emotionality) changes during academic testing as a function of feedback and test importance. *Journal of Educational Psychology, 68,* 817–824.

Morris, L. W., & Liebert, R. M. (1970). Relationship of cognitive and emotional components of test anxiety to physiological arousal and academic performance. *Journal of Consulting and Clinical Psychology, 35,* 332–337.

Morris, L. W., & Liebert, R. M. (1973). Effects of negative feedback, threat of shock, and level of trait anxiety on the arousal of two components of anxiety. *Journal of Counseling Psychology, 20,* 321–326.

Mould, D. E. (1975). Differentiation between depression and anxiety. *Journal of Consulting and Clinical Psychology, 43,* 592.

Multon, K. D., Brown, S. D., & Lent, R. W. (1991). Relation of self-efficacy beliefs to academic outcomes: A meta-analytic investigation. *Journal of Consulting Psychology, 38,* 30–38.

Nadler, A. (1983). Objective self-awareness, self-esteem, and causal attribution for success and failure. *Personality and Individual Differences, 4,* 9–15.

Nasby, W. (1985). Private self-consciousness, articulation of the self-schema, and recognition memory of trait adjectives. *Journal of Personality and Social Psychology, 49,* 704–709.

Nation, J. R., & Cooney, J. B. (1980). The change and maintenance effectiveness of persistence training regarding the treatment of laboratory-induced and naturally occurring depression. *Bulletin of the Psychonomic Society, 16,* 121–124.

Nation, J. R., & Massad, P. (1978). Persistence training: A partial reinforcement procedure for reversing learned helplessness and depression. *Journal of Experimental Psychology: General, 107,* 436–451.

Nezu, A. M., & Carnevale, G. J. (1987). Interpersonal problem solving and coping reactions of Vietnam veterans with posttraumatic stress disorder. *Journal of Abnormal Psychology, 96,* 358–367.

Nicholls, J. G. (1978). The development of the concepts of efforts and ability, perception of academic attainment, and the understanding that difficult tasks require more ability. *Child Development, 49,* 800–814.

Noel, J. G., Forsyth, D. R., & Kelley, K. N. (1987). Improving the performance of failing students by overcoming their attributional biases. *Basic and Applied Social Psychology, 8,* 151–162.

Noel, N. E., & Lisman, S. A. (1980). Alcohol consumption by college women following exposure to unsolvable problems: Learned helplessness or stress induced drinking? *Behavior Research and Therapy, 18,* 429–440.

Nowack, K. M. (1989). Coping style, cognitive hardiness, and health status. *Journal of Behavioral Medicine, 12,* 145–158.

Oakes, W. F., & Curtis, N. (1982). Learned helplessness not dependent upon cognitions, attributions, or other such phenomenal experiences. *Journal of Personality, 50,* 387–408.

O'Leary, M. R., Donovan, D. M., Krueger, K. J., & Cysewski, B. (1978). Depression and the perception of reinforcement: Lack of differences in expectancy change among alcoholics. *Journal of Abnormal Psychology, 87,* 110–112.

Orbach, I., & Hadas, Z. (1982). The elimination of learned helplessness deficits as a function of induced self-esteem. *Journal of Research in Personality, 16,* 511–523.

O'Rourke, T. M., Tryon, W. W., & Raps, C. S. (1980). Learned helplessness, depression, and positive reinforcement. *Cognitive Therapy and Research, 4,* 201–209.

Overmaier, J. P., & Seligman, M. E. P. (1967). Effects of inescapable shock on subsequent escape and avoidance responding. *Journal of Comparative and Physiological Psychology, 63,* 28–33.

Parkes, K. R. (1984). Locus of control, cognitive appraisal and coping in stressful episodes. *Journal of Personality and Social Psychology, 46,* 655–668.

Parsons, J. E., & Ruble, D. (1977). The development of achievement related expectancies. *Child Development, 48,* 1075–1079.

Pasahow, R. J. (1980). The relation between an attributional dimension and learned helplessness. *Journal of Abnormal Psychology, 89,* 358–367.

Paz, D. (1989). *Anxiety and categorization.* Unpublished master's thesis, Bar-Ilan University, Israel.

Pearlin, L. I., Lieberman, M. A., Menaghan, E. G., & Mullan, J. T. (1981). The stress process. *Journal of Health and Social Behavior, 22,* 337–356.

Pearlin, L. I., & Schooler, C. (1978). The structure of coping. *Journal of Health and Social Behavior, 19,* 2–21.

Pennebaker, J. W., & Susman, J. R. (1988). Disclosure of traumas and psychosomatic processes. *Social Science and Medicine, 26,* 327–332.

Perry, R. P., & Penner, K. S. (1990). Enhancing academic achievement in college students through attributional retraining and instruction. *Journal of Educational Psychology, 82,* 262–271.

Peterson, C. (1978). Learning impairment following insoluble problems: Learned helplessness or altered hypothesis pool? *Journal of Experimental Social Psychology, 14,* 53–68.

Peterson, C. (1980). Recognition of noncontingency. *Journal of Personality and Social Psychology, 38,* 727–734.

Peterson, C. (1985). Learned helplessness: Fundamental issues in theory and research. *Journal of Social and Clinical Psychology, 3,* 248–254.

Peterson, C., & Barrett, L. C. (1987). Explanatory style and academic performance among university freshmen. *Journal of Personality and Social Psychology, 53,* 603–607.

Peterson, C., & Bossio, L. M. (1989). Learned helplessness. In R. C. Curtis (Ed.), *Self-defeating behaviors.* New York: Plenum.

Peterson, C., & Seligman, M. E. P. (1983). Learned helplessness and victimization. *Journal of Social Issues, 39,* 103–116.

Peterson, C., & Seligman, M. E. P. (1984). Causal explanations as a risk factor for depression: Theory and evidence. *Psychological Review, 91,* 347–374.

Peterson, P. L., Swing, S. R., Braverman, M. T., & Buss, R. R. (1982). Students' aptitudes and their reports of cognitive processes during direct instruction. *Journal of Educational Psychology, 74,* 535–547.

Phares, E. J. (1957). Expectancy change in chance and skill situations. *Journal of Abnormal and Social Psychology, 54,* 339–342.

Phares, E. J. (1961). Expectancy changes under conditions of relative massing and spacing on expectancies. *Psychological Reports, 8,* 199–206.

Phares, E. J. (1966). Delay, anxiety, and expectancy changes. *Psychological Reports, 18,* 679–682.

Pintrich, P. R. (1989). The dynamic interplay of student motivation and cognition in the college classroom. In C. Ames & M. Maehr (Eds.), *Advances in motivation and achievement* (Vol. 6, pp. 117–160). Greenwich, CT: JAI Press.

Pittman, N. L., & Pittman, T. S. (1979). Effects of amount of helplessness training and internal-external locus of control on mood and performance. *Journal of Personality and Social Psychology, 37,* 39–47.

Pittman, T. S., & D'Agostino, P. R. (1985). Motivation and attribution: The effects of control deprivation on subsequent information processing. In J. Harvey & G. Weary (Eds.), *Current perspectives on attribution research* (Vol. 1, pp. 117–138). New York: Academic Press.

Pittman, T. S., & D'Agostino, P. R. (1989). Motivation and cognition: Control deprivation and the nature of subsequent information processing. *Journal of Experimental Social Psychology, 25,* 465–480.

Pittman, T. S., & Heller, J. F. (1987). Social motivation. *Annual Review of Psychology, 38,* 461–489.

Pittman, T. S., & Pittman, N. L. (1980). Deprivation of control and the attribution process. *Journal of Personality and Social Psychology, 39,* 377–389.

Pittner, M. S., & Houston, B. K. (1980). Response to stress, cognitive coping strategies and the Type A behavior pattern. *Journal of Personality and Social Psychology, 39,* 147–157.

Pittner, M. S., Houston, B. K., & Spiridigliozzi, G. A. (1983). Control over stress, Type A behavior pattern, and response to stress. *Journal of Personality and Social Psychology, 44,* 627–637.

Plutchik, R. (1980). *Emotion: A psychoevolutionary synthesis.* New York: Harper & Row.

Polaino, L. A., & Villamisar, D. A. (1984). Experimental analysis of motivational and cognitive deficits due to learned helplessness in a sample of nondepressed adolescents. *Cuadernos de Psicologia, 8,* 7–34.

Porterfield, A. L., Mayer, F. S., Dougherty, K. G., & Kredich, K. E. (1988). Private self-consciousness, canned laughter, and responses to humorous stimuli. *Journal of Research in Personality, 22,* 409–423.

Price, K. P., Tryon, W. W., & Raps, C. S. (1978). Learned helplessness and depression in a clinical population: A test of two behavioral hypotheses. *Journal of Abnormal Psychology, 87,* 113–121.

Prindaville, P., & Stein, N. (1978). Predictability, controllability, and inoculation against learned helplessness. *Behavior Research and Therapy, 16,* 263–271.

Pryor, J. B., Gibbons, F. X., Wicklund, R. A., Fazio, R., & Hood, R. (1977). Self-focused attention and self-report validity. *Journal of Personality, 45,* 513–527.

Pyszczynski, T. A., & Greenberg, J. (1981). Role of disconfirmed expectancies in the instigation of attributional processing. *Journal of Personality and Social Psychology, 40,* 31–38.

Pyszczynski, T., & Greenberg, J. (1983). Determinants of reduction of intended effort as a strategy for coping with anticipated failure. *Journal of Research in Personality, 17,* 412–422.

Pyszczynski, T., & Greenberg, J. (1985). Depression and preference for self-focusing stimuli after success and failure. *Journal of Personality and Social Psychology, 49,* 1066–1075.

Pyszczynski, T., & Greenberg, J. (1986). Evidence for a depressive self-focusing style. *Journal of Research in Personality, 20,* 95–106.

Pyszczynski, T., & Greenberg, J. (1987). Self-regulatory perseveration and the depressive self-focusing style: A self awareness theory of reactive depression. *Psychological Bulletin, 102,* 1–17.

Rachman, S. (1980). Emotional processing. *Behavior Research and Therapy, 18,* 51–60.

Ramirez, E., Maldonado, A., & Martos, R. (1992). Attributions modulate immunization against learned helplessness in humans. *Journal of Personality and Social Psychology, 62,* 139–146.

Rapaport, D. (1942). *Emotion and memory.* New York: Science Editions.

Raps, C. S., Reinhard, K. E., & Seligman, M. E. P. (1980). Reversal of cognitive and affective deficits associated with depression and learned helplessness by mood elevation in patients. *Journal of Abnormal Psychology, 89,* 342–349.

Raynor, J. (1970). Relationships between achievement-related motives, future orientation, and academic performance. *Journal of Personality and Social Psychology, 15,* 28–33.

Reid, M. K., & Borkowski, J. G. (1987). Causal attribution of hyperactive children: Implications for training strategies and self-control. *Journal of Educational Psychology, 79,* 296–307.

Rhodewalt, F., Saltzman, A. T., & Wittmer, J. (1984). Self-handicapping among competitive athletes: The role of practice in self-esteem protection. *Basic and Applied Social Psychology, 5,* 197–210.

Rholes, W. S., Blackwell, J., Jordan, C., & Walters, C. (1980). A developmental study of learned helplessness. *Developmental Psychology, 16,* 616–624.

Rholes, W. S., Michas, L., & Smith, S. (1987). *Depression, action control, and coping.* Unpublished manuscript, Texas A & M University.

Rich, A. R., & Woolever, D. K. (1988). Expectancy and self-focused attention: Experimental support for the self-regulation model of test anxiety. *Journal of Social and Clinical Psychology, 7,* 246–259.

Rippetoe, P. A., & Rogers, R. W. (1987). Effects of components of protection-motivation theory on adaptive and maladaptive coping with a health threat. *Journal of Personality and Social Psychology, 52,* 596–604.

Riskind, J. H. (1984). They stoop to conquer: Guiding and self-regulatory functions of physical posture after success and failure. *Journal of Personality and Social Psychology, 47,* 479–493.

Riskind, J. H., Castellon, C. S., & Beck, A. T. (1989). Spontaneous causal explanations in unipolar depression and generalized anxiety: Content analysis of dysfunctional thought diaries. *Cognitive Therapy and Research, 13,* 97–108.

Robins, C. J. (1988). Attributions and depression: Why is the literature so inconsistent? *Journal of Personality and Social Psychology, 54,* 880–897.

Rocklin, T., & Thompson, J. M. (1985). Interactive effects of test anxiety, test difficulty, and feedback. *Journal of Educational Psychology, 77,* 368–372.

Rodin, J. (1986). Aging and health: Effects of the sense of control. *Science, 233,* 1271–1276.

Rolnick, A., & Lubow, R. E. (1991). Why is the driver rarely motion sick? The role of controllability in motion sickness. *Ergonomics, 34,* 867–879.

Roseman, I. J. (1984). Cognitive determinants of emotion: A structural theory. In P. Shaver (Ed.), *Review of personality and social psychology* (Vol. 5, pp. 11–36). Beverly Hills, CA: Sage.

Roseman, I. J., Spindel, M. S., & Jose, P. E. (1990). Appraisals of emotion-eliciting events: Testing a theory of discrete emotions. *Journal of Personality and Social psychology, 59,* 899–915.

Rosenbaum, M., & Ben-Ari, K. (1985). Learned helplessness and learned resourcefulness: Effects of noncontingent success and failure on individuals differing in self-control skills. *Journal of Personality and Social Psychology, 48,* 198–215.

Rosenbaum, M., & Jaffe, Y. (1983). Learned helplessness: The role of differences in learned resourcefulness. *British Journal of Social Psychology, 22,* 215–225.

Rosenfield, D., & Stephan, W. G. (1978). Sex differences in attributions for sex-typed tasks. *Journal of Personality, 46,* 244–259.

Roth, S. (1980). A revised model of learned helplessness in humans. *Journal of Personality, 48,* 103–133.

Roth, S., & Bootzin, R. R. (1974). Effects of experimentally induced expectancies of external control: An investigation of learned helplessness. *Journal of Personality and Social Psychology, 29,* 253–264.

Roth, S., & Cohen, L. J. (1986). Approach, avoidance, and coping with stress. *American Psychologist, 41,* 813–819.

Roth, S., & Kubal, L. (1975). Effects of noncontingent reinforcement on tasks of differing importance: Facilitation and learned helplessness. *Journal of Personality and Social Psychology, 32,* 680–691.

Rothbart, M. K., & Derryberry, D. (1981). Development of individual differences in temperament. In M. E. Lamb & A. L. Brown (Eds.), *Advances in developmental psychology* (Vol. 1, pp. 37–86). Hillsdale, NJ: Erlbaum.

Rothbaum, F., Weisz, J. R., & Snyder, S. S. (1982). Changing the world and changing the self: A two-process model of perceived control. *Journal of Personality and Social Psychology, 42,* 5–37.

Rothwell, N., & Williams, J. M. (1983). Attributional style and life events. *British Journal of Clinical Psychology, 22,* 139–140.

Rotter, J. B. (1954). *Social learning and clinical psychology.* Englewood Cliffs, NJ: Prentice-Hall.

Rotter, J. B. (1966). Generalized expectancies for internal versus external control of reinforcement. *Psychological Monographs, 80*(Whole No. 69).

Rotter, J. B., Liverant, S., & Crowne, D. P. (1961). The growth and extinction of expectancies in chance controlled and skilled tasks. *Journal of Psychology, 52,* 161–177.

Rozensky, R. H., Tovian, S. M., Stiles, P. G., Fridkin, K., & Holland, M. (1987). Effects of learned helplessness on Rorschach responses. *Psychological Reports, 60,* 1011–1016.

Russell, D., & McAuley, E. (1986). Causal attributions, causal dimensions, and affective reactions to success and failure. *Journal of Personality and Social Psychology, 50,* 1174–1185.

Rychlack, J. F. (1958). Task influence and the stability of generalized expectancies. *Journal of Experimental Psychology, 55,* 459–462.

Sadowski, C. J., & Blackwell, M. W. (1987). The relationship of locus of control to anxiety and coping among student teachers. *College Student Journal, 21,* 187–189.

Sarason, I. G. (1975). Anxiety and self preoccupation. In I. G. Sarason & C. D. Spielberger (Eds.), *Stress and anxiety* (Vol. 2, pp. 27–44). Washington, DC: Hemisphere.

Sarason, I. G. (1984). Stress, anxiety, and cognitive interference: Reactions to tests. *Journal of Personality and Social Psychology, 46,* 929–938.

Sarason, I. G., Sarason, B. R., Keefe, D. E., Hayes, B. E., & Shearin, E. N. (1986). Cognitive interference: Situational determinants and traitlike characteristics. *Journal of Personality and Social Psychology, 51,* 215–226.

Sarason, I. G., & Stoops, R. (1978). Test anxiety and the passage of time. *Journal of Consulting and Clinical Psychology, 46,* 102–109.

Sarfati, O. (1992). *The influence of positive emotion on cognitive processes.* Unpublished doctoral dissertation, Bar-Ilan University, Israel.

Scheier, M. F. (1976). Self-awareness, self-consciousness, and angry aggression. *Journal of Personality, 44,* 627–644.

Scheier, M. F. (1980). Effects of public and private self-consciousness on the public expression of personal beliefs. *Journal of Personality and Social Psychology, 39,* 514–521.

Scheier, M. F., Buss, A. H., & Buss, D. M. (1978). Self-consciousness, self-report of aggressiveness and aggression. *Journal of Research in Personality, 12,* 133–140.

Scheier, M. F., & Carver, C. S. (1977). Self-focused attention and the experience of emotion: Attraction, repulsion, elation, depression. *Journal of Personality and Social Psychology, 35,* 625–636.

Scheier, M. F., & Carver, C. S. (1982). Self-consciousness, outcome expectancy, and persistence. *Journal of Research in Personality, 16,* 409–418.

Scheier, M. F., & Carver, C. S. (1988). A model of behavioral self-regulation: Translating intention into action. In L. Berkowitz (Ed.), *Advances in experimental social psychology* (Vol. 21, pp. 303–346). New York: Academic Press.

Scheier, M. F., Carver, C. S., & Gibbons, M. F. (1981). Self-focused attention and reactions to fear. *Journal of Research in Personality, 15,* 1–15.

Scheier, M. F., Carver, C. S., & Matthews, K. A. (1982). Attentional factors in the perception of bodily states. In J. Cacciopo & R. Petty (Eds.), *Social psychophysiology* (pp. 510–542). New York: Guilford.

Scheier, M. F., Weintraub, J. K., & Carver, C. S. (1986). Coping with stress: Divergent strategies of optimists and pessimists. *Journal of Personality and Social Psychology, 51,* 1257–1264.

Scherer, K. R. (1984). Emotion as a multicomponent process: A model with some cross-cultural data. In P. Shaver (Ed.), *Review of personality and social psychology* (Vol. 5, pp. 37–63). Beverly Hills, CA: Sage.

Schmolling, P. (1984). Human reactions to the Nazi concentration camp. *Journal of Human Stress, 10*, 108–120.

Schontz, F. C. (1975). *The psychological aspects of physical illness and disability.* New York: Macmillan.

Schultz, R. (1980). Aging and control. In J. Garber & M. E. P. Seligman (Eds.), *Human helplessness: Theory and applications* (pp. 261–277). New York: Academic Press.

Schunk, D. (1985). Self-efficacy and school learning. *Psychology in the Schools, 22*, 208–223.

Schwartz, J. C. (1966). Influences upon expectancy during delay. *Journal of Experimental Research in Personality, 1*, 211–220.

Sedek, G., & Kofta, M. (1990). When cognitive exertion does not yield cognitive gain: Toward an informational explanation of learned helplessness. *Journal of Personality and Social Psychology, 58*, 729–743.

Seligman, M. E. P. (1975). *Helplessness: On depression, development and death.* San Francisco: Freeman.

Seligman, M. E. P., Abramson, L. Y., Semmel, A., & Von Baeyer, C. (1979). Depressive attributional style. *Journal of Abnormal Psychology, 88*, 242–247.

Seligman, M. E. P., & Maier, S. F. (1967). Failure to escape traumatic shock. *Journal of Experimental Psychology, 74*, 1–9.

Seligman, M. E. P., Maier, S. F., & Geer, J. (1968). The alleviation of learned helplessness in the dog. *Journal of Abnormal Psychology, 73*, 256–262.

Seligman, M. E. P., Maier, S. F., & Solomon, R. L. (1971). Unpredictable and uncontrollable aversive events. In F. R. Brush (Ed.), *Aversive conditioning and learning.* New York: Academic Press.

Seligman, M. E. P., Nolen-Hoeksema, S., Thornton, N., & Thornton, K. M. (1990). Explanatory style as a mechanism of disappointing athletic performance. *Psychological Science, 1*, 143–146.

Semel, E., & Newman, M. (1991). *The effects of relaxation techniques on the learned helplessness effect.* Unpublished manuscript, Bar-Ilan University, Israel.

Seta, J. J., & Seta, C. E. (1982). Personal equity: An intrapersonal comparator system analysis of reward value. *Journal of Personality and Social Psychology, 43*, 222–235.

Shaver, P., Schwartz, J., Kirson, D., & O'Connor, C. (1987). Emotion knowledge: Further exploration of a prototype approach. *Journal of Personality and Social Psychology, 52*, 1061–1086.

Shefet, M., & Eilam, N. (1991). *Self concept and learned helplessness.* Unpublished manuscript, Bar-Ilan University, Israel.

Shell, D. F., Murphy, C. C., & Bruning, R. H. (1989). Self-efficacy and outcome expectancy mechanisms on reading and writing achievement. *Journal of Educational Psychology, 81*, 91–100.

Shepperd, J. A., & Arkin, R. M. (1989). The moderating roles of public self-consciousness and task importance. *Personality and Social Psychology Bulletin, 15*, 252–265.

Sherman, S. J., Skov, R. B., Hervitz, E. F., & Stock, C. B. (1981). The effects of explaining hypothetical future events: From possibility to probability to actuality and beyond. *Journal of Experimental Social Psychology, 17*, 142–158.

Sherrod, D. R., & Downs, R. (1974). Environmental determinants of altruism: The effects of stimulus overload and perceived control on helping. *Journal of Experimental Social Psychology, 10*, 468–479.

Shrauger, J. S., & Rosenberg, S. E. (1970). Self-esteem and the effect of success and failure feedback on performance. *Journal of Personality, 38*, 404–417.

Shrauger, J. S., & Sorman, P. (1977). Self-evaluations, initial success and failure, and improvement as determinants of persistence. *Journal of Consulting and Clinical Psychology, 45*, 784–795.

Sigall, H., & Gould, R. (1977). The effects of self-esteem and evaluator demandingness on effort expenditure. *Journal of Personality and Social Psychology, 35*, 12–20.

Silver, R. L., Boon, C., & Stones, M. H. (1983). Searching for meaning in misfortune: Making sense of incest. *Journal of Social Issues, 39*, 81–101.

Silver, R. L., Wortman, C. B., & Klos, D. S. (1982). Cognitions, affect, and behavior following uncontrollable outcomes: A response to current human helplessness research. *Journal of Personality, 50,* 480–514.

Skinner, E. A. (1985). Action, control judgments, and the structure of control experience. *Psychological Review, 92,* 39–58.

Skinner, N. E. (1979). Learned helplessness: Performance as a function of task significance. *Journal of Psychology, 102,* 77–82.

Slapion, M. J., & Carver, C. S. (1981). Self-directed attention and facilitation of intellectual performance among persons high in test anxiety. *Cognitive Therapy and Research, 5,* 115–121.

Slyker, J. P., & McNally, R. J. (1991). Experimental induction of anxious and depressed moods: Are Velten and musical procedures necessary? *Cognitive Therapy and Research, 15,* 33–45.

Smith, C. A. (1990). The self, appraisal, and coping. In C. R. Snyder & D. R. Forsyth (Eds.), *Handbook of social and clinical psychology* (pp. 116–137). New York: Pergamon.

Smith, D. S., & Strube, M. J. (1991). Self-protective tendencies as moderators of self-handicapping impressions. *Basic and Applied Social Psychology, 12,* 63–80.

Smith, T. W., & Greenberg, J. (1981). Depression and self-focused attention. *Motivation and Emotion, 5,* 323–331.

Smith, T. W., Ingram, R. E., & Roth, D. L. (1985). Self-focused attention and depression: Self-evaluation, affect, and life stress. *Motivation and Emotion, 9,* 323–331.

Smith, T. W., Snyder, C. R., & Handelsman, M. M. (1982). On the self-serving function of an academic wooden leg: Test anxiety as a self-handicapping strategy. *Journal of Personality and Social Psychology, 42,* 314–321.,

Smolen, R. C. (1978). Expectancies, mood, and performance of depressed and nondepressed psychiatric inpatients on chance and skill tasks. *Journal of Abnormal Psychology, 87,* 91–101.

Snyder, C. R., & Higgins, R. L. (1988). Excuses: Their effective role in the negotiation of reality. *Psychological Bulletin, 104,* 24–35.

Snyder, C. R., Higgins, R. L., & Stucky, R. J. (1983). *Excuses: Masquerades in search of grace.* New York: Wiley.

Snyder, C. R., & Smith, T. W. (1982). Symptoms as self-handicapping strategies: The virtues of old wine in a new bottle. In G. Weary & H. L. Mirels (Eds.), *Integrations of clinical and social psychology* (pp. 104–127). New York: Oxford University Press.

Snyder, C. R., & Smith, T. W. (1986). On being "shy like a fox": A self-handicapping analysis. In W. H. Jones, J. M. Cheeck, & S. R. Briggs (Eds.), *A sourcebook on shyness: Research and treatment* (pp. 161–172). New York: Plenum.

Snyder, C. R., Smith, T. W., Augelli, R. W., & Ingram, R. E. (1985). On the self-serving function of social anxiety: Shyness as a self-handicapping strategy. *Journal of Personality and Social Psychology, 48,* 970–980.

Snyder, M. L., Smoller, B., Strenta, A., & Frankel, A. (1981). A comparison of egotism, negativity, and learned helplessness explanation for poor performance after unsolvable tasks. *Journal of Personality and Social Psychology, 40,* 24–30.

Snyder, M. L., Stephan, W. G., & Rosenfield, D. (1978). Attributional egotism. In J. H. Harvey, W. J. Ickes, & R. F. Kidd (Eds.), *New directions in attribution research* (Vol. 2). Hillsdale, NJ: Erlbaum.

Solomon, Z., Avitzur, E., & Mikulincer, M. (1989). Coping resources and social functioning following combat stress reaction: A longitudinal study. *Journal of Social and Clinical Psychology, 8,* 87–96.

Solomon, Z., Mikulincer, M., & Avitzur, E. (1988). Coping, locus of control, social support, and combat-related posttraumatic stress disorder: A prospective study. *Journal of Personality and Social Psychology, 55,* 279–285.

Solomon, Z., Mikulincer, M., & Benbenishty, R. (1989). Locus of control and combat-related posttraumatic stress disorder: The intervening role of battle intensity, threat appraisal, and coping. *British Journal of Clinical Psychology, 28,* 131–144.

Solomon, Z., Mikulincer, M., & Flum, H. (1988). Negative life events, coping responses, and combat-related psychopathology: A prospective study. *Journal of Abnormal Psychology, 97,* 302–307.

Stanley, M. A., & Maddux, J. E. (1986). Self-efficacy expectancy and depressed mood: An investigation of causal relationships. *Journal of Social Behavior and Personality, 1,* 575–586.

Steele, C. M. (1988). The psychology of self-affirmation: Sustaining the integrity of the self. In L. Berkowitz (Ed.), *Advances in experimental social psychology* (Vol. 21). New York: Academic Press.

Steenbarger, B. N., & Aderman, D. (1979). Objective self-awareness as a nonaversive state: Effects of anticipating discrepancy reduction. *Journal of Personality, 47,* 330–339.

Stein, N. L., & Levine, L. J. (1989). The causal organization of emotional knowledge: A developmental study. *Cognition and Emotion, 3,* 343–378.

Stephenson, B., & Wicklund, R. A. (1983). Self-directed attention and taking the other's perspective. *Journal of Experimental Social Psychology, 19,* 58–77.

Stevens, L., & Jones, E. E. (1976). Defensive attribution and the Kelley cube. *Journal of Personality and Social Psychology, 34,* 809–820.

Stiensmeier-Pelster, J. (1989). Attributional style and depressive mood reactions. *Journal of Personality, 57,* 581–599.

Stipeck, D. J. (1984). Sex differences in children's attributions for success and failure on math and spelling tests. *Sex Roles, 11,* 969–981.

Stone, A. A., & Neale, J. M. (1984). New measure of daily coping: Development and preliminary results. *Journal of Personality and Social Psychology, 46,* 892–906.

Strack, S., Blaney, P. H., Ganellen, R. J., & Coyne, J. C. (1985). Pessimistic self-preoccupation, performance deficits, and depression. *Journal of Personality and Social Psychology, 49,* 1076–1085.

Strelau, J. (1983). *Temperament, personality, and activity.* London: Academic Press.

Strickland, B. R. (1978). Internal–external expectancies and health-related behaviors. *Journal of Consulting and Clinical Psychology, 46,* 1192–1211.

Strube, M. J., & Lott, C. L. (1985). Type A behavior pattern and the judgment of noncontingency: Mediating roles of mood and perspective. *Journal of Personality and Social Psychology, 49,* 510–519.

Strube, M. J., & Werner, C. (1985). Relinquishment of control and the Type A behavior pattern. *Journal of Personality and Social Psychology, 48,* 688–701.

Swann, W. B., Stephenson, B., & Pittman, T. S. (1981). Curiosity and control: On the determinants of the search for social knowledge. *Journal of Personality and Social Psychology, 40,* 635–642.

Sweeney, P. D., Anderson, A., & Bailey, S. (1986). Attributional style in depression: A meta-analytic review. *Journal of Personality and Social Psychology, 50,* 974–911.

Tallis, F. (1989). *Worry: A cognitive analysis.* Unpublished doctoral dissertation, University of London.

Taylor, S. E. (1983). Adjustment to threatening events: A theory of cognitive adaptation. *American Psychologist, 38,* 1161–1173.

Taylor, S. E., & Brown, J. D. (1988). Illusion and well-being: A social psychological perspective on mental health. *Psychological Bulletin, 103,* 193–210.

Taylor, S. E., & Fiske, S. T. (1978). Salience, attention, and attribution: top of the head phenomena. In L. Berkowitz (Ed.), *Advances in experimental social psychology* (Vol. 10). New York: Academic Press.

Taylor, S. E., Wood, J. V., & Lichtman, R. R. (1983). It could be worse: Selective evaluation as a response to victimization. *Journal of Social Issues, 39,* 19–40.

Teasdale, J. D. (1978). Effects of real and recalled success on learned helplessness and depression. *Journal of Abnormal Psychology, 87,* 155–164.

Teasdale, J. D., & Rezin, V. (1978). The effects of reducing frequency of negative thoughts on the mood of depressed patients: Tests of a cognitive model of depression. *British Journal of Social and Clinical Psychology, 17,* 65–74.

Tennen, H., Drum, P. E., Gillen, R., & Stanton, A. (1982). Learned helplessness and the detection of contingency. *Journal of Personality, 50,* 426–441.

Tennen, H., & Eller, S. J. (1977). Attributional components of learned helplessness and facilitation. *Journal of Personality and Social Psychology, 35*, 265–271.

Tennen, H., & Gillen, R. (1979). The effect of debriefing on laboratory-induced helplessness: An attributional analysis. *Journal of Personality, 47*, 629–642.

Tennen, H., Gillen, R., & Drum, P. E. (1982). The debilitating effect of exposure to noncontingent escape: A test of the learned helplessness model. *Journal of Personality, 50*, 409–425.

Thayer, R. E. (1987). Energy, tiredness, and tension effects of a sugar snack versus moderate exercise. *Journal of Personality and Social Psychology, 52*, 119–125.

Thompson, S. C. (1985). Finding positive meaning in a stressful event. *Basic and Applied Social Psychology, 6*, 279–295.

Thompson, S. C. (1991). The search for meaning following a stroke. *Basic and Applied Social Psychology, 12*, 81–96.

Thornton, J. W., & Jacobs, P. D. (1972). The facilitating effects of prior inescapable unavoidable stress on intellectual performance. *Psychonomic Science, 26*, 185–187.

Thornton, J. W., & Powell, G. D. (1974). Immunization to and alleviation of learned helplessness in man. *American Journal of Psychology, 87*, 351–367.

Tiggemann, M. (1981). Noncontingent success versus noncontingent failure in human subjects. *Journal of Psychology, 109*, 233–238.

Tiggemann, M., Barnett, A., & Winefeld, A. H. (1983). Uncontrollability versus perceived failure as determinants of subsequent performance deficits. *Motivation and Emotion, 7*, 257–268.

Tiggemann, M., & Winefeld, A. H. (1978). Situation similarity and the generalization of learned helplessness. *Quarterly Journal of Experimental Psychology, 30*, 725–735.

Tiggemann, M., & Winefeld, A. H. (1987). Predictability and timing of self-report in learned helplessness experiments. *Personality and Social Psychology Bulletin, 13*, 253–264.

Tobacyk, J. J., & Downs, A. (1986). Personal construct threat and irrational beliefs as cognitive predictors of increases in musical performance anxiety. *Journal of Personality and Social Psychology, 51*, 779–782.

Tobin, D. L., Holroyd, K. A., Reynolds, R. V., & Wigal, J. K. (1989). The hierarchical factor structure of the Coping Strategies Inventory. *Cognitive Therapy and Research, 13*, 343–361.

Tolman, E. C. (1932). *Purposive behavior in animals and man.* New York: Appleton-Century-Crofts.

Tomkins, S. S. (1962). *Affect, imagery, consciousness* (Vol. 1). New York: Springer-Verlag.

Torestad, B., Magnusson, D., & Olah, A. (1990). Coping, control, and experience of anxiety: An interactional perspective. *Anxiety Research, 3*, 1–16.

Trice, A. S., & Woods, P. J. (1979). The role of pretest and test similarity in producing helplessness or reactant responding in humans. *Bulletin of Psychonomic Society, 14*, 457–459.

Tuffin, K., Hesketh, B., & Podd, J. (1985). Experimentally induced learned helplessness: How far does it generalize? *Social Behavior and Personality, 13*, 55–62.

Turner, R. G., Scheier, M. F., Carver, C. S., & Ickes, W. (1978). Correlates of self-consciousness. *Journal of Personality Assessment, 42*, 285–289.

Tverski, A., & Kahneman, D. (1973). Availability: A heuristic for judging frequency and probability. *Cognitive Psychology, 5*, 207–232.

Uleman, J. S., & Bargh, J. A. (Eds.). (1989). *Unintended thought.* New York: Guilford.

Vaillant, G. E. (1977). *Adaptation to life.* Boston: Little Brown.

Valins, S. (1966). Cognitive effects of false heart-rate feedback. *Journal of Personality and Social Psychology, 1*, 400–408.

Valle, V. A., & Frieze, I. H. (1976). The stability of causal attribution as a mediator in changing expectations of success. *Journal of Personality and Social Psychology, 33*, 579–587.

Van-Overwalle, F. (1989). Structure of freshmen's causal attributions for exam performance. *Journal of Educational Psychology, 81*, 400–407.

Watson, D., & Clark, L. A. (1984). Negative affectivity: The disposition to experience aversive emotional states. *Psychological Bulletin, 96*, 465–490.

Wegner, D. M., & Giuliano, T. (1980). Arousal-induced attention to self. *Journal of Personality and Social Psychology, 38,* 719–726.

Wegner, D. M., & Giuliano, T. (1983). On sending artifact in search of artifact: Reply to McDonald, Harris, and Maher. *Journal of Personality and Social Psychology, 44,* 290–293.

Wegner, D. M., Schneider, D. J., Carter, S., & White, L. (1987). Paradoxical effects of thought suppression. *Journal of Personality and Social Psychology, 53,* 5–13.

Wegner, D. M., Schneider, D. J., Knutson, B., & McMahon, S. R. (1991). Polluting the stream of consciousness: The effect of thought suppression on the mind's environment. *Cognitive Therapy and Research, 15,* 141–152.

Weidner, G. (1980). Self-handicapping following learned helplessness treatment and the type A coronary-prone behavior pattern. *Journal of Psychosomatic Research, 24,* 319–325.

Weiner, B. (1972). *Theories of motivation: From mechanism to cognition.* Chicago: Rand McNally.

Weiner, B. (1979). A theory of motivation for some classroom experiences. *Journal of Educational Psychology, 71,* 3–25.

Weiner, B. (1985). An attributional theory of achievement motivation and emotion. *Psychological Review, 92,* 548–573.

Weiner, B. (1986). Attribution, emotion, and action. In R. M. Sorrentino & E. T. Higgins (Eds.), *Handbook of motivation and cognition* (pp. 281–312). New York: Guilford.

Weinburg, A. (1990). *Self-awareness and reactions to failure.* Unpublished master's thesis, Bar-Ilan University, Israel.

Weiner, B., Graham, S., Stern, P., & Lawson, M. E. (1982). Using affective cues to infer causal thoughts. *Developmental Psychology, 18,* 278–286.

Weiner, B., Nierenberg, R., & Goldstein, M. (1976). Social learning (locus of control) versus attributional (causal stability) interpretations of expectancy of success. *Journal of Personality, 44,* 52–68.

Weiner, B., & Sierad, J. (1975). Misattribution for failure and the enhancement of achievement strivings. *Journal of Personality and Social Psychology, 31,* 415–421.

Weisman, A. D., & Worden, J. W. (1975). Psychological analysis of cancer death *Omega, 6,* 61–75.

Weiss, J. M., Glazer, H. I., & Pohorecky, L. A. (1974). Neurotransmitters and helplessness: A chemical bridge to depression? *Psychology Today, 18,* 58–62.

Weisz, J. R. (1979). Perceived control and learned helplessness among mentally retarded children: A developmental analysis. *Developmental Psychology, 15,* 311–319.

Welker, R. L. (1976). Acquisition of a free operant appetitive response in pigeons as a function of prior experience with response-independent food. *Learning and Motivation, 7,* 394–405.

Wenzlaff, R. M., Wegner, D. M., & Roper, D. W. (1988). Depression and mental control: The resurgence of unwanted negative thoughts. *Journal of Personality and Social Psychology, 55,* 882–892.

Wickless, C., & Kirsch, I. (1988). Cognitive correlates of anger, anxiety, and sadness. *Cognitive Therapy and Research, 12,* 367–377.

Wicklund, R. A. (1986). Orientation to the environment versus preoccupation with human potential. In R. M. Sorrentino & E. T. Higgins (Eds.), *Handbook of motivation and cognition* (pp. 64–95). New York: Guilford.

Wicklund, R. A., & Braun, O. L. (1987). Incompetence and the concern with human categories. *Journal of Personality and Social Psychology, 53,* 373–382.

Willis, M. H., & Blaney, P. H. (1978). Three tests of the learned helplessness model of depression. *Journal of Abnormal Psychology, 87,* 131–136.

Wilner, P., & Neiva, J. (1986). Brief exposure to uncontrollable but not to controllable noise biases the retrieval of information from memory. *British Journal of Clinical Psychology, 25,* 93–100.

Wilson, T. D., & Linville, P. W. (1982). Improving the academic performance of college freshmen: Attribution therapy revisited. *Journal of Personality and Social Psychology, 42,* 367–376.

Wilson, T. D., & Linville, P. W. (1985). Improving the performance of college freshmen with attributional techniques. *Journal of Personality and Social Psychology, 49,* 287–293.

Wine, J. (1971). Test anxiety and direction of attention. *Psychological Bulletin, 76*, 92–104.

Winefeld, A. H. (1983). Cognitive performance deficits induced by exposure to response-independent positive outcomes. *Motivation and Emotion, 7*, 145–155.

Winefeld, A. H., Barnett, A., & Tiggemann, M. (1985). Learned helplessness deficits: Uncontrollable outcomes of perceived failure? *Motivation and Emotion, 9*, 185–195.

Winefeld, A. H., & Fay, P. M. (1982). Effects of an institutional environment on responses to uncontrollable outcomes. *Motivation and Emotion, 6*, 103–112.

Winefeld, A. H., & Jardine, E. (1982). Effects of differences in achievement motivation and amount of exposure on responses to uncontrollable rewards. *Motivation and Emotion, 6*, 245–257.

Winefeld, A. H., & Norris, P. J. (1981). Effects of exposure to uncontrollable events as a function of achievement motivation and initial expectation of success. *Motivation and Emotion, 5*, 235–248.

Wong, P. T., & Weiner, B. (1981). When people ask "why" questions and the heuristics of attributional search. *Journal of Personality and Social Psychology, 40*, 650–663.

Wood, J. V., Saltzberg, J. A., & Goldsamt, L. A. (1990). Does affect induce self-focused attention? *Journal of Personality and Social Psychology, 58*, 899–908.

Wood, J. V., Saltzberg, J. A., Neale, J. M., Stone, A. A., & Rachmiel, T. B. (1990). Self-focused attention, coping responses, and distressed mood in everyday life. *Journal of Personality and Social Psychology, 58*, 1027–1036.

Wortman, C. B., & Brehm, J. W. (1975). Responses to uncontrollable outcomes: An integration of reactance theory and the learned helplessness model. In L. Berkowitz (Ed.), *Advances in experimental social psychology* (Vol. 8, pp. 278–336). New York: Academic Press.

Wortman, C. B., & Dintzer, L. (1978). Is an attributional analysis of the learned helplessness phenomenon viable? *Journal of Abnormal Psychology, 87*, 75–90.

Wortman, C. B., Panciera, L., Shusterman, L., & Hibscher, J. (1976). Attributions of causality and reactions to uncontrollable outcomes. *Journal of Experimental and Social Psychology, 12*, 301–316.

Wurtele, S. K. (1986). Self-efficacy and athletic performance: A review. *Journal of Social and Clinical Psychology, 4*, 290–301.

Young, P. T. (1961). *Motivation and emotion: A survey of the determinants of human and animal activity.* New York: Wiley.

Zeigarnik, B. (1927). Ueber das behalten von erledigten und unerledugten handlungen. *Psychologishen Forsh, 9*, 1–85.

Zoeller, C. J., Mahoney, G., & Weiner, B. (1983). Effects of attribution retraining on the assembly task performance of mentally retarded adults. *American Journal of Mental Deficiency, 88*, 109–112.

Zuckerman, M. (1979). Attribution of success and failure revisited. *Journal of Personality, 47*, 245–287.

Zuroff, D. C. (1980). Learned helplessness in humans: An analysis of learning processes and the roles of individual and situational differences. *Journal of Personality and Social Psychology, 39*, 130–146.

INDEX

Abortion, 154
Academic failure, 123, 271
Achievement need, 112, 117, 175, 176, 182,
   183
  and LH effects, 190–191
Action tendencies, 142
Actual self, 145
Adaptation hypothesis, 21
Aerobic exercise, 169
Affect Intensity Measure, 161
Alloplastic adaptation, 37, 39, 122, 143, 162,
   211, 240, 241
Associative memory network, 72, 73, 75
Associative pathways, 66, 77, 90
Attribution-relevant cues, 79, 80
Attribution training, 131, 132
Attributional (explanatory) style, 112, 114, 130,
   154, 222
Attributional Style Questionnaire (ASQ), 130,
   131, 133, 197
Automatic Thought Questionnaire, 216
Autoplastic adaptation, 37, 122, 143, 211, 241

Backward warning system, 141
Battered women, 271
Behavioral persistence, 22, 132
Behavioral system, 178
Belief perseverance 217–218
Bogus feedback, 169, 170

Causal attribution
  dimensions 112–114
  global–specific, 112, 113, 122, 125
    and expectancy change, 114–115

Causal attribution (*Cont.*)
  global–specific (*Cont.*)
    and task performance, 133–135
  internal–external, 100, 114, 176, 196
    and LH effects, 196–198
  spontaneous attributions, 113
  stable–unstable, 112, 113, 122
    and amount of failure, 117
    and expectancy change, 106, 114, 117
    and prior expectancy, 118
    and task performance, 129–135
Child abuse, 163
Childbirth, 154
Chronic illness, 123
Cognition Checklist, 152
Cognitive autonomy, 66, 73
Cognitive confusion, 78
Cognitive context, 69, 88 ,90, 91, 213
Cognitive interference, 24, 51, 140, 259
Cognitive Interference Questionnaire (CIQ), 78,
   83, 85, 125, 182
Cognitive operations, 79, 80
Cognitive system, 72
Cognitively generated motivation, 120
Commitment, 179, 186, 228
Completion tendency, 74
Concern, 240
Concept Learning task, 168
Conditional inattention, 23
Conflict escalation, 163
Consumer behavior, 114
Contingency learning, 106
Coping
  acceptance, 35, 38, 165

Coping (*Cont.*)
  and amount of failure, 45–49
  and appraisal, 48
  approach, 35, 36
  avoidance, 35, 36, 40–42, 43, 45, 46, 47,
    63, 121, 122
    and adaptational outcomes, 54–56
    and amount of failure, 46–48
    behavioral, 41, 43, 45
    cognitive, 40, 41, 44
    and helplessness training, 44–45
    and LH deficits, 62–63
    and performance, 59
    and reappraisal, 41
    and reorganization, 41–42, 57
    self-handicapping, 25, 41
  coping potential, 120
  definition, 34
  emotion-focused, 35, 36
  and helplessness training, 42–45
  off-task, 25, 28, 50, 122, 126, 127
  problem solving (problem-focused), 25, 35,
    36, 37, 38, 39, 63, 67, 76, 77, 80, 81,
    90–91, 121, 122,126, 140
    and adaptational outcomes, 50–52
    and amount of failure, 46–48
    cognitive exhaustion, 51
    and helplessness training, 44, 45
    and LH deficits, 60–61
    and performance, 59
    and reactance, 60–61
    and reappraisal, 52–53
  reappraisal, 25, 35, 36, 38–40, 41, 63, 123
    and adaptational outcomes, 52–54
    and amount of failure, 46–48
    claimed self-handicap, 40
    cognitive adaptation, 39
    compensatory cognitions, 40
    downward comparisons, 53
    excuse making, 25, 39, 40, 44
    focusing on the positive, 39–40
    and helplessness training, 44
    and LH deficits, 60–61
    negotiation with reality, 39
    and performance, 59
    positive social comparisons, 53
    and reactance, 60–61
    and reorganization, 36
  reorganization, 36, 37–38, 63, 121, 122
    and adaptational outcomes, 56–58
    adaptive changes, 38

Coping (*Cont.*)
  reorganization (*Cont.*)
    and amount of failure, 46–48
    completion tendency, 37
    grief work, 37
    and helplessness training, 45
    and LH deficits, 62–63
    and performance, 59
    and problem solving, 38
    work of worrying, 37
  support seeking, 36
  taxonomy, 34–36
  Ways of Coping Checklist, 34, 60, 61
  wishful thinking, 35, 123, 180
Core relational theme, 142
Cue utilization, 82

Declarative memory, 68, 213
Deductive reasoning, 118
Deliberative thinking, 65, 70, 78
Demand characteristics, 132
Desire for control, 176, 178

Egotism, 25, 48, 187, 194
Emotion
  anger
    and amount of failure, 157–158
    and anxiety, 163
    and coping, 162–164
    and expectancy of control, 150–152
    and helplessness training, 146–149
    and mental rumination, 162–164
    and self-efficacy, 156–157
    and task performance, 162–164
  anxiety
    and amount of failure, 157–158
    and coping, 164–170
    and depression, 155–156
    and expectancy of control, 152–159
    and helplessness training, 146–149
    and mental rumination, 164–170
    and self-efficacy, 156–157
    and stable/specific attribution, 153–154
    and task performance, 164–170
  and appraisal, 141–142
  and avoidance, 143–144
  and coping, 140–141, 142–143, 160–162
  depression
    and amount of failure, 157–158
    and coping, 164–170
    and expectancy of control, 152–159

Emotion (*Cont.*)
  depression (*Cont.*)
    and helplessness training, 146–149
    and mental rumination, 164–170
    and self-efficacy, 156–157
    and stable/specific attribution, 153–154
    and task performance, 164–170
    and expectancy of control, 149–150
    and helplessness training, 144–145
    as interfering force, 143–144
    and mental rumination, 160–162
    and task performance, 159–162
    and theories of LH, 145
Emotional distance, 163
Epistemic activity
  and causal attribution, 119–120
  and expectancy of control, 118–120
  and prior expectancies, 119
Evaluation check, 142
Expectancy of control
  and amount of failure, 115–118
  and coping, 102, 120–122, 126
  and coping strategies, 122–124
  and helplessness training, 101–105
  and mental rumination, 124–126
  and persistence in test tasks, 105–108
  and self-efficacy expectancy, 100–101
  and task performance, 126–129
Expectancy-outcome congruence, 196
Expectancy-outcome discrepancy, 145

Fear conditioning, 22
Future expectancy, 120

Galvanic Skin Responses, 146
Gender differences, 133, 195
Goal-directed actions, 68
Goal hierarchy, 67, 68 ,70, 174, 178, 179, 180,
  186, 211
Goal orientation, 204
  and LH effects, 198–199
Guilt, 159

Heart disease, 163
Hidden-figure test, 133
Hudson's Uses of Objects test, 190
Hypertension, 163
Hypnotic suggestion, 167
Hypothesis testing, 119, 130

Ideal self, 145
Illusion of control, 217

Imprisonment, 154
Inaction, 164
Incentive level, 174
Incompatible motor responses, 22
Inertial tendencies, 205
Inhibitory mechanisms, 73, 88, 89, 159
Inner resources, 266–267
Institutionalization, 271
Intellectual Achievement Responsibility (IAR)
  Scale, 130
Intention, 68, 69, 89, 124, 125
Interfering emotions, 80

Learned helplessness
  animal experiments, 3–5
  animal theories, 21–23
  application, 271–273
  and coping process, 239–242
  and coping strategies, 246–250
  direct and indirect antecedents, 250–255
  distal factors, 27, 28, 99, 139
  early human experiments, 5–7
  and emotions, 247–248
  and expectancy of control, 245–247
  experimental setting, 12–13
  functional and dysfunctional aspects, 260–263
  generalization, 16–18, 263–265
  helplessness-prone personality, 266–268
  helplessness state, 82, 255–258, 259–260
  immunization, 5, 7, 267
  LH deficits, 15–16
  LH theory, 23–24, 126, 127, 251
  mediational sequence, 242–250
  and mental rumination, 248–249
  proximal factors, 27
  and psychopathology, 268–271
  reactance state, 258–259, 260
  and self-focus, 244–245
  subjective meaning, 13–14
  and task value, 244
  terminology, 2–3
  therapy, 5, 134
  triadic design, 4
  vicarious experience, 6
Learning goals, 178, 182, 185, 198, 199,
  204
Letter cancellation, 30, 58, 82, 92, 95, 161,
  163, 225, 231
Life Orientation Test (LOT), 123
Locus of control, 105, 123, 134
  and LH deficits, 135–137

Meaning analysis, 142
Mehrabian's test, 190
Mental rumination
  action
    and cue utilization, 83
    and excuse making, 70
    and helplessness training, 80–82 83, 84,
      86, 88
    and information processing, 92–94
    and LH deficits, 96–97
    metastatic function, 68
    and problem solving, 70, 71, 88, 94
    and reactance, 94
    and reappraisal, 70, 71, 88, 94
    and task performance, 80, 88, 89, 90, 95
  and amount of failure, 76, 80–84
  and coping, 69–70, 77–78
  and generalization of LH, 91, 94–95
  and helplessness training, 76–80
  and primacy effect, 85–86
  and stereotypical thinking, 85–86
  and task performance, 88–91
  mind wandering, 78, 92, 96
  state
    and avoidance, 70, 71–72
    catastatic function, 68
    editing function, 68
    and helplessness training, 78, 81, 82, 83,
      84, 85
    and information processing, 92–94
    and LH deficits, 94, 95, 96–97
    and problem solving, 88, 91
    and reorganization, 68, 70, 71, 88
    self-preoccupative worry, 78, 92, 93, 125,
      182
    subtypes, 67, 70
    and task performance, 80, 88, 89, 90, 95
  task-irrelevant
    and avoidance, 70, 71
    and helplessness training, 78, 81, 82, 83,
      85, 86
    and LH deficits, 95–96
    and problem solving, 88, 91
    and task performance, 80, 88, 89, 90,
      92
Mental withdrawal, 24, 180
Metacognitive strategies, 131
Mindfulness, 66, 77, 79, 80, 88
Motion sickness, 272
Multiple Affect Adjective Checklist (MAACL),
  146, 157, 220

Need for cognitive closure, 78
Need satisfaction, 175
Negative reactivity, 266
Norepinephrine, 23

Outcome expectancy, 100, 105, 107, 108, 123,
  151, 204

Paranoid reactions, 269–270
Parole decisions, 114
Perceived self-relevance
  and coping processes, 179–181
  and coping strategies, 181
  definition, 176–178
  and emotions, 183–185
  and LH deficits, 185–188
  and mental rumination, 181–183
  and reactance, 185–188
Perceived task importance
  and coping processes, 179–181
  and coping strategies, 181
  definition, 174–176
  and emotions, 183–185
  and expectancy of control, 202–204
  and helplessness training, 204–207
  and LH deficits, 185–188
  and mental rumination, 181–183
  and perceived self-relevance, 178–179, 201
  and reactance, 185–188
Perception of control, 106, 117, 122
  and amount of failure, 110
  and helplessness training, 109–112
  and self-efficacy, 111
Performance goals, 178, 182, 185, 198, 199,
  204
Personal domain, 152
Personal helplessness, 100, 107, 110, 137
Personal Interest Questionnaire, 190
Persuasion ability, 131
Positive mood, 80
Posttrauma, 51–52, 68
Predictability, 196
Primacy effect, 85, 86
Primary appraisal, 142, 174, 243
Production rules, 119
Pseudohallucinations, 72

Reactance, 18, 20, 24, 25, 26, 27, 28, 29, 46,
  51, 52, 60–63, 80, 91, 99, 145, 163,
  186, 226
Reinforcement value, 174
Resourcefulness, 267–268

Response–outcome (non)contingency, 102, 107, 110, 111, 118, 137, 193
Response repertoire, 77, 93
Response retardation, 93
Response unavailability, 153
Resource allocation, 164
Rokeach's Value scale, 201

Schedule of reinforcement, 131, 132
Scripts, 89
Secondary appraisal, 120, 142, 150
Self-Consciousness Scale, 213, 219, 224
Self-discrepancies, 145
Self-efficacy, 100, 105, 107, 111, 122, 123, 128, 129, 137, 151, 153, 156, 159, 199, 204
Self-esteem, 137–138, 142, 151, 165, 177, 200, 222, 229–230
Self-focus
  and coping process, 212–214
  and coping strategies, 213, 214–215
  definition, 210–212
  and emotions, 213, 218–220, 230–231, 235–237
  and expectancy of control, 213, 216–218, 227–230
  and helplessness training, 232–235
  and LH effects, 223–227
  and mental rumination, 213, 215–216
  and task value, 213, 220–222, 231–232
Self-identity, 67, 69, 70, 93, 150, 151, 158, 163, 174, 176, 178, 179, 180, 186, 195, 199, 204, 205, 211, 212, 233, 235
  and LH effects, 199–201
Self-protective devices, 128
Self-punishment, 68
Self-regulation, 68, 212
Self-representations, 144, 176, 179, 211
Self-reward, 68
Self-schema, 70, 213
Self-state, 69, 84
Self-system, 69, 70, 178

Semantic sorting, 92, 93
Sensitization hypothesis, 22
Shame, 159
Skill/chance tasks, 105–106
Smith's achievement test, 190
Social evaluative cues, 166
Social performance, 131
Social persuasion, 114
Somatic hyperactivity, 72
Spielberger Trait Anger Scale, 163
Sport performance, 131
Spread of activation, 90
States of action readiness, 142
Stereotypical thinking, 85, 86
Systolic blood pressure, 149

Task attractiveness, 174
Task cues, 82, 83
Task difficulty instructions
  and LH effects, 193–196
Task importance instructions
  and coping strategies, 189–190
  and emotions, 189–190
  and LH effects, 188–190
  and mental rumination, 189–190
TAT, 182, 226
Threat appraisal, 180
Tolerance for ambiguity, 78
TOTE, 211
Thought Occurrence Questionnaire (TOQ), 92, 95
Thought suppression paradigm, 86
Type A personality, 175, 176, 180, 183
  and LH effects 191–193

Universal helplessness, 100, 107, 137

Velten's self-statements, 169, 219

War, 123
Working memory, 66, 89, 90, 91, 93